Subject Guide
to U.S. Government
Reference Sources

Subject Guide
to U.S. Government
Reference Sources

Second Edition

Gayle J. Hardy
Associate Librarian
Lockwood Library
State University of New York at Buffalo
E-mail: ghardy@acsu.buffalo.edu

Judith Schiek Robinson
Associate Professor
School of Information and Library Studies
State University of New York at Buffalo
E-mail: lisrobin@acsu.buffalo.edu

1996
Libraries Unlimited, Inc.
Englewood, Colorado

To *Cecil* and *Bruce*.
And to pets everywhere, particularly
Smudge and *Redd*; *Molly*, *Sheba*, and *Barney*;
Pie and *Puny*;
who can be blessed in early October each year at
the National Cathedral in Washington, D.C.

■

Copyright © 1996 Libraries Unlimited, Inc.
All Rights Reserved
Printed in the United States of America

LIBRARIES UNLIMITED, INC.
P.O. Box 6633
Englewood, CO 80155-6633
1-800-237-6124

Production Editor: Kevin W. Perizzolo
Copy Editor: Jan Krygier
Typesetter: Kay Minnis
Indexer: Linda Running Bentley

Library of Congress Cataloging-in-Publication Data

Hardy, Gayle J., 1942-
    Subject guide to U.S. government reference sources /
Gayle J. Hardy, Judith Schiek Robinson. -- 2d ed.
    xxi, 358 p. 17x25 cm.
    Includes index.   **3 1969 00877 8200**
    ISBN 1-56308-189-X
    1. Reference books--Government publications--Bibliography.
2. Government publications--United States--Bibliography.
3. Bibliography--Bibliography--Government publications.
4. Government information--United States--Computer network
resources. I. Robinson, Judith Schiek, 1947-   . II. Title.
Z1223.Z7R63   1996
025.17'34--dc20   96-17543
                                                CIP

Contents

PART THREE
Science and Technology

16—AGRICULTURE (*continued*)

17—ASTRONOMY 197

18—BIOLOGICAL SCIENCES 201

19—EARTH SCIENCES 205

20—ENERGY 213

Acknowledgments

The authors wish to thank the graduate students from the School of Information and Library Studies at the State University of New York at Buffalo who assisted in the bibliographic searching in support of this book. We are also very grateful to the University Libraries staff, in particular the Government Documents Department in Lockwood Library, for their help and patience in answering our many research questions.

A portion of Ms. Hardy's research for this work was made possible by a grant from the New York State/United University Professions Professional Development and Quality of Working Life Committee and a sabbatical leave from the State University of New York at Buffalo.

Introduction

This one-volume compendium helps readers identify and understand the scope of key government reference sources. Its underlying philosophy is *access, not format*. Thus, this updated edition describes titles of lasting value available in depository libraries, along with nonbook sources like specialized information clearinghouses and Internet sites.

The sources described differ from other reference materials in only one key respect: They were produced by the U.S. government. Like nongovernment publications, they are in familiar reference formats: Atlases, bibliographies, directories, catalogs, dictionaries, handbooks, indexes and abstracts, statistical compendiums, and their newer electronic cousins. These reference sources provide a wealth of ready-reference and in-depth information on a wide range of subjects, and, for the most part, are meant to be consulted for specific information rather than read from cover to cover.

This volume is selective rather than comprehensive, intended to serve as a handy one-volume guide. Included are seminal works, unique historical guides, comprehensive titles, and sources of first resort for reference searches. The focus is on materials readily available coast to coast: Depository materials, free information, Internet hubs. The first chapter notes key nongovernment titles that supplement federal information collections.

Prior knowledge of government documents is not required to use this book. Although it will be especially useful to reference and documents librarians, many other information seekers, including students, researchers, teachers, government officials, and the general public, will find it helpful for identifying government information. It can be used as a compact companion to the biennial *Government Reference Books*, a comprehensive guide to government reference materials, also published by Libraries Unlimited.

SCOPE

Emphasis is on depository titles at least 80 pages long (with some shorter, related titles noted in the annotations). Exceptions to these criteria were judiciously incorporated. Key *nongovernment* references are described in chapter 1, Bibliographic Aids, comprising solely commercial references. A special effort was made to cite agency publications catalogs, although most are exceptions to the 80-page rule. Not only do these pamphlets list titles sometimes omitted from the *Monthly Catalog* and PRF, but they are also often available free from their issuing agencies. Many agency telephone directories have also been included (remember that these are often duplicated in agency home pages on the Internet).

Valuable titles were identified by perusing the documents themselves, agency publications lists and Internet sites, GPO sales catalogs, the *Library of Congress Information Bulletin*, Library of Congress *Publications in Print*, *SIGCAT CD-ROM Compendium*, daily depository shipping lists, depository library *Administrative Notes*, Sears and Moody's *Using Government Information Sources*, the *List of Classes* available to depository libraries, the *Census Catalog and Guide, Government Reference Books,* and publications columns in *Booklist, Journal of Government Information, Government Information Quarterly, Collection Building*, and *Library Journal.*

FORMATS

Entries span the range of government information options, from traditional reference books to up-to-the-minute formats: CD-ROMs, diskettes, Internet sites, databases, agency bulletin boards, and even specialized information clearinghouses. In many cases, a title is available in several formats, and these options are noted. Some sources are also available through commercial vendors: These are not itemized but can be identified using sources like the *Gale Directory of Databases.*

Because of the "access, not format" philosophy underlying this book, access has also been enhanced with notes about availability of free copies from the issuing agency or through the Internet; please note that either may change, however. Such notes are especially useful because key bibliographies such as the *Monthly Catalog* and PRF rarely alert users that free copies are available or provide Internet addresses for full-text equivalents of print titles. For conciseness, mailing addresses do not repeat the agency name.

Titles available in print and formats other than print, include the *"also available in [format]"* statement below the citation or in the annotation. Titles available solely in microform include a note to this effect in the citation. When available to depositories in either print or microform, the microform option is not noted.

 # Additions and Changes

OVERLAP WITH FIRST EDITION

More than two-thirds of the entries in this edition are new: 894 titles are making their debut. Historical, outdated, or ceased titles omitted from this update can be identified by consulting the 1985 edition.

ARRANGEMENT

Entries are arranged under four broad subjects (General Reference Sources, Social Sciences, Science and Technology, and Humanities), with further subject subdivision under each. Titles are listed in alphabetical order by the first letter in the citation except when chronological or some other logical order is more helpful.

BIBLIOGRAPHIC CITATIONS

All bibliographic information, including material repeated from the first edition, has been newly verified. When possible, Serial Set numbers have been provided for House and Senate documents and reports.

Although they may vary from library to library, Dewey and LC classification numbers have been provided as general browsing aids. OCLC and LC control numbers, helpful in searching bibliographic databases, have also been included.

Prices and GPO stock numbers have been omitted because they date quickly. ISBN/ISSNs have also been omitted because (1) they tend to vary with changes in issuing agency and titles; (2) many documents lack them; and (3) they often identify a single annual issue. ISBN/ISSNs have been included for the commercial titles in chapter 1, however.

Except in chapter 1, the place of publication (usually Washington, D.C.), has been omitted to save space.

When coverage dates differ from publication dates, this has been noted in the annotation.

Bibliographic elements are detailed in the "How to Use This Book" section (see page xix), although not all elements appear in every citation.

ANNOTATIONS

All annotations are based on firsthand examination of materials. Written to be concise but thorough, annotations do not repeat information in the author statement, title, or subtitle. The focus instead is on new information not readily evident: Scope, omissions, background notes, companion sources, former and popular titles (both accessible through the index), typical citation formats, abbreviations, and differentiation between similar titles.

INDEX

The title and subject index has been augmented with entries for popular or variant titles, famous editors, acronyms, and abbreviations. Index entries refer to entry numbers rather than pages.

SUBJECT BIBLIOGRAPHIES

A complete index to these helpful bibliographies of GPO publications is provided in the appendix to this book.

How to Use This Book

Entries include the following items (when appropriate) in the order shown below.

1. Entry number

2. Issuing agency (or author, in the case of nongovernmental titles)

3. Title

4. Senate/House Report/Document number

5. Personal author, editor, etc.

6. Volume statement

7. Availability information and date of publication (or city of publication, publisher, and date of publication, in the case of nongovernmental titles). Abbreviations used are GPO (Government Printing Office), NTIS (National Technical Information Service), or the initials of the agency from where the item may be obtained.

8. Address for free items, or for those available from the Library of Congress

9. Frequency

10. Edition/format

11. Pagination

12. ISBN/ISSN (for nongovernmental titles)

13. Library of Congress control number

14. Library of Congress classification number

15. Dewey Decimal classification number

16. OCLC number

17. Serial Set number

18. Superintendent of Documents (SuDocs) classification number

SAMPLE ENTRY*
(showing most bibliographic elements)

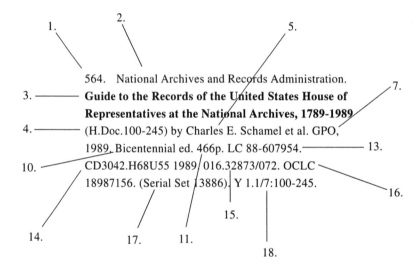

*Numbers in sample reference the list on pages xix and xx.

Access to Materials

This book's coverage emphasizes materials available (as of November 1995) through depository library collections, requests for single free copies, or the Internet. Although every effort has been expended to make this book as complete, accurate, and current as possible, it should be noted that government information is constantly in flux. New points of access are constantly emerging; others wither without fanfare. Changes can be monitored in part by using the Internet addresses and publications catalogs described in this book.

Addresses have been given for titles available free from agencies, along with many agency toll-free telephone numbers and E-mail addresses.

DEPOSITORY LIBRARIES

Federal depository libraries dispersed geographically throughout the United States make government publications accessible free of charge to the public. To locate the depository closest to you, send for the free list of depositories available from the Superintendent of Documents (entry 107 in this book) or call the reference desk at your local library and ask about nearby depository locations.

Many depositories use the Superintendent of Documents classification number (SuDocs number) to shelve federal documents. Do not assume that the library does not own a document if it is not on the shelves under SuDocs number, however. It may be out on loan or shelved with the general book collection, with reference materials, in microform, or in another special location. It is always best to ask the documents librarian for assistance when you cannot locate a document.

PART ONE

General Reference Sources

Bibliographic Aids

GENERAL WORKS

1. Evinger, William R., ed. **Guide to Federal Government Acronyms**. Phoenix, AZ: Oryx Press, 1989. 279p. ISBN 0-89774-458-6. LC 89-34235. JK464.1989. 353/.000148. OCLC 19778265.

The terms in this dictionary of federal acronyms, initialisms, and abbreviations are searchable by their shortened or full form. Terms represent agency names, products, services, programs, projects, surveys and data collections, position titles, laws, the legislative and regulatory process, budgeting, and online systems, along with terms found in publication titles. The department or agency associated with the term is noted.

2. Garner, Diane L., and Diane H. Smith. **The Complete Guide to Citing Government Information Resources: A Manual for Writers & Librarians**. Bethesda, MD: Congressional Information Service, 1993. rev. ed. 222p. ISBN 0-88692-254-2. LC 93-16059. Z7164.G7G37 1993. 016.015. OCLC 28149726.

This manual outlines citation styles for U.S. federal, state, local, and regional titles, as well as electronic sources and publications of other national governments.

BIBLIOGRAPHIES

3. American Library Association. Government Documents Round Table. **Guide to Official Publications of Foreign Countries**. Bethesda, MD: Congressional Information Service, 1990. 359p. LC 90-187873. Z7164.G7G83 1990. 011/.53. OCLC 22197467.

Annotated entries describe books and serials in subject areas, along with bibliographies and catalogs, census data, government directories, and sources of general information for each country. Sources of availability are noted.

4. Bailey, William G. **Guide to Popular U.S. Government Publications**. Englewood, CO: Libraries Unlimited, 1993. 3d ed. 289p. ISBN 1-56308-031-1. LC 93-17573. Z1223.Z7B35 1993. 015.73/053. OCLC 28112610.

This annotated, subject compilation of popular and best-selling general-interest titles notes issuing agency, imprint, collation, GPO stock number and price, and SuDocs number. Includes subject and title indexes, and a list of publications catalogs. Updates Walter L. Newsome's *New Guide to Popular Government Publications* (1978).

5. **Bibliographic Guide to Government Publications—Foreign**. Boston: G. K. Hall, 1975- . ISSN 0360-280X. LC 76-646764. Z7164.G7N54 1972 Suppl. 011. OCLC 2368564.

This is a compilation of reproduced catalog copy for non-U.S. government titles acquired during the year by The Research Libraries of the New York Public Library, with additional LC MARC-tape entries. Publications emanating from developing countries, international and regional agencies, state and provincial governments, and major cities include official parliamentary debates and papers, session laws, foreign relations correspondence, treaties, departmental reports, censuses, and statistical compendiums. Access is by main entry, with added entries for subject, title, author, series, and some conference/meetings.

6. **Bibliographic Guide to Government Publications—U.S.** Boston: G. K. Hall, 1975- . Annual. ISSN 0360-2796. LC 76-646765. Z7164.G7N54 1972 Suppl. 2. 015/.73. OCLC 5754678.

This is a compilation of reproduced catalog copy for federal, state, and regional government publications acquired during the year by The Research Libraries of the New York Public Library, with additional LC MARC-tape entries. Access is by main entry, with added entries for subject, title, author, series, and some conference/meetings.

7. Body, Alexander C. **Annotated Bibliography of Bibliographies on Selected Government Publications and Supplementary Guides to the Superintendent of Documents Classification System**. Kalamazoo, MI: Western Michigan University, 1967. 181p. ISSN 0198-6996. LC 67-28593. Z1223.Z7B65. 016.015/73. OCLC 953372.

> Supplement 1. 1968.
> Supplement 2. 1970.
> Supplement 3. 1972.
> Supplement 4. 1974.
> Supplement 5 compiled by Gabor Kovacs. 1977.
> Supplement 6 compiled by Gabor Kovacs. 1980.
> Supplement 7 compiled by Gabor Kovacs. 1982.
> Supplement 8 compiled by Gabor Kovacs. 1984.
> Supplement 9 compiled by Gabor Kovacs. 1986.
> Supplement 10 compiled by Gabor Kovacs. 1988.
> Supplement 11 compiled by Mary L. Alm. 1990.

This is a bibliography of agency catalogs, published computer searches, subject bibliographies, and library catalogs listed in the *Monthly Catalog* and available to depository libraries. Annotated entries are arranged by SuDocs number and include OCLC number and *Monthly Catalog* entry number. Indexed by titles and subjects. Supplements are issued every two to three years.

8. Geahigan, Priscilla C., and Robert F. Rose, eds. **Business Serials of the U.S. Government**. Chicago: American Library Association, 1988. 2d ed. 86p. ISBN 0-83893-349-1. LC 88-3428. Z7165.U5B88 1988. 016.330973. OCLC 17547833.

An annotated subject guide for small and medium-sized public and academic libraries, "especially those who cannot afford to subscribe to the *American Statistics Index (ASI)*." Government and commercial indexes covering each serial are noted.

9. **Government Reference Books**. Englewood, CO: Libraries Unlimited, 1969- . Biennial. ISSN 0072-5188. LC 76-146307. Z1223.Z7G68. 015/.73. OCLC 1028303.

GRB is an annotated subject guide to government-issued atlases, bibliographies, compendiums, dictionaries, directories, guides, handbooks, indexes, and manuals. It includes GPO and non-GPO materials. Arrangement is by subject, with indexes for authors, titles, and subjects. Coverage began with 1968.

10. **Guide to U.S. Government Publications**. McLean, VA: Documents Index, 1973- . Annual. ISSN 0092-3168. LC 74-646648. Z1223.Z7A574. 015/.73. OCLC 1795366.

"Andriot" (popularly known by its editor's name) is a bibliography of key federal periodicals, series, and reference materials issued within series, with a complete listing of SuDocs classification stems since the turn of the century. Entries include SuDocs number stem (with SuDocs classification number history), depository item number, frequency, selected annotations, title changes, and ISSN. An "Agency Class Chronology" records the history of SuDocs classification stems and corresponding agencies. Includes title, keyword in title, and agency indexes and *A Practical Guide to the Superintendent of Documents Classification System* (GP 3.29:Pr 88).

11. Schwarzkopf, LeRoy C. **Government Reference Serials**. Englewood, CO: Libraries Unlimited, 1988. 344p. ISBN 0-87287-451-6. LC 87-37846. Z1223.Z7S338 1988. 015.73/053. OCLC 17353510.

This annotated subject guide describes reference periodicals and serials. A companion to *Government Reference Books* (entry 9), it offers the same subject arrangement.

12. **U.S. Government Periodicals Index**. Bethesda, MD: Congressional Information Service, 1993- . Quarterly. ISSN 1076-3163. LC 94-640854. Z1223.Z7U5227. 070.5/09753. OCLC 30094729.

This subject and author index to federal periodicals is available in print, CD-ROM, or magnetic tape. A retrospective issue covers the years 1988–93.

13. Williams, Wiley J. **Subject Guide to Major United States Government Publications**. Chicago: American Library Association, 1987. 2d ed. 257p. ISBN 0-83890-475-0. LC 87-1152. Z1223.Z7J32 1987. 015.73/053. OCLC 15411326.

This annotated, subject compilation of seminal historical and contemporary titles is aimed at librarians and scholars. Appendixes list guides, catalogs, indexes, and directories of government information sources, and Subject Bibliographies. Updates Ellen Jackson's 1968 edition of the same title.

14. Zink, Steven D. **United States Government Publications Catalogs**. Washington, DC: Special Libraries Association, 1988. 2d ed. 292p. ISBN 0-87111-335-X. LC 87-32353. Z1223.A12Z56 1988. 015.73/053. OCLC 17202276.

This is an annotated bibliography of federal agencies' own catalogs, bibliographies, and publications lists, including lists of audiovisual and electronic information.

DIRECTORIES

15. American Library Association. Government Documents Round Table. **Directory of Government Document Collections & Librarians**. Washington, DC: Congressional Information Service, 1974- . Irregular. ISSN 0276-959X. LC 81-645853. Z1223.Z7D57. 011/.53. OCLC 3998563.

This state and city directory of U.S. documents collections and libraries gives addresses, telephone and fax numbers, E-mail addresses, and information about collections, depository status, subject specialties, and staff names. Indexes allow searching by library name, type of documents collected (state, local, international, and foreign), special collections (subject specialties, collection strengths, regional emphases), and library staff. Other sections list library school documents faculty; people and agencies administering state documents programs; organizations involved in government document activities and government agencies with sales programs; and subject terms, agency names, and acronyms.

16. Evinger, William R. **Federal Statistical Source: Where to Find Agency Experts & Personnel**. Phoenix, AZ: Oryx Press, 1991. 29th ed. 161p. ISBN 0-89774-673-2. LC 91-31174. HA37.U55E85 1991. 353.0081/9. OCLC 24285012.

This is a directory of people working with federal statistics in the executive branch, independent agencies, and selected agencies outside the executive branch. Arrangement is by agency name, augmented by a personal name index. Each entry notes agency address, telephone number, and area of expertise (including the surveys, data series, or publications on which he or she works). Organizational entries also list agency library and publications office staff. Appendixes list frequently called numbers, Census Bureau State Data Center Lead Agencies, Bureau of Justice Statistics Statistical Analysis Centers, and National Agricultural Statistics Service State Statisticians-in-Charge. Supersedes *Federal Statistical Directory: The Guide to Personnel and Data Sources*. From 1944 to 1987, the *Federal Statistical Directory* was published by GPO (C 1.75:).

17. Evinger, William R., ed. **Directory of Federal Libraries**. Phoenix, AZ: Oryx Press, 1993. 2d ed. 373p. ISBN 0-89774-674-0. LC 92-33458. Z731.E93 1993. 027.5/025/73. OCLC 26858095.

Profiles of federal government libraries in the U.S. and other nations include address, telephone and fax numbers, with information about staff, depository status, automated operations, services and collections, and publications. Includes library type, subject, and geographic indexes.

18. **Government Research Directory**. Detroit: Gale Research, 1985- . ISSN 0882-3766. LC 85-647549. Q179.98.G68. 001.4/025/73. OCLC 11826223.

Research facilities operated by or for the federal government are listed, with address, director, telephone and fax numbers, official acronym or initialism, description, databases, publications, and special collections. Includes alphabetical, subject, and geographic (by state and city) indexes.

19. Lovinger, King F., comp. **The Federal Government Subject Guide**. Jefferson, NC: McFarland, 1987. 139p. ISBN 0-89950-238-5. LC 86-43179. JK411.L68.1987. 353/.00025. OCLC 15107407.

This subject directory of federal agency specialties includes addresses and telephone numbers.

20. National Historical Publications and Records Commission. **Directory of Archives and Manuscript Repositories in the United States**. Phoenix, AZ: Oryx Press, 1988. 2d ed. 853p. ISBN 0-89774-475-6. LC 87-30157. CD3020.D49.1988. 016.091/025/73. OCLC 16984463.

Repositories of historical research materials in the United States, Puerto Rico, and the Virgin Islands are described, noting address, size, telephone number, hours of service, user fees, access restrictions, and holdings (including photographs, sound recordings, machine-readable files, films, architectural drawings, and microfilms). Indexed by subject and repository names.

21. Washington Researchers Publishing. **Who Knows, A Guide to Washington Experts**. Washington, DC: Washington Researchers, 1992. Edition XII. 373p. ISBN 1-56365-014-2. OCLC 26998210.

This directory of federal offices and staff focuses on information sources for markets, competition, law and policy, economics, and the social environment. Gives addresses and telephone numbers for experts in administrative agencies, cabinet departments, the judiciary, and the legislative branch.

22. Zwirn, Jerrold, comp. **Access to U.S. Government Information: Guide to Executive and Legislative Authors and Authority**. New York: Greenwood, 1989. 158p. ISBN 0-31326-851-7. LC 89-27373. Z1223.Z7Z87 1989. 015.73/053. OCLC 20422724.

Searching by subject allows identification of executive and legislative agencies with jurisdiction over that area. Includes indexes to parent agencies, agency subunits, and congressional committees.

GUIDES

23. Boyd, Anne Morris. **United States Government Publications**. New York: Wilson, 1952. 3d ed. revised by Rae Elizabeth Rips. 627p. LC 55-694. Z1223.Z7B7 1952. 015.73. OCLC 1932283.

Still useful for historical information on the history, organization, and functions of government agencies as they pertain to printing, publishing, and distribution of documents. Includes subject and title indexes.

24. Ekhaml, Leticia T., and Alice J. Wittig. **U.S. Government Publications for the School Library Media Center**. Englewood, CO: Libraries Unlimited, 1991. rev. ed. 172p. ISBN 0-87287-822-8. LC 90-20016. Z1223.A12E38 1991. 015.73/053. OCLC 22629818.

This annotated guide to documents for elementary and secondary school libraries emphasizes titles sold by the GPO and includes an overview of federal government information. Most entries include SuDocs number, GPO stock number, and price.

25. Herman, Edward. **Locating U.S. Government Information: A Guide to Print and Electronic Sources**. Buffalo, NY: William Hein, [expected publication date, 1996]. 2d ed.

This guide to locating U.S. government information in print and electronic sources includes the Internet, bibliographic sources, indexes to historical documents, legislative materials, statutory and regulatory sources, statistical sources, technical reports, the Freedom of Information and Privacy Acts, and directories. Illustrated, with questions and answers presented in a workbook style.

26. Kelly, Melody S. **Using Government Documents: A How-To-Do-It Manual for School Librarians**. New York: Neal-Schuman, 1992. 160p. ISBN 1-55570-106-X. LC 92-11729. Z688.G6K44 1992. 025.2/8. OCLC 25547569.

This guide to documents collection development includes a list of recommended titles for school and public libraries.

27. Lavin, Michael R. **Understanding the Census: A Guide for Marketers, Planners, Grant Writers, and Other Data Users**. Kenmore, NY: Epoch, 1996. 545p. ISBN 0-96295-861-1. LC 96-146991. HA201.1990ar. 304.6/0723. OCLC 34536389.

This in-depth manual explains print and electronic Census publications, definitions, concepts, and practices with sample tables, examples, tips, and other user aids.

28. Lavin, Michael R., Jane Weintrop, and Cynthia Cornelius. **Subject Index to the 1990 Census of Population and Housing**. Kenmore, NY: Epoch Books, [expected publication date, October 1996]. approx. 140p.

This is a detailed table locator for major print and electronic products of the 1990 Census. Part A provides a composite Table Finding Guide covering every 1990 print report. Part B offers a variety of indexes (alphabetical, numerical, subject, and coverage universe) for STF 1 and STF 3, the major CD-ROM series for 1990. Part C contains an abbreviated glossary of key Census terms.

29. Morehead, Joe. **Introduction to United States Government Information Sources**. Englewood, CO: Libraries Unlimited, 1996. 5th ed. 333p. ISBN 1-56308-485-6. LC 96-6246. Z1223.M674 1996. 015.73/053. OCLC 34318432.

This is a classic guide to federal government publishing, the GPO, and depository libraries, with introductions to key titles, including technical reports, statistics, geographic information, and government periodicals and serials.

30. Robinson, Judith Schiek. **Tapping the Government Grapevine: The User-Friendly Guide to U.S. Government Information Sources**. Phoenix, AZ: Oryx Press, 1993. 2d ed. 227p. ISBN 0-89774-712-7. LC 92-40201. Z1223.Z7R633 1993. 025.17/34. OCLC 27108990.

This clearly written guide to government information includes descriptions of key information resources, search tips, glossaries, summary tables, and practice exercises. It covers GPO and depository libraries and key sources, including scientific, statistical, nonprint, and primary resources. It includes a chapter on foreign and international documents and a list of SuDocs numbers for key federal titles.

31. Schmeckebier, Laurence Frederick, and Roy B. Eastin. **Government Publications and Their Use**. Washington, DC: Brookings Institution, 1969. 2d rev. ed. 502p. ISBN 0-81577-736-1. LC 69-19694. Z1223.Z7S3 1969. 025.17/3. OCLC 52095.

This is a standard reference describing historical U.S. government publishing and tracing historical materials. It discusses basic guides to government publications, including indexes, catalogs and bibliographies, compilations, and series.

32. Schorr, Alan Edward. **Federal Documents Librarianship, 1879-1987**. Juneau, AK: Denali, 1988. 215p. ISBN 0-93873-714-7. LC 87-73054. Z675.D63S36 1988. 015.73053. OCLC 17595326.

This comprehensive bibliography of literature on U.S. government documents and government information policy includes books, articles, chapters, editorials, conference proceedings, theses and dissertations, reviews, columns, news, and miscellaneous contributions. It is arranged by subject, with an author index.

33. Sears, Jean L., and Marilyn K. Moody. **Using Government Information Sources: Print and Electronic**. Phoenix, AZ: Oryx Press, 1994. 2d ed. 539p. ISBN 0-89774-670-8. LC 93-30859. Z1223.Z7S4 1994. 015.73/053. OCLC 28631325.

This manual for identifying and using government information sources is arranged by type of search, with sources and search strategies thoroughly explained.

General Works

GENERAL WORKS

34. Congress. Joint Committee on Printing. **A Directory of U.S. Government Depository Libraries**. GPO, 1985- . Free: Government Printing Office, Washington, DC 20402. Annual. LC 91-642133. Z675.D4D56. 027/.0025/73. OCLC 13202927. Y 4.P 93/1-10: .

> Also available on the Internet: *Federal Bulletin Board* (entry 35): Select *Federal Depository Library Files/Depository Library Files/profiles.dbf.*

Lists regional and selective depository libraries by state and city, with addresses; telephone, fax, and E-mail numbers; depository library number; designation type, year designated, and size; staff names; and congressional districts. Includes the text of depository laws.

35. Government Printing Office. **Federal Bulletin Board**. GP 3.35: Internet *URL http://fedbbs.access.gpo.gov/* or *URL telnet://fedbbs.access.gpo.gov/.*

The FBB provides access to federal agency electronic products for downloading to personal computers, including CD-ROMs, diskettes, magnetic tapes, and online files. The FBB allows online ordering of GPO sales titles and access to Subject Bibliographies and other free catalogs. Users must register for an ID to use the FBB by calling (202) 512-1387. Request more information from the GPO Office of Electronic Information Dissemination Services (202) 512-1265; fax (202) 612-1262. Also available on GPO Access (entry 104).

36. Library of Congress. **LC MARVEL**. Internet *URL http://www.loc.gov/* or *URL gopher://marvel.loc.gov/70* or *URL http://lcweb.loc.gov.*

MARVEL is LC's gopher for Internet access to LC information and other resources on the Internet, including numerous government and commercial information resources.

37. Library of Congress. **Library of Congress Publications in Print**. LC, 19??- . Free: Office Systems Services, Printing and Processing Section, Washington, DC 20540-5446. Biennial. LC 06-35005. Z733.U57B15. 015.73. OCLC 2561502. LC 1.12/2-3: .

> Also available on the Internet on LC MARVEL (entry 36): Select *Services and Publications/Library of Congress Publications.*

This is a bibliography of books, pamphlets, serials, and audio and video recordings published by LC, with availability information and an index.

38. Library of Congress. **Respectfully Quoted: A Dictionary of Quotations Requested from the Congressional Research Service** edited by Suzy Platt. GPO, 1989. 520p. LC 86-600157. PN6081.R435 1989. 081. OCLC 13642402. LC 14.2:D 56.

Quotations accumulated over the past 50 years in the "Quote File" of the Congressional Reading Room cite sources and note attribution. With author and subject indexes.

39. National Technical Information Service. **FedWorld**. Internet *URL telnet://fedworld.gov* or *URL http://ftp.fedworld.gov/* or *URL http://www.fedworld.gov/*.

This "electronic marketplace of U.S. and foreign government information" is a gateway to federal agency online systems, online ordering of government reports, and access to government databases, files, documents, and federal job listings.

40. Smithsonian Institution. Press. **Complete Catalog**. SI, 19??- . Free: Box 1579, Washington, DC 20560. Annual. LC sn87-42145. OCLC 14395211. SI 1.17/4: .

This annotated list of in-print titles is updated by the free supplement New Titles (SI 1.17/2:Sm 6). It is issued alternatively with *New Books* (SI 1.17/2:Sm 6/1), also free.

41. Superintendent of Documents. Office of the Assistant Public Printer. **Inactive or Discontinued Items from the 1950 Revision of the Classified List**. GPO, 1953- . Annual. LC sn85-949. 011. OCLC 4128255. GP 3.24/2: .

This update to the List of Classes (entry 42) is arranged by item number, with class title, SuDocs number stem and issuing agency are noted. There is no index or cross-references.

42. Superintendent of Documents. Office of the Assistant Public Printer. **List of Classes of United States Government Publications Available for Selection by Depository Libraries**. GPO, 1960- . Quarterly. LC 90-649584. Z1223.A7L57. 015.73/053. OCLC 5529709. GP 3.24: .

Also available on the Internet: *Federal Bulletin Board* (entry 35).

This listing of all categories ("classes") of materials available to federal depository libraries is organized according to issuing agencies and SuDocs number stems. Each class is identified by a depository item number and its SuDocs number stem. A code indicates the format of distribution. There are indexes converting item numbers and issuing agencies to SuDocs number stems, plus lists of deleted or inactive classes.

BIBLIOGRAPHIES
BY GEOGRAPHIC REGION

Africa

43. Library of Congress. African Section. African and Middle Eastern Division. **Africa South of the Sahara: Index to Periodical Literature. Third Supplement**. LC, 1985. Free to U.S. Libraries and Institutions: Office Systems Services, Printing and Processing Section, Washington, DC 20540-5446. 306p. LC 85-18068. Z3503.U47 Suppl. 3. 016.967/005. OCLC 12370934. LC 41.12:Af 8.

Volumes 1-4. 1900-1970. Available in microfilm from Macmillan Publishing.

First Supplement. 1973. Available in microfilm from Macmillan Publishing.

Second Supplement. 1982. Available in microfilm from Macmillan Publishing.

This is a subject bibliography of journal articles omitted from standard periodical indexes and about any African country except Algeria, Egypt, Libya, Morocco, and Tunisia. Volumes 1-4 cover the years 1900–70. The first supplement covers articles published during the period 1971–June 1972 and the second covers the period June 1972–December 1976. The third supplement, covering those articles published in 1977, will be the last and is the only one available free.

44. Library of Congress. African Section. **Sub-Saharan Africa: A Guide to Serials.** LC, 1970. Free: Office Systems Services, Washington, DC 20540. 409p. LC 70-607392. Z3503.U49. 016.9167/03. OCLC 102654. LC 2.8:Af 8/2.
This bibliography of publications related to Africa south of the Sahara includes monographic series, annual reports, yearbooks, and directories. The publications cited are in Western languages, or in African languages using the Roman alphabet, and are owned by the Library of Congress or other American libraries represented in the *National Union Catalog*. Many serials have "indexed in" notations, guiding readers to appropriate indexing and abstracting services.

45. Library of Congress. African Section. **U.S. Imprints on Sub-Saharan Africa: A Guide to Publications Cataloged at the Library of Congress.** GPO, 1985- . Biennial. LC 86-658057. Z3509.U18. 016.967. OCLC 13521020. LC 41.12/2: .
> Vol. 1. 1985. Free to U.S. Libraries and Institutions: Office Systems Services, Printing and Processing Section, Washington, DC 20540-5446.
> Vol. 2. 1986. Free to U.S. Libraries and Institutions: Office Systems Services, Printing and Processing Section, Washington, DC 20540-5446.
> Vol. 3. 1987. Free to U.S. Libraries and Institutions: Office Systems Services, Printing and Processing Section, Washington, DC 20540-5446.
> Vol. 4/5. 1988/89. Free to U.S. Libraries and Institutions: Office Systems Services, Printing and Processing Section, Washington, DC 20540-5446.
> Vol. 6/7. 1990/91. GPO.

This bibliography reproduces the Library of Congress's catalog copy for U.S.-published or -distributed monographs about sub-Saharan Africa. Includes a list of titles and an index of subjects, geographic terms, and personal authors.

46. Library of Congress. **Arabic-English and English-Arabic Dictionaries in the Library of Congress** compiled by George Dimitri Selim. GPO, 1992. 213p. LC 92-147161. Z7052.S4 1992. 016.492/7321. OCLC 25755852. LC 41.9:Ar 1/3.
Lists general language and special subject dictionaries, glossaries, and vocabularies, along with multilingual dictionaries that include Arabic and English entries. With name and title indexes.

47. Library of Congress. Library of Congress Office, Nairobi, Kenya. **Accessions List, Eastern Africa.** LC, 1968- . Free to Libraries: Field Director, Karachi-LOC, U.S. Department of State, Washington, DC 20520. Bimonthly. LC 76-607943. Z3516.U52. 016.9167. OCLC 2403577. LC 1.30/8: .
This record of publications received in the Library of Congress Office, Eastern Africa, is supplemented by an *Annual Serial Supplement* listing all serials received by the office (LC 1.30/8-2:) and *Annual Publisher's Directory*, a cumulated list of publishers listed in individual issues (LC 1.30/8-3:). There is an annual cumulative index.

48. Library of Congress. Serial and Government Publications Division. **African Newspapers in the Library of Congress** compiled by John Pluge, Jr. LC, 1984. Free to U.S. Libraries and Institutions: Office Systems Services, Printing and Processing Section, Washington, DC 20540-5446. 2d ed. 144p. LC 84-600992. Z6959.Z9L53 1984. 015.68/035. OCLC 10779261. LC 6.9:Af 8.

This is an inventory of LC holdings of newspapers from 52 countries in Africa through June 1983. Entries note frequency, first year of publication, and holdings. Includes a title index.

Asia

49. Library of Congress. African and Middle Eastern Division. **Persian and Afghan Newspapers in the Library of Congress, 1871-1978** by Ibrahim V. Pourhadi. LC, 1979. Free to U.S. Libraries and Institutions: Office Systems Services, Printing and Processing Section, Washington, DC 20540-5446. 101p. LC 79-12160. Z6958.I65P875. 016.079/55. OCLC 4857473. LC 1.12/2:P 43/871-978.

This is an alphabetical inventory of Library of Congress holdings of newspapers from Iran and Afghanistan, with short annotations. An introductory essay describes the 13 categories of newspapers in the collection and their significance. A chronological index shows place and first year of publication. There is also an index of editors, publishers, and newspaper owners.

50. Library of Congress. Asian Division. **Chinese Periodicals in the Library of Congress** compiled by Han Chu Huang and David H. G. Hsu. LC, 1988. Free to U.S. Libraries and Institutions: Office Systems Services, Printing and Processing Section, Washington, DC 20540-5446. 814p. LC 87-600394. Z6958.C5L52 1988. 015.51034. OCLC 16922527. LC 17.9:C 44/2.

This is a list of periodicals issued during the years 1868–1986 and held in LC's Chinese and Korean Section, Asian Division. Location and call numbers are provided. Titles are given in Chinese and romanized English. Those about law, technical agriculture, or clinical medicine are omitted. Law serials are held in the Far Eastern Law Division of LC's Law Library; technical agriculture and clinical medicine in the National Agricultural Library and the National Library of Medicine. Also omitted are periodicals on microform in the Chinese Collection.

51. Library of Congress. Asian Division. **Vietnamese Holdings in the Library of Congress: A Bibliography** compiled by A. Kohar Rony. LC, 1982. Free to U.S. Libraries and Institutions: Office of Systems Services, Printing and Processing Section, Washington, DC 20540-5446. 236p. LC 81-2847. Z3228.V5L52 1982. 016.9597. OCLC 7329336. LC 17.9:V 67.
     Vietnamese Holdings in the Library of Congress. Supplement, 1979-1985. LC 17.9:V 67/SUPP./979-85.

This bibliography of Vietnamese language materials in the Library of Congress's Asian Division lists books, serials, and newspapers, with subject, title, and issuing body indexes.

52. Library of Congress. **Chinese Newspapers in the Library of Congress: A Bibliography = [Kuo Hui Tou Shu Kuan Tsoang Chung Wen Pao Koan Mu Lu]** compiled by Han-chu Huang and Hseo-chin Jen. LC, 1985. Free to U.S. Libraries and Institutions: Office Systems Services, Printing and Processing Section, Washington, DC 20540-5446. 206p. LC 84-600306. Z6958.C5L52 1985. 011/.35. OCLC 11289393. LC 17.9:C 44.

This comprehensive list of Chinese-language newspapers published in either paper or microform since the 1870s and held in LC's Chinese and Korean Section includes general, official government, special interest, and special subject newspapers. Titles are romanized in the Wade-Giles system and in Chinese characters, with place of publication, frequency, and holdings. Includes location and title indexes (strokes of the first character of each title), along with a Pinyin conversion table.

53. Library of Congress. **Guide to Japanese Reference Books: Supplement** by Nihon no Sanko Tosho Henshu Iinkai. LC, 1979. Free to U.S. Libraries and Institutions: Office Systems Services, Printing and Processing Section, Washington, DC 20540-5446. English-language edition. 300p. LC 77-608084. Z1035.8.J3.N55 1966 Suppl. 011/.02. OCLC 3069592. LC 1.12/2:J 27/2.

This title supplements *Guide to Japanese Reference Books* (1966, American Library Association), and covers works published during the years 1964–70. Notes Japanese and translated titles, with English annotations for some titles.

54. Library of Congress. **Japanese Children's Books at the Library of Congress: A Bibliography of Books from the Postwar Years, 1946-1985** compiled by Tayo Shima and edited by Sybille A. Jagusch. GPO, 1987. 57p. LC 87-600327. Z1037.8.J3L53 1987. 016.8956/09/9282. OCLC 16682456. LC 1.12/2:J 27/4.

Japanese children's books and magazines, reprints of prewar books, history and criticism, exhibition catalogs, and reference periodicals are listed. Includes title, author, and artist indexes.

55. Library of Congress. Library of Congress Office, Cairo. **Accessions List, Middle East**. LC, 1974- . Free to Libraries: Field Director, Karachi-LOC, Department of State, Washington, DC 20520. Bimonthly. LC 75-644385. Z3013.U54. 015/.56. OCLC 2452246. LC 1.30/3: .

   Annual Index. LC 1.30/3: .

ALME is a record of Middle Eastern and Iranian commercial and government publications acquired by the Library of Congress Cairo and Karachi offices. The Cairo office collects Arab publications from the Arab world, Europe, Turkey, and Cyprus, plus titles in Armenian and Kurdish from non-Arab countries. Excluded are publications of Mauritania and of Djibouti and Somalia, which are cited in *Accessions List, Eastern Africa* (entry 47). A cumulative author index is issued at the year's end, and a cumulative serials list in July/August.

56. Library of Congress. Library of Congress Office, New Delhi. **Accessions List, South Asia**. LC, 1981- . Free to Libraries: Field Director, New Delhi-LOC, U.S. Department of State, Washington, DC 20520. Monthly. LC 81-644186. Z3185.L52a. 015.59. OCLC 6674270. LC 1.30/10-3: .

This is a record of publications from Afghanistan, Bangladesh, Bhutan, India, Maldives, Nepal, Pakistan, and Sri Lanka acquired by the Library of Congress offices in New Delhi, India, and Karachi, Pakistan. Includes monographs, serials, and special materials. Monthly issues and the December cumulative index include author, title, and subject indexes. Beginning with V. 24, no. 103, bibliographic entries for Burma, Cambodia, Laos, and Thailand will also be included; these were formerly listed in *Accessions List, Southeast Asia* (LC 1.30/10:), which has been discontinued.

57. Library of Congress. Orientalia Division. **Chinese-English and English-Chinese Dictionaries in the Library of Congress: An Annotated Bibliography** compiled by Robert Dunn. LC, 1977. Free to U.S. Libraries and Institutions: Office Systems Services, Printing and Processing Section, Washington, DC 20540-5446. 140p. LC 76-608329. Z3109.U53 1977. 495.1/3/21. OCLC 2596898. LC 17.2:C 43/5.

An annotated list of Library of Congress holdings of Chinese-English and English-Chinese dictionaries and glossaries on all subjects, plus polyglot and multilingual dictionaries with English and Chinese entries. Includes vocabularies, word lists, syllabaries, sci/tech glossaries, and lists of names, nomenclature, phrases, sayings, and proverbs. Not included are Chinese dictionaries limited to the Chinese language or with equivalents in languages other than English.

58. Library of Congress. **Philippine Holdings in the Library of Congress, 1960-1987: A Bibliography** compiled by A. Kohar Rony. GPO, 1993. 702p. LC 92-3438. Z3299.L53 1993. 016.9599. OCLC 25317397. LC 17.9:P 53.

This is a comprehensive, computer-generated subject bibliography of books and maps in the LC collections issued by or about the Philippines.

59. Library of Congress. Southern Asia Section. **Southeast Asia: Western-Language Periodicals in the Library of Congress** compiled by A. Kohar Rony. LC, 1979. Free to U.S. Libraries and Institutions: Office Systems Services, Printing and Processing Section, Washington, DC 20540-5446. 201p. LC 79-607777. Z3221.U524 1979. 016.959. OCLC 5474230. LC 17.2:As 4/4.

This is an alphabetical list of Library of Congress holdings of periodicals published both in and outside Southeast Asia containing information on Southeast Asia. Subject and issuing body indexes are included.

60. Library of Congress. **The Near East National Union List** compiled by Dorothy Stehle. 1v. LC, 1988. Free to U.S. Libraries and Institutions: Office Systems Services, Printing and Processing Section, Washington, DC 20540-5446. LC 87-600398. Z3015.N4 1988. 015.956. OCLC 16950660. LC 41.12:N 27/v.1.

The NENUL is a bibliography of pre-1979 publications, manuscripts, and serials in Arabic, Persian, and Turkish reported to the *National Union Catalog* by libraries in the U.S. and Canada, including the Library of Congress's Near East Section.

Europe

61. Library of Congress. **Finland and the Finns: A Selective Bibliography** by Elemer Bako. LC, 1993. 276p. LC 93-16151. Z2520.B33 1993. 016.94897. OCLC 27382885. LC 43.9:F 49.

This is a subject list of LC holdings (largely in English) of maps, books, and serials by Finns, Americans, Scandinavians, and others, issued from before 1945 to 1991. Includes name indexes (authors, translators, editors, illustrators, subjects of research, etc.), a topical guide to chapters, and an abbreviation/acronyms list.

62. Library of Congress. **Hidden Research Resources in the Dutch-Language Collections of the Library of Congress: A Selective Bibliography of Reference Works = Verborgen Onderzoeks-Bronnen in de Nederlandstalige Collectie van de Library of Congress** by Margrit B. Krewson. LC, 1993. Free: European Division, Washington, DC 20540-5530. 74p. LC 93-772. Z2401.K74 1993. 016.9492. OCLC 27812455. LC 1.12/2:D 95.

This list of minimally cataloged Dutch materials in the LC collections is arranged by subject, with title and author indexes. About two-thirds are available only at the Library of Congress.

63. Library of Congress. **Hidden Research Resources in the German Collections of the Library of Congress: A Selective Bibliography of Reference Works** by Margrit B. Krewson. LC, 1992. Free: European Division, Washington, DC 20540-5530. 170p. LC 92-31469. Z2000.K74 1992. 016.943. OCLC 26396013. LC 1.12/2:G 31/7.

Lists reference sources contained in LC's German collection, the largest and most diverse in North America. Includes incunabula, books, personal papers, music, maps, and posters. Two related pamphlets, *The German Collections of the Library of Congress: Chronological Development* (LC 1.2:G 31/2/994) and *Deutschsprachige Bestande in der*

KongreBbibliothek: Chronologische Entrwicklung, are free from Library of Congress, European Division, Washington, DC 20540-5530.

64. Library of Congress. Manuscript Division. **The Portuguese Manuscripts Collection of the Library of Congress: A Guide** compiled by Christopher C. Lund and Mary Ellis Kahler and edited by Mary Ellis Kahler. LC, 1980. Free to U.S. Libraries and Institutions: Office Systems Services, Printing and Processing Section, Washington, DC 20540-5446. 187p. LC 80-607039. Z6621.U582P68. 091. OCLC 6093542. LC 1.6/4:P 83.

This guide describes items in the LC Manuscript Division, many of them originals dating from the 15th to the 20th century.

65. Library of Congress. Slavic and Central European Division. **The Federal Republic of Germany: A Selected Bibliography of English-Language Publications** compiled by Arnold H. Price. LC, 1978. Free to U.S. Libraries and Institutions: Office Systems Services, Printing and Processing Section, Washington, DC 20540-5446. 2d rev. ed. 116p. LC 77-608128. Z2240.3.P75 1978. 016.943. OCLC 3088710. LC 35.2:G 31/3/978.

This unannotated bibliography reflects opinions of American scholars on developments in Germany between 1966 and 1976, with entries arranged by subject.

66. Library of Congress. **The Netherlands and Northern Belgium, A Selective Bibliography of Reference Works** by Margrit B. Krewson. LC, 1988. Free: European Division, Washington, DC 20540-5530. rev. ed. 152p. LC 88-600438. Z2431.K73 1989. 016.949.2. OCLC 18836997. LC 1.12/2:N 38/3.

This list of current resources (focusing on the 1980s) includes works in Dutch, English, French, and German held in the LC collections. It is arranged by subjects, with a name index and a list of scholarly U.S. institutions, fraternal societies, and other sources of information on the Netherlands and Northern Belgium.

Latin America

67. Library of Congress. Library of Congress Office, Rio de Janeiro. **Accessions List, Brazil and Uruguay.** LC, 1989- . Free to Libraries: Field Director, Karachi-LOC, Department of State, Washington, DC 20520. Bimonthly. LC 88-641051. Z1671.U53a. 015/.81. OCLC 18678777. LC 1.30/11: .

Annual List of Serials. LC 1.30/11-3: .

This record of the Brazilian and Uruguayan publications acquired by the Library of Congress's Rio de Janeiro Office lists commercial, institutional, and government monographs and serials. It continues *Accessions List Brazil* (1975-88).

Soviet Union

68. Library of Congress. European Division. **The USSR and East Central and Southeastern Europe; Periodicals in Western Languages** compiled by Janina W. Hoskins. LC, 1979. Free to U.S. Libraries and Institutions: Office Systems Services, Printing and Processing Section, Washington, DC 20540-5446. 4th ed. rev. ed. 87p. LC 78-22038. Z2483.H63 1978. 016.94/005. OCLC 4504699. LC 35.2:P 41/979.

This is an annotated list of social science and humanities periodicals about the Soviet Union and satellite countries, through 1977, with discontinued titles. The journals covered include articles in West European languages on Albania, the Baltic countries, Bulgaria,

Romania, Yugoslavia, and the Soviet Union. Supersedes *The USSR and Eastern Europe: Periodicals in Western Languages*, first published in 1958 and considered an essential research tool through each of its previous three editions.

69. Library of Congress. Reference Department. **Half a Century of Soviet Serials, 1917-68: A Bibliography and Union List of Serials Published in the USSR** compiled by Rudolf Smits. 2v. LC, 1968. Free to U.S. Libraries and Institutions: Central Services Division, Library of Congress, Washington, DC 20540. 1661p. LC 68-62169. Z6956.R9S58. 016.057. OCLC 453552. LC 29.2:So 8/3/v.1-2.

A list of serials (except newspapers) in the Soviet Union since 1917, in all except oriental languages. Some serials that the Library of Congress has classified separately as monographs are included. Entries are arranged alphabetically by title or issuing body, with the language (when not Russian), place of publication, issuing body (for title entries), frequency, title changes, temporary suspensions of publication, and library holdings in the United States and Canada. Supersedes *Serial Publications of the Soviet Union, 1939-57*, without the English-language subject index included in the earlier edition.

BIBLIOGRAPHIES OF GOVERNMENT PUBLICATIONS

Africa

70. Library of Congress. African and Middle Eastern Division. **Libya, 1969-1989: An American Perspective: A Guide to U.S. Official Documents and Government-Sponsored Publications** by Julian W. Witherell. GPO, 1990. 180p. LC 91-184151. Z3971.W57 1990. 016.9612. OCLC 25131837. LC 41.9:L 61.

This is an annotated bibliography of government-sponsored publications on Libya issued since September 1, 1969, located in the Library of Congress, other federal collections, and American libraries. Citations are grouped by subject and include location and holdings information. Includes an index, a list of "African and Middle Eastern Division Publications on the Middle East, 1978-1990," and a map of Libya.

71. Library of Congress. African Section. **French-Speaking Central Africa; A Guide to Official Publications in American Libraries** compiled by Julian W. Witherell. LC, 1973. Free: Office Systems Services, Printing and Processing Section, Washington, DC 20540-5446. 314p. LC 72-5766. Z3692.W5. 015/.67. OCLC 379298. LC 2.8:Af 8/3.

This is a bibliography of government records of former Belgian and French possessions, national governments, and regional and provincial administrations, along with League of Nations and UN documents on Ruanda-Urundi and Cameroon, through 1970.

72. Library of Congress. African Section. **Ghana; A Guide to Official Publications, 1872-1968** compiled by Julian W. Witherell and Sharon B. Lockwood. LC, 1969. Free: Office Systems Services, Printing and Processing Section, Washington, DC 20540-5446. 110p. LC 74-601680. Z3785.W5. 015/.667. OCLC 30009. LC 2.8:G84/872-968.

A bibliography of official documents holdings of the Library of Congress and other American libraries, including publications of the Gold Coast (1872-1957) and Ghana (1957-68); British government documents related to the Gold Coast, Ghana, and British Togoland; and League of Nations and UN publications on British Togoland. Indexed by author and subject.

73. Library of Congress. African Section. **Kenya: Subject Guide to Official Publications** compiled by John Bruce Howell. LC, 1978. Free: Office Systems Services, Printing and Processing Section, Washington, DC 20540-5446. 423p. LC 78-1915. Z3587.H68. 015/.676/2. OCLC 3728868. LC 2.7/2:K 42.

This unannotated bibliography of racial publications of Kenya between 1886 and 1975 is arranged by subject. Locations in the Library of Congress and North American libraries are given.

74. Library of Congress. African Section. **Madagascar and Adjacent Islands: A Guide to Official Publications** compiled by Julian W. Witherell. LC, 1965. Free: Office Systems Services, Printing and Processing Section, Washington, DC 20540-5446. 58p. LC 65-61703. Z3702.U5. OCLC 576807. LC 2.8:M 26.

This is a bibliography of local government publications and selected French and British government documents about their possessions. Includes publications of the French in Madagascar (1896-1958), the Comoro Islands, and Réunion, and British publications issued in Mauritius and the Seychelles Islands.

75. Library of Congress. African Section. **Official Publications of British East Africa**. 4v. LC, 1960-1963. Free: Office Systems Services, Printing and Processing Section, Washington, DC 20540-5446. LC 61-60009. Z3582.U5. 015.676. OCLC 1446417. LC 2.2:Af 8/4/pt.1-4.

> Part 1. **The East Africa High Commission and Other Regional Documents** compiled by Helen F. Conover. 1960. 67p.
>
> Part 2. **Tanganyika** compiled by Audrey A. Walker. 1962. 134p.
>
> Part 3. **Kenya and Zanzibar** compiled by Audrey A. Walker. 1962. 162p.
>
> Part 4. **Uganda** compiled by Audrey A. Walker. 1963. 100p.

Part 1 lists papers and reports of the High Commission, including the Conference of Governors and other official bodies concerned with East Africa as a unit before 1948, with a selection of British official documents. Parts 2-4 are bibliographies of official publications, arranged by author (personal and governmental). Each volume has its own author/subject index.

76. Library of Congress. African Section. **Official Publications of Sierra Leone and Gambia** compiled by Audrey A. Walker. LC, 1963. Free: Office Systems Services, Printing and Processing Section, Washington, DC 20540-5446. 92p. LC 63-60090. Z3553.S5U5. OCLC 1028633. LC 2.2:Si 1/2.

A bibliography of publications dating from the establishment of the central government in both Sierra Leone (part 1) and Gambia (part 2), with some pertinent British government publications, listed alphabetically by author and title. Library of Congress holdings are emphasized. Indexed by subject and author.

77. Library of Congress. African Section. **Uganda: Subject Guide to Official Publications** compiled by Beverly Ann Gray. LC, 1977. Free to U.S. Libraries and Institutions: Office Systems Services, Printing and Processing Section, Washington, DC 20540-5446. 271p. LC 77-608126. Z3586.G7. 015/.676/1. OCLC 3166676. LC 2.8:Ug 1.

This list of official Ugandan publications spanning the years 1893-1974 is arranged under general subjects, with locations in the Library of Congress and other libraries noted.

78. Library of Congress. **East African Community: Subject Guide to Official Publications** compiled by John Bruce Howell. LC, 1976. Free: Office Systems Services, Printing and Processing Section, Washington, DC 20540-5446. 272p. LC 76-608001. Z3516.H68. 015/.67. OCLC 2021205. LC 1.12/2:Af 8.

This is a subject bibliography of official publications of the East African Community and its predecessors, 1926-74, and of the East African region, 1859-1974, issued by Great Britain or one of the three partner states.

79. Library of Congress. **The United States and Sub-Saharan Africa: Guide to U.S. Official Documents and Government-Sponsored Publications, 1976-1980** compiled by Julian W. Witherell. LC, 1984. Free to U.S. Libraries and Institutions: Office Systems Services, Printing and Processing Section, Washington, DC 20540-5446. 721p. LC 84-600009. Z3501.W58 1984. 016.967. OCLC 10458116. LC 41.12:Un 3.

This bibliography of unclassified publications issued by or for the U.S. government lists holdings in the Library of Congress and other institutions. It omits bills, resolutions, Congressional Research Service reports, most preliminary or progress reports on government contracts, and material issued by American cultural centers in Africa. It includes an index and a list of LC publications on Africa covering the years 1965-84. It updates *The United States and Africa: Guide to U.S. Official Documents and Government Sponsored Publications on Africa, 1785-1975* (LC 1.2:Af 8/2/785-975).

Asia

80. Library of Congress. **Afghanistan: An American Perspective: A Guide to U.S. Official Documents and Government-Sponsored Publications** by Julian W. Witherell. LC, 1986. Photoduplication Service, Washington, DC 20540-5230. 158p. LC 86-167382. Z3016.W58 1986. 016.958/104. OCLC 13651278. LC 41.9:Af 3.

This is an annotated bibliography of government-sponsored publications on Afghanistan issued between 1920 and 1984, located in the Library of Congress, other federal collections, and American libraries. Citations are grouped by subject and include location and holdings information. Indexed.

81. Library of Congress. **Censored Japanese Serials of the Pre-1946 Period: A Checklist of the Microfilm Collection = Ken'etsu Wazasshi (1945-Nen Izen): Maikurofirumu Chekkurisuto** compiled by Yoshiko Yoshimura. GPO, 1994. 367p. LC 93-20511. Z6958.J3L53 1994. 015.52034. OCLC 27895680. LC 17.9:J 27/3.

This is a checklist (largely in Japanese) of suppressed or prohibited Japanese government serials transferred from the WDC collection of the Washington Document Centre to the Japanese Section of LC's Asian Division (the MOJ 76 Microfilm Collection). Serially issued government reports are omitted. Includes name, publisher, subject, and title indexes.

82. Library of Congress. **Japanese Government Documents and Censored Publications: A Checklist of the Microfilm Collection = Nihon No Keobunsho Oyobi Ken Etsu Shiryeo (1954-Nen Izen): Maikurofirumu Chekkurisuto** compiled by Yoshiko Yoshimura. GPO, 1992. 531p. LC 89-600094. Z3309.L53 1992. 015.52/053. OCLC 19630408. LC 17.9:J 27/2.

This is a list of Japanese government documents and censored monographs seized during the Occupation of Japan and converted to microfilm, transferred from the WDC collection of the Washington Document Centre to the Library of Congress. The materials are primarily newspapers and serials (with some pre-1946 archival materials). Titles appear in Japanese with English titles in brackets and a brief abstract. There are name, subject, and title indexes.

83. Library of Congress. **Japanese National Government Publications in the Library of Congress: A Bibliography** compiled by Thaddeus Y. Ohta. LC, 1981. Free to U.S. Libraries and Institutions: Office Systems Services, Printing and Processing Section, Washington, DC 20540-5446. 402p. LC 80-607001. Z3305.U54 1981. 015.52. OCLC 7673066. LC 1.12/2:J 27/3.

This inventory of official Japanese government publications added to the LC collections through 1977 includes publications of Japanese legislative, executive, and judicial agencies and of commercial publishers serving the government or quasi-governmental bodies. Most are serials.

84. Library of Congress. **The Republic of Turkey: An American Perspective: A Guide to U.S. Official Documents and Government-Sponsored Publications** by Julian W. Witherell. LC, 1988. Free to U.S. Libraries and Institutions: Office Systems Services, Printing and Processing Section, Washington, DC 20540-5446. 211p. LC 87-600428. Z6465.U5W56 1988. 016.3034/8273/0561. OCLC 17259995. LC 1.6/4:T 84.

This is an annotated bibliography of government-sponsored publications on Turkey issued between 1919 and 1986, located in the Library of Congress, other federal collections, and American libraries. Citations are grouped by subject and include location and holdings information. There is an index, a "List of Library of Congress Publications on the Middle East," and a map of Turkey.

Soviet Union

85. Library of Congress. **Russian Imperial Government Serials on Microfilm in the Library of Congress: A Guide to the Uncataloged Collection** compiled by Harold M. Leich et al. LC, 1985. Free: Office Systems Services, Printing and Processing Section, Washington, DC 20540-5446. 135p. LC 85-600026. Z6956.S65L52 1985. 015.47053. OCLC 11867047. LC 43.8:R 92.

This checklist to a collection of uncataloged government and nongovernment publications and irregular serials of the Czarist period notes titles and LC holdings, with corporate and place of publication indexes. All of the prerevolutionary titles listed are preserved on microfilm that may be purchased from LC's Photoduplication Service.

United States

General

86. Library of Congress. Serial & Government Publications Division. **Popular Names of U.S. Government Reports: A Catalog** compiled by Bernard A. Bernier, Jr. and Karen A. Wood. LC, 1984. Free to U.S. Libraries and Institutions: Office Systems Services, Printing and Processing Section, Washington, DC 20540-5446. 4th ed. 272p. LC 84-603923. Z1223.A199B47 1984. 015/.73/053. OCLC 11430066. LC 6.2:G 74/984.

This source translates the short, popular names of GPO and non-GPO reports into official titles and issuing agencies, with reproductions of their Library of Congress catalog cards, including SuDocs number and *Monthly Catalog* entry number. Citations to older reports include a reference to *Checklist of United States Public Documents, 1789-1909* or *Document Catalog*. Includes a subject index. Updated by: Bengtson, Marjorie C. "Popular Names of U.S. Government Reports: A Supplement" *Illinois Libraries* 69 (September

1987):472-77; Bengtson, Marjorie C. "Popular Names of U.S. Government Reports: Second Supplement" *Illinois Libraries* 75 (April 1993):161-65; Graf, Jeffrey and Louise Malcomb. "Identifying Unidentified U.S. Government Reports" *Journal of Government Information* (March/April 1994):105-28.

Retrospective

87. Congress. **A Descriptive Catalogue of the Government Publications of the United States, September 5, 1774-March 4, 1881** (S.Misc.Doc.V.67) compiled by Benjamin Perley Poore. GPO, 1885. 1392p. LC 01-9291. Z1223.A1885. OCLC 1105499. (Serial Set 2268). [no SuDocs number].

Technically, Poore's Catalogue was the first guide to publications from all three branches of government, although it heavily emphasizes Congress and is considered weak for departmental materials. It is arranged chronologically, with executive and judicial publications at the beginning of each yearly section, followed by congressional publications, listed by the date printing was ordered. Each entry gives title, author, date, and a brief annotation, with a reference for locating the publication in the Serial Set. The general index is most useful for identifying specific publications. Subject entries are lumped together with no indication of contents, making it necessary to check entries on each page cited.

88. Department of the Interior. Division of Documents. **Comprehensive Index to the Publications of the United States Government, 1881-1893** (H.Doc.754) by John G. Ames. 2v. GPO, 1905. LC 05-32405. Z1223.A 1905. OCLC 1217011. (Serial Set 4745, 4746). I 15.2:In 2/2-3.

"Ames" bridges the gap between Poore's *Descriptive Catalogue* and the *Document Catalog*. Despite the "comprehensive" label in the title, many departmental publications were omitted and the focus is on congressional materials. Arranged by subjects and title keywords, information is presented in a three-column format. Authors/issuing agencies are listed in the left column (with a personal name index at the end of volume 2). The main subject entry is in the center: A brief description of contents and the date of publication. The contents of some books were listed separately under subject headings. Documents citations in the right column note report type (S.M. = Senate miscellaneous report; S.E. = Senate executive report), congress-session, and report number.

89. Superintendent of Documents. **Catalogue of the Public Documents of the . . . Congress and of All Departments of the Government of the United States for the Period from . . . to . . . .** 25v. GPO, 1895-1940. LC sn87-28582. OCLC 2477063. GP 3.6: .

The Document Catalog cites departmental and congressional publications from the 53d Congress (1893/94) through the 76th Congress (1939/40). It was issued biennially with each volume covering a single Congress, except for volumes 2 and 3, which covered the first and second sessions of the 54th Congress. This dictionary catalog contains entries for subjects, personal and departmental authors, and some titles. Congressional Serial Set numbers are noted.

90. Superintendent of Documents. **Checklist of United States Public Documents, 1789-1909: Congressional to Close of Sixtieth Congress, Departmental to End of Calendar Year 1909**. GPO, 1911. 3d ed., rev. and enl. 1707p. LC 12-35731. Z1223.A113. OCLC 759306. GP 3.2:C 41/2.

Based on the Public Documents Library collection, the 1909 Checklist is a list of congressional publications from the first through 60th Congresses and departmental publications 1789-1909, compiled in shelflist arrangement by SuDocs number. Also listed are the American State Papers (reprints of documents from the first 14 Congresses), proceedings and miscellaneous congressional publications, and committee reports. Citations include notes about editions, numbers and/or volumes issued for periodicals, and dates of publication. A brief history is given for each agency or department, including name changes or departmental transfers. Citations to the Serial Set are accessed by congress and session, noting for each serial number the volume, part, numbers of reports or documents included, and a brief description of contents. Individual items in Serial Set volumes are not listed, nor are individual titles for series (such as Geological Survey bulletins).

91. Superintendent of Documents. **Index to the Reports and Documents of the 54th Congress, 1st Session—72d Congress, 2d Session, Dec. 2, 1895-March 4, 1933 with Numerical Lists and Schedule of Volumes.** 43v. GPO, 1897-1933. LC 06-20448. Z1223.A14. OCLC 1025843. GP 3.7:1-43.

The "Document Index" lists House and Senate documents and reports from the 54th to 72nd Congresses. The index, issued at the end of each congressional session, contains numerical lists of reports and documents, plus a schedule of Serial Set volumes showing the reports and documents bound in each, along with a subject index. It was superseded by *Numerical Lists and Schedule of Volumes* (entry 101).

92. Superintendent of Documents. **Tables of and Annotated Index to the Congressional Series of United States Public Documents.** GPO, 1902. 769p. LC 02-13262. Z1223.A1902. OCLC 2562645. GP 3.2:P 96.

This is a selected, not a comprehensive, list of congressional publications. Part 1, "Tables," listing documents and reports from the 15th through 52d Congresses (1817–93) arranged by series number, was superseded by the 1909 Checklist (entry 90). Part 2, the "Index," is still useful for locating pre-1893 congressional materials, citing each document and report and its Congressional Serial Set number. However, it does not give the number or session of the Congress.

Current

93. Consumer Information Center. **Consumer Information Catalog.** CIC, 1977- . Free: P.O. Box 100, Pueblo, CO 81002. Quarterly. LC sn87-43042. OCLC 3458485. GS 11.9: .

Also available on the Internet *URL http://www.gsa.gov/staff/pa/cic/cic.html.*

This list of free and inexpensive booklets on popular topics is aimed at the general public and offers only rudimentary bibliographic information: Title, date, and issuing agency. Topics covered include cars, children, food, health, money management and travel. About 40 percent of the titles are free. A Spanish version is available (Lista de Publicaciones Federales en Espanol para el Consumidor). Multiple copies for distribution giveaways can be requested by nonprofit groups.

94. Library of Congress. Exchange and Gift Division. **Monthly Checklist of State Publications.** GPO, 1943-1994. Monthly. LC 10-8924. Z1223.5.A1U5. 015.73. OCLC 2553426. LC 30.9: .

This was a record of state documents received by the Library of Congress, arranged by state and issuing agency. It cited monographs; publications of regional organizations and associations of state officials; library surveys, studies, manuals, and statistics; and periodicals. College catalogs, loose-leaf additions, and slip laws were omitted. Citations usually included LC card number, price, and issuing agency or title changes. There were subject and issuing-agency indexes. Formerly titled *Monthly List of State Publications* (1910–20) and *Monthly Check-List of State Publications* (1921–43).

95. Superintendent of Documents. **GPO Sales Publications Reference File**. GPO, 197?- . Bimonthly with monthly supplement. Microfiche. LC sn86-16446. 015. OCLC 6343237. GP 3.22/3: .

The PRF is a microfiche catalog of GPO sales titles, along with some titles from other sources, such as ERIC. Issued bimonthly with a monthly supplement (*GPO New Sales Publications* GP 3.22/3:), each PRF cumulation completely supersedes the last. Regional depositories receive a weekly update. The Publications Reference File can be searched by GPO stock number, SuDocs number, or keyword (there is no authority list), title, agency series and report number, or personal author. The PRF is also searchable through commercial vendors, with the option of online ordering. The complete PRF master file can be purchased on magnetic tape from GPO (GP 3.22/3-2:). GPO is exploring electronic modes of delivery for the PRF.

96. Superintendent of Documents. **Out-of-Print GPO Sales Publications Reference File**. GPO, 1981- . Annual. Microfiche. LC sn86-16448. OCLC 9474648. GP 3.22/3-3: .

The *OPRF* is a cumulative listing of out-of-stock GPO sales titles. There have been two six-year cumulations: The *Exhausted GPO Sales Publications Reference File, 1980* (*EPRF*), covering the years 1972–78, and the OPRF 1986, covering the years 1979–84. Cumulative supplements in 1989 and 1994 will eventually be superseded by a third six-year cumulation. All six-year cumulations should be kept for a complete record of out-of-stock titles.

97. Superintendent of Documents. **Monthly Catalog of United States Government Publications**. GPO, 1895- . Monthly, with semiannual and annual indexes and periodicals supplement. LC 04-18088. Z1223.A18. 015. OCLC 2264351. GP 3.8: .

As the most comprehensive bibliography of general U.S. government publications, MoCat offers the most inclusive coverage of unclassified agency and departmental information products. It lists both depository and nondepository, GPO and non-GPO titles, in various formats. Bibliographic entries include SuDocs number, depository item number, LC control number, LC and Dewey class numbers, OCLC number, and Library of Congress subject headings. There are author, title, subject (LCSH), series/report number, and keyword indexes, plus semiannual indexes to SuDocs numbers and GPO stock numbers (S/N).

The annual Periodicals Supplement (GP 3.8/5:), which lists federal periodicals and indexes to them, usually appears as the first issue of the year. The preliminary pages list "Title Changes," "Discontinued Periodicals," and "Classification Changes." It was formerly titled Serial Supplement.

The *Monthly Catalog* is sold in hard copy or microfiche from the GPO, and on CD-ROM from commercial publishers (under various titles). MoCat is also searchable online through commercial vendors.

Three supplements issued in 1947 and 1948 list 1941-1946 titles received late and some declassified World War II materials. GPO decennial and quinquennial cumulative indexes refer to the year and entry number (or page, prior to 1948) of the entry. These indexes provide subject, title, author, and series access but omit personal authors between 1941 and 1960. GPO issued cumulated indexes for the years 1941-50, 1951-60, 1961-65, 1966-70, and 1971-76 (GP 3.8/3:). GPO index cumulations for 1976-80 and 1981-85 are in microfiche (GP 3.8:). Records since January 1995 are available at *http://www.access. gpo.gov/su_docs/index.html*

98. Superintendent of Documents. **New Products from the U.S. Government**. GPO, 1994- . Free: Mail Stop, SSOM, Washington, DC 20402-9373. Bimonthly. LC sn95-27237. OCLC 32033700. GP 3.17/6: .

This roster of new titles added to GPO's sales inventory during the previous two months gives price, GPO stock number, and occasionally SuDocs number, but no annotations. Formerly *New Books.*

99. Superintendent of Documents. **U.S. Government Subscriptions**. GPO, 1993- . Free: Superintendent of Documents, U.S. Government Printing Office, Stop: SSOP, Washington, DC 20402-9328. Quarterly. LC 93-648228. Z1223.A1U15. 015.73/053/05. OCLC 27901339. GP 3.9: .

> Also available on the Internet *URL http://www.access.gpo.gov/su_docs/sale/subs 031.html*; or a free electronic copy can be downloaded from the *Federal Bulletin Board* (entry 35).

This annotated list of government periodicals and loose-leaf subscriptions for sale from the GPO gives title, frequency, price, GPO stock number, and SuDocs number stem. Formerly titled *Government Periodicals and Subscription Services* and still popularly known as "Price List 36."

100. Congress. **United States Congressional Serial Set**. GPO, 1817- . Irregular. LC 92-643101. J66. Serial. OCLC 3888071. Y 1.1/2: .

The Serial Set is a serially numbered compilation of House and Senate Reports and Documents since 1789 (plus the House and Senate Journals through 1952). House and Senate Reports and Documents are issued individually throughout each Congress, and later permanently bound and serially numbered in the Serial Set. The Serial Set includes congressional committee reports, Senate Executive Reports since the 97th Congress (1980), House and Senate Documents, and Senate Treaty Documents since the 96th Congress (1978–79). House and Senate Reports since 104-1, 1995 are also available on GPO Access (entry 104).

101. Superintendent of Documents. **Numerical Lists and Schedule of Volumes of the Reports and Documents of the . . . Congress . . . Session**. GPO, 1934-1980. Annual. LC sn88-26770. 015.73. OCLC 1768667. GP 3.7/2: .

From 1933 (73d Congress) to 1980 (96th Congress), the *Numerical Lists and Schedule of Volumes* referred from congressional Document and Report numbers to the Serial Set volume where the text of the Report or Document could be found (numerical lists), and from serial numbers to the Reports and Documents in each Serial Set volume (schedule of volumes). It was searchable by Report, Document, and serial numbers only, not by subjects or names. Preceded by *Index to the Reports and Documents of the 54th Congress, 1st Session—72d Congress, 2d Session, Dec. 2, 1895-March 4, 1933 with Numerical Lists and Schedule of Volumes*; superseded by the *Monthly Catalog of United States Government Publications. United States Congressional Serial Set Supplement* (entry 102).

102. Superintendent of Documents. **Monthly Catalog of United States Government Publications. United States Congressional Serial Set Supplement**. 1v. GPO, 1982. Biennial. LC 85-646142. Z1223.A18. 016.32873. OCLC 11463577. GP 3.8/6: .

For a short time, this finding aid superseded the *Numerical Lists and Schedule of Volumes* and was issued as a *Monthly Catalog* supplement following each Congress. This source had author, title, subject, series/report number, bill number, GPO stock number, and title keyword indexes. It was superseded by the *United States Congressional Serial Set Catalog. Numerical Lists and Schedule of Volumes* (entry 103).

103. Superintendent of Documents. **United States Congressional Serial Set Catalog. Numerical Lists and Schedule of Volumes**. GPO, 1984- . Biennial. LC 89-649623. Z1223.A18. 016. OCLC 17745498. GP 3.34: .

Since the 98th Congress (1983-84) the *Serial Set Catalog: Numerical Lists and Schedule of Volumes* (also known as the *Serial Set Index*) has been the access tool for the Serial Set. Issued after all items from a two-year congress have been printed, it includes a numerical list of congressional Reports and Documents, a schedule of serial set volume contents, and *Monthly Catalog* Report/Document entries enhanced with serial set numbers added in bold type. It is indexed by author, title, subject, series/report and bill numbers. It supersedes *Monthly Catalog of United States Government Publications. United States Congressional Serial Set Supplement* (entry 102).

> Superintendent of Documents Home Page: *URL http://www.access.gpo.gov/su_docs/.*

104. Government Printing Office. **GPO Access**. Internet *URL http://www.access. gpo.gov/su_docs/aces/aaces00/.html.* 1994- .

GPO's electronic dissemination system provides online access to the *Congressional Record*, the *Congressional Record Index*, full text of introduced bills and public laws of the current congress, the *U.S. Code*, the *Federal Register*, the Unified Agenda of Federal Regulations, and the Lobby List. It is available on subscription, and free in depository libraries and authorized Internet "gateways" co-sponsored by GPO and individual depository libraries (these can be accessed locally and through the Superintendent of Documents Home Page: *URL http://www.access.gpo.gov/su_docs/*).

105. Special Interest Group on CD-ROM Applications and Technology (SIGCAT), GPO Office of Electronic Information and Dissemination Services, and U.S. Geological Survey Library. **SIGCAT CD-ROM Compendium**. GPO, 1992- . Annual. LC 93-644452. Z286.O68S552. OCLC 26390202. GP 3.22/6: .

This is an annotated list of federal or commercial CD-ROMs containing substantial federal government information. Information on documentation and vendors is included, with agency and vendor indexes, and a bibliography.

106. Superintendent of Documents. **Electronic Information Products**. GPO, 19??- . Free: GPO, P.O. Box 371954, Pittsburgh, PA 15250-7954. LC sn91-23206. OCLC 24860219. GP 3.22/5: .

This annotated list of CD-ROMs and magnetic tapes for sale from GPO includes price and GPO stock number. It is Subject Bibliography #314 (see appendix).

107. Superintendent of Documents. **Subject Bibliography: SB**. GPO, 1975- . Free: Stop: SSOP, Washington, DC 20402; U.S. Fax Watch (202) 512-1716. Irregular. LC sn86-22744. OCLC 2520276. GP 3.22/2: .

    Also available on the Internet *URL http://www.access.gpo.gov/su_docs/sale/sale 105.html*, or through the *Federal Bulletin Board* (entry 35).

Subject Bibliographies (SBs) are free subject lists of government information products sold by GPO. They provide document title, publication date, stock number, price, ISBN, and in some cases, SuDocs number and an annotation. An order form is included in each. The free Subject Bibliography Index, *A Guide to Government Information*, identifies SBs for general topics. It is reprinted in *U.S. Government Subscriptions* and has been included in Appendix A of this book. Subject Bibliographies are regularly revised and reissued under the same SB numbers.

108. Superintendent of Documents. **United States Government Information: Publications, Periodicals, Electronic Products**. GPO, 1994- . Free: Stop SM, Washington, DC 20401. Semiannual. LC sn95-27268. OCLC 32041723. GP 3.17/5: .

This free, annotated catalog of information products for sale from GPO is organized under broad subjects. Citations include price, GPO stock number, and occasionally SuDocs numbers. Formerly *U.S. Government Books*.

LIBRARY OF CONGRESS CATALOGS AND UNION LISTS

Catalogs

109. Library of Congress. **National Union Catalog, Pre-1956 Imprints: A Cumulative Author List Representing Library of Congress Printed Cards and Titles Reported by Other American Libraries**. 754v. London: Mansell, 1968-1981. LC 67-30001. Z881.A1U518. 021.6/4. OCLC 935967. [no SuDocs number].

This set of more than 700 volumes is a cumulative *National Union Catalog* through 1956. These volumes list the NUC holdings before 1956 and replace the separate sets published earlier: *A Catalog of Books Represented by Library of Congress Printed Cards [Issued from August 1898 Through July 1942]*; its *Supplement: Cards Issued August 1, 1942-December 31, 1947*; and *The Library of Congress Author Catalog: A Cumulative List of Works Represented by Library of Congress Cards, 1948-52*.

110. Library of Congress. Catalog Publication Division. **National Union Catalog**. New York: Roman and Littlefield, 1956-1982. Nine monthly issues, three quarterly cumulations, annual cumulations for four years, and a quinquennial cumulation in the fifth year. ISSN 00280348. LC 56-60041. Z881.A1U372. OCLC 1759445. LC 30.8/2: .

NUC is a cumulative list of books, pamphlets, periodicals, serials, and other formats cataloged by the Library of Congress or other U.S. and Canadian libraries. Since 1990 it has omitted records reported to utilities such as OCLC, RLIN, or WLIN. Arranged by authors, entries are photographic reproductions of printed catalog cards. Indexes to names, titles, subjects, and series include brief bibliographic information and refer to the complete bibliographic record by its register number. The register contains full bibliographic records in sequential order, including ISBN, price, Dewey class number, collation, notes, and added entries. The 1982 annual cumulation was the last published in book format: Since January 1983, NUC has been available only on microfiche. It now appears in three segments, each with its own author, title, subject, and series indexes. These are: *NUC Books* (entry 112), *NUC Audiovisual Materials* (entry 111), and *NUC Cartographic Materials* (entry 113). These microfiche publications supersede *Subject Catalog, Chinese Cooperative Catalog, Audiovisual Materials*, and *Monographic Series*. The *NUC Register of Additional Locations* (cumulative microform edition) continues to supplement the NUC. Quinquennial cumulations through 1972 include *Register of Additional Locations, Motion Pictures and Filmstrips*, and *Music and Phono-Records*. Cumulations for 1973-77 include *Films and Other Materials for Projection* and *Music, Books on Music, and Sound Recordings*.

111. Library of Congress. **National Union Catalog. Audiovisual Materials**. Cataloging Distribution Service, 1983- . Quarterly. Microfiche. LC sn82-6948. OCLC 8829434. LC 30.8/4: .

This catalog of motion pictures, video recordings, filmstrips, transparency and slide sets, and kits cataloged by the Library of Congress since 1983 provides a register of full bibliographic records and separate cumulative indexes: Name, title, subject, and series. It continues *Audiovisual Materials* (1979–82), *Films and Other Materials for Projection* (1973–77), and *Library of Congress Catalog: Motion Pictures and Filmstrips; A Cumulative List of Works Represented by Library of Congress Printed Cards* (1953–72).

112. Library of Congress. **National Union Catalog. Books.** Cataloging Distribution Service, 1983- . Monthly. Microfiche ed. LC 88-657036. OCLC 8829353. LC 30.26: .

Contains bibliographic records for books, pamphlets, manuscripts, map atlases, microform masters, and monographic government publications from the U.S. and other nations cataloged since 1983. It includes four separate cumulative indexes: Name, title, subject, and series. Since 1990, NUC has omitted records reported to utilities such as OCLC, RLIN, or WLIN. After 1983, this catalog replaced *Monographic Series* (LC 30.8/9:), *Chinese Cooperative Catalog* (LC 30.18:), and *Subject Catalog* (LC 30.8/3:).

113. Library of Congress. **National Union Catalog. Cartographic Materials**. Cataloging Distribution Service, 1983- . Quarterly. Microfiche. LC 93-640487. 912. OCLC 8808363. [no SuDocs number].

This includes the complete retrospective Library of Congress maps database together with entries cataloged by the Library of Congress for single maps, map sets, and atlases and maps treated as serials, plus records for atlases cataloged by participating libraries. There are five separate cumulative indexes: Name, title, LC subject, LC series, and geographic classification code (based on the *Library of Congress Classifications Schedule G* and expanded Cutter lists for place names). The Register is a separate section.

114. Library of Congress. **National Union Catalog of Manuscript Collections**. Cataloging Distribution Service, 1961-1994. Annual. LC 62-17486. Z6620.U5N3. OCLC 1759448. LC 9.8: .

Also available as a MARC database from the Library of Congress.

NUCMC lists collections of manuscripts, personal papers, and records of public and private organizations held in U.S. repositories and open to the public for research. The form, extent, and location of the manuscripts are noted. The index cites names, places, subjects, and occupations, along with some form and genre terms reported in the catalog entries. Coverage began with 1959/61, with the 29th issue (volume for 1993) being the last in print. The Library of Congress will continue to enter NUCMC data for smaller institutions without RLIN or OCLC access into RLIN's Archival and Manuscripts file, and it is also available through OCLC and WLIN. Additional electronic avenues are being explored.

115. Library of Congress. Catalog Publication Division. **National Register of Microform Masters**. Cataloging Distribution Service, 1965-1983. Annual. LC 65-29419. Z1033.M5N3. 011. OCLC 936298. LC 30.8/8: .

NRMM is a catalog of library materials for which master negatives exist for making microform copies, including master preservation microforms stored under optimum conditions by nonprofit institutions. In print from 1965–83, it is now a data file of masters for foreign and U.S. books, pamphlets, serials, and foreign doctoral dissertations. Omitted are masters for technical reports, typescript collections, U.S. dissertations and master's theses, and newspapers (covered in *Newspapers in Microform*). Archival materials and manuscripts are covered in the *National Union Catalog of Manuscript Collections* (entry 114). Because most of the entries in the Register are duplicated in the *National Union Catalog* (entry 110), full bibliographic data are given in the latter. Entries include author, condensed title, imprint, collation, and location code.

116. Library of Congress. General Reading Rooms Division. **Microform Collections and Selected Titles in Microform in the Microform Reading Room** edited by Anna Keller and Eugene Ferguson. LC, 1987. Photoduplication Service, Washington, DC 20540-5230. 3d ed. 82p. LC 88-142485. Z1033.M5L54 1987. 011/.36. OCLC 17754207. LC 1.2:M 58/4.

    . . . **First Supplement**. 1991. 207p. Free: Humanities and Social Sciences Division.

This is a selected, annotated list of microforms of books, serials, manuscripts, dissertations, government documents, and archival records added to the collections during the period 1987–89. Includes subject and format indexes.

117. Library of Congress. **Special Collections in the Library of Congress: A Selective Guide** compiled by Annette Melville. LC, 1980. Free to U.S. Libraries and Institutions: Office Systems Services, Printing and Processing Section, Washington, DC 20540-5446. 464p. LC 79-607780. Z733.U58U54 1980. 027.5753. OCLC 5474180. LC 1.6/4:C 68.

This guide introduces some of the most prized research material in the Library of Congress's special collections, including books, pamphlets, drawings, films, manuscripts, maps, prints, music, musical instruments, photographs, sound recordings, and videotapes. Arranged according to divisions within LC, it focuses on 269 thematically related groups of materials maintained as separate units and identified as rare or of scholarly interest. Brief essays describe the history, content, scope, subject strengths, and organization of each collection. Updating is available through other LC publications, such as the *Library of Congress Information Bulletin* and *Library of Congress Publications in Print*. It updates *A Guide to the Special Book Collections in the Library of Congress* (1949).

118. Library of Congress. **The Library of Congress Main Reading Room Reference Collection Subject Catalog** compiled and edited by Katherine Ann Gardner. LC, 1980. Free to U.S. Libraries and Institutions: Office Systems Services, Printing and Processing Section, Washington, DC 20540-5446. 2d ed. 1236p. LC 80-19478. Z1035.1 U526 1980. 011/.02. OCLC 6555179. LC 1.12/2:R 22/980.

This subject catalog to one of the world's largest general reference collections lists every title in the general reference collection of the Library of Congress main reading room, with holdings as of August 1980. Entries are arranged alphabetically by subject heading and by main entry.

Copyright

> Copyright information since 1978: Internet *URL telnet://locis.loc.gov*; *URL gopher://marvel.loc.gov* and select the copyright menu; *URL http://lcweb.loc.gov/copyright*.

119. Library of Congress. Copyright Office. **Catalog of Copyright Entries. 4th Series**. GPO, 1979-1982. Microfiche. LC 91-643704. Z1219.U58. 019/.1. OCLC 11733091. LC 3.6/6: .

    Part 1. **Nondramatic Literary Works**.

    Part 2. **Serials and Periodicals**.

    Part 3. **Performing Arts**.

Part 4. **Motion Pictures.**

Part 5. **Visual Arts.**

Part 6. **Maps.**

Part 7. **Sound Recordings.**

Part 8. **Renewals.**

120. Library of Congress. Copyright Office. **Catalog of Copyright Entries. 3rd Series.** GPO, 1947-1977. Frequency varies. LC 6-35347. Z1219.U58. OCLC 6481719. LC 3.6/5:vol./nos.

Part 1. **Books and Pamphlets, Including Serials and Contributions to Periodicals.**

Part 2. **Periodicals.**

Parts 3-4. **Dramas and Works Prepared for Oral Delivery.**

Part 5. **Music.**

Part 6. **Maps and Atlases.**

Parts 7-11A. **Works of Art, Reproductions of Works of Art, Scientific and Technical Drawings, Photographic Works, Prints, and Pictorial Illustrations.**

Part 11B. **Commercial Prints and Labels.**

Parts 12-13. **Motion Pictures and Filmstrips.**

Part 14. **Sound Recordings.**

CCE was a catalog of copyright registrations divided into eight parts based on formats. Citations include author and copyright claimant, title, dates of creation and deposit, ISBN, ISSN, and related works. The fourth series, covering 1978-82, was the last released. Copyright registrations and renewals since 1978 are now searchable on LC's online database, SCORPIO, available through MARVEL (entry 36).

121. Library of Congress. Copyright Office. **Catalog of Copyright Entries.** GPO, 1891-1906; New Series 1906-1946. Frequency varies. LC 6-35347. Z1219.U58. OCLC 6467863. LC 3.6./1-4:vol./nos.

Part 1, **Books** covered pamphlets, maps, dramatic compositions, and motion pictures

Part 2, **Periodicals and Newspapers**

Part 3, **Musical Compositions**

Part 4, **Works of Art.**

122. Library of Congress. **Federal Copyright Records, 1790-1800** compiled by Elizabeth Carter Wills. LC, 1987. Free to U.S. Libraries and Institutions: Office Systems Services, Printing and Processing Section, Washington, DC 20540-5446. 166p. LC 86-600334. Z642.W54 1987. 015.73. OCLC 14214989. LC 23.16:C 79.

Entries for copyright deposits between 1790 and 1800 are arranged by the district court and department ledgers (Departments of State and Interior) in which they were recorded. Information given includes ledger citation, deposit date, title, imprint, and notes.

123. Library of Congress. Copyright Office. **Publications on Copyright.** LC, 1994. Free: Publications Section, LM-455, Copyright Office, Library of Congress, Washington, DC 20559. 15p. OCLC 31909289. LC 3.4/2:2/994-2.

This is a list, with some annotations, of publications available from the Library of Congress (some are free), National Technical Information Service, and Government Printing Office.

Included are information circulars, reports on hearings and conferences, a general guide to the Copyright Act, studies of copyright issues, copies of the law, registration catalogs, and judicial decisions.

Serials and Newspapers

124. Library of Congress. Catalog Publication Division. **Newspapers in Microform.** LC, 1973-1983. Annual. LC 75-644000. Z6945.U515b. 016.07. OCLC 1354452. LC 30.20: .

This title listed foreign and U.S. newspapers on microform that are permanently housed in U.S., Canadian, and foreign libraries or in vaults of commercial microform producers. Location codes and brief bibliographic identifications were given. It supplemented *Newspapers in Microform: Foreign Countries, 1948-1983* (LC 30.20/2:) and *Newspapers in Microform: United States, 1948-1983* (LC 30.20/3:).

125. Library of Congress. Joint Committee on the Union List of Serials. **New Serial Titles**. Cataloging Distribution Service, 1953- . Eight monthly issues, three quarterly issues, and an annual cumulation. LC 53-60021. Z6945.U5S42. 016.05. OCLC 1759958. LC 1.23/3: .

    1950-70 Cumulation. (R.R. Bowker)

    1971-75 Cumulation.

    1976-80 Cumulation.

    1981-85 Cumulation.

    1986-90 Cumulation.

    1990 Cumulation.

    1991 Cumulation.

    1992 Cumulation.

NST, the primary authority for serials bibliographic and location information, is a union list of titles cataloged by CONSER members, regardless of publication date. Entry arrangement is alphabetical by title (or issuing body for undistinctive titles), with place of publication, beginning date, title changes, cessation date, Library of Congress control number, International Standard Serial Number (ISSN), country codes, and notes on abstracting and indexing sources. It includes NUC location symbols for U.S. and Canadian libraries. Each issue includes an ISSN index. NST continues *Union List of Serials in Libraries of the United States and Canada* and supersedes *Serial Titles Newly Received*. A companion source, *CONSER Microfiche*, contains the same bibliographic records in microfiche.

126. Library of Congress. Serial and Government Publications Division. **Newspapers Received Currently in the Library of Congress**. LC, 1972- . Free to U.S. Libraries and Institutions: Office Systems Services, Printing and Processing Section, Washington, DC 20540-5446. Biennial. LC 82-647098. Z6945.U5N42. 016.07. OCLC 7093410. LC 6.7: .

This directory lists U.S. and foreign newspapers permanently received by the Library of Congress, along with U.S. and foreign newspapers retained.

MATERIALS FOR THE BLIND

Materials from the Library of Congress's National
Library Service for the Blind and Physically Handi-
capped are available through LC MARVEL (entry 36):
Select *Services and Publications/National Library
Service to the Blind and Physically Handicapped.*
E-mail: *nlsbph@mail.loc.gov.*

127. Library of Congress. National Library Service for the Blind and Physically
Handicapped. **Braille Books**. LC, 1981- . Free: National Library Service for the
Blind and Physically Handicapped, Washington, DC 20542-5304. Biennial. LC
82-644735. Z5346.Z9U62a. 011/.63. OCLC 7586764. LC 19.9/2: .
An annotated bibliography of fiction and nonfiction in braille for adults and teens, arranged
by subject. Entries include author, title, number of volumes, code number, and publication
date. Indexed by author and title. Coverage for the series began in 1980.

128. Library of Congress. National Library Service for the Blind and Physically
Handicapped. **Cassette Books**. LC, 1978- . National Library Service for the Blind
and Physically Handicapped, Washington, DC 20542-5304. Annual. LC 79-
645707. Z5347.U59b. 011. OCLC 5173930. LC 19.10/3: .
This annotated bibliography of fiction and nonfiction cassette books is arranged by subject.
Entries include author, title, number of cassettes, code number, and publication date. There
is an index to best-sellers. Books for teens and books in foreign languages are included.
Published in large print and also available on phonodisc. Updated by the bimonthly *Talking
Book Topics* (new recorded books and program news, LC 19.10:). Coverage for the series
began in 1977.

129. Library of Congress. National Library Service for the Blind and Physically
Handicapped. **For Younger Readers: Braille and Talking Books**. LC, 1965- .
Free: National Library Service for the Blind and Physically Handicapped, Washington, DC 20542-5304. Biennial. LC 73-4220. Z5346.A2F6. 028.52/05. OCLC
1569687. LC 19.11/2: .
An annotated bibliography of fiction and nonfiction on cassette and in braille available to
children and teens from the NLS, arranged by subject. Entries include author, title, grade
level, number of cassettes or braille volumes, code number, and publication date. Published
in large print and also available on phonodisc. Coverage for the series began in 1964.

130. Library of Congress. National Library Service for the Blind and Physically
Handicapped. **Library Resources for the Blind & Physically Handicapped**. LC,
1977- . Free: National Library Service for the Blind and Physically Handicapped,
Washington, DC 20542-5304. Annual. LC 76-640140. Z675.B6L52. 027.6/63/02573.
OCLC 2977219. LC 19.16: .
This is a state-by-state directory of the network libraries and machine-lending agencies
providing free braille and recorded materials. These libraries circulate materials by
postage-free mail, offer reference, readers' advisory, and other services, and may loan
playback equipment and accessories. The directory gives address; telephone, fax, TDD,
and WATS numbers; name of librarian; and description of services, including hours,
publications, assistive devices, special collections, and services. The directory lists other

national library resources and features appendixes with statistics on readership, circulation, budget, staff, and collections.

131. Library of Congress. National Library Service for the Blind and Physically Handicapped. **Magazines in Special Media**. LC, 1978- . National Library Service for the Blind and Physically Handicapped, Washington, DC 20542-5304. Biennial. LC 87-659032. Z5346.A29. 016.3624/1/05. OCLC 8924224. LC 19.11/2-2: .

This is an annotated list of periodicals available in braille, cassette, computer disk, disc, large print, and moon type and available from NLS cooperating libraries or from other sources. Includes title, subject, and media indexes. Updated by magazine announcements in *Braille Book Review* (new braille books and program news, LC 19.9:) and *Talking Book Topics* (new recorded books and program news, LC 19.10:).

132. Library of Congress. National Library Service for the Blind and Physically Handicapped. **Reference Books in Special Media** by Carol Keys. LC, 1983. 74p. OCLC 9568136. LC 19.4/2:82-4.
    Reference Books in Special Media: Addendum compiled by Mary A. Barber. 1987.

A bibliography of reference books grouped by medium (braille, cassette, disc, large type). Availability is noted, including that through the National Library Service for the Blind and Physically Handicapped, a free loan source for qualified users.

133. Library of Congress. National Library Service for the Blind and Physically Handicapped. **Tactile Maps: A Listing of Maps in the National Library Service for the Blind and Physically Handicapped Collection**. LC, 1987. Free: National Library Service for the Blind and Physically Handicapped, Washington, DC 20542-5304. 133p. LC 87-600240. Z6028.L52 1987. 016.912. OCLC 16226100. LC 19.2:T 11.

Describes circulating tactile geographical, thematic, and mobility maps.

134. Library of Congress. National Library Service for the Blind and Physically Handicapped. **Volunteers Who Produce Books**. LC, 19??- . Free: National Library Service for the Blind and Physically Handicapped, Washington, DC 20542-5304. Irregular. LC 78-9942. HV1790.V64. 362.4/1/02573. OCLC 5116203. LC 19.21: .

This directory of individuals and volunteer groups who transcribe and record materials is arranged alphabetically by state and indexed according to the specialized talents of the volunteers. It is also available in braille and large print.

MUSEUMS

135. National Park Service. **Museum Handbook. Part I, Museum Collections**. 1v. GPO, 1991. OCLC 23845298. I 29.9/2:M 97/2.

This loose-leaf manual is a guide to managing museum collections, with information on storage, conservation, emergency preparedness, and professional ethics.

STYLE MANUALS

136. Government Printing Office. **Style Manual**. GPO, 1984. 28th ed. 479p. LC 84-600037. Z253.U58 1984. 808/.02. OCLC 10532947. GP 1.23/4:St 9/984.

This GPO printer's stylebook includes rules for submission of copy to GPO, standardizing grammar, punctuation, type size, and other printing techniques. This edition reflects the newer language of electronic photocomposition but retains traditional printing terminology to bridge the gap between the old and new printing methods. It includes tables of scientific terms, titles, and foreign money. Supplemented by *Patents and Trademarks Style Manual* (entry 138) and *Word Division: Supplement to United States Government Printing Office Style Manual* (entry 137).

137. Government Printing Office. **Word Division: Supplement to United States Government Printing Office Style Manual.** GPO, 1987. 142p. GP I.23/4:St 9/supp.987.

This booklet provides word divisions, spelling, pronunciation, word-break rules, line-ending rules, and pronunciation guidance for names of new countries.

138. Patent and Trademark Office. **Patents and Trademarks Style Manual: A Supplement to the United States Government Printing Office Style Manual**. GPO, 1984. 137p. OCLC 11326990. C 21.14/2:St 9/984/supp.

This supplement to U.S. Government Printing Office *Style Manual* (entry 136) is a guide to composing and publishing PTO publications, including patent grants, trademark certificates, and the patent and trademark *Official Gazettes*.

Biographical Sources

139. Air Force. Office of Air Force History. **Makers of the United States Air Force** edited by John L. Frisbee. GPO, 1987. 347p. LC 87-600206. UG626.M35 1987. 358.4/0092/2aB. OCLC 16004834. D 301.96:M 28.
Contians biographical essays about Benjamin Foulois, Frank Andrews, Harold George, Hugh Knerr, George Kenney, William Kepner, Elwood Quesada, Hoyt Vandenberg, Benjamin Davis, Nathan Twining, Bernard Schriever, and Robinson Risner.

140. Customs Service. **A Biographical Directory of the United States Customs Service, 1771-1989.** 2v. CS, 1985-1986. 1st ed. LC 85-603304. HJ6731.U18 1985. 353.0072/46/025. OCLC 16648656. T 17.15/2:B 52/771-989 v.1,2.
These biographical sketches of Collectors, Surveyors, Comptrollers (Navy Officers), or Appraisers of Customs include some who also served as President, cabinet officers, congressmen, and military officers. Related titles are *Commissioners of Customs* (T 17.2:C 73) and *The First Officers of the United States Customs Service Appointed by President George Washington in 1789* (T 17.2:Of 2).

141. Department of State. Bureau of Public Affairs. **Nicaraguan Biographies: A Resource Book.** DS, 1988. rev. ed. 98p. LC 88-602952. E840.U614b no.174.F1528.2. 909. OCLC 17512012. S 1.129:174/rev.
These biographical sketches of people involved in the Nicaraguan human rights movement, religion, culture, business, labor, politics, and history are arranged in three categories: The Sandinista Regime, the Nicaraguan Resistance, and the Society. They were compiled using interviews, publications, and diplomatic cables.

142. Library of Congress. Hispanic Division. **National Directory of Latin Americanists: Biographies of 4,915 Specialists** edited by Inge Maria Harman. LC, 1985. Free to U.S. Libraries and Institutions: Office Systems Services, Printing and Processing Section, Washington, DC 20540-5446. 3d ed. 1011p. LC 84-600356. F1409.8.A2N37 1985. 980/.0072022. OCLC 11519057. LC 24.11:L 34.
Biographical sketches note birth date and birthplace, education, positions held and memberships, research, publications, languages spoken, and address for U.S. scholars with knowledge of Latin America, including specialists in agriculture, natural resources, and the physical and biological sciences. Includes an index of subject specialties and an index of area specialties with languages noted.

Library Science

Library of Congress: *URL gopher://marvel.loc.gov/*or
URL http://lcweb.loc.gov or *URL http://www.loc.gov.*

GENERAL WORKS

143. Library of Congress. **LOCIS**. (Library of Congress Information System). Internet
URL telnet://locis.loc.gov or *URL telnet://140.147.254.3.*
LC's online database includes the LC catalog; copyright registration records; holdings
records for braille, large print, and audios; abstracts of foreign laws and regulations and
of legal journal articles; referral to organizations; and the Bill Digest, an online version
of the discontinued *Digest of Public General Bills and Resolutions* (LC 14.16:), summarizing all bills, joint and concurrent resolutions, and simple resolutions emanating from
the House and Senate since 1973 (the 93d Congress).

144. Library of Congress. **For Congress and the Nation: A Chronological History of
the Library of Congress Through 1975** by John Y. Cole. GPO, 1979. 196p. LC
76-608365. Z733.U6C565. 027.5753. OCLC 2633473. LC 1.2:C 76/6.
Spanning the years 1774 to 1975, this chronology details the origins of the Library's
principal collections, services, and administrative units. Emphasis is on the early development of collections and how the Library acquired its many functions.

145. Library of Congress. **Library of Congress Information Bulletin**. LC, 1972- .
Free to U.S. Libraries and Institutions: Office Systems Services, Printing and
Processing Section, Washington, DC 20540-5446. Biweekly. LC 83-641631.
Z733.U57I6. 027.573. OCLC 2566556. LC 1.18: .
> Also available on the Internet *URL gopher://marvel.loc.gov*; from the main
> menu choose *Events, Facilities, Programs and Services/LC Publica-
> tions and Products/Library of Congress Information Bulletin* or *URL
> http://lcweb.loc.gov/.*

The official Library of Congress newsletter reviews events at LC and in the library world.
An annual *Index to the Information Bulletin* is sold by Index Orders, Library of Congress
Professional Association, Library of Congress, Washington, DC 20540-9991.

BIBLIOGRAPHY

146. Library of Congress. **Thomas Jefferson's Library: A Catalog with the Entries in His Own Order** edited by James Gilreath and Douglas L. Wilson. GPO, 1989. 149p. LC 88-607928. Z997.J48 1989. 017/.6. OCLC 19124971. LC 1.2:T 36.

Jefferson's own classified list of the books he sold to the government to rebuild the Library of Congress after the War of 1812 is organized under three broad topics (memory, philosophy, and fine arts) and subtopics. Includes references.

CATALOGING AND CLASSIFICATION

147. Library of Congress. Catalog Publication Division. **Name Authorities**. Cataloging Distribution Service, 1979- . Quarterly. Cumulative Microform Edition. LC 79-647358. Z695.1.P4. OCLC 5996698. LC 30.21: .

This is a compilation of MARC authority records established since 1977 for personal, corporate, conference, and geographic names. Each issue completely supersedes its predecessor. Available in CD-ROM and as a computer file.

148. Library of Congress. Cataloging Distribution Service. **Descriptive Cataloging of Rare Books**. LC, 1991. 2d ed. 113p. LC 91-6988. Z695.74.U54 1991. 025.3/416. OCLC 23141521. LC 30.2:R 18.

DCRB is a manual for cataloging rare materials. It is a revision of *Bibliographic Description of Rare Books* (1981). Includes a glossary.

149. Library of Congress. Cataloging Distribution Service. **Symbols of American Libraries**. LC, 1969- . Irregular. LC 33-13797. Z881.U49U6. 018/.1. OCLC 3423023. LC 30.32: .

This standard in the field lists the short alphabetical codes developed by the Library of Congress for identifying libraries and information organizations in union catalogs, databases, and other compilations. It is the only comprehensive list of library symbols, including obsolete and variant forms. Includes alphabetical, NUC symbol, and organization indexes.

150. Library of Congress. Cataloging Distribution Service. **The Complete Catalog**. LC, 1991- . Free: Customer Services Section, Washington, DC 20541-5017. LC sn91-23104. OCLC 23273691. LC 30.27/2: .

Also available on the Internet *URL http://www.loc.gov/cds.*

This catalog describes and lists prices for products in various formats, with title and subject indexes.

151. Library of Congress. Cataloging Policy and Support Office. **Free-Floating Subdivisions: An Alphabetical Index**. Cataloging Distribution Service, 1989- . Annual. LC 90-656294. Z696.U4L53a. OCLC 22199173. LC 30.2:F 87/yr.

This is a list of free-floating subject headings appearing in *Subject Cataloging Manual* (LC 26.8/4:), with references to the Manual.

152. Library of Congress. Geography and Map Division. **Map Cataloging Manual**. 1v. Cataloging Distribution Service, 1991. LC 91-6987. Z695.6.L52 1991. 025.3/46. OCLC 23141516. LC 30.25:M 32.

This is a manual of interpretation of the Anglo-American Cataloging Rules and Library of Congress cataloging policy and practice in map cataloging.

153. Library of Congress. Office for Subject Cataloging Policy. **LC Classification Outline**. Cataloging Distribution Service, 1990. 6th ed. 47p. LC 90-23319. Z696.U42 1990. 025.4/33. OCLC 22767116. LC 26.10:C 56/990.
This is an outline of the topics and subtopics in the LC classification system.

154. Library of Congress. Office for Subject Cataloging Policy. **LC Period Subdivisions Under Names of Places: Compiled from the Online Subject Authority File**. Cataloging Distribution Service, 1990. 4th ed. 130p. LC 90-5636. Z695.1.G4L52 1990. 025.4/992. OCLC 21119126. LC 26.2:P 41/980.
This list of subject headings for places, with date subdivisions, was compiled from LC's online subject authority file and is current through January 1994.

155. Library of Congress. Office for Subject Cataloging Policy. **Library of Congress Classification**. Cataloging Distribution Service, 1917- . LC 26.9: .
The LC classification scheme is used to classify and physically arrange library collections. Changes are reported in the quarterly *LC Classification, Additions and Changes* (LC 26.9/2:). Publications are as follows:

A	General Works. 4th ed. 1973.
B-BJ	Philosophy. Psychology. 4th ed. 1989.
BL, BM, BP, BQ	Religion: Religions. Hinduism, Judaism, Islam, Buddhism. 3d ed. 1984.
BR-BV	Religion: Christianity, Bible. 1987.
BX	Religion: Christian Denominations. 1985.
C	Auxiliary Sciences of History. 4th ed. 1993.
D-DJ	History (General), History of Europe, Part 1. 3d ed. 1990.
DJK-DK	History of Eastern Europe: General, Soviet Union, Poland. 1987.
DL-DR	History of Europe, Part 2. 3d ed. 1990.
DS	History of Asia. 1987.
DT-DX	History of Africa, Australia, New Zealand, etc. 1988.
E-F	History, America (Western Hemisphere). 4th ed. 1995.
G	Geography. Maps. Anthropology. Recreation. 4th ed. 1976.
H	Social Sciences. 1994.
J	Political Science. 1995 ed. 1995.
K	Law (General). 1977.
KD	Law of the United Kingdom and Ireland. 1973.
KDZ, KG-KH	Law of the Americas, Latin America, and the West Indies. 1984.
KE	Law of Canada. 1976.
KF	Law of the United States. Prelim. ed. 1969.
KJ-KKZ	Law of Europe. 1989.
KJV-KJW	Law of France. 1985.
KK-KKC	Law of Germany. 1982.

KL-KWX	Law of Asia and Eurasia, Africa, Pacific Area and Antarctica. 1st ed. 1993.
L	Education. 1995 ed. 1995.
M	Music and Books on Music. 3d ed. 1978.
N	Fine Arts. 4th ed. 1970.
P-PZ	Language and Literature Tables. Supersedes the tables in the P Schedules. 1982.
P-PA	Philology, Linguistics, Classical Philology, Classical Literature. 1928. Reissue with supplementary pages, 1968.
PA	Supplement: Byzantine and Modern Greek Literature. Medieval and Modern Latin Literature. 1942. Reissue with supplementary pages, 1968.
PB-PH	Modern European Languages. 1933. Reissue with supplementary pages, 1966.
PG	Russian Literature. 1948. Reissue with supplementary pages, 1965.
PJ-PK	Oriental Philology and Literature, Indo-Iranian Philology and Literature. 2d ed. 1988.
PL-PM	Languages of Eastern Asia, Africa, Oceania; Hyperborean, Indian, and Artificial Languages. 2d ed. 1988.
P-PM	Supplement: Index to Languages and Dialects. 4th ed. 1991.
PN, PR, PS, PZ	General Literature, English and American Literature, Fiction in English, Juvenile Belles Lettres. 3d ed. 1988.
PQ	Part 1: French Literature. 1992.
PQ	Part 2: Italian, Spanish, and Portuguese Literature. 1937. Reissue with supplementary pages, 1965.
PT	Part 1: German Literature. 1989.
PT	Part 2: Dutch and Scandinavian Literatures. 2d ed. 1992.
Q	Science. 7th ed. 1989.
R	Medicine. 1995.
S	Agriculture. 4th ed. 1982.
T	Technology. 1995 ed. 1995.
U	Military Science. 5th ed. 1992.
V	Naval Science. 4th ed. 1993.
Z	Bibliography and Library Science. 1995 ed. 1995.

156. Library of Congress. Office for Subject Cataloging Policy. **Library of Congress Subject Headings**. Cataloging Distribution Service, 1990. Annual. LC 91-643512. Z695.Z8L524a. 025.4/9. OCLC 22238028. LC 26.7: .

LCSH is a dictionary list of subject headings used in the Library of Congress catalog since 1898, with cross-references. The "red book" includes a list of headings canceled since the previous edition, with their replacements noted. Updated by *L.C. Subject Headings Weekly Lists* (LC 26.7/2-2:); the quarterly microfiche LCSH, *Library of Congress Subject Headings Cumulative Microform Edition* (LC 26.7/2:); the quarterly CD-ROM subject authority file, CDMARC SUBJECTS; and *Cataloging Service Bulletin* (LC 30.7/2:). This title continues *Subject Headings Used in the Dictionary Catalogues of the Library of Congress.*

157. Library of Congress. Prints and Photographs Division. **Thesaurus for Graphic Materials**. Cataloging Distribution Service, 1995. 556p. LC 94-40967. Z695.27.L52 1995. 025.3/47. OCLC 31712198. LC 25.2:SU 1/995.

Terms for indexing prints, photographs, drawings, photomechanical prints, and pictorial ephemera allow description of activities, objects, people, events, and places depicted.

158. Library of Congress. Processing Services. **Library of Congress Filing Rules**. Cataloging Distribution Service, 1980. 111p. LC 80-607944. Z695.95.U533 1980. 025.3/17. OCLC 7597849. LC 1.6:F 47.

Filing rules are described, with examples. Supersedes *Filing Rules for the Dictionary Catalogs of the Library of Congress* (1956).

159. Library of Congress. Subject Cataloging Division. **Subject Headings in Microform**. Cataloging Distribution Service, 1976- . Quarterly. Microfiche. LC 79-641066. OCLC 3454199. LC 26.7/2: .

New headings are integrated into the constantly growing LC subject authority database, creating the equivalent of a new edition each quarter. The introduction is available separately in book form, not in microform. Each issue is cumulative.

160. Superintendent of Documents. Depository Administration Branch. **An Explanation of the Superintendent of Documents Classification System**. GPO, 1990. rev. 14p. OCLC 22518303. GP 3.2:C 56/8/990.

This general introduction to SuDocs numbers describes their derivation and components.

161. Superintendent of Documents. Library Programs Service. **GPO Classification Manual: A Practical Guide to the Superintendent of Documents Classification System** edited by Marian W. MacGilvray. GPO, 1993. rev. 102p. OCLC 27402634. GP 3.29:P 88/993.

This detailed librarian's guide to constructing SuDocs numbers is often referred to as "the Classification manual." Automated versions are available on the *Federal Bulletin Board* (entry 35).

162. Superintendent of Documents. Library Programs Service. **Government Printing Office Cataloging Guidelines**. 1v. GPO, 1990. 3d ed. OCLC 22266110. GP 3.29:C 28/990.

A cataloger's guide to applying Anglo-American Cataloging Rules to government monographs, serials, and maps.

PRESERVATION OF MATERIALS

163. Library of Congress. **Bookbinding and the Conservation of Books: A Dictionary of Descriptive Terminology** by Matt T. Roberts and Don Etherington. GPO, 1982. 296p. LC 81-607974. Z266.7.R62 1982. 686.3/03. OCLC 7555465. LC 1.2:B 64/3.

This is a comprehensive nomenclature of bookbinding and archival conservation, with definitions and explanations, biographical vignettes, and a bibliography. It is enhanced by color plates of endpapers and rare bindings.

164. Library of Congress. Preservation Directorate. **Boxes for the Protection of Books: Their Design and Construction** compiled by Lage Carlson et al.; illustrated by Margaret Brown. 1v. GPO, 1994. LC 93-1994. Z701.3.B64B68 1994. 676./32. OCLC 28147809. LC 1.2:B 69/994.

Features step-by-step instructions and illustrations for constructing protective boxes for books, folded manuscripts, matted items, and other library materials.

STATISTICS

165. National Center for Education Statistics. **Academic Libraries**. GPO, 19??- . Biennial. LC sn95-27345. OCLC 26103871. ED 1.328/3:L 61/3/ .

> Data are also available from NCES's National Data Resource Center (entry 342).

This is a biennial report on holdings, staffing, operations, and expenditures of public and private college and university libraries in each state and nationwide. Data are from the Integrated Postsecondary Education Data System (IPEDS).

166. National Center for Education Statistics. **Public Libraries in the United States**. GPO, 19??- . Annual. LC sn93-33502. Z731.P83. OCLC 28208330. ED 1.328/3:L 61/2/.

> Data are also available from NCES's National Data Resource Center (entry 342).

Data from the 50 states and the District of Columbia are compiled from reports filed with state libraries and submitted to the NCES. State and national figures are given for population served, library outlets, FTE staff, budget, staffing, income and expenditures, capital outlays, collections, public service hours, circulation, attendance and reference transactions, and interlibrary loans. The information in this volume is also available from the GPO on diskette in *Public Library Data [year]* (ED 1.334/3:). The report and data files are available on the Internet *URL gopher://gopher.ed.gov* and select *Educational Research, Improvement, and Statistics (OERI & NCES)/National Center for Education Statistics (NCES)/Library Statistics Program/Surveys and Studies/Public Library Statistics* or *URL gopher://gopher.ed.gov:10000/11/data/library/public*. Current data and custom data analyses are also available from NCES's National Data Resource Center (entry 342). Background information is available in *Report on Coverage Evaluation of the Public Library Statistics Program* (ED 1.102:L 61), *Evaluation of Definitions Used in the Public Library Statistics Program*, and *Finance Data in the Public Library Statistics Program* (ED 1.328/7:F 49). Formerly titled *Public Libraries in 50 States and the District of Columbia.*

167. National Center for Education Statistics. **School Library Media Centers in the United States: 1990-91** by Richard M. Ingersoll. GPO, 1994. 52p. LC 95-131709. LB3044.72.I54 1994. 371.3/078. OCLC 31885228. ED 1.378:SCH 6.

Data from the *Schools and Staffing Survey* (entry 361) report the availability and role of libraries in public and private schools, staffing levels, and a historical overview.

PART TWO

Social Sciences

Economics and Business

GENERAL WORKS

> Commerce Department: *URL http://www.doc.gov.*

168. Department of Commerce. **Commerce Business Daily**. GPO, 19??- . Daily (Mon.-Fri.). LC 79-643799. JK1673.A24. 353.007/12. OCLC 4506910. C 1.76: .

> Also available on the Internet *URL http://www.stat-usa.gov/* (access to the WWW version requires a low-cost subscription).

CBD is a list of government procurement invitations, contracts, subcontracting leads, surplus property sales, and foreign business opportunities. Each Monday edition includes a "Reader's Guide" with CBD's Numbered Notes, an index of the Classification Codes, and other information. Also available through commercial vendors.

169. Department of Commerce. Economics and Statistics Administration. **Economic Bulletin Board**. Available through NTIS or the Internet *URL http://www.stat-usa.gov/* or *URL telnet://ebb.stat-usa.gov* (user ID = guest).

EBB is a fee-based service providing online access to news releases, statistics, and economic news from the Commerce Department and other government agencies. Data files are replaced as new information becomes available. EBB includes the Consumer Price Index, Gross National Product, employment data, and Daily Trade Opportunities for Exporters.

170. Department of Commerce. Economics and Statistics Administration. **National Trade Data Bank [computer file]: NTDB**. DC, 1990- . Monthly. CD-ROM. LC 92-644644. HF1009.5. 382. OCLC 24445375. C 1.88: .

> Also available on the Internet *URL http://www.stat-usa.gov* (access to the WWW version requires a low-cost subscription).

NTDB is the government's most comprehensive source of world trade and economic data. It includes the full text of selected government publications, tables, and time series from numerous federal statistical agencies and from the Massachusetts Institute for Social and Economic Research (MISER). Most of the data on the NTDB CD-ROM are available on the Internet through STAT-USA (entry 171).

171. Department of Commerce. Economics and Statistics Administration. **STAT-USA**. Internet *URL http://www.stat-usa.gov* (access to the WWW version requires a low-cost subscription).

This "Internet version" of the *National Trade Data Bank* (entry 170), contains comprehensive economic, business, social, and environmental data from federal agencies, including books, magazines, reports, and statistics. It contains most (about 95 percent) of the data on the NTDB CD-ROM. Depository libraries are eligible for free subscriptions to STAT-USA.

172. Department of Commerce. Office of Business Analysis. **National Economic, Social & Environmental Data Bank [computer file]: NESE-DB**. DC, 1992-1995. Quarterly. CD-ROM. LC 93-644284. HC101. 551/11. OCLC 25918230. C 1.88/2: .

> The CD-ROM version is no longer published. Available on the Internet *URL http://www.stat-usa.gov/BEN/Services/nesehome.html.*

NESE-DB is the domestic counterpart to the National Trade Data Bank, containing statistics and the full text of government publications about the U.S. economy, society, and the environment, as well as spreadsheets, diagrams, tables, and time series from various government agencies.

173. General Services Administration. **Federal Information Resources Management Regulation and Bulletins Through Transmittal Circular . . . [computer file]: FIRMR; Federal Acquisition Regulation and Circulars Through Federal Acquisition Circular . . . : FAR**. GPO, 1991- . Quarterly. CD-ROM. LC 93-648713. KF844.7u. 353. OCLC 24516350. GS 12.15/2: .

FAR/FIRMR on CD-ROM provides procurement laws and regulations from Federal Acquisition Regulation (D 1.6/11:) and Federal Information Resources Management Regulation (GS 12.19:). FAR regulates federal agency supply and services procurements and subcontracting. FIRMR procurement and contracting regulations are used for ADP and telecommunications requests.

174. Office of Management and Budget. **Catalog of Federal Domestic Assistance**. GPO, 1969- . Annual. LC 73-600118. HC110.P63U53a. 338.973. OCLC 2239457. PrEx 2.20: .

> Also available on the Internet *URL http://www.sura.net/main/members/ gsa.shtml.*

The CFDA describes federal programs, projects, services, and activities providing assistance to individuals; state and local governments; U.S. territories and possessions; private, public, and quasi-public organizations; and specialized groups. Entries list program sponsor, contacts, eligibility, application and award process, financial information, and matching requirements. Includes indexes by agency and program name, eligibility category, deadlines, function, and subject. Appendixes include a directory of federal agency regional and local offices, a chronology of program titles and changes since 1965, and a guide to writing grant proposals. A loose-leaf *Update to the Catalog of Federal Domestic Assistance* (Pr Ex 2.20:[year]-2) is issued in December. The catalog is also available on floppy diskettes and online as Federal Assistance Program Retrieval System (FAPRS), from the Federal Domestic Assistance Catalog Staff, General Services Administration. It is also available on MARVEL (entry 36): Select *Federal government information/Federal Information Resources/Information by agency/General information resources* or *URL http://lcweb.loc.gov/global/executive/general_resources.html.*

175. Office of the Federal Register. National Archives and Records Service. **Guide to Record Retention Requirements**. GPO, 1955- . Irregular. LC 80-644936. KF70.G84. OCLC 2481622. AE 2.108:R 24/yr.
This guide for business, organizations, and the general public includes the text of regulations from the *Code of Federal Regulations* (arranged in CFR citation format) describing what records must be kept, by whom, and for how long.

176. Patent and Trademark Office. Office of Electronic Information Products and Services. **Trademarks. Assignment Data [computer file]**. PTO, 19??- . Bimonthly. CD-ROM. OCLC 25704652. C 21.2-2:T 67/3.
> Not available for sale. Available for public use at U.S. Patent Depository Libraries.

TRADEMARKS/ASIGN contains the text of assignment deeds changing trademark ownership, along with the *Trademark Manual of Examining Procedure* (C 21.14/2:T 67).

177. Patent and Trademark Office. Office of Electronic Information Products and Services. **Trademarks. Trademark Pending Applications [computer file]**. PTO, 19??- . Bimonthly. CD-ROM. OCLC 25701555. C 21.2-2:T 67.
> Not available for sale. Available for public use at U.S. Patent Depository Libraries.

The "Trademark Pending File" contains the text of pending trademarks plus the *Trademark Manual of Examining Procedure* (C 21.14/2:T 67).

178. Not used.

179. Patent and Trademark Office. Office of Electronic Information Products and Services. **Trademarks. Trademark Registrations [computer file]**. PTO, 19??- . Bimonthly. CD-ROM. OCLC 25701637. C 21.2-2:T 67/2.
> Not available for sale. Available for public use at U.S. Patent Depository Libraries.

TRADEMARKS/REGISTERED gives the text of active U.S. trademarks, along with the *Trademark Manual of Examining Procedure* (C 21.14/2:T 67).

180. Patent and Trademark Office. **Official Gazette of the United States Patent and Trademark Office. Trademarks**. GPO, 1975- . Weekly. LC 75-641793. T223.V13A34. 602/.75. OCLC 2240594. C 21.5/4: .
This illustrated record of registered trademarks includes an index of registrants (the companies, organizations, and people owning the trademarks), trademark notices, marks published for opposition, and registrations. The *Index of Trademarks* (entry 181) is an annual index to its contents.

181. Patent and Trademark Office. **Index of Trademarks Issued from the United States Patent and Trademark Office**. GPO, 1974- . Annual. LC 75-646550. T223.V4A2. 602/.75. OCLC 2243146. C 21.5/3: .
This annual index to the *Official Gazette: Trademarks* is arranged alphabetically by registrants' names, with address and registration information.

Bibliographies

182. Bureau of Economic Analysis. **User's Guide to BEA Information**. BEA, 198?- . Free: Economics and Statistics Administration, Washington, DC 20230. Annual. LC sn92-23758. OCLC 19232828. C 59.8:B 89/ .

This is an annotated list of publications, products, and services related to national, regional, and international economics and other tools for economic analysis. It includes order forms, BEA telephone contacts, and press release dates.

183. Bureau of Labor Statistics. **BLS Publications on Productivity and Technology.** BLS, 1994. 24p. OCLC 31224503. L 2.71:876.

This is a catalog of studies, international comparisons, and bibliographies issued since 1982, arranged by subject.

184. Bureau of Labor Statistics. **Productivity, A Selected, Annotated Bibliography.** GPO, 1971- . Irregular. LC 80-644049. Z7164.E2P76. 016/338/06. OCLC 6413509. L 2.3:no .

These annotated bibliographies of books, articles, and doctoral dissertations published since 1965 deal with productivity concepts and methods, measurement, sources of change, economic growth, and relationship to economic variables such as wages and employment. They are numbered according to their BLS Bulletin number: Bulletins 1226 (1958), 1514 (1966), 1776 (1971), 1933 (1977), 2051 (1980), 2212 (1984), and 2360 (1990).

185. Department of Commerce. **Commerce Publications Update: A Biweekly Listing of Latest Titles from the U.S. Department of Commerce.** GPO, 1980- . Bi-weekly. LC sn83-10652. 353. OCLC 6504692. C 1.24/3: .

Contains descriptions of new publications and press releases issued during the preceding two weeks, along with highlights of special interest publications. The list also provides the latest figures for "Key Business Indicators," including personal income, the Consumer Price Index, employment, and housing.

186. Office of Personnel Management. Library. **Personnel Literature.** GPO, 1941-March 1995. Monthly, with annual index. LC 79-644985. Z7164.C81U45683. 016.3501. OCLC 4792386. PM 1.16: .

This is a current awareness list of personnel administration articles in journals received by the U.S. Office of Personnel Management Library.

187. Superintendent of Documents. **United States Government Information for Business.** GPO, 1995?. Free: Washington, DC 20401. 6th ed. 23p. GP 3.22:B 96/11.

This annotated catalog of publications, periodicals, and electronic products for sale from the Government Printing Office is organized by broad subjects. Citations include price and GPO stock number.

Dictionaries

188. Bureau of the Census. **Concordance Between the Standard Industrial Classifications of the United States and Canada: 1987 United States SIC—1980 Canadian SIC.** GPO, 1991. 252p. LC 91-600900. HF1042.C67 1991. 338/.02/012. OCLC 25633713. C 3.2:C 74.

The 1987 U.S. and 1980 Canadian SICs are correlated at some or all of four classification levels showing divisions, major groups, industry groups, and industries. Products shown by SIC number include crops; metal mining; coal mining; construction; paint, glass, and wallpaper stores; special trade contractors; food; tobacco; textiles; lumber and wood; and florists, lawn, and garden centers. Classifications appear in numerically arranged tables, allowing comparison of industrial data between the two countries.

189. Bureau of the Census. Economic Census and Surveys Division. **Industry and Product Classification Manual.** GPO, 19??- . Quinquennial. LC sn90-30050. OCLC 3943888. C 3.6/2:IN 2/2/ .

This guide for classifying establishments by industrial activity is organized like the 1987 *Standard Industrial Classification Manual* (entry 192).

190. Employment and Training Administration. **Selected Characteristics of Occupations Defined in the Revised Dictionary of Occupational Titles.** 1v. GPO, 1993. LC 93-231193. HB2595.S45 1993. 331.7/0012. OCLC 28233759. L 37.2:OC 1/4.

SCO supplements the *Dictionary of Occupational Titles* (entry 191) with more detailed occupational data, including job placement, career guidance, occupational research, the labor market, curricula development, and long-range job planning. Part of the data in the 1981 edition of SCO are included in and superseded by the 1991 DOT, however. SCO lists data on training time, physical demands, and environmental conditions for jobs defined in DOT and grouped according to interest factors identified in *Guide for Occupational Exploration* (entry 308). It includes an index of titles by DOT code.

191. Employment Service. **Dictionary of Occupational Titles.** 2v. GPO, 1991. 4th ed., rev. 1991. LC 91-601686. HB2595.D53 1991. 331.7/003. OCLC 24424019. L 37.2:Oc 1/2/991/v.1-2.

DOT presents snapshots of job content within occupations. Each occupational definition includes the occupational code number and title, industry designation, alternate titles, undefined related titles, and definition. Includes a glossary, a list of revisions from the fourth edition (1977), and indexes of industries, occupational titles, and occupational titles arranged by industry designation. The 1991 edition will be the last in print format.

192. Office of Management and Budget. **Standard Industrial Classification Manual: 1987.** GPO, 1987. 705p. LC 87-602335. HF1042.S73 1987. 338/.02/0973. OCLC 17676154. PrEx 2.6/2:In 27/987.

Classifies and defines industries by activity, segmenting the U.S. economy into categories, major groups, and industries with their Standard Industrial Classification (SIC) codes. This edition supersedes the 1972/77 edition and includes an appendix with a conversion table between the two editions.

Directories

193. Bureau of Industrial Economics. **Franchise Opportunities Handbook.** GPO, 1972- . Irregular. LC 79-640923. HF5429.3.F694. 381/.13/02573. OCLC 2430498. C 1.108/2:yr.

This directory of nondiscriminatory franchisers summarizes franchise terms, requirements, and conditions. It also includes general information on franchising, government and nongovernment assistance programs, and sources of information. Includes alphabetical and category indexes.

194. Department of Commerce. **United States Department of Commerce Telephone Directory.** GPO, 1933- . Annual. LC sn89-23283. OCLC 2653317. C 1.37: .

Identifies staff by office and last name, with telephone and office numbers provided. Includes a list of state district offices, with director, address, and telephone number.

195. Department of Labor. **Telephone Directory.** GPO, 1992- . Annual. LC sn93-27916. OCLC 28186878. L 1.67: .

Lists telephone and fax numbers alphabetically and by organizational unit, with an organization chart and telephone numbers for departmental support services.

196. Department of State. Foreign Affairs Document and Reference Center. **Key Officers of Foreign Service Posts.** GPO, 19??- . Triannual. LC 64-61222. JX1705.A255. 353. OCLC 1783120. S 1.40/5: .

Officers at embassies and missions, consulates general, and consulates with whom U.S. businesses would be most likely to interact are listed by country, with address, telephone number, telex number, and fax number. Includes listings for the mission's chief and deputy chief; officers for commercial, tourism, economic, political, labor, consular, administrative, security, agricultural, and public affairs; scientific, legal, or financial attachés, and others. Includes foreign service post zip codes. Also available on *U.S. Foreign Affairs on CD-ROM* (entry 605).

197. Small Business Administration. **National Directory of Women-Owned Construction Firms.** SBA, 1992. 166p. LC 92-243113. HD9715.U52N32 1992. OCLC 28147430. SBA 1.13/4:W 84/4.

Lists those small U.S. construction businesses that are (1) at least 51 percent owned by women, (2) gross more than one million dollars yearly, and (3) have been in business for at least three years under SIC groups, with address, telephone number, specialties, number of employees, and SIC, FSC, and DUNS numbers.

198. Small Business Administration. Office of Procurement Assistance and the Office of Women's Business Ownership. **National Directory of Women-Owned Manufacturing Firms.** 1v. SBA, 1991. OCLC 25521354. SBA 1.13/4:W 84/3.

Manufacturing companies at least 51 percent owned by women and grossing more than one million dollars yearly are listed under SIC groups, with address, owner, number of employees, products, and SIC, FSC, and DUNS numbers.

199. Women's Bureau. **Directory of Non Traditional Training and Employment Programs Serving Women.** GPO, 1991. 157p. LC 92-215862. HD6095.D58 1991. OCLC 24535753. L 36.116:T 68.

This state-by-state listing of programs that help women find training and jobs in the skilled trades and apprenticeships gives name, address, telephone number, contact person, a description of services, and eligibility requirements.

Small Business

SBA Online: *URL http://www.sbaonline.sba.gov.*

200. Internal Revenue Service. **Tax Guide for Small Business.** IRS, 1956- . Free from local IRS offices, state IRS Forms Distribution Centers, or from (800) 829-3676. Annual. LC 57-60150. KF6491.A73I5. 336.2. OCLC 1768450. T 22.19/2-3: .

This is a guide to tax laws for sole proprietorships, partnerships, corporations, and Subchapter S corporations. It contains sections on business organization and accounting, accounting for business assets, figuring business income, and rules for selling or exchanging assets or investment property.

201. Library of Congress. Business Reference Services. **The Entrepreneur's Reference Guide to Small Business Information.** LC, 1994. Free: Washington, DC 20540-5446. 78p. LC 95-131690. Z7164.C81E58 1994. 016.65802/2. OCLC 32179117. [SuDocs number not available].

This annotated bibliography of books, reference sources, journals, indexes, and databases useful to small businesses includes an index.

202. Small Business Administration. Office of Advocacy. **Handbook of Small Business Data, 1988**. GPO, 1988. 344p. LC 88-600379. HD2346.U5H37 1988. 338.6/42/0973021. OCLC 18557700. SBA 1.19:D 26.

Data from the SBA's Small Business Data Base describe small businesses at the national and state levels. Data are compared with statistics from *County Business Patterns, Enterprise Statistics,* and *Employment and Earnings.*

203. Small Business Administration. Office of Business Development. **SBA Directory of Business Development Publications: "Building Excellence in Enterprise."** SBA, 1990. 2p. OCLC 21568006. SBA 1.13/4:B 96/990.

This is a short, annotated list of inexpensive pamphlets about financial management, general management and planning, crime prevention, marketing, personnel management, and new product innovation.

204. Small Business Administration. Office of Business Initiatives. **Resource Directory for Small Business Management: Publications and Videotapes for Starting and Managing a Successful Small Business**. SBA, 19??- . Free: 409 Third St., S.W., Washington, DC 20416. OCLC 33004656. SBA 1.40:115 C.

This is a short, annotated list of inexpensive pamphlets and videos about starting a business, financial management, planning, marketing, and personnel management.

205. Small Business Administration. **The States and Small Business: Programs and Activities**. SBA, 1983- . Annual. LC 84-641308. HD2346.U5D57. 353.9/382048/025. OCLC 10165466. SBA 1.34: .

This directory of state and local programs, agencies, laws, and activities supporting small business in the U.S., Puerto Rico, and the U.S. Virgin Islands lists addresses, contact people, and phone numbers. Appendixes list Small Business Development Centers, State Regulatory Flexibility Acts, SBA Regional Advocates, and District Offices.

Statistics

206. Bureau of Economic Analysis. **National Income and Product Accounts of the United States**. GPO, 1958- . Irregular. LC sn93-27161. OCLC 27245948. C 59.11/5: .
   Also available on CD-ROM, C 59.11/1: .

This major statistical publication, which serves as a supplement to the *Survey of Current Business* (entry 209), presents the full set of national income and product account (NIPA) tables. It includes statistical conventions and the definitions and classifications underlying the NIPAs. Volume 1 covers the years 1929-58; Volume 2 covers the years 1959-88. Also available through the *National Trade Data Bank* (entry 170) and the *National Economic, Social & Environmental Data Bank* (entry 172). Summary tables of source data and estimating methods are also included regularly in *Survey of Current Business* (entry 209) and updated by *National Income and Product Accounts of the United States, [date]: Statistical Tables* (C 59.11/4:In 2/), issued approximately every five years.

207. Bureau of Economic Analysis. Office of Business Economics. **Business Statistics**. GPO, 1951-1992. Biennial. LC 90-643805. HC101.A13122. OCLC 1227582. C 59.11/3: .

A supplement to the *Survey of Current Business* (entry 209), this compendium of historical data on the U.S. economy included sales, inventories, and orders; prices; employment and unemployment; construction; banking and finance; and transportation. In 1994, BEA discontinued compiling these data series, making the 27th edition (1992) the last to be published. It presented the full set of national income and product account (NIPA) tables, with statistical conventions and the definitions and classifications underlying the NIPAs. Summary tables of source data and estimating methods are included regularly in *Survey of Current Business* (entry 209), and are updated by *National Income and Product Accounts of the United States, [date]: Statistical Tables* (C 59.11/4:In 2/), issued approximately every five years. BEA statistics are also available online through the *National Trade Data Bank* (entry 170) and the *National Economic, Social & Environmental Data Bank* (entry 172).

208. Bureau of Economic Analysis. Regional Economic Measurement Division. **REIS [computer file]: Regional Economic Information System**. BEA, 1990- . Annual. CD-ROM. LC 93-644283. HT388u. OCLC 24674014. C 59.24:yr./CD.

Local area estimates of personal income and employment retrospective to 1969 are given by 1-2 digit SIC, region, state, county, and MSA. Data include total and per capita income, employment and earnings, transfer payments, BEAR-FACTS income profiles, and farm income and expenses (excluded for MSAs). Income statistics also appear quarterly in *Survey of Current Business* (entry 209).

209. Bureau of Economic Analysis. **Survey of Current Business**. GPO, 1921- . Monthly. LC 21-26819. HC101.A13. 330.5. OCLC 1697070. C 59.11: .

The BEA's "journal of record" provides estimates and analyses of U.S. economic activity, in full or summary form. It contains the latest estimates and analyses of U.S. national, regional, and international economic activity. Also included are estimates of the gross national product (GNP), GNP price measures, personal income and outlays, regional economic activity, and international transactions and investment. It reviews economic developments in the "Business Situation"; includes regular and special articles about national, regional, and international economic accounts; and features two statistical sections: "Business Cycle Indicators" (analyzing current cyclical developments) and "Current Business Statistics" (describing general business activities and specific industries). A separate section presents business cycle indicators formerly published in BCD, *Business Conditions Digest* (C 59.9:), which ceased in 1990. The business cycle indicators are available through STAT-USA (entry 171) on the Internet *URL http://www.stat-usa.gov.* The January or February issue includes "User's Guide to BEA Information" (entry 182). June and December issues include a subject index; the January issue, an NIPA index; and the October issue, an index to C-Pages. An index to S-Pages (the Current Business Statistics section) appeared in every issue until 1994, when the S-pages were discontinued. The back cover announces upcoming BEA news releases. Selected articles from *Survey of Current Business* and BEA news releases are available online on the Commerce Department's *Economic Bulletin Board* (entry 169). BEA statistics are also available electronically through the *National Trade Data Bank* (entry 170) and the *National Economic, Social & Environmental Data Bank* (entry 172).

210. Bureau of Labor Statistics. **Productivity Measures for Selected Industries and Government Services**. GPO, 1986- . Annual. LC 88-647395. HC110.L3U54a. 331.11/8/0973021. OCLC 17827206. L 2.3/20: .

This bulletin updates all indexes in the BLS industry productivity measurement program. Tables and charts show total and per employee hourly output for selected industries and government functions. The bulletin includes a list of BLS publications on productivity and technology, and an index of industries. Continues *Productivity Indexes for Selected Industries* (L 2.3:) and *Productivity Measures for Selected Industries*. A related title is *Productivity and the Economy: A Chartbook* (L 2.3:2431).

211. Bureau of Labor Statistics. **Working Women: A Chartbook**. GPO, 1991. 53p. LC 92-191638. HD6094.W67 1991. 331.4/0973. OCLC 24800650. L 2.3:2385.
Presents charts, tables, and descriptions of working women today and over the past 30 years, including employment characteristics, occupational patterns and earnings, unemployment figures, and family background. A related title is *Where to Find BLS Statistics on Women* (L 2.71:762).

212. Bureau of the Census. **Census of Construction Industries**. C 3.245/ .
This is an enumeration of U.S. establishments that act as general contractors and builders; special trade contractors; land subdividers and developers; and heavy construction general contractors. Data are presented by industry and geography, with statistics on number of establishments, value of work done, payrolls, value added, capital expenditures, depreciable assets, and costs for fringe benefits, subcontracting, materials, power, machinery rental, buildings, and inventory. Also available in *1992 Economic Census* on CD-ROM (entry 218).

213. Bureau of the Census. **Census of Retail Trade**. C 3.255/ .
Data on public sale of services or personal or household merchandise are gathered from businesses and grouped by SIC codes for the nation, states, District of Columbia, American Samoa, Guam, Puerto Rico, the Northern Marianas, the Virgin Islands, metropolitan areas, counties, incorporated places, and five-digit zip codes. Information is collected on the kind of business, sales, payroll, and employment. Also available in *1992 Economic Census* on CD-ROM (entry 218).

214. Bureau of the Census. **Census of Service Industries**. C 3.257/ .
Data on businesses providing amusements, accommodations, education, repairs, and other services are gathered from businesses and grouped by SIC code and type of operation for the nation, states, District of Columbia, Guam, Puerto Rico, the Northern Marianas, the Virgin Islands, metropolitan areas, counties, incorporated places, and five-digit zip codes. Information is collected on the kind of business, federal tax status, receipts and revenues, payroll, size, and employment. Also available in *1992 Economic Census* on CD-ROM (entry 218).

215. Bureau of the Census. **Census of Wholesale Trade**. C 3.256/ .
Data on the sale of merchandise to retailers, contractors, farmers, wholesalers, and governments are gathered from businesses and grouped by SIC code and type of operation for the nation, states, District of Columbia, Guam, Puerto Rico, the Northern Marianas, the Virgin Islands, metropolitan areas, counties, and incorporated places. Information is collected on the kind of business, sales, payroll, operating expenses, inventory, and employment. Also available in *1992 Economic Census* on CD-ROM (entry 218).

216. Bureau of the Census. **County Business Patterns**. GPO, 1946- . Annual. LC 49-45747. HC101.A184. OCLC 2475762. C 3.204/3 (nos.):yr.
Also available on CD-ROM, C 3.204/4:, through CENDATA (entry 758), and on diskette.
CBP-90 contains data on number of establishments, employees, and payroll, presented by industry for the nation, states, counties, the District of Columbia, and Puerto Rico. Included are agriculture, forestry, and fisheries; mining; contract construction; manufacturing; transportation and public utilities; wholesale and retail trade; finance, insurance, and real estate; and services. Omitted are most government employees, the self-employed, railroad and ocean liner employees, and farm and domestic workers. CBP reports were issued irregularly during the years 1946-63, and yearly since 1964.

217. Bureau of the Census. Data User Services Division. **1990 Census of Population and Housing. Equal Employment Opportunity File [computer file]**. BC, 1993. CD-ROM. OCLC 27720263. C 3.283:CD 90-EEO-2.

Contains detailed job and education data for the nation, states, metropolitan areas, counties, county subdivisions in some states, and places with population of more than 50,000, which can be used as a primary resource for personnel recruitment and affirmative action program planning. Technical documentation for the file is available in C 3.283:EQ 2/3/DOC.

218. Bureau of the Census. Data User Services Division. **1992 Economic Census [computer file]**. BC, 1995. CD-ROM. OCLC 32730300. C 3.277:CD-EC 92-nos.

Data are from the Censuses of Retail and Wholesale Trade; Service, Construction, and Mineral Industries; Manufactures, Transportation, and Agriculture; and related statistical programs.

219. Bureau of the Census. **Guide to the 1987 Economic Censuses and Related Statistics**. BC, 1990. Free: Census Customer Services, Washington, DC 20233-8300; (301) 763-4100. 130p. LC 89-600742. HA37.U55G87 1990. 330.973/0927/027. OCLC 21248354. C 3.253:EC 87-R-2.

Describes scope, coverage, classifications, data, and products for the Censuses of Retail and Wholesale Trade; Service, Construction, and Mineral Industries; and Manufactures, Transportation, and Agriculture. Economic data from other censuses and surveys are also described. An explanation of the classification system and geographic detail are included. Descriptions of individual programs include scope, summaries of report series and products, and representative tables. Appendixes include a list of Standard Industrial Classification (SIC) short titles, Metropolitan Statistical Areas (MSA), economic census publication schedule, and economic subject specialists. Also available on microfiche.

220. Bureau of the Census. **History of the . . . Economic Censuses**. GPO, 19??- . Quinquennial. LC sn92-23763. OCLC 25992681. C 3.253/3: .

Background on planning, mailing of questionnaires, data handling, geographic coding, censuses in outlying areas, special programs, publications and public information, and evaluation is provided, along with a list of published reports and questionnaire facsimiles.

221. Bureau of the Census. **1987 Economic Censuses: Survey of Minority-Owned Business Enterprises**. 4v. GPO, 1990-1991. LC 88-600232. HD2346.U5A17 1990. 338.6/422/0973021. OCLC 18192426. C 3.258:yr.-nos.

The *Survey of Minority-Owned Business Enterprises* contains data for the nation and for selected metropolitan areas, counties, and cities. The data, classified by SIC 2-digit code, organization type, industry division, and size, include type and legal form of business, place, size (employment and receipts), number of firms, gross receipts, number of employees, and annual payroll. A summary is available (C 3.258:87-4). Individual analyses are available for Blacks (C 3.258:87-1), Hispanics (C 3.258:87-2), and Asian Americans, American Indians, and other minorities (C 3.258:87-3). Also available through CENDATA (entry 758).

222. Bureau of the Census. **1992 Economic Census. Geographic Reference Manual**. GPO, 1993. 352p. LC 94-170500. HC106.8.E265 1992. 330.973/0928/072. OCLC 31739755. C 3.253:EC 92-R-1.

The Geographic Reference Manual lists the set of geographic unit codes used in the 1992 Economic Census, including those for states, metropolitan areas, counties, incorporated places, selected large northeastern towns and townships, Guam, the Northern Marianas, Puerto Rico, and the Virgin Islands.

223. Congress. Joint Committee on the Economic Report. **Economic Indicators**. GPO, 1948- . Monthly. LC 48-46615. HC101.A186. 330.973/005. OCLC 1567401. Y 4.Ec 7:Ec 7/date.
      Also available on GPO ACCESS (entry 104).
Prepared for Congress's Joint Economic Committee by the Council of Economic Advisors, the report includes monthly, quarterly, and annual data for the nation on prices, wages, production, business activity, purchasing power, credit, money, federal finance, and international statistics. Tables show 6- to 15-year trends in addition to current data.

224. Department of Labor. Women's Bureau. **1993 Handbook on Women Workers: Trends and Issues**. DL, 1994. 273p. LC 94-223038. HD6094.A17 1994. OCLC 31710109. L 36.108:W 84/3.
This comprehensive statistical summary discusses working women's occupations, earnings, education and training, occupational safety, and legal rights, along with information on minorities, business owners, families, changes in industry, workstyle diversity, and older women. It includes projections and an index.

225. Equal Employment Opportunity Commission. **Indicators of Equal Employment Opportunity—Status and Trends**. EEOC, 1990- . Irregular. LC sn94-28085. OCLC 25278224. Y 3.EQ 2:2 IN 2/ .
Data as of 1988 about the labor force, employment, unemployment, gender and minority occupational patterns, and earnings are shown in tables, charts, and graphs.

226. Equal Employment Opportunity Commission. **Job Patterns for Minorities and Women in Private Industry**. EEOC, 1966- . Annual. LC 76-600741. HD4903.5. U58A543. 331.13/3/0973. OCLC 1461615. Y 3.Eq 2:12-7/ .
These annual reports show sex, race, and ethnic data by industry for the nation, states, and MSAs.

227. Equal Employment Opportunity Commission. **Job Patterns for Minorities and Women in State and Local Government**. GPO, 198?- . Annual. LC 91-641533. JK2480.M5M56. 353.9/3104/021. OCLC 22971116. Y 3.EQ 2:12-4/ .
Presents data for full- and part-time workers and new hires by state, race, sex, job, salary, and government.

228. International Trade Administration. **U.S. Global Trade Outlook**. GPO, 1995- . Annual. LC sn95-27449. OCLC 32379018. C 61.34/2: .
This analysis of world economic and trade trends discusses the fastest growing export markets, identifying opportunities for key U.S. manufacturing and service industries. Following the Standard Industrial Classification (SIC) system, the Outlook provides reviews, forecasts, industry profiles, trends, projection tables, and trade data. It describes domestic and international markets, with tables and charts showing industry revenues, employment, production, market share, and trade patterns. Excerpts are available electronically through the *National Trade Data Bank* (entry 170), *STAT-USA* (entry 171), *and* the *National Economic, Social & Environmental Data Bank* (entry 172). This title incorporates the former *U.S. Industrial Outlook* (C 62.34:) which ceased after the 1994 edition.

229. President. **Economic Report of the President Transmitted to the Congress**. GPO, 1950- . Annual. LC 47-32975. HC106.5.A272. 330.973. OCLC 1193149. PR__.9: (numbered individually for each president).
The President's report to Congress on the nation's economic condition is presented, along with descriptions of economic policies and statistical tables. It includes the Annual Report

of the Council of Economic Advisors, which reviews the economy and proposed spending, along with key economic data, many retrospective to the late 1920s. Also available on the *National Economic, Social & Environmental Data Bank* (entry 172). From 1947-49 this was titled *Economic Report of the President to the Congress.*

230. Not used.

COMMERCE AND TRADE

General Works

231. Bureau of Economic Analysis. **Foreign Direct Investment in the United States: 1987 Benchmark Survey, Final Results**. 1v. GPO, 1990. LC 90-602547. OCLC 22570495. C 59.2:F 76/4/final.

Also available on diskette.

The BEA's benchmark surveys are their most comprehensive studies. Data on the financial structure and operations of the U.S. affiliates of foreign investors in 1987 are classified by industry, country, and, for selected data, by industry and state. Preliminary data from a 1992 benchmark study are available in *Foreign Direct Investment in the United States: 1987 Benchmark Survey, Preliminary Results* (C 59.2:F 76/4/992/Prelim.); also available on diskette.

232. Bureau of Economic Analysis. **Foreign Direct Investment in the United States: Operations of U.S. Affiliates**. GPO, 1980- . Annual. LC 87-644253. HG4501.F65. 332.6/73/0973. OCLC 14089580. C 59.20: .

Also available on diskette.

Data since 1977 from the BEA's annual survey include information on the financial structure and activities of nonbank U.S. affiliates of foreign direct investors. Data are classified by industry, country, and sometimes by state. Preliminary estimates of the annual surveys precede revised estimates, released one year later. Data are briefly summarized in the *Survey of Current Business* (entry 209).

233. House. Committee on Ways and Means. **Overview and Compilation of U.S. Trade Statutes**. GPO, 1987- . Biennial. LC 94-644114. KF1975.A29U55. 343.73/087. OCLC 21016243. Y 4.W 36: .

This is an overview and compilation of key federal laws related to international trade, with foreign trade data. Discussion and compilations cover trade and customs laws, trade remedy laws, import and export laws, reciprocal agreements, organization of trade policy functions, authorities, and profiles of major multilateral trade organizations. Includes a subject index.

234. President. **North American Free Trade Agreement Between the Government of the United States of America, the Government of Canada, and the Government of the United Mexican States**. 6v. GPO, 1993. LC 94-124498. KDZ944.A41992A2 1993. 343.7/087. OCLC 28818607. PrEx 1.2:T 67/V.1-6.

Volume 1. **The NAFTA.**

Volume 2. **Specific Rules of Origin.**

Volume 3. **Tariff Schedule of Canada.**

Volume 4. **Tariff Schedule of Mexico.**

Volume 5. **Tariff Schedule of the United States.**

Volume 6. **NAFTA Supplemental Agreements.**

Includes NAFTA objectives, guidelines, rules of international law, rules of origin, supplemental agreements, and the tariff schedules for Canada, Mexico, and the United States.

Foreign Commerce

235. Bureau of Economic Analysis. International Investment Division. **U.S. Direct Investment Abroad: Operations of U.S. Parent Companies and Their Foreign Affiliates.** BEA, 19??- . Annual. LC 81-602504. HG4538.U2. 332.6/7373/00212. OCLC 7832049. C 59.20/2: .

Also available on diskette.

This survey of world operations of U.S. multinational companies provides data on the financial structure and operations of U.S. parent companies and of their foreign affiliates, classified by country and industry. Preliminary estimates are followed by revised estimates one year later. Summarized in *Survey of Current Business* (entry 209).

236. Bureau of Economic Analysis. **The Balance of Payments of the United States: Concepts, Data Sources, and Estimating Procedures.** GPO, 1990. 146p. LC 90-602246. HG3883.U7U53 1990. 382/.17/0973. OCLC 22329440. C 59.2:P 29.

An overview of basic concepts, methodologies, definitions, and data sources.

237. Bureau of Economic Analysis. **U.S. Direct Investment Abroad: 1989 Benchmark Survey, Final Results.** 1v. GPO, 1992. OCLC 27480951. C 59.2:IN 8/4/1989/FINAL.

Also available on diskette.

Data from the BEA's comprehensive survey cover balance sheets, income statements, employment, employee compensation, U.S. merchandise trade, sales, research and development costs, property, plant, equipment, and taxes. Data are classified by industry and country.

238. Bureau of the Census. **Guide to Foreign Trade Statistics.** GPO, 1967- . Irregular. LC 74-642459. HF105.B73a. 382/.0973. OCLC 1792725. C 3.6/2:F 76/yr.

This guide to sources of foreign trade data describes the content and format of publications, tabulations, computer tapes, CD-ROMs, and microfiche. Includes an index. An overview of the history of foreign trade statistics and references to additional sources of historical trade are given in *Historical Statistics of the United States* (entry 782). A related title is *Foreign Trade Statistics* (Factfinder for the Nation no. 14; C 3.252:14/yr.), available free from the Census Bureau.

239. Bureau of the Census. **U.S. Exports of Merchandise [computer file].** Customer Services, 1989- . Monthly, with annual summary. CD-ROM. LC 91-655128. HF3003. 382. OCLC 23886398. C 3.278/3: .

Also known as Foreign Trade Data, this provides U.S. export statistics since 1989 for domestic and foreign merchandise, including nonmonetary gold and silver and both government and nongovernment shipments. Data cover U.S. Customs districts, U.S. Foreign Trade Zones, and the Virgin Islands.

240. Congress. Joint Committee Print. **Country Reports on Economic Policy and Trade Practices: Report Submitted to the Committee on International Relations, Committee on Ways and Means of the U.S. House of Representatives and the Committee on Foreign Relations, Committee on Finance of the U.S. Senate by the Department of State in Accordance with Section 2202 of the Omnibus Trade Competitiveness Act of 1988**. GPO, 1989- . Biennial. LC 93-642434. HF1410.C69. 338.9/005. OCLC 21537224. Y 4.IN 8/21:C 83.

Reports submitted to Congress by the Department of State under the Omnibus Trade and Competitiveness Act of 1988 summarize economic indicators, policies, structure and exchange rate policies, debt management, U.S. export and investment barriers, export subsidies, intellectual property protection, and worker rights in foreign countries.

241. Department of Commerce. **A Basic Guide to Exporting**. 1v. DC, 1992. LC 92-203380. HF1416.5.B36 1992. 658.8/48/0973. OCLC 25560408. C 61.8:Ex 7/3/992.

This manual describes exporting costs, strategies, and risks. Includes a glossary, directories of sources of assistance, U.S. and overseas contacts for major foreign markets, and a bibliography.

242. Department of Commerce. **International Business Practices**. GPO, 1993. 297p. LC 93-203487. HD2755.5.I5368 1993. OCLC 27967064. C 1.2:B 96/9.

This country directory describes organizations, exporting, commercial policies, foreign investments, intellectual property protection, taxes, regulation, and contacts.

243. Department of Labor. Bureau of International Labor Affairs. **Foreign Labor Trends**. GPO, 19??- . Annual. OCLC 25104887. L 29.16: .

Summaries prepared by American embassies provide narrative and tabular country reports on labor conditions, usually for the previous two years. Data include employment and unemployment, wages and income, GNP, benefits, unions, productivity, poverty rate, and work accidents, plus demographic and socioeconomic statistics. Also available through the *National Trade Data Bank* (entry 170).

244. Internal Revenue Service. Office of International Programs. **Sources of Information from Abroad**. IRS, 1993. rev. 2-93. 361p. LC 93-203481. JF1521.S67 1993. OCLC 28360857. T 22.2/15:6743.

A directory of information sources for foreign nations' public records access, U.S and foreign national government officials and agencies, commercial sources, economic research, and tax treaties.

245. International Trade Administration. Office of Trade and Economic Analysis. **U.S. Foreign Trade Highlights**. GPO, 19??- . Annual. LC 85-643059. HF3000.U173. 382/.0973/021. OCLC 12309860. C 61.28/2: .

Tables of data depict U.S. international trade in goods and services, including imports, exports, trade balances, and shifts in commodity composition. This is the only Department of Commerce publication providing detailed, longitudinal export and import commodity data. Data are presented on the basis of Balance of Payments, census, or National Income and Products Accounts.

246. Small Business Administration. Office of International Trade. **Exporter's Guide to Federal Resources for Small Business**. GPO, 1992. 3d rev. ed. 122p. LC 91-37967. HF1455.E935 1991. 016.382/6. OCLC 24669930. SBA 1.19:Ex 7/3/992.

This directory of federal programs assisting small businesses in exporting lists contacts, telephone numbers, program descriptions, speakers, and a bibliography of key federal publications on international trade. A related guide is *USA, Export Programs: A Business Directory of U.S. Government Resources* (C 1.2:Ex 7/5/993).

Manufacturing

247. Bureau of the Census. **Annual Survey of Manufactures**. C 3.24/9-[no.]: .
The ASM is conducted in years not covered by the Census of Manufactures, updating statistics on key manufacturing measures for industry groups and individual industries. Data cover employment, payroll, work hours, supplemental labor costs, value of shipments for classes of products, energy data, and value added by manufacture.

248. Bureau of the Census. **Census of Manufactures**. GPO, 1810- . Quinquennial. C 3.24/ .
Conducted in years ending in 2 and 7, the Census of Manufactures provides detailed statistics on manufacturing for small geographic areas, industries, products shipped, and materials consumed. Data are provided on employment, payroll, supplementary labor costs, assets, rents, depreciation, cost of materials, fuel consumption, shipment values, value added by manufacture, capital expenditures, and inventories. Selected data are included in CENDATA (entry 758). Also available in *1992 Economic Census* on CD-ROM (entry 218). *Guide to the 1987 Census of Agriculture and Related Statistics* is a user guide and overview. Updated by the *Annual Survey of Manufactures* (entry 247).

249. Bureau of the Census. **Current Industrial Reports**. C 3.158: .
CIR provides timely data on production, inventories, and orders for 5,000 products representing 40 percent of all U.S. manufacturing. Data appear in SIC categories for clothing and leather; chemicals, rubber, and plastic; metals; metal products; lumber, furniture, and paper products; machinery; stone, clay, glass, and concrete products; and textiles. One component, the Survey of Manufacturing Technology (SMT) series, presents data on the use of advanced manufacturing technology. Most CIR monthly and quarterly reports are no longer available in print. They are available online, on paper by special request, or via the Census Bureau's FastFax service: (900) 555-2FAX.

250. Bureau of the Census. **1987 Census of Manufactures and Census of Mineral Industries. Numerical List of Manufactured and Mineral Products**. GPO, 1989. 296p. LC 88-600090. HD9725.A54 1989. 338/.02/0973. OCLC 17732660. C 3.24/2:P 94/5/987.
Describes products and services for the 1987 Census of Manufactures and Census of Mineral Industries, plus data collected monthly, quarterly, and annually in the Current Industrial Reports program. Product classifications are given within their 4-digit SIC code industries; industries are given within their 2-digit major groups. A concordance of 1987 and 1982 codes is included.

251. International Trade Commission. **Harmonized Tariff Schedule of the United States**. GPO, 1987- . Annual. LC 91-643710. KF6654.599.U55. 343.7305/6. OCLC 17427157. ITC 1.10: .
HTS classifies and shows rates of duty for imported and exported commodities. Commodity listings include 10-digit classification number, description, unit of measurement, and rates of duty. Formerly *Tariff Schedules of the United States, Annotated*.

Transportation

252. Army. Corps of Engineers. **Water-Borne Commerce of the United States**. GPO, 1953- . Annual. Microfiche. OCLC 27252540. D 103.1/2: .
WCUS is an annual report on commercial domestic freight transport through waterways, with traffic types, direction, and commodity class. The report is issued in five separate parts, one for each of four U.S. regions and a national summary.

COMMUNICATIONS

General Work

253. Federal Communications Commission. **Statistics of Communications Common Carriers**. GPO, 1957- . Annual. LC sn79-3710. 384. OCLC 3124984. CC 1.35: .
SOCC provides financial and operating statistics for telephone and telegraph companies, controlling companies, and the Communications Satellite Corporation (COMSAT). Data from reports filed with the FCC show assets, liabilities, income, taxes, expenses, dividends, operating revenues, facilities, services, employment, and employee compensation. Includes subject and company indexes. SOCC replaced *Statistics of the Communications Industry in the U.S.* in 1957.

Postal Guides

254. Postal Service. **Domestic Mail Manual**. GPO, 1979- . Quarterly. LC sn82-2716. HE6311.A355. 383. OCLC 5153904. P 1.12/11: .
DMM is a compilation of Postal Service regulations governing domestic mail services, including rates and postage, services, and wrapping requirements. Includes subject and form indexes.

255. Postal Service. **International Mail Manual**. GPO, 1981- . Annual. LC 88-659312. HE6445.I58. 383/.23/0973. OCLC 8269582. P 1.10/5: .
IMM details the policies, regulations, and procedures governing mail to other countries through the U.S. Postal Service.

256. Postal Service. **National Five Digit Zip Code and Post Office Directory**. GPO, 1982- . Annual. LC 82-641753. HE6361.N37. 383/.145. OCLC 8135572. P 1.10/8: .
> Also available on the Internet *URL http://www.usps.gov*. Select "Your post office", ZIP Codes, and ZIP Code Lookup.

Also known as Publication 65, this lists postal zip codes for towns and streets in every state. Also included is an alphabetical list of post offices, a numerical list of post offices by zip code and three-digit service area, new zip codes, discontinued postal units, and information on mail services and U.S. Postal Service organization.

CONSUMER INFORMATION GUIDE

256a. White House Office of the Special Assistant for Consumer Affairs. **Consumer's Resource Handbook**. Consumer Information Center, 1979- . Free: U.S. Office of Consumer Affairs, Office of the Special Advisor to the President for Consumer Affairs, Pueblo, CO 81009. Biennial. LC 89-659022. HC110.C63C652. 381.3/3/02573. OCLC 8872676. HE 1.508/2: .

This directory of federal, state, and local government agencies fielding complaints about goods or services gives addresses, phone numbers (some toll–free), and descriptions of responsibilities, with information on consumer laws and rights.

EMPLOYMENT AND LABOR

Bibliographies

257. Bureau of Labor Statistics. **BLS Publications**. GPO, 1886- . OCLC 15369657. L 2.3-9x: .
This is an unannotated bibliography of BLS reports and bulletins (listed by number and title), with a subject index. It supplements Bulletin 1990, covering the years 1972-77, and Bulletin 1749, covering the years 1886-1971. Updated by *BLS Update* (entry 258).

258. Bureau of Labor Statistics. **BLS Update**. BLS, 1988- . Irregular. LC sn88-18246. 331. OCLC 17911529. L 2.131: .
Lists BLS bulletins, reports, news releases, and other publications issued during the quarter.

Labor-Management Relations

259. Bureau of Labor Statistics. **Displaced Workers**. GPO, 19??- . Irregular. LC sn92-25340. OCLC 24297004. L 2.3: .
Presents data on workers displaced because of plant closings or cutbacks.

260. Bureau of Labor Statistics. **Employee Benefits in a Changing Economy: A BLS Chartbook**. BLS, 1992. 72p. OCLC 27030551. L 2.3:2394.
Consists of a historical review of worker benefits, details on medical and retirement plans, and recent developments in employer-provided benefits.

261. Bureau of Labor Statistics. **Employee Benefits in Small Private Establishments**. GPO, 1990- . Biennial. LC 92-648847. HD4928.N62U63343. 331.25/5/097305. OCLC 25193519. L 2.3:no.
Also known as the Employee Benefits Survey (EBS), this provides data on worker benefits in businesses with fewer than 100 employees. The report for 1990 (issued in 1991) was Bulletin 2388. Two related reports are *Employee Benefits in Medium and Large Firms* (L 2.3/10:) and *Employee Benefits in State and Local Governments* (L 2.3/10-2:).

262. Bureau of Labor Statistics. **Employment Cost Indexes and Levels**. GPO, 1988- . Annual. LC 90-649250. HD4973.E48. 331.2/0973/021. OCLC 20082561. L 2.3:no.
Gives data on wages, salaries, and benefits and on two BLS compensation measures: The Employee Cost Index (ECI) and the Employer Costs for Compensation series. The report for 1975-92 (1992) was Bulletin 2413.

263. Bureau of Labor Statistics. **Geographic Profile of Employment and Unemployment**. GPO, 19??- . Annual. LC 73-603091. HD8051.A7876 subser. 331.1/08 s. OCLC 2806807. L 2.3/12: .
Presents data on labor force, employment, and unemployment in states and substate areas, including annual average labor force estimates by age, race, sex, and Hispanic origin, with economic data for the employed and unemployed.

264. Bureau of Labor Statistics. Office of Compensation and Working Conditions. **Compensation and Working Conditions.** GPO, 1991- . Monthly. LC 91-656642. HD4973.A275. 331. OCLC 23898753. L 2.44: .

CWC reports wage and benefit changes from collective bargaining agreements, expiring agreements, and strikes or lockouts. It also reports wages, salaries, benefits, and safety and health changes. Formerly *Current Wage Developments.*

265. Department of Labor. Office of Administrative Law Judges. **Whistleblower Library and Judges' Benchbooks on Alien Labor Certification, Black Lung & Longshore.** GPO, 1994. CD-ROM. OCLC 32006595. L 1.89:W 57/CD.

Contains the text of Secretary of Labor decisions; *Decisions of the Office of Administrative Law Judges and Office of Administrative Appeals* (L 1.5/2:); texts of regulations and laws, with legislative history; and Judges' Benchbooks, covering alien labor certification, the Black Lung Benefits Act, and the Longshore and Harbor Workers' Compensation Act; and the Benefits Review Board's Black Lung Deskbook. It also includes finding aids: Digests of decisions related to nuclear or environmental employee protection provisions and the employee protection provision of the Surface Transportation Assistance Act, and a caselist organized by docket number.

266. Employment Standards Administration. Office of Workers' Compensation Programs. **State Workers' Compensation Laws.** ESA, 19??- . Semiannual. LC 87-642053. KF3615.Z9L3. 344.73/021. OCLC 10305575. L 36.2:W 89/4/.

Tables depicting laws in the states, the District of Columbia, and territories show coverage of agricultural workers, payment methods, burial allowances, waiting periods, attorney fees, and work-related hearing loss statistics.

267. Unemployment Insurance Service. **Fifty Years of Unemployment Insurance—A Legislative History, 1935-1985** by James M. Rosbrow. UIS, 1986. 97p. LC 87-601117. HD7096.U5U637 no.86-5. 368.4/4/00973. OCLC 15298871. L 37.20:86-5.

This history of unemployment compensation describes the current compensation system, programs before 1935, Titles III and IX of the Social Security Act, and subsequent program changes, with a legislative chronology and notes on laws.

Labor Organizations

268. National Labor Relations Board. **Decisions and Orders of the National Labor Relations Board.** GPO, 1936- . Irregular. LC 37-26136. 331.154. OCLC 1768562. LR 1.8: .

Provides the text of decisions and orders of the Board, along with an alphabetical table of cases and a cross-reference table from advance sheet numbers to page numbers in the *Decisions* volume. Coverage for the series began December 7, 1935.

269. National Labor Relations Board. Legal Research and Policy Planning Branch. **Classified Index of National Labor Relations Board Decisions and Related Court Decisions.** GPO, 19??- . Irregular. LC 73-647147. KF3362.7.C55. 344/.73/0102648. OCLC 1789332. LR 1.8/6: .

This is a subject index to selected Board decisions and to related court decisions printed in *Decisions and Orders of the National Labor Relations Board* (entry 268). Board decisions are cited by volume and folio number, for example, 304 NLRB No. 24. Decisions are classified according to numerical codes from the *Classification Outline with Topical Index for Decisions of the National Labor Relations Board and Related Court Decisions* (LR 1.8/7:). A supplement is published irregularly.

Occupational Safety

270. National Institute for Occupational Safety and Health. Division of Standards Development and Technology Transfer. **NIOSH Publications Catalog**. NIOSH, 1987. 7th ed. 653p. OCLC 17869662. HE 20.7114:P 96/2/987.

This cumulative list of all NIOSH titles includes numbered publications, hazard evaluations and technical reports, industry studies, control technology reports, and contract and miscellaneous reports, indexed by subject. Unannotated entries include ordering information. A related publication, listing basic reference titles, is *NIOSH Bookshelf* (HE 20.7114:B 29/991).

271. National Institute for Occupational Safety and Health. Division of Standards Development and Technology Transfer. **NIOSH Publications on Noise and Hearing**. NIOSH, 1991. 106p. LC 92-198754. Z6675.N5N37 1991. 363.7/4. OCLC 24639314. HE 20.7114:N 69/2.

Part 1 is a bibliography of NIOSH publications on workplace noise, most of which are available from NTIS. Included are numbered publications, hazard evaluations and technical reports, industry studies, control technology reports, and contract and miscellaneous reports. Part 2 contains both full text and abstracts of many of the materials cited in part 1, including testimony, research results, and recommendations.

272. National Institute for Occupational Safety and Health. **NIOSH Pocket Guide to Chemical Hazards**. GPO, 1994. 398p. OCLC 31992459. HE 20.7108:C 42/994.

Information on federally regulated workplace chemicals or chemical types includes name and synonyms, exposure limits, properties, analytical methods, protective equipment, symptoms of exposure, and emergency treatment. For more comprehensive guidelines consult *Occupational Health Guidelines for Chemical Hazards* and supplements (entry 273).

273. National Institute for Occupational Safety and Health. **NIOSH/OSHA Occupational Health Guidelines for Chemical Hazards** edited by Frank W. Mackison, R. Scott Stricoff, and Lawrence J. Partridge, Jr. GPO, 1981. 1545p. OCLC 7855161. HE 20.7108:C 42/3.

NIOSH/OSHA Occupational Health Guidelines for Chemical Hazards summarizes safety and health information for federally regulated workplace chemicals. Chemical notations include an introduction, chemical names and synonyms, exposure limits, chemical and physical properties, symptoms of overexposure, environmental and medical monitoring, respiratory and personal protection, management of leaks and spills, sanitation, control measures, and first aid. The volume also provides a "Summary of NIOSH Recommendations for Occupational Health Standards" for each chemical. Updated by supplements (HE 20.7108:C 42/3/supp.no.-OHG).

274. Occupational Safety and Health Administration. **OSHA CD-ROM [computer file]**. GPO, 1991- . Quarterly. CD-ROM. LC 92-660645. HD7654. 363. OCLC 25363814. L 35.26: .

The OSHA CD-ROM is an electronic text of OSHA regulations, documents, and technical information. It includes Title 20 of the Code of Federal Regulations (CFR), parts 1900-1990; an index to *Federal Register* notices since 1971; memoranda, testimony, settlement agreements, fact sheets, standards interpretations, the *OSHA Field Operations Manual* and the *OSHA Technical Manual*; and information about 1,200 workplace chemicals.

275. Occupational Safety and Health Administration. **OSHA Publications and Audiovisual Programs**. OSHA, 19??- . Free: Publications Office, Room N3101, 200 Constitution Ave., N.W., Washington, DC 20210. Irregular. LC sn90-20087. OCLC 21020794. L 35.16:P 96/2/yr.

This is a short annotated list of OSHA publications, posters, and audiovisuals.

Statistics

276. Bureau of Economic Analysis. **Fixed Reproducible Tangible Wealth in the United States, 1925-89**. GPO, 1993. 452p. LC 93-198516. HC110.C3F487 1993. OCLC 27665602. C 59.2:W 37/925-89.

Provides estimates of wealth, based on durable equipment and structures and durable goods owned in the U.S.

277. Bureau of Labor Statistics. **BLS Handbook of Methods**. GPO, 1982- . LC 88-646297. HD8064.2.U54a. 331/.0723. OCLC 9114103. L 2.3: .

Volume 1 provides explanations of BLS statistical series, describing the background of each major program, concepts and definitions, data sources and collection, analysis, uses and limitations, publication, and sources of additional technical information. Volume 2 gives a detailed description of the Consumer Price Index, with appendixes showing changes in the CPI since 1980, relative importance of components, non-POPS nonhousehold sample designs, pricing cycles for sample areas, and seasonal adjustment methods.

278. Bureau of Labor Statistics. **Consumer Expenditure Survey**. GPO, 1987- . LC 92-659091. HD6983.C558. 339.4/7/0973021. OCLC 25196986. L 2.3-11X: .

Presents information related to consumer spending and income, with annual expenditures classed by such characteristics as income, age, housing, residence, and occupation.

279. Bureau of Labor Statistics. **CPI Detailed Report**. GPO, 1974- . Monthly. LC 75-641423. HB235.U6U54b. 339.4/2/0973. OCLC 2251913. L 2.38/3: .

The most comprehensive report on monthly consumer price indexes and rates of change. A companion title, *Relative Importance of Components in the Consumer Price Index* (L 2.3/9:), provides data on the value weights of CPI components.

280. Bureau of Labor Statistics. **Employment and Earnings**. GPO, 1969- . Monthly. LC 83-645868. HD5723.A4532. 331.12/5/0973. OCLC 2610713. L 2.41/2: .

E&E gives monthly statistics for the nation, states, and local areas. It includes household and business establishment data, seasonably and not seasonably adjusted, and provides timely analyses of labor force development.

281. Bureau of Labor Statistics. **Employment, Hours, and Earnings, States and Areas, [date]**. GPO, 1982- . Quinquennial. LC 87-658036. HD8051.A62. 331/.0973 s. OCLC 10672299. L 2.3-6x: .

This statistical companion to *Employment, Hours, and Earnings, United States* (entry 282) gives monthly and annual averages for employment, earnings, and hours worked for states, the District of Columbia, Puerto Rico, the Virgin Islands, and MSAs. Data are provided for industries and selected SIC codes. Does not include information on farm, military, self-employed and domestic workers, and unpaid family workers. There is also an annual *Supplement to Employment, Hours, and Earnings, States and Areas, Data for. . .* (L 2.3/7x:).

282. Bureau of Labor Statistics. **Employment, Hours, and Earnings, United States, 1909-[year]**. GPO, 1984- . Irregular. LC 92-649503. HD8051.A62. 331. OCLC 12000403. L 2.3:1312.

This compilation of annual and monthly averages for nonfarm employment, earnings, and hours provides national data only. Compilations, issued every three to five years, are updated by the annual supplement *Employment and Earnings* (L 2.41/2-2:).

283. Bureau of Labor Statistics. **Handbook of Labor Statistics**. GPO, 1926-1989. Irregular. LC 27-328. HD8051.A62. 331/.0973. OCLC 1768204. L 2.3/5:nos. vary.

This compilation of major BLS labor force statistical series includes information on employment, unemployment, earnings, and benefits. Tables begin with the earliest reliable data for the nation, with some state and area data. Includes a section on foreign labor statistics. Coverage for the series began in 1924, with the last statistical series issued in 1989. BLS plans to divert *Handbook* information to other BLS publications until the title is released in CD-ROM format.

284. Bureau of Labor Statistics. **Monthly Labor Review**. GPO, 1918- . Monthly. LC 15-26485. HD8051.A78. 331/.0973. OCLC 5345258. L 2.6: .

MLR articles focus on employment, the labor force, wages, prices, productivity, economic growth, and occupational injuries and illnesses. Regular features include a review of industrial relations developments, research summaries, convention reports, book reviews, and labor statistics. The back cover announces release dates for BLS statistical series.

285. Bureau of Labor Statistics. **Occupational Injuries and Illnesses in the United States by Industry**. GPO, 1973- . Annual. LC 78-641536. HD7262.5.U6U54a. 614.8/52/0973. OCLC 4072093. L 2.3/11: .

This annual report on the number and frequency of private sector occupational injuries and illnesses is based on employer logs. Data are reported for SIC industry classifications. A brief summary, *Survey of Occupational Injuries and Illnesses* (L 2.2:Su 7/2/yr.), is issued annually.

286. Bureau of Labor Statistics. Office of Prices and Living Conditions. **Producer Price Indexes**. GPO, 1985- . Monthly. Expanded Version. LC 85-644268. HB235.U6A472. 338.5/28/0973. OCLC 11962976. L 2.61: .

PPI is a comprehensive report on wholesale prices of farm and industrial commodities, by industry and stage of processing, using text, statistical tables, and technical notes. An annual supplement, *Producer Price Indexes, Data for [year]* (L 2.61/11:), provides monthly data for the year, annual averages, and information on weights. PPI information is also available through the BLS electronic news release and on diskette or computer tapes. A monthly PPI summary is also included in *Monthly Labor Review* (entry 284). Background is provided in *Data Collection Manual: Producer Price Index* (L 1.7:D 26/990).

287. Central Intelligence Agency. Directorate of Intelligence. **Handbook of International Economic Statistics**. GPO, 1992- . Annual. LC 94-649698. HA155.U54a. 330.9/04. OCLC 27990932. PrEx 3.16: .

Basic statistics for comparing worldwide economic performance since 1970 include data on aggregate trends, the Organization for Economic Co-operation and Development (OECD), country trends, energy, agriculture, minerals and metals, chemicals and manufactures, environment, foreign trade and aid, regional trade, and aid to emerging states. Excerpts are included in the *National Trade Data Bank* (entry 170). Formerly *Handbook of Economic Statistics* (PrEx 3.10/7-5:).

FINANCE AND BANKING

288. Board of Governors of the Federal Reserve System. **Federal Reserve Bulletin.** GPO, 1915- . Monthly. LC 15-26318. HG2401.A5. 332.1/1/0973. OCLC 1606526. FR 1.3: .

Topical articles, announcements, and statistical data focus on the current U.S. financial situation and outlook, and feature national and international statistics. Issues include a guide to statistical releases and special tables; an index to statistical tables; a list of the Board of Governors and staff and the Federal Open Market Committee, staff, and advisory councils; maps of the Federal Reserve System; and lists of Federal Reserve banks, branches, and offices. June and December issues list periodic release dates, and the December issue includes an annual index.

289. House. Committee on Banking, Finance, and Urban Affairs. **Give Yourself Credit: (Guide to Consumer Credit Laws).** GPO, 1992. 230p. LC 92-173697. KF1039.A25 1992. 346.73/073. OCLC 25696355. Y 4.B 22/1:C 86/17/992.

This introduction to credit and federal consumer protection laws describes how to apply for and use credit, rights and obligations, types of loans, and managing debts. It includes the text of consumer protection laws and a glossary.

290. House. Committee on Banking, Finance, and Urban Affairs. **A Reference Guide to Banking and Finance** prepared by the Congressional Research Service, Library of Congress. GPO, 1983. 2d rev. ed. 102p. LC 83-602064. HG151.R43 1983. 332.1/03/21. OCLC 9437606. Y 4.B 22/1:B22/27/983.

This guide defines terms, describes organizations, and summarizes key laws.

291. Securities and Exchange Commission. **Directory of Companies Required to File Annual Reports with the Securities and Exchange Commission Under the Securities Exchange Act of 1934, Alphabetically and by Industry Groups.** GPO, 1976- . Annual. LC 77-644292. HG4057.A216. 338.7/4/02573. OCLC 3172888. SE 1.27: .

This is a directory of companies with stocks listed on national securities exchanges and which have registered under the Securities Exchange Act of 1934 (but not investment companies registered under the Investment Company Act of 1940). Section 1-2 lists industry groups with corresponding SIC codes; Section 3 is an alphabetical company list, with industry group and sector, docket number, and end of company fiscal year; and Section 4 lists companies by industry, with docket number, identification number, and end of company fiscal year. SEC filings since January 1, 1994 are available on EDGAR through the Internet *URL http://www.sec.gov/edgarhp.htm.*

INSURANCE

Social Security

> Social Security Administration: *URL*
> *gopher://gopher.ssa.gov; URL http://www.ssa.gov.*

292. Social Security Administration. **Annual Statistical Supplement . . . to the Social Security Bulletin.** GPO, 1992- . Annual. LC sn93-28651. OCLC 28328831. HE 3.3/3: .

This compendium of historical and current data on Social Security augments the monthly and quarterly tables in the *Social Security Bulletin* (entry 296). It includes an overview, statistical tables, technical notes, abbreviations, glossary, and an index. The supplement is included with the subscription to *Social Security Bulletin* or may be purchased separately.

293. Social Security Administration. **Author, Title, and Subject Index to the Social Security Bulletin, 1938-79** prepared by Associate Consultants, Inc. GPO, 1982. 132p. OCLC 8448044. HE 3.3/5:938-79.

> **Author, Title, and Subject Index to the Social Security Bulletin, 1980-88** complied by Phyllis A. Marbray. GPO, 1989. 34p. OCLC 23439921. HE 3.3/5:980-88.

This is a cumulative index to articles, notes, commentary, book reviews, research summaries, historical reprints, and statistical tables published in the *Bulletin*. Annual author and title indexes appear in the *Bulletin's* December issue.

294. Social Security Administration. **Compilation of the Social Security Laws: Including the Social Security Act, As Amended, and Related Enactments Through. . . .** GPO, 19??- . Biennial. LC sn87-41069. OCLC 11883898. Y 4.W 36:10-3/.

This compilation, printed for the Ways and Means Committee, features the text of the Social Security Act, as amended, with an index to it; selected provisions of the Internal Revenue Code; and provisions of laws cited in and affecting the Social Security Act (listed by *U.S. Code* citations, public law numbers, and short titles).

295. Social Security Administration. Office of Policy. **Rulings. Cumulative Edition: Social Security Rulings on Federal Old-Age, Survivors, Disability, Supplemental Security Income, and Black Lung Benefits**. GPO, 1980- . Annual. LC 86-641567. KF3646.A2S6. 344.73/023. OCLC 8540051. HE 3.44/2: .

Social Security Rulings is a compilation of precedential case decisions published in the *Federal Register* as Social Security Rulings or Acquiescence Rulings. Rulings emerge from administrative adjudication, federal court decisions, Commissioner's decisions, General Counsel opinions, and other policy interpretations. Acquiescence Rulings explain how the Social Security Administration (SSA) applies U.S. Courts of Appeals decisions that vary from SSA's policies in adjudicating claims. This cumulation compiles the year's rulings from *Social Security Rulings* (known as SSR, HE 3.44:) that were not superseded or rescinded.

296. Social Security Administration. Office of Policy. **Social Security Bulletin**. GPO, 1938- . Quarterly. LC 40-29327. HD7123.S56. 368.4/00973. OCLC 1640226. HE 3.3: .

This official journal for reporting Social Security program statistics, research, and data includes monthly and quarterly tables on the history and status of Social Security. Indexed by *Author, Title, and Subject Index to the Social Security Bulletin* (entry 293).

297. Social Security Administration. Office of Research and Statistics. **Social Security Programs in the United States**. GPO, 1994. 82p. OCLC 31255045. HE 3.2:SO 13/21/1993.

This guide to publicly funded cash and in-kind income support programs under the Social Security Act discusses historical and current program provisions of the old-age, survivors, and disability program (OASDI), Supplemental Security Income (SSI), Aid to Families with Dependent Children (AFDC), Medicare, unemployment insurance, workers' compensation, and temporary disability programs.

298. Social Security Administration. Office of Research and Statistics. **SSA Research and Statistics Publications Catalog**. SSA, 1991. Free: Room 921, Universal North Bldg., 1875 Connecticut Ave., N.W., Washington, DC 20009. HE 3.38/5: .

This annotated bibliography of statistical releases and compilations, commission reports and legislative summaries, data files, and research includes author and subject indexes. A new edition is expected.

299. Social Security Administration. **Social Security Handbook**. GPO, 1969- . Irregular. LC 86-645860. HD7123.A214. 344.73/023/05. OCLC 8082609. SSA 1.8/3: .

Also available on the Internet *URL http://www.ssa.gov/handbook*

A summary of legislation, regulations, and rulings related to federal retirement, survivors, disability, black lung, supplemental security income, health insurance, public assistance, and related programs. Related titles are *Fast Facts and Figures About Social Security* (HE 3.94:993) and *Understanding Social Security* (HE 3.2:Un 2/2/993-2).

300. Social Security Administration. **Social Security Programs Throughout the World**. GPO, 1958- . Biennial. LC hew62-40. HD7091.U62. 368.4/005. OCLC 1588903. HE 3.49/3: .

This comprehensive, worldwide survey highlights the principal features of programs in more than 140 countries and territories. Country summaries describe types and dates of programs, coverage, funding, qualifying conditions, benefits for insured workers, disability and medical benefits for dependents, and administrative organization. Issued periodically since 1937.

OCCUPATIONS

General Work

301. Bureau of the Census. **1990 Census of Population and Housing. Alphabetical Index of Industries and Occupations**. GPO, 1992. 370p. OCLC 25615331. C 3.223/22:90-R-3.

Used to classify census-respondent occupations and industry, the index lists current and former industry and occupation titles, with their code numbers. A companion source is *Classified Index of Industries and Occupations* (C 3.223/22:90-R-4).

Career Guides

302. Bureau of Labor Statistics. **Career Guide to Industries**. GPO, 1992- . Annual. LC 93-642799. HF5382.5.U5C316. 331.7/02/05. OCLC 27055382. L 2.3/4-3: .

This companion to *Occupational Outlook Handbook* (entry 303) describes job opportunities for 40 industries, including the nature of the industry, employment, working conditions, occupations, training and advancement, earnings and benefits, and outlook.

303. Bureau of Labor Statistics. **Occupational Outlook Handbook**. GPO, 1949- . Biennial. LC sn88-40069. 331. OCLC 1773253. L 2.3/4: .

Also available from the GPO on CD-ROM L 2.3/4-4: .

The federal government's premier career guide describes job duties, working conditions, level and places of employment, education and training, prospects, earnings, and related occupations. Occupations are tagged with *Dictionary of Occupational Titles* (DOT) codes. *Occupational Outlook Quarterly* (L 2.70/4:) updates the handbook with articles, statistics, and publication and news notes about new careers, training, salary trends, and career counseling.

304. Bureau of Labor Statistics. **Occupational Projections and Training Data**. GPO, 1971- . Biennial. LC 80-649629. HD5723.U54c. 331.12/0973. OCLC 5133145. L 2.3/4-2: .

Statistical and technical data supporting the information in *Occupational Outlook Handbook* (entry 303) are presented along with occupational rankings by employment growth, earnings, unemployment susceptibility, separation rates, and part-time work.

305. Bureau of Labor Statistics. **Outlook, 1990-2005**. GPO, 1992. 144p. OCLC 26060713. L 2.3:2402.

Provides economic and employment projections for specific industries and occupations based on three alternate growth patterns.

306. Department of Commerce. Office of Federal Statistical Policy and Standards. **Standard Occupational Classification Manual**. GPO, 1980. LC 81-601243. HB2595.S7 1980. 331.7/0012. OCLC 8953905. C 1.8/3:0c 1/980.

The SOC Manual provides a coding system and nomenclature for classifying occupations. It features a mechanism for cross-referencing and aggregating occupation-related data collected in statistical reporting programs. The occupational groupings include a list of *Dictionary of Occupational Titles* codes and titles descriptive of the group.

307. Department of Defense. **Military Careers**. DOD, 1992- . Biennial. LC 93-648162. UB147.M56. OCLC 27117642. D 1.6/15: .

Descriptions of enlisted careers include what titleholders do, training, work environment, civilian counterparts, opportunities, qualifications, and physical demands, with profiles of typical 20-year military careers. Includes a glossary and indexes by *Dictionary of Occupational Titles* number and by occupation and title.

308. Employment and Training Administration. **Guide for Occupational Exploration**. GPO, 1979. 715p. LC 81-601909. HF5382.G85 1979. 331.7/02/0973. OCLC 11728122. L 37.8:Oc 1/2.

This supplement to the *Dictionary of Occupational Titles* (entry 191) translates areas of interest into types of work, with descriptions of the aptitudes, adaptabilities, and other requisites of occupational groups. Appendixes relate the *Guide* to the DOT and to the General Aptitude Test Battery.

309. Employment and Training Administration. **The Revised Handbook for Analyzing Jobs**. 1v. GPO, 1991. LC 92-600034. HF5549.5.J6R5 1991. 658.3/06. OCLC 25354839. L 1.7/2:J 57/6/991.

This is a guide to techniques for job analysis and recording.

310. Office of Personnel Management. **Federal Career Directory: The U.S. Government, Find Out Why It's Becoming the First Choice!: Career America**. 1v. GPO, 1990. OCLC 22784428. PM 1.2:C 18/8.

Profiles of executive and judicial branch units and independent agencies include mission, functions, and typical entry-level college majors and degrees recruited. Includes an index of college majors and study areas.

311. Office of Personnel Management. **Operating Manual for Qualification Standards for General Schedule Positions**. 1v. GPO, 1994. OCLC 31467890. PM 1.8/14: .

The Qualification Standards Handbook describes educational, experience, and other qualifications required for General Schedule (GS and GM) federal jobs. It includes indexes and information about medical, written, and performance test requirements. Supersedes Handbook X-118. Information about job duties in General Schedule occupational series is available in the *Handbook of Occupational Groups and Series* (PM 1.8/2:) and the *Position Classification Standards* (PM 1.30:990/pt.).

TAXES

312. House. Committee on Ways and Means. **Overview of the Federal Tax System: Including Data on Tax and Revenue Measures Within the Jurisdiction of the Committee on Ways and Means**. GPO, 1990- . Annual. LC 94-655041. KF6275.5.O93. 343.7304. OCLC 23737106. Y 4.W 36: .

Provides background and statistics on taxes and revenue, expenditures, taxing authority, information sources, historical tables, legislative histories, taxpayer rights, tax provisions that expired, and distribution of income and taxes.

313. Internal Revenue Service. **A Selection of . . . Internal Revenue Service Tax Information Publications**. IRS, 1982- . Annual. LC 87-649141. KF6301.A33S45. 343.7304. OCLC 10261132. T 22.44/2:1194/ .

This 5-volume compendium contains the text of frequently requested IRS publications. Indexed by subject. A related title is *IRS Printed Product Catalog* (T 22.2/15:).

314. Internal Revenue Service. **Bulletin Index-Digest System: Service 1-4**. GPO, 1953. Irregular. LC 76-645237. KF6362.3.I5. 343/.73/05202648. OCLC 2403463. T 22.25/5: .

This is a cumulative index and digest to the *Internal Revenue Bulletin* (entry 317) since 1952. Summaries (digests) of official IRS rulings and procedures, Supreme Court decisions, adverse Tax Court decisions, Executive Orders, Treasury decisions and orders, Delegation Orders, and laws are arranged topically, with finding aids to Internal Revenue Code, Statement of Procedural Rules, Supreme Court Decisions, Tax Court Decisions, Revenue Rulings and Procedures, miscellaneous items, public laws, and tax conventions. It is divided into four Services: Service no. 1, Income Tax, Publication 641; Service no. 2, Estate and Gift Taxes, Publication 642; Service no. 3, Employment Taxes, Publication 643; and Service no. 4, Excise Taxes, Publication 644. Each Service consists of a basic volume and its cumulative supplement. Formerly *Index-Digest Supplement*.

315. Internal Revenue Service. **Cumulative List of Organizations Described in Section 170 (c) of the Internal Revenue Code**. GPO, 19??- . Annual with cumulative quarterly supplements. LC 55-61341. HJ4653.D4A3. OCLC 2457127. T 22.2/11: .

Also known as Publication 78, this is an alphabetical list of nonprofit organizations to which donations are tax deductible, with city and state identified. Three cumulative supplements are published annually, listing new organizations on the Exempt Organizations/Business Master File.

316. Internal Revenue Service. **Federal Tax Forms [computer file]**. GPO, 1993- . Annual. CD-ROM. LC sn94-27718. OCLC 29894562. T 22.51/4: .

Contains hundreds of IRS forms and instructions for the current and previous year that can be printed from the disc and searched by keyword.

317. Internal Revenue Service. **Internal Revenue Bulletin**. GPO, 1922- . Weekly. LC 22-26051. 336.2. OCLC 2447728. T 22.23: .

I.R.B. is the official announcement organ for IRS rulings and procedures, including those superseded, revoked, modified, or amended. Permanent rulings and procedures are cumulated semiannually in *Internal Revenue Cumulative Bulletin* (entry 318).

318. Internal Revenue Service. **Internal Revenue Cumulative Bulletin**. GPO, 1922- . Semiannual. LC 85-642251. KF6282.A2I495. 343.7304/02646. OCLC 2779188. T 22.25: .

C.B. consolidates permanent IRS rulings and procedures previously published in the weekly *Internal Revenue Bulletin* (entry 317). It includes finding lists, notices of proposed rulemaking, a disbarments and suspensions list, and an index.

319. Internal Revenue Service. **IRS Facsimile Directory**. IRS, 1993- . Irregular. LC sn93-27766. OCLC 28103149. T 22.2/15:7159/yr.

This is a telephone and fax number directory for IRS regional, district, and service center offices.

320. Internal Revenue Service. **Reference Listing of Federal Tax Forms and Publications**. IRS, 198?- . Annual. LC sn89-25610. OCLC 15157014. T 22.44/2: 1200/ .

Lists forms, with descriptions, by number and subject, along with a toll-free IRS telephone number for requesting them.

321. Internal Revenue Service. Statistics of Income Division. **Individual Income Tax Returns**. GPO, 1989- . Annual. LC sn92-40731. OCLC 27062126. T 22.35/8: .

Information on taxpayers' income, exemptions, deductions, credits, and taxes is based on a sample drawn from individual income tax returns. The report also includes data on sources of income, adjusted gross income, taxable income, tax withheld, foreign and domestic dividends, capital gains and losses, and selected income and tax items for states. Classifications are by tax status, size of adjusted gross income, marital status, form of deduction, and state of residence. This report has more comprehensive and complete data than those published earlier in *SOI Bulletin* (entry 323).

322. Internal Revenue Service. Statistics of Income Division. **Statistics of Income. Corporation Income Tax Returns**. GPO, 1954- . Annual. LC 61-37568. HJ4653.C7A3. 336.243. OCLC 2687847. T 22.35/5: .

Data on U.S. and foreign business income, assets, liabilities, dividends and other deductions, credits, and taxes are based on a sample drawn from corporate tax returns. Based on *Corporation Source Book of Statistics of Income* (T 22.35/2:C 81/), this report has more comprehensive and complete data than those published earlier in *SOI Bulletin* (entry 323).

323. Internal Revenue Service. Statistics of Income Division. **Statistics of Income. SOI Bulletin**. GPO, 1981- . Quarterly. LC 81-649949. HJ4653.S7S73. 336.2/00973. OCLC 7904895. T 22.35/4: .

SOI Bulletin presents the earliest published financial statistics from individual and corporate income tax returns in text, tables, and graphs. It also includes information from analytical studies, personal income and tax data by state, historical data for types of taxpayers, and data on tax collections, refunds, and other tax-related items. The Internal Revenue Service's Statistics of Income (SOI) Bulletin Board provides access to many *SOI Bulletin* tables, and SOI data can be purchased on magnetic tape; it is also accessible through FedWorld (entry 39). Related publications are the annual *Partnership Source Book* (T 22.35/6-2:), with data from partnership tax returns; the quinquennial *Sole Proprietorship Source Book* (T 22.35/5-3:) with data on nonfarm businesses; and the quinquennial

Compendium of Studies of International Income and Taxes (T 22.35/2:In 8), with data on foreign activities of U.S. corporations, foreign corporations in the U.S., and foreign-controlled U.S. corporations.

324. Internal Revenue Service. **Your Federal Income Tax for Individuals**. IRS, 1951- . Free from local IRS offices, state IRS Forms Distribution Centers, or from (800) 829-3676. Annual. LC 44-40552. KF6369.A425. 336.242. OCLC 1695426. T 22.44: .

This publication explains the tax law, how to prepare forms, exemptions and deductions, taxable income, income and deductions from investment properties, capital gains and losses, and other regulations. Examples, an index, and sample forms and schedules are provided.

Education

> Department of Education/OERI Gopher:
> *URL gopher://gopher.ed.gov* or *URL http://www.ed.gov/*
> or *URL ftp://ftp.ed.gov* (logon anonymous).

BIBLIOGRAPHIES

325. Department of Education. Captioning and Adaptation Branch. **Catalog of Captioned Educational Videos and Films**. DE, 1994- . Free: Captioned Films/Videos, Modern Talking Picture Service, 5000 Park St. North, St. Petersburg, FL 33709. Annual. LC sn93-44085. OCLC 29332314. ED 1.209/2-2: .
This annotated list of materials for the hearing impaired provides bibliographic and availability information, including grade level. Includes a subject index.

326. Department of Education. Captioning and Adaptation Branch. **Catalog of General Interest Films/Videos**. DE, 199?- . Free: Captioned Films/Videos, Modern Talking Picture Service, 5000 Park St. North, St. Petersburg, FL 33709. Annual. LC sn94-28568. OCLC 31682267. ED 1.209/2: .
This annotated list provides bibliographic and availability information for features, continuing education, short subjects, and videos for the hearing impaired and available for school loans. Includes a subject index.

327. Department of Education. Office of Educational Research and Improvement. Educational Research Library. **Early American Textbooks, 1775-1900: A Catalog of the Titles Held by the Educational Research Library**. DE, 1985. (ED 264601). 287p. LC 86-601410. Z5817.U57 1985. OCLC 29387864. ED 1.2:T31/2.
This bibliography of titles in the Early American Textbook Collection lists texts used or published in the U.S. during the 18th and 19th centuries. It includes a historical review and author and subject indexes. It supplements the 1976 edition of *Fifteenth to Eighteenth Century Rare Books in Education* (HE 19.213:R 18).

Machine-Readable Data

328.   Educational Resources Information Center. **ERIC [computer file]**. ERIC, 1966- for RIE subfile; 1969- for CIJE subfile. Updated monthly.
Contains citations and abstracts of journal and report literature announced in *Resources in Education* and *Current Index to Journals in Education* in all areas of education. Available online and on CD-ROM from numerous commercial vendors.

Office of Education Catalogs

329.   Educational Resources Information Center. **AskERIC**. E-mail: *askeric@ericir. syr.edu*; Internet *URL http://ericir.syr.edu*.
AskERIC answers E-mailed questions and maintains a full-text resource collection related to K-12 education and information technology, including guides and directories.

330.   Educational Resources Information Center. **Catalog of ERIC Clearinghouse Publications**. ERIC, 19??- . Irregular. LC sn93-28072. OCLC 28297366. ED 1.302:C 58/ .
Lists publications available from the ERIC Clearinghouses with order number and price. Includes a subject index.

331.   Educational Resources Information Center. **Recent Department of Education Publications in ERIC**. Department of Education, 1992- . Free: 555 New Jersey Ave., N.W., Washington, DC 20208-5641. Annual. LC 93-664120. Z5815.U5U68a. 016.370/.973/05. OCLC 26141194. ED 1.317/2: .
This is a selected, annotated list of publications produced or sponsored by the Department of Education, arranged by subject category. Includes a title index and ERIC control number for each entry.

DIRECTORIES

332.   Department of Education. **A Teacher's Guide to the U.S. Department of Education**. DE, 1995. 3d ed. 140p. OCLC 32841039. ED 1.8:T 22/3/995.
Also available on the Internet *URL http://www.ed.gov*.
Responsibilities, grant programs, and services of USDE offices are described, along with a list of clearinghouses funded by the USDE.

333.   Department of Education. Office of Educational Research and Improvement. **Guidebook to Excellence**. GPO, 1993- . Annual. National Edition. LC 94-648604. QA13.G82. OCLC 30763176. ED 1.330:M 42.
Provides descriptions, addresses, and telephone numbers for federal offices, programs, and facilities supporting K-12 math and science education. There are also 10 regional guidebooks. All are also available online from the Eisenhower National Clearinghouse gopher *URL http://www.enc.org* or ftp site at *infor@enc.org*.

334.   Department of Health and Human Services. Head Start Bureau. **Directory of Local Head Start Programs**. DHHS, 1983- . LC 86-646980. LC4091.D48. 372/.21/02573. OCLC 11389620. HE 23.1113: .
This is a state and city directory of public and private nonprofit organizations awarded grants to operate Head Start programs for three- to five-year-olds, special programs for migrant and Native American children, and Parent and Child Centers for children up to

age three. Appendixes list Head Start Technical Assistance Support Centers, Head Start Resource Access Projects, and all grantees by state, with their delegates.

335. Educational Resources Information Center. **Directory of ERIC Information Service Providers**. ERIC, 1986- . Irregular. LC 87-644520. LB1028.27.U6D57. 370/.7/8073. OCLC 14923688. ED 1.30/2:ED 8/ .

Organizations providing ERIC database searches or maintaining collections of ERIC microfiche or printed publications are described, with hours and charges for special services noted.

336. Educational Resources Information Center. **ERIC Directory of Education-Related Information Centers**. ERIC, 1990- . Annual. LC 93-664356. L901.E76. 370/.78/02573. OCLC 23587171. ED 1.310/2: .

Federal and nonfederal organizations providing education-related information, database building, reference, referral, and user services are indexed by organization name, subject, and location.

DISABILITIES

337. American Council on Education. HEATH Resource Center. **Resource Directory**. ACE, 198?- . Free: One Dupont Circle, Suite 800, Washington, DC 20036-1193. Biannual. LC sn88-15607. OCLC 13380255. ED 1.310/2: .

Provides addresses, telephone numbers, and descriptions of organizations focusing on postsecondary education and disability.

338. American Council on Education. **National Clearinghouse on Postsecondary Education for Individuals with Disabilities**. HEATH, One Dupont Circle, Suite 800, Washington, DC 20036-1193; (800) 544-3284; (202) 939-9320; E-mail: *HEATH@ace.nche.edu*.

The HEATH Resource Center provides information, referral, free publications, and listings of educational and training opportunities related to post high school education and training of disabled people.

339. Department of Education. Office of Special Education and Rehabilitative Services. **Directory of Selected Early Childhood Programs**. DE, 1988- . Irregular. LC 94-664002. LC4031.H36. 371. OCLC 19840530. ED 1.30/2:C 43/ .

This state-by-state directory of programs for disabled children lists Office of Special Education and Rehabilitative Services projects and personnel, with grant information, sponsoring agency, address, telephone and fax numbers, and a project description. Indexed by program category and state.

340. **National Information Center for Children and Youth with Disabilities**. Box 1492, Washington, DC 20013; (800) 695-0285; E-mail: *nichcy@capcon.net*.

NICHCY is an information and referral center providing free information on childhood (through age 22) disabilities and related issues.

STATISTICS

341. Department of Education. Office of Educational Research and Improvement. **Adult Literacy in America: A First Look at the Results of the National Adult Literacy Survey** by Irwin S. Kirsch et al. GPO, 1993. 2d ed. 150p. LC 94-133275. LC5251.A6437 1993. 374/.012. OCLC 28768301. ED 1.302:AD 9/4.

Literacy of people over age 15 (including prison populations) is depicted by educational level, age, race, region, and sex. Data are also correlated to health, illness and disabilities, parents' education, work and poverty status, sources of income, newspaper reading, information sources, and voting. First in a projected series of reports on the National Adult Literacy Survey (NALS).

342. Department of Education. Office of Educational Research and Improvement. **National Center for Education Statistics**. 555 New Jersey Ave., N.W., Washington, DC 20208.

NCES collects data on the condition of U.S. education, including vocational education and elementary through postsecondary education into the workforce. NCES releases publications, operates the OERI [Office of Educational Research and Improvement] Electronic Bulletin Board of statistical and research results, and archives unpublished, computerized data. NCES's National Data Resource Center (NDRC) provides current statistics and free data analysis of data sets. Contact the NDRC by mail through NCES; telephone (202) 219-1642; fax (202) 219-1679; or Internet *URL http://ndrc@inet.ed.gov/* or *URL gopher: //gopher.ed.gov/* or *URL http://www.ed.gov* or *URL ftp://ftp.ed.gov*. The ED/OERI Internet gopher server provides access to announcements, publications (including the Department of Education telephone directory), and data: *URL http://www.ed.gov* or *URL gopher://gopher.ed.gov* or *URL ftp://ftp.ed.gov* (logon: anonymous). The annual *Programs and Plans of the National Center for Education Statistics* (ED 1.302:P 94/5/yr.) describes NCES surveys and statistical programs, with a list of publications, data files, and contact people. The annual *OERI Directory of Computer Data Files* (ED 1.330:C 73/yr.) describes data files and special tabulations sold by OERI (E-mail: *almanac@inet.ed.gov*). *Current and Forthcoming Publications* (nondepository) announces publications and tapes issued during last year and the next three months, with a calendar for the next release of NCES key statistics.

343. National Center for Education Statistics. **Classification of Instructional Programs** by Robert L. Morgan, E. Stephen Hunt, and Judith M. Carpenter. GPO, 1991. 333p. LC 92-201350. LB1570.M657 1991. 375/.00973. OCLC 24302663. ED 1.102:C 56/1990.

As the federal government standard for federal and state educational surveys, CIP provides a standard classification system and curriculum descriptions for instructional programs.

344. National Center for Education Statistics. **Common Core of Data (CCD) School Years 1987-1988 Through 1992-1993**. GPO, 1995. CD-ROM. OCLC 34082349. ED 1.334/2:C 73/CD.

CCD data include school, state, and agency records, with financial, nonfiscal, and Census school district boundary data.

345. National Center for Education Statistics. **Digest of Education Statistics**. GPO, 1975- . Annual. LC 88-647233. L11.D48. 370/.973. OCLC 3133477. ED 1.326: .

This statistical profile from nursery school to graduate school is the primary compendium of American education statistics. Most data are from the past three years, covering topics like number of schools, colleges, teachers, and graduates; enrollment; educational attainment; population characteristics; opinion polls; finances; libraries; international education; and research and development. Some tables show historical statistics from as early as 1870. The *Digest* is more comprehensive than *Condition of Education* (entry 353). Highlights are summarized in *Mini-Digest of Education Statistics* (ED 1.326:), free from OERI, Department of Education, Room 610, 555 New Jersey Ave., N.W., Washington, DC 20208-5521. Also available as *EDsearch, Education Statistics on Disk* (entry 346) and on the *National Economic, Social & Environmental Data Bank* (entry 172) and *STAT-USA* (entry 171).

346. National Center for Education Statistics. **EDsearch, Education Statistics on Disk [computer file]**. GPO, 1994. CD-ROM. OCLC 31364280. ED 1.334/2:ST 2/CD. Also available on computer disks.

Education Statistics on Disk (EDsearch) is a compilation of the tables, charts, and text from *Condition of Education* (entry 353), *Digest of Education Statistics* (entry 345), *Youth Indicators* (entry 747), *Projections of Education Statistics* (entry 350), *120 Years of American Education: A Statistical Portrait* (entry 349), *Historical Trends: State Education Facts 1969-1989* (entry 347), and *Education in States and Nations* (entry 356).

347. National Center for Education Statistics. **Historical Trends: State Education Facts**. NCES, 1988- . LC 90-649134. LA209.2.H563. 370/.973/021. OCLC 18530651. ED 1.302:H 62/ .

National, state, and regional data are compared for public elementary and secondary education (including enrollment, disabled children, graduates, number and salaries of teachers and staff, and expenditures), and higher education (including enrollment, salaries, degrees, and expenditures).

348. National Center for Education Statistics. **National Household Education Surveys Data Files and Electronic Codebook [computer file]**. GPO, 199?- . Biennial. CD-ROM. LC sn94-28669. OCLC 31752815. ED 1.334/5: .

Data are also available from NCES's National Data Resource Center (NCES; entry 342).

Presents raw data from the 1991 (NHES:91) and 1993 (NHES:93) telephone surveys of U.S. households regarding school readiness, safety and discipline, early childhood education, and adult education. Note: This is not a survey of home schooling.

349. National Center for Education Statistics. **120 Years of American Education: A Statistical Portrait** edited by Thomas D. Snyder. NCES, 1993. 107p. LC 93-211278. LA209.A16 1993. 370/.973/021. OCLC 28039199. ED 1.302:ED 8/12.

A compendium of historical statistics about American elementary, secondary, and higher education between the years 1790 and 1991/92.

350. National Center for Education Statistics. **Projections of Education Statistics to...[year]**. GPO, 1984- . Annual. LC 67-62767. LA 210.A28. 371/.00973. OCLC 3075606. ED 1.120: .

Twelve-year projections that forecast the nation's enrollment, graduates, degrees, teachers, expenditures in public and private elementary and secondary schools and institutions of higher education; with expenditures during the past 15 years. Includes a discussion of methodology explaining models and assumptions, and a glossary. The projections are summarized in *Pocket Projections* (ED 1.302:2004/Pock), free from NCES. *Projections of Education Statistics to 2004* is also available on CD-ROM as *EDsearch, Education Statistics on Disk* (entry 346).

351. National Center for Education Statistics. **Reading Literacy in the United States: Findings from the IEA Reading Literacy Study**. [expected publication date, 1996].

Data depict ability in narrative, expository, and document reading for American fourth graders and ninth graders, the U.S. portion of the international Reading Literacy Study (published by the International Reading Association in *How in the World Do Students*

Read?, with results for 32 countries). A companion volume, *Reading Literacy in the United States: Technical Report* (ED 1.328/7:R 22), describes data design and analysis.

352.   National Center for Education Statistics. **State Comparisons of Education Statistics 1969-70 to 1993-94** by Thomas D. Snyder and Charlene M. Hoffman. GPO, 1995. 232p. OCLC 33944787. ED 1.126:95-122.

Also available through the Internet *URL http://gopher.ed.gov:10000/*.

Data for elementary, secondary, and higher education includes enrollments, teacher salaries, expenditures per FTE student and by function, special education, size of school districts, and public college tuition/per capita income.

353.   National Center for Education Statistics. **The Condition of Education**. GPO, 1975- . Annual. LC 75-643861. L112.N377a. 370/.973. OCLC 2241465. ED 1.109: .

This congressionally mandated statistical report depicts the health of elementary, secondary, and higher education in text, tables, charts, and graphs, with a glossary and sources of data. It is also available on CD-ROM as *EDsearch, Education Statistics on Disk* (entry 346). Highlights are summarized in *The Pocket Condition of Education* (ED 1.302:P 75/4), free from OERI, Department of Education, Room 610, 555 New Jersey Ave., N.W., Washington, DC 20208-5521; E-mail: *almanac@inet.ed.gov*.

354.   National Commission on Migrant Education. **Invisible Children: A Portrait of Migrant Education in the United States: A Final Report of the National Commission on Migrant Education**. GPO, 1992. 166p. LC 93-110926. LC5151.I58 1992. 371.96/75. OCLC 26998395. ED 1.2:M 58/2.

This final report of the National Commission on Migrant Education describes the demographics of migrant worker families; reviews federal programs to assist in their education; discusses administration and costs; and provides a legislative summary and recommendations.

COMPARATIVE EDUCATION

355.   Department of Education. Office of Educational Research and Improvement. **Japanese Education Today = [Nihon Kyoiku No Genjro]**. GPO, 1987. 95p. LC 87-600798. LA1312.J325 1987. 370/.952. OCLC 23180397. ED 1.2:J 27.

Describes the history; cultural foundations; academic juku; teachers; family; pre-elementary, compulsory, upper secondary, and higher education; employment; and reform as they relate to education in Japan. Includes a bibliography.

356.   National Center for Education Statistics. **Education in States and Nations: Indicators Comparing U.S. States with the OECD Countries in 1988** by Laura Herch Salganik et al. GPO, 1993. 129p. LC 94-139435. LB2846.E249 1993. OCLC 29552055. ED 1.102:N 21.

Comparisons between U.S. states and other nations of the Organization for Economic Co-operation and Development (OECD) are shown in tables, graphs, and text. State and international data are related to background, participation, outcomes, and financing of education. Includes an index and a glossary. Also included in the CD-ROM *EDsearch, Education Statistics on Disk* (entry 346).

ELEMENTARY AND SECONDARY EDUCATION

Directory

357. National Center for Education Statistics. **Directory of Public Elementary and Secondary Education Agencies.** GPO, 1986- . Annual. LC 89-647202. L901.E35. 371/.01/02573. OCLC 16903389. ED 1.111/2: .

Local public school systems and education agencies in each state are listed, noting the county, address, telephone number, metropolitan status code, grade span, and number of students, graduates, teachers, and schools operated by the agency. State education agency addresses are given in an appendix.

Statistics

358. National Center for Education Statistics. **America's Teachers: Profile of a Profession** by Susan P. Choy et al. GPO, 1993. 189p. LC 93-246218. LB2832.2.A44 1993. 371.1/00973/021. OCLC 28468622. ED 1.302:T 22/6.

This statistical compendium is based on surveys conducted by NCES in the period 1987-88; the results describe teachers, schools, and students; supply and demand; education and qualifications; human and fiscal resources; instructional practices; compensation; opinions about their schools and the profession; and projected trends.

359. National Center for Education Statistics. **High School and Beyond [computer file].** GPO, 19??- . CD-ROM. LC 94-660814. LB2846. 373. OCLC 29526716. ED 1.334:980-86/CD.

> Data are also available from NCES's National Data Resource Center (NCES; entry 342).

HS&B surveyed public and private school sophomores in 1980, with follow-up studies in 1982, 1984, 1986, and 1992 (*High School and Beyond Fourth Follow-Up [Sophomore Cohort]: HS&B 1992*, known as *HS&B:92* [ED 1.334/2:H 53/2/CD]). Data depict demographics, education and employment, goals, attitudes, extracurricular activities, attendance, and study methods. Also includes data from principals and information about postsecondary education.

360. National Center for Education Statistics. **Private Schools in the United States: A Statistical Profile, with Comparisons to Public Schools** by Peter Benson and Marilyn Miles McMillen. GPO, 1991. 162p. OCLC 23190718. ED 1.102:P 93/2.

Data on private elementary and secondary schools cover orientation (religion, nonsectarian), levels, tuition, and programs; teachers; students; resources and student outcomes; and parental choice. Tables show various periods between 1979 and 1988, often presented by school level, orientation, years of operation, and enrollment size, and allow comparisons with public schools.

361. National Center for Education Statistics. **Schools and Staffing Survey . . . Electronic Codebook and Public Use Data [computer file].** GPO, 1991- . Triennial. CD-ROM. LC sn94-28667. OCLC 31752520. ED 1.332:SCH 6/2/ .

> Data are also available from NCES's National Data Resource Center (NCES; entry 342).

This SASS package includes teacher, principal, school, and school district data from public and private elementary and secondary schools and 1991-92 Teacher Followup Survey data.

Related publications for 1990-91 data are *1990-91 Schools and Staffing Survey: Data File User's Manual* (ED 1.332:Sch 6/990-91/vol.), *SASS by State, Schools and Staffing Survey: Selected State Results* (ED 1.302:Sch 6/14), and *An Overview of the SASS and TF's (Schools Staffing Survey)* (ED 1.102:Sch 6/5; free from OERI: #NCES 94-440).

362. National Center for Education Statistics. **Vocational Education Electronic Table Library [computer file]**. GPO, 1993. Computer Disk. OCLC 30373511. ED 1.334/2:V 85/FLOPPY/INST.

Contains data on all phases of vocational education from the following NCES publications: *Vocational Education in the United States: 1969-1990* (ED 1.302:Ed 8/10), *Participation in Secondary Vocational Education: 1982-1987* (ED 1.328/5:P 25), *A Comparison of Vocational and Non-Vocational Public School Teachers of Grades 9 to 12* (ED 1.310/2:341874), *Teachers of Secondary Vocational and Nonvocational Classes in Public Schools* (ED 1.328:T 22), and *The Postsecondary Vocational Education of 1980 High School Seniors: The Two-Year Associate of Arts Degree* (ED 1.310/2:309821 or ED 1.328:V 85). Tables can be searched by subject, keyword, or table title.

HIGHER EDUCATION

Directory

363. National Center for Education Statistics. **Directory of Postsecondary Institutions**. GPO, 1986- . Biennial. LC 87-658180. L901.E34. 378. OCLC 15610434. ED 1.111/4: .

This is a comprehensive listing of colleges and universities in the United States, District of Columbia, and outlying areas. It gives address, telephone number, affiliation, tuition and fees, highest degree offered, types of programs, and nationally recognized accreditations. It contains no evaluative information. Volume 1 covers four-year and two-year institutions; volume 2, fewer-than-two-year institutions.

Financial Aid

364. Department of Education. **Higher Education Opportunities for Minorities and Women, Annotated Selections**. GPO, 1982. LC 87-640637. LB2338.H48. 378/.34/02573. OCLC 9513842. ED 1.42: .

Lists sources of financial aid for undergraduate, graduate, and postdoctoral education, along with addresses for further information. Includes general information about seeking financial assistance, and a bibliography of publications describing educational opportunities for minorities and women.

365. Department of Education. Office of Student Financial Assistance. **Federal Student Financial Aid Handbook**. DE, 1982- . Annual. LC 82-640139. LB2337.4.F42. 378.3/0973. OCLC 8054682. ED 1.45/4: .

This guide for college and university financial aid administrators describes programs and eligibility, with detailed instructions for completing application forms and the Student Aid Report (SAR).

366. Department of Education. Student Financial Assistance Programs. **Counselor's Handbook for High Schools**. DE, 19??- . Annual. LC 92-662038. LB2337.4.C68. 379.1/214/0973. OCLC 25208426. ED 1.8:C 83/2/yr.

This handbook for guidance counselors provides information about federal financial aid for college, including application procedures.

367. Department of Education. Student Financial Assistance Programs. **Counselor's Handbook for Postsecondary Schools**. DE, 19??- . Annual. LC sn92-23116. OCLC 25454494. ED 1.8:C 83/3/yr.

This guide for financial aid administrators provides information about federal financial aid for college, including application procedures and recent changes in laws. It includes a directory of state agencies administering the State Student Incentive Grant Program.

368. Department of Education. Student Financial Assistance Programs. **The Student Guide**. DE, 19??- . Annual. LC sn87-42944. OCLC 11025475. ED 1.8/2: .

Offers tips for choosing a college and obtaining student aid, with information about federal grant, work-study, and loan programs, including Pell Grants, Supplemental Educational Opportunity Grants, Work-Study, Perkins Loans, and Guaranteed Student Loans.

Statistics

369. Department of Education. Office of Educational Research and Improvement. **Trends in Degrees Conferred by Institutions of Higher Education: 1984-85 Through 1990-91** by Frank Morgan. DE, 1993. 54p. LC 93-234085. LB2390.M67 1993. 378.2/4/0973. OCLC 29000629. ED 1.328/3:T 72/2.

Presents data on degrees awarded by sex, race, Hispanic origin, state, discipline, and other characteristics. Formerly *Race/Ethnicity Trends in Degrees Conferred by Institutions of Higher Education*.

370. National Center for Education Statistics. **Historically Black Colleges and Universities, 1976-90** by Charlene M. Hoffman, Thomas D. Snyder, and Bill Sonnenberg. GPO, 1992. 93p. LC 92-212341. LC2781.H64 1992. 378.73/021. OCLC 26249069. ED 1.302:B 56.

This statistical compendium summarizes data on enrollment, degrees, staff, faculty, salaries, revenues, and expenditures in traditionally black institutions, with information on all public and private colleges for comparisons. Consists largely of tables, with an executive summary and guide to sources.

371. National Center for Education Statistics. **Integrated Postsecondary Education Data System [computer file]: IPEDS**. GPO, 1990- . Annual. CD-ROM. LC sn94-28222. OCLC 30631461. ED 1.334/4: .

> Data are also available from NCES's National Data Resource Center (NCES; entry 342); on diskette; and through the Internet *URL http://www.ed.gov/* or *URL ftp://ftp.ed.gov*.

IPEDS collects data on colleges, universities, and vocational schools pertaining to institutional characteristics; finances; faculty salaries, tenure, and fringe benefits; staff; fall enrollment; libraries; and completions. In 1986 IPEDS replaced the Higher Education General Information Survey. The *Integrated Postsecondary Education Data System Glossary* (ED 1.2:In 8/4/992) and *Integrated Postsecondary Education Data System, Guide to Surveys* (NCES 93-195) are supporting documents. Current data and custom data analyses are also available from NCES's National Data Resource Center (NCES; entry 342).

372. National Center for Education Statistics. **National Postsecondary Student Aid Study [computer file]**. GPO, 19??- . Irregular. CD-ROM. LC 94-660799. LB2337.4u. 378. OCLC 26676054. ED 1.333: .

> Data are also available from NCES's National Data Resource Center (NCES; entry 342).

NPSAS describes how full- and part-time students pay for private and public college education. Data are drawn from administrative records, student interviews, and parent surveys, covering academic years 1986-87, 1989-90, and 1992-93.

373. National Center for Education Statistics. **1991 Survey of Recent College Graduates [computer file]: Public Release File**. GPO, 1995. CD-ROM. OCLC 32689015. ED 1.334/2:SU 7/CD.

One year after their 1989 or 1990 graduation, college graduates were surveyed about their job and educational experiences. Methodology for the study is available via Internet *URL http://gopher.ed.gov:70/*.

374. National Center for Education Statistics. **State Higher Education Profiles**. GPO, 1985- . Annual. LC 88-655086. LB2342.S74. 379.1/214/0973. OCLC 16949313. ED 1.116/3: .

SHEP uses statistics and indicators to profile state involvement, support, and performance in higher education for the nation, the 50 states, the District of Columbia, and Puerto Rico. Each state statistic is indexed to a national average, and state rankings are provided for selected statistics.

RESEARCH

375. Smithsonian Institution. Office of Fellowships and Grants. **Smithsonian Opportunities for Research and Study in History, Art, Science**. SI, 1972- . Annual. LC 73-646897. Q11.S8S86. 001.4/3/O9753. OCLC 1789143. SI 1.44: .

This directory outlines purpose, research fields, eligibility, appointment duration, and application for fellowships and internships, and describes units, staff research interests, and research resources in the Smithsonian Institution. Includes an index.

RESEARCH REPORTS

376. Department of Education. Office of Educational Research and Improvement. **Resources in Education**. GPO, 1975- . Monthly. LC 75-644211. Z5813.R4. 016.370/78. OCLC 2241688. ED 1.310: .

RIE provides abstracts of recent research and project reports, technical reports, speeches, unpublished manuscripts, and books. Its companion abstract journal, *Current Index to Journals in Education* (CIJE) is published commercially. Both are available through the ERIC database (entry 328). Semiannual issues were discontinued in 1995. A cumulative annual index is published commercially. Continues *Research in Education*.

Geography

GENERAL WORKS

377. Defense Mapping Agency. **Digital Chart of the World [computer file]**. DMA, 1992. Edition 1. CD-ROM. OCLC 26783779. D 5.358: .

DCW is a 1:1,000,000-scale vector global base map, with geographic, attribute, and textual data that can be manipulated on personal computers. Elements shown include major airports, boundaries, coasts, contours, elevation, geographic names, international boundaries, land cover, ports, railroads, roads, major drainage systems, major utility networks, populated places, topography, transmission lines, and waterways. Includes an index of geographic names to aid in location.

378. Defense Mapping Agency. **Gazetteer of [country]**. D 5.319: .

These dictionaries of places and features include names approved by the United States Board of Geographic Names, with cross-references to variant names, latitude, longitude, area code number, Universal Transverse Mercator Grid Reference, and Joint Operations Graphic (JOG) map number. A list of countries covered is available in the free catalog *Defense Mapping Agency Public Sale Topographic Maps and Publications* (entry 385).

379. Geological Survey. National Mapping Division. **GNIS [computer file]: Geographic Names Information System**. GS, 1991- . CD-ROM. OCLC 31299079. I 19.120:G 25/CD.

Also available as a database.

GNIS lists the proper names for U.S. places, features, and areas. Each name is identified by geographic coordinates, the 1:24,000-scale USGS topographic map on which it appears, and elevation in feet. Products include the National Geographic Names Data Base (NGNDB), which lists names for geographic features in the U.S. and its territories, and the Topographic Map Names Data Base (TMNDB), a digital inventory of USGS topographic maps.

THE AMERICAS

General Work

380. Library of Congress. Geography and Map Division. **Maps and Charts of North America and the West Indies, 1750-1789: A Guide to the Collections in the Library of Congress** compiled by John R. Sellers and Patricia Molen Van Ee. LC, 1981. Free to U.S. Libraries and Institutions: Office Systems Services, Printing and Processing Section, Washington, DC 20540-5446. 495p. LC 80-607054. Z6027.N68U54 1981. 016.912/7. OCLC 6223077. LC 1.6/4:M 32/2/750-789.

This annotated guide is a comprehensive list of the Geography and Map Division's holdings of maps and charts of North America and the West Indies for the years 1750-89. Photographic copies of many of them may be ordered from the Library of Congress.

United States

General Work

381. Department of the Interior. Bureau of Land Management. **General Land Office Automated Records Project [computer file]: Pre-1908 Homestead & Cash Entry Patents**. GPO, 1993. CD-ROM. I 53.57: .

Legal land descriptions and property transfers from the government to private owners can be traced using this database of land patents/certificates/documents from the BLM Eastern States Repository, containing the Interior Secretary's official copies of General Land Office records. Documents dating from the late 1700s to 1908 can be searched by document number or type, title transfer authority, county, patentee name, land office, or legal land description. Individual states are on separate CD-ROMs.

Atlases

382. Geological Survey. **National Atlas of the United States of America** edited by Arch C. Gerlach. GS, 1970. 417p. LC 79-654043. G1200.U57 1970. 912.73. OCLC 127112. I 19.2:N 21a.

The National Atlas—the first U.S. national atlas ever produced—included general, physical, historical, economic, sociocultural, and administrative thematic maps, along with discussions of mapping, charting, and the world. Although now out of print, selected National Atlas maps are still sold by the USGS, which will send a price list on request.

383. Library of Congress. Map Division. **A List of Geographical Atlases in the Library of Congress, with Bibliographical Notes**. 8v. LC, 1909-1992. LC 09-35009. Z6028.U56. 016.912. OCLC 557867. LC 5.2:G 29/vol.

Vols. 1-8. Photoduplication Service, Washington DC 20540-5230.

Vol. 9. **Comprehensive Author List** compiled by Clara Egli LeGear. GPO.

Atlases are described in detail, with tables of contents for many volumes. Volumes 1 and 2 are a complete list of atlases held by the Library of Congress up to 1909, with author and subject indexes. Volumes 3 and 4 list new additions to the collection, with a cumulative author index in volume 4. The remaining volumes are: volume 5, world atlases; volume 6, Europe, Asia, Africa, Oceania, and the polar regions of the ocean; volume 7, western hemisphere and countries of North and South America; volume 8, index to volume 7; and volume 9, comprehensive author list.

Boundaries

384. Geological Survey. **The National Gazetteer of the United States of America. United States Concise 1990.** GPO, 1990. 526p. LC 90-3796. E154.N38 1990. 917.3/003. OCLC 21909961. I 19.16:1200-US.
This gazetteer provides a standard for names, with the United States Concise volume describing significant places, features, and areas throughout the nation and its territories. Separate volumes are issued for states, territories, and other special listings, all published as USGS Professional Paper 1200 (I 19.16:1200-no.) and collectively called the *National Gazetteer of the United States of America.*

Maps

385. Defense Mapping Agency. **Defense Mapping Agency Public Sale Topographic Maps and Publications**. Geological Survey, 1993- . Annual. Free: USGS, 508 National Center, Reston, VA 22092. OCLC 30603913. D 5.351/3: .
This is a descriptive catalog of DMA public sale maps, publications, and databases, which are distributed by the USGS. Information is given on availability, price, and ordering.

386. Geological Survey. **An Album of Map Projections** by John P. Snyder and Philip M. Voxland. GPO, 1989. 249p. LC 86-600253. GA110.S575 1989. 526.8. OCLC 13946170. I 19.16:1453.
Basic map projections and modifications are described, including cylindrical, pseudocylindrical, conic, azimuthal, and miscellaneous projections. Includes an index. A related title is *Bibliography of Map Projections* (I 19.3:1856), which includes references since ancient times in numerous languages.

387. Geological Survey. **Catalog of Topographic and Other Published Maps**. GS, 19??- . Irregular. OCLC 18439568. I 19.41/6-2: .
The catalogs, issued for individual states, list USGS topographic, U.S., state, satellite image, and world maps. Map type, scale, dates, and prices are noted. Also included are lists of map products from Earth Science Information Centers (ESICs), map dealers, and map reference libraries in the state. To identify each map available for a state, use the *Index to Topographic and Other Map Coverage [state]* (entry 390).

388. Geological Survey. **Map Projections—A Working Manual** by John P. Snyder. GPO, 1987. 383p. LC 87-600250. GA110.S577 1987. 526.8. OCLC 16226163. I 19.16:1395.
Details characteristics and uses of cylindrical, pseudocylindrical, conic, azimuthal, space, and miscellaneous projections, along with nonmathematical phases, formulas, and tables. Includes an index.

389. Geological Survey. **Maps for America: Cartographic Products of the U.S. Geological Survey and Others** by Morris M. Thompson. GS, 1987. 3d ed. 265p. LC 87-600339. GA405.T46 1987. 526/.0973. OCLC 16830994. I 19.2:M 32/12/987.
This is a comprehensive, illustrated guide to maps available from the USGS and other agencies, with a history of U.S. mapping; descriptions of types of maps and map data; map symbols; and sources of maps and cartographic information. An index, a list of standard map series, a glossary, and an agency address list are included. The first edition (1979) was published as a U.S. Geological Survey Centennial Volume, 1879-1979.

390.   Geological Survey. National Mapping Program. **Index to Topographic and Other Map Coverage [state]**. GS, 19??. I 19.41/6-3: .

Each state index identifies named grids representing mapping of the entire state, along with maps of counties in the state.

391.   Library of Congress. Geography and Map Division. **Panoramic Maps of Cities in the United States and Canada: A Checklist of Maps in the Collections of the Library of Congress, Geography and Map Division** by John R. Hebert and Patrick E. Dempsey. GPO, 1984. 2d ed. 181p. LC 82-600316. Z6027.U5L5 1984. 016.912/7. OCLC 8953194. LC 5.2:P 19.

This is a checklist of LC's panoramic map collection, the largest in North America. Citations to "bird's-eye views" of U.S. and Canadian cities note date, LC call number, artist, publisher, lithographer, and size. Supersedes *Panoramic Maps of Anglo-American Cities: A Checklist of Maps in the Collections of the Library of Congress, Geography and Map Division.*

392.   Library of Congress. **Railroad Maps of North America: The First Hundred Years** by Andrew M. Modelski. LC, 1984. Free to U.S. Libraries and Institutions: Office Systems Services, Printing and Processing Section, Washington, DC 20540-5446. 186p. LC 82-675134. G1106.P3M6 1984. 912/.1385/097. OCLC 10578102. LC 5.2:R 13/2.

Selected maps of the United States, Canada, and Mexico from the Library of Congress's collection are reproduced, including surveys, promotional maps, land-grant and right of way maps, and route guides. Includes a history of the first century of railroad mapping and a name/place index.

393.   National Archives and Records Service. **Guide to Cartographic Records in the National Archives** by Charlotte M. Ashby and others. GPO, 1971. 444p. LC 76-611061. Z6028.U575. 016.91273. OCLC 238759. GS 4.6/2:C 24.

Although dated, this guide continues to be the key to the National Archives's general collections of aerial photographs and maps. It is a finding aid for maps and aerial photographs in the Cartographic and Architectural Branch, as well as other maps filed with related textual records held in other National Archives units.

History and Area Studies

GENERAL WORKS

394. Central Intelligence Agency. **The World Factbook**. GPO, 1981- . Annual. LC 81-641760. G122.U56a. 910/.5. OCLC 7390695. PrEx 3.15: .

> Also available through the *National Trade Data Bank* (entry 170) and through the CIA's home page: *URL http://www.odci.gov/cia/*.

Brief national profiles describe the geography, people, government, economy, communications, and defense, with national maps. This is a good source of information on small and Third World countries. Appendixes cover the United Nations System, international organizations, weights and measures, and a cross-reference list of geographic names. It continues *National Basic Intelligence Factbook*.

395. Department of State. Office of Public Communication. **Department of State Publication. Background Notes Series**. GPO, 1980- . Irregular. LC sn90-3091. 321. OCLC 7437325. S 1.123: .

Background Notes are short, factual pamphlets about foreign countries, geographic entities, and international organizations with overviews of politics, culture, economics, history, and travel tips. Full text is available on CIDS, the State Department's online service; on *U.S. Foreign Affairs on CD-ROM* (entry 605); through the *National Trade Data Bank* (entry 170); and on the GPO *Federal Bulletin Board* (entry 35). Subject Bibliography 93 lists in-print issues with stock number and price.

396. Library of Congress. Federal Research Division. **Country Study** Series. GPO, 19??- . D 101.22:550-nos.

Country Studies are basic introductions to a nation's history, society, economy, government, politics, and military, with a focus on history and culture. Each contains maps, charts, photos, tables, bibliographies, and an index. Country Studies are prepared by the Library of Congress Country Studies Program, sponsored by the U.S. Department of the Army, and are updated irregularly. A list of in-print titles, stock numbers, and prices is available in SB-166 and in *Library of Congress Publications in Print* (entry 37), or by writing to the Country Studies Program, Federal Research Division, Library of Congress, Washington, DC 20540. Also known as Area Handbooks.

> Afghanistan D 101.22:550-65/2/986.
>
> Albania D 101.22:550-98/994.
>
> Algeria D 101.22:550-44/994.

Angola D 101.22:550-59/990.

Argentina D 101.22:550-73/985.

Armenia, Azerbaijan, and Georgia D 101.22:550-111.

Australia D 101.22:550-169.

Austria D 101.22:550-176/994.

Bangladesh D 101.22:550-175/989.

Belgium D 101.22:550-170/985.

Bolivia D 101.22:550-66/991.

Brazil D 101.22:550-20/4.

Bulgaria D 101.22:550-168/993.

Burma D 101.22:550-61/3.

Cambodia D 101.22:550-50/990.

Cameroon D 101.22:550-166.

Chad D 101.22:550-159/990.

Chile D 101.22:550-70/994.

China D 101.22:550-60/988.

Columbia D 101.22:550-26/990.

Commonwealth Caribbean, Islands of the D 101.22:550-33.

Congo D 101.22:550-91.

Costa Rica D 101.22:550-90/2.

Cote D'Ivoire (Ivory Coast) D 101.22:550-69/991.

Cuba D 101.22:550-152/987.

Cyprus D 101.22:550-22/993.

Czechoslovakia D 101.22:550-158/989.

Dominican Republic and Haiti D 101.22:550-36.

Ecuador D 101.22:550-52/991.

Egypt D 101.22:550-43/991.

El Salvador D 101.22:550-150/990.

Ethiopia D 101.22:550-28/993.

Finland D 101.22:550-167/990.

Germany, East D 101.22:550-155/987.

Germany, Federal Republic of D 101.22:550-173/2.

Ghana D 101.22:550-153.

Greece D 101.22:550-87/986.

Guatemala D 101.22:550-78/2.

Guinea D 101.22:550-174.

Guyana and Belize D 101.22:550-82/993.

Honduras D 101.22:550-151/995.

Hungary D 101.22:550-165/991.

India D 101.22:550-21.

Indian Ocean D 101.22:550-154/2.

Indonesia D 101.22:550-39.

Iran D 101.22:550-68/989.

Iraq D 101.22:550-31/990.

Israel D 101.22:550-25/990.

Italy D 101.22:550-182/985.

Japan D 101.22:550-30/992.

Jordan D 101.22:550-34/991.

Kenya D 101.22:550-56/3.

Korea, North D 101.22:550-81/994.

Korea, South D 101.22:550-41/992.

Laos D 101.22:550-58/985.

Lebanon D 101.22:550-24/989.

Liberia D 101.22:550-38/3.

Libya D 101.22:550-85/989.

Malawi D 101.22:550-172.

Malaysia D 101.22:550-45/4.

Mauritania D 101.22:550-161/990.

Mexico D 101.22:550-79/985.

Mongolia D 101.22:550-76/991.

Morocco D 101.22:550-49.

Mozambique D 101.22:550-64/3.

Nepal and Bhutan D 101.22:550-35/993.

Nicaragua D 101.22:550-88/994.

Nigeria D 101.22:550-157/4.

Oceania D 101.22:550-94/2.

Pakistan D 101.22:550-48/4.

Panama D 101.22:550-46/989.

Paraguay D 101.22:550-156/990.

Persian Gulf States D 101.22:550-185/994.

Peru D 101.22:550-42/993.

Philippines D 101.22:550-72/993.

Poland D 101.22:550-162/994.

Portugal D 101.22:550-181/994.

Romania D 101.22:550-160/991.

Rwanda and Burundi D 101.22:550-37.

Saudi Arabia D 101.22:550-51/993.

Senegal D 101.22:550-70.

Sierra Leone D 101.22:550-180.

Singapore D 101.22:550-184/991.

Somalia D 101.22:550-86/993.

South Africa D 101.22:550-93/2.

Soviet Union D 101.22:550-95/991.

Spain D 101.22:550-179/990.

Sri Lanka D 101.22:550-96/990.

Sudan D 101.22:550-27/992.

Syria D 101.22:550-47/987.

Tanzania D 101.22:550-62/2.

Thailand D 101.22:550-53/989.

Tunisia D 101.22:550-89/987.

Turkey D 101.22:550-80/996.

Uganda D 101.22:550-74/992.

Uruguay D 101.22:550-97/992.

Venezuela D 101.22:550-71/993.

Vietnam D 101.22:550-32.

The Yemens D 101.22:550-183/986.

Yugoslavia D 101.22:550-99/992.

Zaire D 101.22:550-67/994.

Zambia D 101.22:550-75.

Zimbabwe D 101.22:550-171/2.

397. Library of Congress. **Folklife Sourcebook: A Directory of Folklife Resources in the United States** prepared by Peter T. Bartis and Hillary Glatt. LC, 1994. Free: American Folklife Center, Library of Congress, Washington, DC 20540-8100. 2d ed. rev. and expanded. 165p. LC 93-4839. GR37.B37 1994. 398/.025/73. OCLC 28257325. LC 39.9:14.

Also available on LC MARVEL (entry 36).

This is a state-by-state directory of federal and public agencies, organizations, archives, university programs, societies, serials, book publishers, and book and recording mail order dealers. Entries for agencies give address and telephone number, date of establishment, access information, collection size and format, and key collections. Includes an index by state and introductions to resources in Canada and Mexico.

398. Library of Congress. **Library of Congress Manuscripts: An Illustrated Guide**. GPO, 1993. 63p. LC 93-2529. Z6621.U58L53 1993. 016.091/0973. OCLC 28336360. LC 4.8:M 31.

This guide to collections in LC's Manuscript Division, and in the Music, Rare Book, and Area Studies divisions, covers the nation's founding, presidency, congress, federal judiciary, military affairs, foreign policy, arts and literature, science and medicine, African-American history and culture, and women's history. The illustrated guide describes personal papers, paintings, photographs, and other materials. A related title is *Manuscripts on Microfilm: A Checklist of the Holdings in the Manuscript Division* (LC 4.2:M 58), published in 1975 and free from Library of Congress, Office Systems Services, Printing and Processing Section, Washington, DC 20540-5446.

399. Library of Congress. Manuscript Division. **Library of Congress Acquisitions. Manuscript Division**. LC, 1979- . Free: Manuscript Division, Washington, DC 20540-4780. Annual. LC 81-646298. Z733.L735L48a. 027.573. OCLC 7264920. LC 4.9: .

This annual report describes selected new acquisitions in depth, with a list of all new holdings in the Manuscript Division. It includes a bibliography of Manuscript Division publications.

400. Library of Congress. Prints and Photographs Division. **A Century of Photographs, 1846-1946: Selected from the Collections of the Library of Congress** compiled by Renata V. Shaw. GPO, 1980. 211p. LC 79-21624. TR6.U62D572. 779/.074/0153. OCLC 5497409. LC 1 .2:P 56/5/846-946.

Essays describe LC collections of photographic prints, negatives, transparencies, and stereographs. Representative images showing the range and beauty of the collections are included.

401. Library of Congress. Prints and Photographs Division. **Viewpoints; A Selection from the Pictorial Collections of the Library of Congress; A Picture Book** by Alan Fern and Milton Kaplan. LC, 1975. Free to U.S. Libraries and Institutions: Office Systems Services, Printing and Processing Section, Washington, DC 20540-5446. 223p. LC 73-18317. E178.5.U54 1974. 973/.022/2. OCLC 740995. LC 25.2:V 67.

Samples from LC's prints and photographs collections are illustrated and described, with the LC negative number for ordering copies. They are arranged in subject sections: World and U.S. history, transportation, the American scene, U.S. architecture, entertainment, and artists' prints.

402. Smithsonian Institution. **Guide to Photographic Collections at the Smithsonian Institution** by Diane Vogt O'Connor. 3v. SI, 1989- . LC 89-600116. Q11.S79 1989. 026/.779/074753. OCLC 19741738. SI 3.10:P 56.

This selected guide to the Smithsonian Institution's vast holdings of still photographs includes photonegatives, photoprints, phototransparencies, and direct positive processes. Entries describe collections, dates of photos, origins, subjects, arrangement, captions, finding aids, and restrictions. Includes indexes to creators, forms and processes, and subjects. Five volumes are planned, including: volume 1, National Museum of American History; volume 2, National Museum of Natural History, National Zoological Park, Smithsonian Astrophysical Observatory, Smithsonian Tropical Research Institute; volume 3, Cooper-Hewitt Museum, Freer Gallery of Art, National Museum of American Art, National Portrait Gallery, Arthur M. Sackler Gallery, Office of Horticulture.

AMERICAN INDIANS

North American Indians

General Works

403. Library of Congress. American Folklife Center. **The Federal Cylinder Project: A Guide to Field Cylinder Collections in Federal Agencies**. GPO, 1984- . LC 82-600289. ML156.4.F5 1984. 016.78026/6. OCLC 8785183. LC 39.11:3/v.1- .

Vol. 1. **Introduction and Inventory** by Erika Brady et al.

Vol. 2. **Northeastern Indian Catalog, Southeastern Indian Catalog** edited by Judith A. Gray, and Dorothy Sara Lee with the assistance of Gregory Pontecorvo.

Vol. 3. **Great Basin Plateau Indian Catalog, Northwest Coast Arctic Indian Catalog** edited by Judith A. Gray with the assistance of Karen R. Moses.

    Vol. 5. **California Indian Catalog, Middle and South American Indian Catalog, Southwestern Indian Catalog—I** edited by Judith A. Gray and Edwin J. Schupman, Jr.

    Vol. 8. **Early Anthologies** edited by Dorothy Sara Lee with the assistance of Gregory Pontecorvo.

This projected eight-volume guide focuses on American Indian collections in the Federal Cylinder Project series, recorded on wax cylinders under the auspices of the Bureau of American Ethnology. Entries give cylinder number, Archive of Folk Culture number, length, quality, description, performer, recording location and date, and notes.

404. Library of Congress. **Portrait Index of North American Indians in Published Collections** by Patrick Frazier. GPO, 1992. 142p. LC 90-13329. E89.F725 1991. 016.970004/97/00222. OCLC 22273494. LC 1.2:P 83/3.

This index to published Indian portraits in the LC collections is arranged by tribe and then by individual name, with access to name variations.

405. National Archives and Records Service. **Cartographic Records of the Bureau of Indian Affairs** compiled by Laura E. Kelsay. NARS, 1977. 187p. LC 77-9434. Z1209.2.U5U53 1977. 016.912/73. OCLC 3034532. GS 4.7:13/3.

The list describes Bureau of Indian Affairs (BIA) cartographic records maintained as central maps files, along with descriptions from BIA divisions, Indian agencies, and field offices. All maps listed may be examined or reproduced.

406. National Archives and Records Service. **Guide to Records in The National Archives of the United States Relating to American Indians** compiled by Edward E. Hill. GPO, 1982. 467p. LC 81-22357. Z1209.2.U5H54 1982. 016.3231/97/073. OCLC 8052651. GS 4.6/2:Am 3.

This is a descriptive list and location guide for materials in the National Archives about American Indians and their relations with the U.S. government and the American people. It focuses on Indians living near the Canadian and Mexican borders and in the former European colonies, along with tribes interacting with the United States through the Bureau of Indian Affairs or military operations. Includes an index. Supplements *Guide to the National Archives of the United States* (entry 427). A related title is *American Indians: A Select Catalog of National Archives Microfilm Publications* (nondepository, 1995).

Handbooks

407. Smithsonian Institution. **Handbook of North American Indians** edited by William C. Sturtevant. GPO, 1978- . Irregular. LC 77-17162. E77.H25. 970/.004/97. OCLC 13240086. SI 1.20/2: .

    Vol. 1. **Introduction**. [not yet published]

    Vol. 2. **Indians in Contemporary Society**. [not yet published]

    Vol. 3. **Environment, Origins, and Population**. [not yet published]

    Vol. 4. **History of Indian-White Relations**. 1988.

    Vol. 5. **Arctic**. 1984.

    Vol. 6. **Subarctic**. 1981.

    Vol. 7. **Northwest Coast**. 1990.

    Vol. 8. **California**. 1978.

    Vol. 9. **Southwest**. 1979.

Vol. 10. **Southwest**. 1983.

Vol. 11. **Great Basin**. 1986.

Vol. 12. **Plateau**. [not yet published]

Vol. 13. **Plains**. [not yet published]

Vol. 14. **Southeast**. [not yet published]

Vol. 15. **Northeast**. 1978.

Vol. 16. **Technology and Visual Arts**. [not yet published]

Vol. 17. **Languages**. [not yet published]

Vol. 18. **Biographical Dictionary**. [not yet published]

Vol. 19. **Biographical Dictionary**. [not yet published]

Vol. 20. **Index**. [not yet published]

This series will be a 20-volume encyclopedic summary of the prehistory, history, and cultures of the aboriginal peoples of North America. Volumes include indexes to illustrations, subjects, and names.

ARCHAEOLOGY, ANTHROPOLOGY, AND ETHNOLOGY

408. National Park Service. Cultural Resources Management Division. **Remote Sensing: A Handbook for Archeologists and Cultural Resource Managers** by Thomas R. Lyons and Thomas Eugene Avery. GPO, 1977. 109p. LC 77-608037. CC76.4.L96. 930/.1/028. OCLC 2815651. I 29.9/2:Se 5.

Several supplements have been published (I 29.9/2:Se 5/Supp.no.):

Supplement 1. **Remote Sensing: Practical Exercises on Remote Sensing in Archeology** by Thomas Eugene Avery and Thomas R. Lyons.

Supplement 2. **Remote Sensing: Instrumentation for Nondestructive Exploration of Cultural Resources** by Stanley A. Morain and Thomas K. Budge.

Supplement 3. **Remote Sensing: Aerial Anthropological Perspectives: A Bibliography of Remote Sensing in Cultural Resource Studies** by Thomas R. Lyons, Robert K. Hitchcock, and Wirth H. Wills.

Supplement 4. **Remote Sensing: A Handbook for Archeologists and Cultural Resources Managers: Basic Manual Supplement: Oregon** by C. Melvin Aikens et al.

Supplement 5. **Remote Sensing: Multispectral Analyses of Cultural Resources, Chaco Canyon and Bandelier National Monument** edited by Thomas R. Lyons.

Supplement 6. **Remote Sensing: Archeological Applications of Remote Sensing in the North Central Lowlands** by Craig Baker and George J. Gumerman.

Supplement 7. **Remote Sensing: Aerial and Terrestial Photography for Archeologists** by Thomas Eugene Avery and Thomas R. Lyons.

Supplement 8. **Remote Sensing: Applications to Cultural Resources in Southwestern North America** by Eileen L. Camilli and Linda S. Cordell.

Supplement 9. **Remote Sensing: The American Great Plains** by W. Raymond Wood, Robert K. Nickel, and David E. Griffin.

Supplement 10. **Remote Sensing: Photogrammetry in Archeology: The Chaco Mapping Project** by Dwight L. Drager and Thomas R. Lyons.

These supplements feature basic principles of remote sensor data gathering, handling, and interpretation, along with photographs, a bibliography, and glossary.

ASIA AND THE MIDDLE EAST

Japan

409. Library of Congress. Asian Division. Japanese Section. **Japanese Local Histories in the Library of Congress: A Bibliography** compiled by Philip M. Nagao. LC, 1988. Free to U.S. Libraries and Institutions: Office Systems Services, Printing and Processing Section, Washington, DC 20540-5446. 324p. LC 86-600328. Z3309.N3413 1988. 016.952. OCLC 14214983. LC 17.9:J 27.

Japanese-language works on regional history cataloged by LC between 1958 and 1980 are arranged according to the 47 Japanese prefectures. Entries give author, imprint, collation, reprint information, and LC classification number. Includes an author-title index.

Middle East

410. Library of Congress. Orientalia Division. **American Doctoral Dissertations on the Arab World, 1883-1974** compiled by George Dimitri Selim. LC, 1976. Free: Office Systems Services, Printing and Processing Section, Washington, DC 20540-5446. 2d ed. 173p. LC 76-7391. Z3013.S43 1976. 016.909/09/74927. OCLC 2119373. LC 1.12/2:Ar 1/883-974.

> **Supplement**. 1975-1981. Free to U.S. Libraries and Institutions: Office Systems Services, Printing and Processing Section, Washington, DC 20540-5446. LC 1.12/2:Ar 1 suppl.

> **Supplement**. August 1981-December 1987. Free to U.S. Libraries and Institutions: Office Systems Services, Printing and Processing Section, Washington, DC 20540-5446. LC 1.12/2:Ar 1 suppl.

These are unannotated lists of U.S. and Canadian dissertations on subjects related to the Arab world.

Turkey

411. Library of Congress. Orientalia Division. **Turkey, Politics and Government: A Bibliography, 1938-1975** compiled by Abraham Bodurgil. LC, 1978. Free: Office Systems Services, Printing and Processing Section, Washington, DC 20540-5446. 156p. LC 78-10790. Z2850.B64 suppl. 016.9561. OCLC 4495897. LC 17.2:T 84/938-75.

This unannotated bibliography covers from Kemal Ataturk's death in 1938 through 1975, listing publications related to Turkey's politics and government, social and economic conditions, religion, geography, and international relations. Half of the references are in Turkish, with the remainder in English and other languages. It supplements *Ataturk and Turkey: A Bibliography, 1919-1938* (1974).

EUROPE

Germany

412.   Holocaust Memorial Council. **Night of Pogroms: "Kristallnacht," November 9-10, 1938**. HMC, 1988. 103p. LC 88-603033. DS135.G33N45 1988. 943.086. OCLC 20492178. Y 3.H 74:2 P 75.
This history of Kristallnacht includes translated German documents, American diplomatic dispatches, news articles, eyewitness accounts, and excerpts from radio broadcasts and literature. Includes a chronology, bibliography, filmography, resource list, and program ideas for schools and communities.

413.   Library of Congress. **German-American Relations: A Selective Bibliography** by Margrit B. Krewson. GPO, 1995. 319p. LC 94-47942. Z6465.U5K74 1995. 016.30348/273043. OCLC 31708911. LC 23.16:G 31.
Works in LC's German collections about the German-American relationship and the German community in the U.S. include reference books, bibliographies, and general works. Coverage dates back as far as the U.S. Colonial period. LC call numbers are provided.

414.   Library of Congress. **The German-Speaking Countries of Europe: A Selective Bibliography** by Margrit B. Krewson. LC, 1989. Free: Office Systems Services, Printing and Processing Section, Washington, DC 20540-5446. 2d ed., rev. and enl. 318p. LC 88-600276. Z2000.K73 1989. 016.940/097531. OCLC 18351848. LC 1.12/2:G 31/2/989.
This is an unannotated bibliography of materials (primarily in English) published in the 1980s about Austria, Germany, Liechtenstein, and Switzerland. Citations are arranged according to topics such as bibliographies and reference works, description and travel, economy, education, history, military, religion, and society. Includes an index.

415.   National Archives and Records Service. **Guides to German Records Microfilmed at Alexandria, Va**. NARS, 1958- . Irregular. LC a58-9982. Z2240.A7. 016.943086. OCLC 12979030. AE 1.112: .
This is a series of finding aids for the National Archives's Collection of Seized Enemy Records, 1941-, microfilmed records seized during World War II from German central, regional, and local government agencies; military commands and units; and the Nazi Party and affiliated organizations. Provenance and contents are described, along with inclusive dates. Also features an index and a glossary. All microfilm is available for use at the National Archives or may be purchased from the National Archives Publications Sales Branch. Guides 1-56 are available in Microfilm Publication T733.

Soviet Union

416.   Library of Congress. **Russia Looks at America: The View to 1917** by Robert V. Allen. LC, 1988. Free: Office Systems Services, Printing and Processing Section, Washington, DC 20540-5446. 322p. LC 88-600001. E183.8.S65A544 1988. 973. OCLC 17479159. LC 1.2:R 92/3.
This treatise on Imperial Russian views of America describes Russian perceptions of U.S. films, literature, agriculture, technology, and education. Includes an annotated bibliography of Russian books and articles and a name index.

Spain

417. Library of Congress. **The Hispanic World, 1492-1898: A Guide to Photorepro-duced Manuscripts from Spain in the Collections of the United States, Guam, and Puerto Rico = El Mundo Hispbanico, 1492-1898: Gubia de Copias Fotogrbaficas de Manuscritos Espanoles Existentes en los Estados Unidos de Amberica, Guam y Puerto Rico** by Estela Guadalupe Jimbenez Codinach. GPO, 1994. 1060p. LC 92-23419. Z2701.C7J55 1994. 016.98. OCLC 26300897. LC 1.6/4:H 62/2.

This guide to reproductions of manuscripts from the Spanish State Archives includes text, illustrations, a directory of repositories, a bibliography, a list of serials, and an index.

418. National Park Service. **Spanish Colonial Research Center Computerized Index of Spanish Colonial Documents** compiled by Joseph P. Sanchez with the assis-tance of William Broughton et al. 3v. NPS, 1991. LC 92-201722. Z1212.S26 1991. 016.97001/6. OCLC 24703766. I 29.82:Sp 2/v.1-3.

The National Park Service's Spanish Colonial Research Center microfilm collection at the University of New Mexico was compiled from documents in the Spanish Colonial archives in Seville, Madrid, and Simancas. This guide notes author, title, description, provenance and location of original document, and places, people, and subjects mentioned in the document.

GENEALOGY

419. Library of Congress. **Genealogies Cataloged by the Library of Congress Since 1986: With a List of Established Forms of Family Names and a List of Genealogies Converted to Microform Since 1983**. Cataloging Distribution Ser-vice, 1991. 1349p. LC 91-39573. Z5313.U5L53 1991. 016.9291. OCLC 24907327. LC 30.27:G 28.

This is a list of genealogies (arranged by family name) cataloged by LC between 1986 and July 1991, plus pre-1986 titles with revised cataloging. It includes a compilation of family surname subject headings cross-referenced to variant spellings, and a list of older genealogies replaced by microfilm copies. This title updates the now out-of-print Kaminkow series by Marion J. Kaminkow: *Genealogies in the Library of Congress: A Bibliography* (1972), its 1977 supplement, and *Genealogies in the Library of Congress, a Bibliography, Second Supplement, 1976-1986*. The LC title and the Kaminkow volumes provide a complete listing of genealogies at the Library of Congress. Related titles from the National Archives are *Using Records in the National Archives for Genealogical Research* (AE 1.113:5/990), *Immigrant and Passenger Arrivals: A Select Catalog of National Archives Microfilm Publications* (nondepository, 1991), *Genealogical and Bio-graphical Research: A Select Catalog of National Archives Microfilm Publications* (non-depository, 1983), and *Guide to Genealogical Research in the National Archives* (nondepository, 1985).

420. Library of Congress. **Generations Past: A Selected List of Sources for Afro-American Genealogical Research** compiled by Sandra M. Lawson. GPO, 1988. 101p. LC 88-600100. Z1361.N39L34 1988. 016.929/1/08996073. OCLC 17732709. LC 1.12/2:Af 8/4.

This guide to Afro-American genealogical research includes state lists of family histories, reference sources, newspapers, magazines, and organizations.

421. Library of Congress. **Polish Genealogy & Heraldry: An Introduction to Research** by Janina W. Hoskins. GPO, 1987. 114p. LC 87-600087. CS872.H67 1987. 929/.1/0899185. OCLC 15488196. LC 35.9:P 75.

A bibliography of sources (Polish and non-Polish), with a brief history of Poland, Polish history chronology from c. 963 to 1952, and a list of Russian, Prussian, and Austrian rulers, 1682-1918.

LATIN AMERICA

422. National Archives and Records Administration. **Guide to Materials on Latin America in the National Archives of the United States** by George S. Ulibarri and John P. Harrison. GPO, 1974. 489p. LC 74-600051. CD3028.L37U54 1974. 016.918. OCLC 899014. GS 4.6/2:L 34a/974.

This is a finding aid for records issued by Congress, the courts, and executive departments between 1774 and the early 1970s, and relating to Latin America and the former Spanish borderlands. Reprinted in 1988 (nondepository).

Cuba

423. Library of Congress. **A Survey of Cuban Revistas, 1902-1958** compiled and annotated by Roberto Esquenazi-Mayo. LC, 1993. 112p. LC 92-20930. PN4937.P4E84 1993. 015.7291034. OCLC 26094752. LC 1.12/2:C 89/2.

Cuban literary, scientific, artistic, and economic publications held in the Library of Congress, elsewhere in the U.S., and abroad are listed. Those held in LC (about one-fifth) are annotated, with notes on their historical and literary importance, first year of publication, missing volumes, and their condition. Includes an index, bibliography, and statistics.

OCEANIA

Antarctica

424. Library of Congress. **Antarctic Bibliography**. 1965- . Irregular. LC 65-61825. Z6005.P7A55. OCLC 1064353. LC 33.9: .

Vol. 1. 1965. Free to U.S. Libraries and Institutions: Office Systems Services, Printing and Processing Section, Washington, DC 20540-5446.

Vol. 2. 1966. Free to U.S. Libraries and Institutions: Office Systems Services, Printing and Processing Section, Washington, DC 20540-5446.

Vol. 3. 1968. Free to U.S. Libraries and Institutions: Office Systems Services, Printing and Processing Section, Washington, DC 20540-5446.

Vol. 4. 1970. Photoduplication Service, Washington, DC 20540-5230.

Vol. 5. 1971. Free to U.S. Libraries and Institutions: Office Systems Services, Printing and Processing Section, Washington, DC 20540-5446.

Vol. 6. 1973. Free to U.S. Libraries and Institutions: Office Systems Services, Printing and Processing Section, Washington, DC 20540-5446.

Vol. 7. 1974. Free to U.S. Libraries and Institutions: Office Systems Services, Printing and Processing Section, Washington, DC 20540-5446.

Vols. 1-7 Index. 1977. Free to U.S. Libraries and Institutions: Office Systems Services, Printing and Processing Section, Washington, DC 20540-5446.

Vol. 8. 1976. Free to U.S. Libraries and Institutions: Office Systems Services, Printing and Processing Section, Washington, DC 20540-5446.

Vol. 9. 1977. Free to U.S. Libraries and Institutions: Office Systems Services, Printing and Processing Section, Washington, DC 20540-5446.

Vol. 10. 1979. Photoduplication Service, Washington, DC 20540-5230.

Vol. 11. 1980. Free to U.S. Libraries and Institutions: Office Systems Services, Printing and Processing Section, Washington, DC 20540-5446.

Vol. 12. 1982. Free to U.S. Libraries and Institutions: Office Systems Services, Printing and Processing Section, Washington, DC 20540-5446.

Vols. 8-12 Index. 1984. Free to U.S. Libraries and Institutions: Office Systems Services, Printing and Processing Section, Washington, DC 20540-5446.

Vol. 13. 1983. Free to U.S. Libraries and Institutions: Office Systems Services, Printing and Processing Section, Washington, DC 20540-5446.

Vol. 14. 1985. Free to U.S. Libraries and Institutions: Office Systems Services, Printing and Processing Section, Washington, DC 20540-5446.

Vol. 15. 1986. Free to U.S. Libraries and Institutions: Office Systems Services, Printing and Processing Section, Washington, DC 20540-5446.

Vol. 16. 1988. Free to U.S. Libraries and Institutions: Office Systems Services, Printing and Processing Section, Washington, DC 20540-5446.

Vol. 17. 1989. GPO.

Vol. 18. 1991. GPO.

Vol. 19. 1992. GPO.

This continuing bibliography of current Antarctic literature is sponsored by the National Science Foundation's Division of Antarctic Programs. It is also available as part of the *Arctic and Antarctic Regions* CD-ROM, and is updated by the monthly *Current Literature, Cold Regions Science and Technology* (formerly *Current Antarctic Literature*). The Navy's *Antarctic Bibliography* (D 202.2:An 8) and *Antarctic Bibliography, 1951-1961* (LC 33.9:951-61) provide retrospective coverage.

UNITED STATES

Archives

> National Archives: *URL http://gopher.nara.gov/*;
> *URL http://www.nara.gov/*.

425. National Archives and Records Administration. **Catalog of Machine–Readable Records in the National Archives of the United States**. NARA, 1977. 37p. LC 75-619120. CD3027.M32 1977. 016.973. OCLC 1342366. GS 4.17/3:R 24.

One of two basic finding aids for machine-readable records in the National Archives, this catalog describes computerized record groups and how to access them. Entries note record group coverage, status, restrictions, and order number. Updated by *Title List: A Preliminary and Partial Listing of the Data Files in the National Archives and Records Administration,* free from NARA's Center for Electronic Records and on the NARA gopher. Copies of most of NARA's data sets may be purchased from the Center. A related title, General Information Leaflet 37, *Information About Electronic Records in the National Archives for Prospective Researchers,* is free from Publications Distribution, National Archives, Room G9, 7th and Pennsylvania Ave., N.W., Washington, DC 20408.

426. National Archives and Records Administration. **Guide to Records in the National Archives: [region].** NARA, 1989-1990. CD3029. AE 1.108:R 24/3/region.

This series describes federal records held in the Regional Archives. Arranged by record group number, entries give description, dates, cubic feet of space the records occupy, agency administrative history, finding aids, and related microfilm records in the Washington, D.C., National Archives collection. Includes an index of agencies and subjects.

427. National Archives and Records Administration. **Guide to the National Archives of the United States.** NARA, 1987. 896p. LC 87-28205. CD3023.U53 1987. 027.573. OCLC 16868200. AE 1.108:N 21.

This, the most comprehensive overview of National Archives holdings, describes all records acquisitioned through June 1970 (except those held in presidential libraries). It includes an introduction to record groups and finding aids, detailed agency administrative histories, and regulations governing use of NARA records. The 1987 edition is a reprint of the 1974 edition with new prefatory material and an appendix of record groups added during the years 1970-77. The 1974 edition was the first revision since the 1948 *Guide to the Records in the National Archives.* A new edition is expected in 1996. It can be previewed on the NARA Gopher *URL http://gopher.nara.gov/*; Select *Information about NARA Holdings/Guide to the National Archives.* Related titles are *Basic Laws and Authorities of the National Archives and Records Administration* (AE 1.102:L 41/991) and General Information Leaflet 17, *Citing Records in the National Archives of the United States* (AE 1.113:17; free from Publications Distribution, National Archives, Room G9, 7th and Pennsylvania Ave., N.W., Washington, DC 20408).

428. National Archives and Records Administration. **Microfilm Resources for Research: A Comprehensive Catalog.** NARA, 1986. 126p. LC 85-15242. CD3026 1986. 027.573. OCLC 12286740. AE 1.102:M 58/2.

> 1990 edition is available on the Internet *URL http://gopher.nara.gov/* or *URL http://www.nara.gov/.*

The National Archives reproduces part of its holdings on microfilm, often with accompanying descriptive guides. This catalog provides short descriptions of these microfilm publications and descriptive guides, also citing indexes and other user tools. Omitted are administrative histories, roll-by-roll lists, and descriptions of microfilm contents. Arranged by record group in the format of *Guide to the National Archives of the United States,* entries include inclusive dates, number of microfilm rolls, and notes on accompanying descriptive pamphlets. Also contains personal and place name and title keyword indexes, plus record group lists arranged alphabetically and numerically. Other microfilm catalogs on specific subjects issued by the National Archives Trust Fund Board are listed in *Select List of Publications of the National Archives and Records Administration* (entry 429).

429. National Archives and Records Administration. **Select List of Publications of the National Archives and Records Administration.** NARA, 1994. Free: Publications Distribution, Room G9, 7th and Pennsylvania Ave., N.W., Washington, DC 20408. (Rev. 1994.) 1994. 53p. OCLC 32043535. AE 1.113:3/yr.

> Internet *URL http://gopher.nara.gov/* or *URL http://www.nara.gov/.*

This is a bibliography of NARA finding aids, information leaflets, professional archival papers and books, and records management publications. Because many National Archives finding aids are published by the National Archives Trust Fund Board and are nondepository, the *Select List* lists useful titles not noted in this *Subject Guide to United States Government Reference Sources.*

430. National Archives and Records Administration. Still Picture Branch. **Guide to the Holdings of the Still Picture Branch of the National Archives and Records Administration** compiled by Barbara Lewis Burger. NARA, 1990. 166p. LC 90-5834. CD3027.S75.1990. 015.753/037. OCLC 21336256. AE 1.108:St 5.

This is a directory of photographic prints, negatives, transparencies, posters, and other visual images in NARA's Still Picture Branch. Pictorial records are described, identifying the time period, subjects, events and people depicted, and photographer. It is intended to be used in conjunction with the *Guide to the National Archives of the United States* (entry 427). Related titles—General Information Leaflet 38, *Information for Prospective Researchers About the Still Picture Branch of the National Archives*, and General Information Leaflet 13, *Ordering Reproductions from the National Archives* (AE 1.108:D 63)—are free from Publications Distribution, National Archives, Room G9, 7th and Pennsylvania Ave., N.W., Washington, DC 20408.

431. National Archives and Records Administration. **The Management of Archives** by T. R. Schellenberg. NARA, 1988. 383p. LC 88-600028. CD950.S29 1988. 025.17/1. OCLC 17508889. AE 1.102:M 31.

This reprint of the classic 1965 edition (Columbia University Press) discusses development and application of archival principles and techniques, and arrangement and description of cartographic and pictorial records. Includes a bibliography and index, along with a foreword by Jane F. Smith, former director of the National Archives Civil Archives Division, focusing on Theodore R. Schellenberg's life and work.

General History

432. Congress. Joint Committee on Printing. **Our Flag.** (H.Doc.100-247). GPO, 1989. 52p. LC 89-603355. JC346.Z3O94 1989. 929.9/2/0973. OCLC 20551255. (Serial Set 13888). Y 1.1/7:100-247.

This illustrated history of the American flag includes discussion of laws and regulations, state and territorial flags, flag stamps, and care and display guidelines. Includes a bibliography.

433. Library of Congress. General Reference and Bibliography Division. **A Guide to the Study of the United States of America; Representative Books Reflecting the Development of American Life and Thought** by Donald H. Mugridge and Blanche P. McCrum. LC, 1960. Photoduplication Service, Washington, DC 20540-5230. 1193p. LC 60-60009. Z1215.U53. 016.9173. OCLC 248042. LC 2.2: Un 3/4.

> **Supplement.** 1956-1965. 1976. Free to U.S. Libraries and Institutions: Office Systems Services, Printing and Processing Section, Washington, DC 20540-5446. LC 2.2:Un 3/4/supp.

This is an annotated bibliography of books reflecting the development of U.S. life and thought in 32 fields of endeavor. The main volume includes works published through 1955, with the supplement extending coverage through 1965. Both volumes include extensive indexes.

434. Library of Congress. **Keys to the Encounter: A Library of Congress Resource Guide for the Study of the Age of Discovery** by Louis De Vorsey, Jr. GPO, 1992. 212p. LC 91-16735. E101.D48 1991. 016.9701. OCLC 23650363. LC 1.6/4:K 52.

This historical narrative of European world exploration, 1450-1580, also provides resource notes for locating incunabula, books, maps, atlases, globes, nautical charts, portraits, manuscripts, photographs, and illustrations in the Library of Congress.

435. Library of Congress. Prints and Photographs Division. **Washingtoniana: Photographs: Collections in the Prints and Photographs Division of the Library of Congress** by Kathleen Collins. GPO, 1989. 310p. LC 87-600421. F195.L66 1989. 016.779/99753. OCLC 17104184. LC 25.8/2:W27.

Photos depicting Washington, D.C., and surrounding communities, nearby Civil War forts and battlefields, and important people are described, including date, photographer, publisher, physical description, arrangement, source, and restrictions. The Prints and Photographs Division browsing files are also described. Includes a bibliography and subject index. This title augments the Prints and Photographs Division Catalog and the Library of Congress's online bibliographic database.

436. National Historical Publications and Records Commission. **Historical Documentary Editions**. NHPRC, 1986- . Free: Room 403, National Archives Bldg., 8th and Pennsylvania Ave., N.W., Washington, DC 20408. Irregular. LC sn93-28292. OCLC 28483946. AE 1.110:H 62/ .

The catalog describes NHPRC's print and microform publications of important historical materials, key documents, and papers of outstanding Americans, including the Adams Papers, First Congress, Franklin Papers, Hamilton Papers, Jefferson Papers, Madison Papers, and the Ratification of the Constitution.

437. National Park Service. **The National Register of Historic Places**. GPO, 1969-1989?. LC 78-603008. E159.N34. 973/.025. OCLC 1759352. I 29.76: .

This listing of properties on the national register is now published commercially and no longer available free to depository libraries.

History by Periods

Pre-Revolutionary

438. Army. Center of Military History. **Soldier-Statesmen of the Constitution** by Robert K. Wright, Jr. and Morris J. MacGregor, Jr. GPO, 1987. 298p. LC 87-1353. E302.5.W85 1987. 973.3/092/2. OCLC 15549460. D 114.19:C 76.

A history of the role of the Army in founding the republic, with the text of selected documents and biographies of Revolutionary War veterans and others who signed the Constitution.

439. Congress. **American Archives: Consisting of a Collection of Authentick Records, State Papers, Debates, and Letters and Other Notices of Publick Affairs, the Whole Forming. . .** compiled by Peter Force. 9v. 1837-1853. LC 2-5529. E203.A51. OCLC 444558. Z 1.1: .

This is a compilation of records, state papers, debates, and letters from the years 1774-76 related to colonial affairs and the Revolution. In six series: Series 1 covers from the discovery and settlement of the colonies to the English Revolution in 1688; series 2 covers from 1688 to the cession of Canada to Great Britain in 1763; series 3 covers the years 1763-74; series 4 covers from 1774 to the signing of the U.S. Declaration of Independence; series 5 covers the years 1776-83; and series 6 covers to the ratification of the U.S. Constitution in 1787.

440. National Archives and Records Administration. **A Guide to Pre-Federal Records in the National Archives** compiled by Howard H. Wehmann; revised by Benjamin L. DeWhitt. NARA, 1989. 375p. LC 88-600400. CD3045.W44 1989. 016.973. OCLC 18627903. AE 1.108:P 91.

This finding aid to records related to the pre-federal United States (before March 4, 1789) includes documents of the Continental and Confederation Congresses, the Constitutional Convention, and the Continental Army and Navy; diplomatic, fiscal, and judicial records; commerce, Indian affairs, postal, and customs records; and records related to pension, bounty land, and other claims. Includes name and subject indexes.

Revolutionary

441. House. **Revolutionary Diplomatic Correspondence of the United States** (H.Misc.Doc.603) edited by Francis Wharton. 6v. GPO, 1889. LC 5-17851. OCLC 493244. (Serial Set 2585-2589). Z 2.4: .

This compilation of the text of correspondence, along with historical and legal notes, includes papers of George Washington, Benjamin Franklin, James Madison, Samuel Adams, John Paul Jones, Arthur Lee, John Langdon, John Adams, and John Jay. Volume 1 contains an index.

442. Library of Congress. Bibliography Section. **Revolutionary America, 1763-1789: A Bibliography** compiled by Ronald M. Gephart. 2v. LC, 1984. Free to U.S. Libraries and Institutions: Office Systems Services, Printing and Processing Section, Washington, DC 20540-5446. LC 80-606802. Z1238.G43 1984. 016.9733. OCLC 7204655. LC 1.12/2:R 32/4/763-789/v.1-2.

This bibliography of primary and secondary publications published through 1972 and held in the Library of Congress includes books, dissertations, collected works, festschriften, pamphlets, and serials. Some have brief annotations. An essay on "The Preservation and Publication of Documentary Sources on the American Revolution" has cross-references to the major series listed in the bibliography. There is a chapter on research aids as well as an index.

443. Library of Congress. General Reference and Bibliography Division. **Periodical Literature on the American Revolution: Historical Research and Changing Interpretations, 1895-1970; A Selective Bibliography** compiled by Ronald M. Gephart. LC, 1971. Free: Office Systems Services, Printing and Processing Section, Washington, DC 20540-5446. 93p. LC 74-609228. Z1238.G4. 016.9733. OCLC 138376. LC 2.2:Am 3/3/895-970.

This is a bibliography of essays, festschriften, collections of essays or lectures, and articles about the Revolutionary period.

444. Library of Congress. General Reference and Bibliography Division. **The American Revolution: A Selected Reading List** prepared by Stefan M. Harrow. LC, 1968. Free: Office Systems Services, Printing and Processing Section, Washington, DC 20540-5446. 38p. LC 68-67236. Z1238.U62. 016.9733. OCLC 736679. LC 1.12/2:R 32.

A bibliography of books dealing with the prewar to postwar years of the 1780s. Citations are listed under broad subjects with separate sections for biographies, personal narratives and documentary sources, children's literature, and fiction. Includes an author index.

445. Library of Congress. **Letters of Delegates to Congress, 1774-1789** edited by Paul H. Smith. GPO, 1976- . Irregular. LC 76-2592. JK1033.L47. 973.3/12. OCLC 2020737. LC 1.34:vol.

    Vol. 1. August 1774-August 1775.

    Vol. 2. September-December 1775.

    Vol. 3. January 1-May 15, 1776.

> Vol. 4. May 16-August 15, 1776.
>
> Vol. 5. August 16-December 31, 1776.
>
> Vol. 6. January 1-April 30, 1777.
>
> Vol. 7. May 1-September 18, 1777.
>
> Vol. 8. September 19, 1777-January 31, 1778.
>
> Vol. 9. February 1-May 31, 1778.
>
> Vol. 10. June 1-September 30, 1778.
>
> Vol. 11. October 1, 1778-January 31, 1779.
>
> Vol. 12. February 1-May 31, 1779.
>
> Vol. 13. June 1-September 30, 1779.
>
> Vol. 14. October 1, 1779-March 31, 1780.
>
> Vol. 15. April 1-August 31, 1780.
>
> Vol. 16. September 1, 1780-February 28, 1781.
>
> Vol. 17. March 1-August 31, 1781.
>
> Vol. 18. September 1, 1781-July 31, 1782.
>
> Vol. 19. August 1, 1782-March 11, 1783.
>
> Vol. 20. March 12-September 30, 1783.

Volumes contain documents written by congressional delegates related to their official tasks during the years 1774-89. This is a new, expanded edition of the original *Letters of Members of the Continental Congress*, edited by Edmund C. Burnett (1921-36). New volumes will be listed in Library of Congress *Publications in Print.*

446. Library of Congress. **Manuscript Sources in the Library of Congress for Research on the American Revolution** compiled by John R. Sellers and others. LC, 1975. Free: Office Systems Services, Printing and Processing Section, Washington, DC 20540-5446. 372p. LC 74-5404. Z1238.U57 1975. 016.9733. OCLC 867944. LC 1.2:M 31/3.

This is a guide to manuscript material dated 1763-89 available for research in the Library of Congress, one of the world's foremost repositories of original American Revolution source material. The collections described include original documents, photostats, transcripts, and microfilm copies. A brochure from the National Archives, *Pictures of the Revolutionary War* (GS 4.2:R 32), is a short, chronological listing of photographic copies of artwork related to the American Revolution.

447. National Archives and Records Administration. **Index, Journals of the Continental Congress 1774-1789** compiled by Kenneth E. Harris and Steven D. Tilley. NARA, 1976. 429p. OCLC 2433402. GS 4.2:C 76/2/774-89.

This is a personal name, place, and subject index to the 34-volume set of journals of the Continental Congress published by the Library of Congress (not to the originals housed in the National Archives). This is a companion to *Index, The Papers of the Continental Congress, 1774-1789* (entry 448).

448. National Archives and Records Administration. **Index, The Papers of the Continental Congress, 1774-1789** compiled by John P. Butler. 5v. GPO, 1978. LC 78-23783. Z1238.B87. 973.3/12/016. OCLC 4493262. GS 4.2:C 76/3/774-89/v.1-5.

Known as Papers of the Continental Congress, this includes records of the Continental and Confederation Congresses and the Constitutional Convention of 1787, all contained in National Archives Record Group 360. The journals and two manuscript indexes are omitted. Names, places, and subjects are indexed, followed by a chronological documents list. Records of the Continental Congress in other record groups are not included. This is a companion to *Index, Journals of the Continental Congress, 1774-1789* (entry 447).

449. Navy. Naval Historical Center. **Naval Documents of the American Revolution**. 9v. GPO, 1964-1986. LC 64-60087. E271.U583. OCLC 426774. D 207. 12: .

    Vol. 1. 1964. American Theatre: Dec. 1, 1774-Sept. 2, 1775; European Theatre: Dec. 6, 1774-Aug. 9, 1775.

    Vol. 2. 1966. American Theatre: Sept. 3-Dec. 7, 1775; European Theatre: Aug.11-Oct. 31, 1775.

    Vol. 3. 1968. American Theatre: Dec. 8, 1775-Feb. 18, 1776; European Theatre: Nov. 1, 1775-Jan. 31, 1776.

    Vol. 4. 1969. American Theatre: Feb. 19-May 8, 1776; European Theatre: Feb. 1-May 25, 1776.

    Vol. 5. 1970. American Theatre: May 9-July 31, 1776.

    Vol. 6. 1972. American Theatre: Aug. 1-Oct. 31, 1776; European Theatre: May 26-Oct. 5, 1776.

    Vol. 7. 1976. American Theatre: Nov. 1, 1776-Feb. 28, 1777; European Theatre: Oct. 6-Dec. 31, 1776.

    Vol. 8. 1980. American Theatre: Mar. 1-May 31, 1777; European Theatre: Jan. 1-May 31, 1777.

    Vol. 9. 1986. American Theatre: June 1-July 31, 1777; European Theatre: June 1-Sept. 30, 1777; American Theatre: August 1-Sept. 30, 1777.

A compilation of full-text original and related manuscripts illustrating the role of the sea in the American Revolution. Maps, illustrations, bibliography, and index are included, and foreign language documents are translated.

War of 1812

450. House. Committee on Energy and Commerce. **Petitions, Memorials, and Other Documents Submitted for the Consideration of Congress, March 4, 1789 to December 14, 1795: A Staff Study**. GPO, 1986. 433p. LC 86-602119. JK1051.P48 1986. 328.73/09. OCLC 13704879. Y 4.En 2/3:99-AA.

Petitions and memorials, a major source of legislation enacted by early Congresses, are described in historical context and then listed individually. Petitions, memorials, and other documents submitted during the first four Congresses were compiled from the 1828 Gales and Seaton editions of the House Journal and arranged by subject. The list is also available as a database in the House Committee on Energy and Commerce.

451. Naval Historical Center. **The Naval War of 1812: A Documentary History** edited by William S. Dudley; Michael J. Crawford, associate editor. 2v. GPO, 1985, 1992. LC 85-600565. E360.N35 1985. 973.5/25. OCLC 12834733. D 207.10/2:H 62/ v.1-2.

This compilation of manuscripts includes headnotes explaining historical background, illustrations, maps, a bibliography, and an index in each volume.

Civil War

452. Army Military History Institute. **The Era of the Civil War—1820-1876** by Louise Arnold. AMHI, 1982. 704p. LC 83-601163. Z1242.U588 1982. 016.9737. OCLC 10558237. D 114.14:11/2.

This bibliography of the MHI Civil War collection includes descriptions of manuscript holdings and the museum collection. Although there has been no printed update, the MHI has placed Civil War unit and battle bibliographies on the Internet *URL http://144.99.192.240/* or E-mail to *MHI-HR@carlisle-EMH2.army.mil.*

453. Library of Congress. Geography and Map Division. **Civil War Maps: An Annotated List of Maps and Atlases in the Library of Congress** compiled by Richard W. Stephenson. GPO, 1989. 2d ed. 410p. LC 83-600031. Z6027.U5L5 1989. 016.9737. OCLC 17508893. LC 5.2:C 49/989.

This is a cartobibliography of maps, charts, atlases, and sketchbooks depicting troop positions and movements, engagements, and fortifications, along with reconnaissance, theater of war, sketch maps, and coastal charts. Entries give title, author, imprint, color, scale, size, and description, keeping entry numbers from the first edition. There are indexes to short titles, battles, places, subjects, cartographers, surveyors, engravers, lithographers, publishers, printers, and other personal names. A related publication issued by the National Archives is *A Guide to Civil War Maps in the National Archives* (1986).

454. Library of Congress. Manuscript Division. **Civil War Manuscripts: A Guide to Collections in the Manuscript Division of the Library of Congress** compiled by John R. Sellers. GPO, 1986. 391p. LC 81-607105. Z1242.L48 1986. 016.9737. OCLC 7836679. LC 4.2:C 49.

This guide to LC Manuscript Division collections related to the Civil War includes some postwar materials related to Lincoln's assassination and conspirators' trials, and the Fitz-John Porter and Henry Wirz trials.

455. National Archives and Records Administration. **Guide to Federal Archives Relating to the Civil War** by Kenneth W. Munden and Henry Putney Beers. NARA, 1962. 721p. LC a62-9432. CD3047.M8. OCLC 795805. GS 4.6/2:C 49.

> Also available on the Internet *URL http://gopher.nara.gov/* or
> *URL http://www.nara.gov/.*

This guide for scholarly study of the Civil War describes official war-related records and is arranged by departments, with a subject index. It was reprinted in 1986 as *The Union: Guide to Federal Archives Relating to the Civil War* (nondepository). Also from the National Archives is the brochure *Pictures of the Civil War* (GS 4.2:C 49/2/981), a short listing of photographs and photographs of artworks, arranged chronologically under four categories: Activities, places, portraits, and Lincoln's assassination. When known, names of photographers or artists are included and compiled in a name index. Includes ordering information.

456. National Archives and Records Administration. **Guide to the Archives of the Government of the Confederate States of America** by Henry Putney Beers. NARA, 1968. 536p. LC a68-7603. CD3047.B4. 016.97371/3. OCLC 390979. GS 4.6/2:C 76.

This is a descriptive guide to official records of both the U.S. government and the government of the Confederate States of America. It lists Confederate records, including those of the central government in Richmond, Congress, the Judiciary, the Presidency, and the Departments of State, Treasury, War, Navy, Post Office, and Justice. It is indexed by subject. Reprinted as *The Confederacy: A Guide to the Archives of the Government of the Confederate States of America* (nondepository, 1986).

457. Naval War Records Office. **Official Records of the Union and Confederate Navies in the War of the Rebellion**. 30v. GPO, 1894-1922. LC sn85-64154. E591.U58. OCLC 5194016. [In the Serial Set under various numbers]. N 16.6: .

Contemporary naval documents include Union and Confederate reports, orders, and correspondence (arranged according to squadrons and flotillas); statistics on all Union and Confederate vessels; materials related to the condition of the Union Army before the war, the construction of the Confederate Navy, and returns of captured war property; and correspondence about naval prisoners. With maps, diagrams, illustrations, and an index.

458. War Department. **The War of the Rebellion: A Compilation of the Official Records of the Union and Confederate Armies**. 70v. in 128. GPO, 1880-1901. LC 3-3452. E464.U6. OCLC 427057. [In the Serial Set under various numbers]. W 45.5: .

Contemporary documents include Union and Confederate military records, reports, orders, and correspondence, arranged by campaign and theater of war.

World War I

459. Army. Center of Military History. **Order of Battle of the United States Land Forces in the World War**. 3v. in 5. CMH, 1988. LC 87-600306. D570.O73 1988. 940.4/12/73. OCLC 16582087. D 114.2:B 32.

This facsimile reprint of volumes originally published in the years 1931-49 provides command rosters, daily order of battle tables, analysis of composition of land forces, and a chronology of events. A new appendix, "Posts, Camps, and Stations Index," is in part 2.

460. Army. Center of Military History. **United States Army in the World War, 1917-1919**. 17v. GPO, 1988. LC 88-600367. D570.U55 1988. 940.4/0973. OCLC 17981006. D 114.8:v.1-17.

Vol. 1. **Organization of the American Expeditionary Forces**.

Vol. 2. **Policy-Forming Documents of the American Expeditionary Forces**.

Vol. 3. **Training and Use of American Units with the British and French**.

Vol. 4-9. **Military Operations of the American Expeditionary Forces**.

Vol. 10. **The Armistice Agreement and Related Documents**.

Vol. 11. **American Occupation of Germany**.

Vol. 12-15. **Reports of the Commander-in-Chief, AEF, Staff Sections and Services**.

Vol. 16. **General Orders, GHQ, AEF**.

Vol. 17. **Bulletins, GHQ, AEF**.

This reprint of a 1948 17-volume compilation of World War I records of the American Expeditionary Forces includes maps and photographs.

461. National Archives. **Handbook of Federal World War Agencies and Their Records, 1917-1921**. GPO, 1943. 666p. LC 43-50551. JK464.1943.A52. 353. OCLC 1648088. AE 1.6:W 19/917-21.

This overall guide to wartime records of emergency war agencies, executive departments, and independent agencies covers from America's entrance into WWI in 1917 to the peace resolution of 1921. Record descriptions include history and functions. Includes a hierarchical list of agencies.

World War II

462. Army. Center of Military History. **American Armies and Battlefields in Europe.**
CMH, 1992. 1st CMH ed. 547p. LC 92-930. D528.A44 1992. 940.4. OCLC
25316157. D 114.2:AR 5/4.
This guide to American Expeditionary Forces battlefields in France and Italy includes an
index and maps. This is a reprint, with a new introduction, of *American Armies and
Battlefields in Europe: A History, Guide, and Reference Book* (1938).

463. Army. Center of Military History. **Manhattan, the Army and the Atomic Bomb**
by Vincent C. Jones. GPO, 1985. 660p. LC 84-12407. QC773.3.U5J65 1985.
355.8/25119/0973. OCLC 10913875. D 114.7:M 31.
This is a history of the Army's participation in the atomic program, 1939-1946.

464. Army. Center of Military History. **U.S. Army Signals Intelligence in World War
II: A Documentary History** edited by James L. Gilbert and John P. Finnegan.
GPO, 1993. 237p. LC 92-43143. D810.S7U7 1993. 940.54/85/0973. OCLC
27068268. D 114.2:SI 2.
This is a collection of declassified World War II documents from Army cryptologic
organizations, largely official histories and government memoranda. They are part of the
materials released to the National Archives as Special Research Histories (SRH) after
declassification by the National Security Agency. The volume also provides an overview
of Army Signals intelligence in World War II, a chronology, glossary, and a dictionary of
people, places, and terms.

465. Army. Center of Military History. **United States Army in World War II.
Reader's Guide** compiled and edited by Richard D. Adamczyk and Morris J.
MacGregor. GPO, 1992. 173p. LC 93-135094. Z6207.W8A34 1992. OCLC
29566614. D 114.7/2:992.
This guide to military information contained in volumes of the U.S. Army in World War
II series covers the Army and War Department roles during the years 1939-45. Includes
brief descriptions of subject coverage in each volume and the chapters, with a topical
index.

466. Army. **Trials of War Criminals Before the Nuernberg Military Tribunals
Under Control Council Law No. 10, Nuremberg, October 1946-April 1949.**
15v. GPO, 1949-1953. LC 49-45929. D804.G42A42. 341.4. OCLC 12799641.
D 102.8: .
These volumes contain materials introduced in evidence at the 12 war crimes trials held
pursuant to Allied Control Council Law No. 10, including indictments, judgments, and
other portions of the record. Indexes of documents and testimony are included. Additional
materials are available at the National Archives (see *Select List of Publications of the
National Archives and Records Administration*, entry 429).

467. Holocaust Memorial Council. **Directory of Holocaust Institutions.** HMC, 1988- .
LC 88-659150. D810.J4D55. 940.53/15/0392402573. OCLC 17797297. Y 3.H
74:11/ .
Entries for each Holocaust institution provide address, telephone number, president's
name, number of staff, organizational features, purpose, activities, collections, hours,
when established, and publications issued. Includes geographical and activity/collection
indexes.

468. International Military Tribunal. **Trial of the Major War Criminals Before the International Military Tribunal, Nuremberg, 14 November 1945-1 October 1946**. 42v. War Department, 1947-1949. LC 47-31575. D804.G42A5. 341.4. OCLC 748042. W 1.2:C 86/ .

This is a record of trial proceedings, with documents introduced in evidence. Additional materials are available at the National Archives (see *Select List of Publications of the National Archives and Records Administration*, entry 429).

469. Library of Congress. **The Largest Event: A Library of Congress Resource Guide for the Study of World War II** by Peter T. Rohrbach. GPO, 1994. 137p. LC 93-16487. Z6207.W8R564 1994. 016.94053. OCLC 27684030. LC 1.6/4:L 32.

This historical narrative of World War II also provides resource notes for locating books, recordings, manuscripts, musical scores, newspaper accounts, interviews, films, photographs, and illustrations in the Library of Congress.

470. National Archives and Records Administration. **Records Relating to Personal Participation in World War II: American Military Casualties and Burials** compiled by Benjamin L. DeWhitt. NARA, 1993. 61p. OCLC 29929400. AE 1.124:82.

Also known as Reference Information Paper 82 (RIP 82), this describes records in the National Archives containing information on soldiers, civilian military employees, and classes of individuals killed or wounded in World War II, including noncombat casualties. Includes an appendix of war casualty statistics and an index.

471. National Archives and Records Administration. **Records Relating to Personal Participation in World War II: American Prisoners of War and Civilian Internees** compiled by Ben DeWhitt and Jennifer Davis Heaps. NARA, 1992. 84p. LC 93-205658. CD3023.A35 no. 80. OCLC 27007752. AE 1.124:80.

Also known as Reference Information Paper 80 (RIP 80), this describes National Archives record groups relating to American military personnel and civilians held by the Axis during World War II. It includes an index and appendixes: "Boxlist for general subject file, 1942-46 (American POW Information Bureau, Records Branch; Record Group 389—Records of the Office of the Provost Marshal General)"; "Index to Files on Japanese-Controlled POW Camps (World War II): From general subject file, 1942-46 (American POW Information Bureau, Records Branch; Record Group 389—Records of the Office of the Provost Marshal General)"; and "Folder List for the series Navy Prisoner of War Board subject files, 1942-45 (Records of the Casualty Section; Record Group 24—Records of the Bureau of Naval Personnel)."

472. National Archives and Records Administration. **Records Relating to Personal Participation in World War II: "The American Soldier" Surveys** compiled by Ben DeWhitt and Heidi Ziemer. GPO, 1992. 20p. OCLC 28770831. AE 1.102:AM 3/3.

Lists National Archives machine-readable data files from the "American Soldier Surveys" of Army personnel, conducted by the Army Research Branch of the Army Services Forces between 1941 and the 1950s. Topics surveyed included race relations, the enemy, allies, training and combat experience, Army broadcasts and films, attitudes about USO clubs and medical care, winter clothing preferences, and postwar job plans.

473. National Archives and Records Administration. **World War II Records in the Cartographic and Architectural Branch of the National Archives** compiled by Daryl Bottoms. NARA, 1992. 87p. LC 93-122766. CD3023.A35 no.79. OCLC 27007184. AE 1.124:79.

This list of war-related maps, charts, aerial photos, architectural drawings, and engineering plans includes civilian and military home front records as well as those related to theaters of war, arranged by record groups (originating department, bureau, or agency). Includes an index of subjects and place names, and a glossary of terms, World War II code names, and jargon.

474. National Archives and Records Service. **Federal Records of World War II**. 2v. NARS, 1951. LC a51-9196. OCLC 1223402. GS 4.2:R 25/2/v.1-2.
This overall guide to wartime records describes materials of civilian and military agencies dating from 1939 to 1945. Includes an index.

475. Naval Historical Center. **Cruise Books of the United States Navy in World War II: A Bibliography** by Dean L. Mawdsley. NHC, 1993. 144p. LC 92-41498. D773.M358 1993. 016.94054/5973. OCLC 27035864. D 221.17:2.
This is a bibliography of World War II ship and naval unit cruise books available in naval, Coast Guard, museum, and research libraries. Part of the Naval History Bibliographies series.

Korean War

476. Army. Center of Military History. **United States Army in the Korean War**. 5v. GPO, 1987-1992. LC 93-213424. DS918.U5246 1987. 951.904/2. OCLC 31709741. D 114.2:K 84/2/vol.
This official history describes Army operations. Each volume has an index. Volume 1: *South to the Naktong, North to the Yalu*, volume 2: *Truce Tent and Fighting Front*, volume 3: *Policy and Direction in the First Year*, volume 4: *Medics War*, volume 5: *Ebb and Flow: November 1950-July 1951*.

Military History

477. Air Force. Historical Research Center. **Personal Papers in the United States Air Force Historical Research Center** compiled and edited by Richard E. Morse et al. AF, 1990. 5th ed. 225p. OCLC 22685063. D 301.26/6:P 19.
This catalog to papers donated by Air Force leaders, aircraft designers, explorers, authors, journalists, and public officials notes collection dates and description, cubic feet of records, donor biography, and location of related materials.

478. Air Force. Office of Air Force History. **Encyclopedia of US Air Force Aircraft and Missile Systems** by Marcelle Size Knaack. 2v- . GPO, 1978- . LC 77-22377. UG1243.K53. 358.4/3. OCLC 3088764. D 301.82/5:B 63.
    Vol. 1. **Post-World War II Fighters, 1943-1973**.
    Vol. 2. **Post-World War II Bombers, 1945-1973**.
Volume 1 describes all Air Force fighters developed between World War II and 1973, giving configurations, aircraft origin, developmental problems and modifications, and production milestones. Volume 2 describes strategic, tactical, and experimental bombers, discussing problems, production, tests, procurement, milestones, and special features. The volumes include indexes, a bibliography, and glossary.

479. Army. Center of Military History. **A Guide to the Study and Use of Military History** edited by John E. Jessup, Jr. and Robert W. Coakley. GPO, 1979. 507p. LC 78-606157. E181.G85. 973/.07/2. OCLC 4131480. D 114.12:St 9.

This guide to the literature provides an overview of military history, with guides to researching specific time periods and descriptions of history programs in the various military branches.

480. Army. Center of Military History. **A Guide to U.S. Army Museums** by R. Cody Phillips. GPO, 1992. 118p. LC 93-122781. U13.U6P45 1992. 355/.0074/73. OCLC 27028890. D 114.12:AR 5.

This is a directory of Army and other military museums, military historical collections, and historic sites. Museums are listed by location, with address, telephone number, hours, travel directions, description, programs and services, and publications. Continues *Guide to U.S. Army Museums and Historic Sites*.

481. Army. Center of Military History. **American Military History**. GPO, 1989. Partially rev. ed. 755p. LC 89-602760. E181.A44 1989. 355/.00973. OCLC 20149794. D 114.19:M 59/2.

This ROTC textbook is a history of the U.S. Army from colonial times to the post-Vietnam era. Includes suggested readings and an index.

482. Army. Center of Military History. **Publications of the U.S. Army Center of Military History**. A, 197?- . Irregular. LC sf93-91896. Z6725.U5A58. OCLC 15061938. D 114.10: .

An annotated bibliography of publications related to U.S. Army history, with GPO stock numbers and ordering information. The list includes all current CMH titles, arranged in reverse chronology by war. Includes an appendix of titles and publication numbers and an author index. A related title is *Military Service Records: A Select Catalog of National Archives Microfilm Publications* (nondepository, 1985).

483. Army. Center of Military History. **Secretaries of War and Secretaries of the Army: Portraits & Biographical Sketches** by William Gardner Bell. GPO, 1992. 177p. OCLC 26812780. D 114.2:Se 2/992.

Presents biographies and color portraits of the Secretaries of War and of the Army from Henry Knox (George Washington's administration) to Michael P. W. Stone (Bush administration), as well as a brief introduction to Army history, illustrated with drawings and photographs of buildings.

484. Army Intelligence and Security Command. History Office. **Military Intelligence: A Picture History** by John Patrick Finnegan. GPO, 1992. 2d ed. 195p. LC 92-36885. UB251.U5F56 1992. 355.3/432/0973. OCLC 26800114. D 101.2:IN 8/10.

This history of the major U.S. intelligence disciplines includes black-and-white photographs.

485. Army. Office of the Inspector General. **The Inspectors General of the United States Army, 1777-1903** by David A. Clary and Joseph W. A. Whitehorne. GPO, 1987. 465p. LC 86-25931. UB243.C56 1987. 355.6/3/0973. OCLC 14360079. D 114.2:In 7.

This history of Inspector General activities from the Revolutionary War to the War Department reorganization in 1903 includes an index and a bibliography.

486. Department of Defense. Office of the Secretary of Defense. Historical Office. **The Pentagon: The First Fifty Years** by Alfred Goldberg. GPO, 1992. 197p. LC 92-20946. UA26.V8G65 1992. 355.6/0973. OCLC 26094776. D 1.2:P 38.

This is an illustrated history of the Department of Defense headquarters building.

487. National Archives and Records Service. **List of Logbooks of U.S. Navy Ships, Stations, and Miscellaneous Units, 1801-1947** compiled by Claudia Bradley et al. NARS, 1978. 562p. LC 78-606194. Z6835.U5U43 1978. 016.973s. OCLC 3728731. GS 4.7:44.

This inventory of National Archives holdings of logbooks of U.S. Navy ships, stations, and miscellaneous units lists vessel or station name, dates covered by the logbooks, and number of logbooks.

488. Naval Historical Center. **Dictionary of American Naval Fighting Ships**. 8v. GPO, 1959- . LC 60-60198. VA61.A53. 359.3/2/50973. OCLC 2794587. D 207.10:v.1-8.
    Vol.1. Part A. **Historical Sketches, Letter A** edited by James L. Mooney. D 207.10:1/pt.A/991- .

Provides histories of U.S. Navy and Continental Navy ships, with descriptions of tonnage, length, beam, draft, speed, armament and class, builder, sponsor, launching, acquisition and commission dates, first commanding officer, and a concise operational record. Volumes also include illustrations, a bibliography, and appendixes for types of ships in the modern and historic Navy. Short biographies of the naval leaders after whom ships were named are also included. Volume 8 (W-Z) includes a guide to the entire series. In 1991 Volume 1-Part A, *Historical Sketches, Letter A* (D 207.10:1/pt.A/991) was updated with new histories of all "A" ships but does not entirely replace the original Volume 1 (A-B).

489. Naval Historical Center. **Historical Manuscripts in the Navy Department Library: A Bibliography** by George W. Emery. NHC, 1994. LC 94-42335. Z1249.N3U53 1994. 016.359/00973. OCLC 31433798. D 221.17:3.

Citations to official and secondary U.S. naval history sources include histories, bibliographies, and journal articles. Entries are arranged by subject within historical periods. Indexed by author, editor, and compiler. Part of the Naval History Bibliographies series.

490. Naval Historical Center. **Naval Historical Publications in Print**. NHC, 1992. Free: Washington Navy Yard, Washington, DC 20374. 23p. OCLC 27664885. D 207.11:H 62/3/992.

Lists, with annotations, of Naval Historical Center microfilm collections and publications in print. A related title is *Naval Historical Foundation Manuscript Collection: A Catalog* (LC 1.2:N 22/2).

491. Naval Historical Center. **United States Naval History: A Bibliography** revised by Barbara A. Lynch and John E. Vajda. NHC, 1993. 7th ed. 173p. LC 92-40017. Z1249.N3U54 1993. 016.359/00973. OCLC 27810411. D 221.17:1.

This is a subject-arranged list of publications about U.S. naval history during the American Revolution, the War of 1812, Civil War, Mexican War, Spanish-American War, World Wars I and II, the Korean War, and the Vietnam War. Part of the Naval History Bibliographies series.

492. **U.S. Army Military History Institute**. Department of the Army, Carlisle Barracks, Carlisle, PA 17013-5008; (717) 245-3611.

The MHI is the Army's central repository of source materials on American military history since colonial times and on allied fields such as international relations, law, science, sociology, medicine, exploration, economics, geography, political science, and literature. Its collection includes books, periodicals, manuscripts, diaries, letters, memoirs, artworks, oral histories, photographs, and audiovisuals.

Law

GENERAL WORKS

493. Department of Justice. **Attorneys General of the United States, 1789-1985.** GPO, 1985. 151p. LC 85-601508. KF372.A77 1985. 353.5/092/2. OCLC 11844112. J 1.2:At 8/6/789-85.
Provides biographical sketches and black-and-white official portraits of U.S. attorneys general, with biographical sketches of the portrait artists. The portraits are displayed in the Department of Justice building. Includes a name index.

494. Department of Justice.
> Department of Justice. **Evaluation of the Handling of the Branch Davidian Stand-Off in Waco, Texas by the United States Department of Justice and the Federal Bureau of Investigation** by Edward S. G. Dennis Jr. GPO, 1993. 63p. LC 94-128972. BP605.B72D45 1993. 363.2/3/0973. OCLC 29138380. J 1.2:W 11/EVALUA.

> Department of Justice. **Lessons of Waco: Proposed Changes in Federal Law Enforcement** by Philip B. Heymann. GPO, 1993. 31p. LC 94-129052. HV8141.H49 1993. 363.2/32/0973. OCLC 29138324. J 1.2:W 11/LESSONS.

> Department of Justice. **Recommendations of Experts for Improvements in Federal Law Enforcement After Waco.** 1v. GPO, 1993. LC 94-128966. HV8141.R38 1993. 363.2/3/0973. OCLC 29138439. J 1.2:W 11/RECOMM.

> Department of Justice. **Report of the Events at Waco, Texas, February 28 to April 19, 1993.** 1v. GPO, 1993. LC 94-129613. BP605.B72R46 1993. 363.2/3/0973. OCLC 29148193. J 1.2:W 11.

The four volumes in this investigation focus on the 1993 Waco Branch Davidian disaster in Waco, Texas.

495. General Accounting Office. Comptroller General of the United States. **Government Auditing Standards.** GPO, 1994. 1994 rev. 109p. LC 94-190843. HJ9801.A3 1994. 350.72/32/0973. OCLC 30611236. GA 1.2:AU 2/14/994.
Government Auditing Standards, more commonly known as the "Yellow Book," is a manual of standards CPA firms must follow during audits of government agencies, programs, activities, and functions. This first revision since 1988 contains financial audit standards effective January 1, 1995.

496. General Accounting Office. Office of the General Counsel. **Principles of Federal Appropriations Law.** GPO, 1991. 2d ed. LC 92-198609. KF6225.A36 1991. 343.73/034. OCLC 25295050. GA 1.14:F 31/991/vol.

Better known as the "Red Book," this is a guide to legal areas in which the Comptroller General renders decisions but that are omitted from other GAO publications. Includes availability and obligation of appropriations, continuing resolutions, liability and relief of accountable officers, and federal assistance information.

497. Library of Congress. **Slavery in the Courtroom: An Annotated Bibliography of American Cases** by Paul Finkelman. LC, 1985. Free to U.S. Libraries and Institutions: Office Systems Services, Printing and Processing Section, Washington, DC 20540-5446. 312p. LC 83-600166. KF4545.S5A123 1985. 016.34273/0873. OCLC 9686320. LC 1.12/2:SI 1/2.

This annotated bibliography cites materials in the Library of Congress, with chapters on free jurisdiction slaves, fugitives, abolition, revolts, the African slave trade, and miscellaneous trials and cases.

498. Secret Service. **Moments in History** by Marcia Roberts. SS, 1990. 52p. OCLC 25186755. T 34.2:H 62/865-90.

Offers highlights of 125 years of the agency, with photos and biographical sketches of the chiefs.

499. Senate. Committee on Governmental Affairs. **Government in the Sunshine Act: History and Recent Issues: A Report of the Committee on Governmental Affairs, United States Senate.** GPO, 1989. 151p. LC 89-603601. KF5105.5.A25 1989. 353.0081/9. OCLC 20701128. Y 4.G 74/9:S.prt.101-54.

Describes issues and judicial decisions related to Public Law 94-409, along with articles from the media and statements printed in the *Congressional Record.*

500. Smithsonian Institution. **The Lawmen: United States Marshals and Their Deputies, 1789-1989** by Frederick S. Calhoun. SI Press, 1989. 370p. LC 89-21806. KF8794.C35 1990. 363.2/82/097309. OCLC 20318943. J 25.2:L 42.

This official history relates key events in American history in which marshals played a role with a discussion of today's marshals. Includes an index and a bibliography.

BIBLIOGRAPHIES

501. Bureau of Alcohol, Tobacco, and Firearms. **ATF Publications.** 1v. BATF, 1987. OCLC 15493577. T 70.13:A 1 1/987.

This is a loose-leaf, unannotated bibliography of titles stocked by ATF distribution centers, with publication numbers.

502. Federal Judicial Center. **Catalog of Publications.** FJC, 19??- . Annual. LC sn88-40013. OCLC 8290120. JU 13.11/2: .

This is a subject-arranged annotated bibliography of reports and products issued since the Center's creation in 1967. Includes author and title indexes.

503. Library of Congress. **Consilia: A Bibliography of Holdings in the Library of Congress and Certain Other Collections in the United States** by Peter R. Pazzaglini and Catharine A. Hawks. GPO, 1990. 154p. LC 89-600323. KJA2145.A2P39 1990. 016.347/05. OCLC 20722175. LC 1.12/2:C 76/2.

This is an unannotated list of U.S. holdings of legal analyses by medieval and Renaissance jurists, printed before 1800. Arranged by author and then chronologically by publication date, with imprint, holdings information, a place names glossary, and an author index.

504. Library of Congress. **The Canon Law Collection of the Library of Congress: A General Bibliography with Selective Annotations** compiled by Dario C. Ferreira-Ibarra. LC, 1981. Free to U.S. Libraries and Institutions: Office Systems Services, Printing and Processing Section, Washington, DC 20540-5446. 210p. LC 81-607964. 016.2629. OCLC 7555441. LC 42.9:C 16.

This selectively annotated bibliography lists the canon law holdings (legislation of the Roman Catholic Church) in the Library of Congress Law Library, classified by subject.

CIVIL RIGHTS

505. Commission on Civil Rights. **Catalog of Publications**. CCR, 19??- . Annual. LC sn95-17094. OCLC 6191162. CR 1.9:C 28/ .

An annotated list of statutory and interim reports, clearinghouse publications, hearings, consultations, conferences, staff reports, state advisory committee reports, and Spanish-language publications.

506. Commission on Civil Rights. **Directory of Private Fair Housing Organizations**. CCR, 1986. 172p. LC 86-602029. KF4755.A83 no.87. 323.4/0973. OCLC 13615297. CR 1.10:87.

This directory lists fair housing organizations by state and city, with addresses, telephone numbers, director names, foundation dates, areas served, and activities. Also features a list of Community Housing Resource Boards.

507. Commission on Civil Rights. **Directory of State and Local Fair Housing Agencies**. CCR, 1985. 231p. LC 85-602170. KF4755.A83 no.86. 323.4/0973. OCLC 12247490. CR 1.10:86.

Names, addresses, and telephone numbers of housing organizations are augmented by information on protected classes, unlawful practices, exemptions, enforcement powers, and staffing for the jurisdiction. An appendix lists the status of individual state and locality fair housing laws as of September 1, 1983.

508. Senate. Committee on the Judiciary. Subcommittee on the Constitution. **Federal Civil Rights Laws: A Sourcebook**. GPO, 1984. 149p. LC 84-604192. KF4744 1984. 342.73/085. OCLC 11503887. Y 4.J 89/2:S.prt.98-245.

This is a compilation of descriptions, legislative histories, and citations to federal and state laws, constitutional amendments, court decisions, and executive orders.

U.S. CONSTITUTION

509. Commission on the Bicentennial of the United States Constitution. **The Bill of Rights and Beyond, 1791-1991**. CBUSC, 1991. 106p. LC 91-76382. KF4750.B52 1991. 342.73/085. OCLC 25057627. Y 3.B 47/2:2 B 49/6.

The first 10 amendments to the U.S. Constitution (the "Bill of Rights") and the seven later amendments are described in historical context. Includes an index and a bibliography.

510. Department of Justice. Federal Justice Research Program. **Bibliography of Original Meaning of the United States Constitution** prepared by the Faculty and Students at the University of San Diego School of Law. GPO, 1988. 287p. LC 88-602460. KF4546.A1B53 1988. 016.34273. OCLC 18299165. J 1.20/2:C 76/2.

This is an unannotated bibliography of materials interpreting provisions of the Constitution and amendments, as understood by its original framers. Cited are debates of the framing and ratifying bodies, early and modern scholarly works, and Supreme Court cases. A related title is *Original Meaning Jurisprudence: A Sourcebook* (J 1.96:J 97).

511. House. **The Constitution of the United States of America, As Amended: Un-ratified Amendments, Analytical Index**. (H.Doc.102-188). GPO, 1992. 81p. OCLC 26646116. [Serial Set number not available]. Y 1.1/7:102-188.

The "Analytical Index" provides the text of the Constitution and amendments, with amendment ratification dates, background on unratified proposed amendments, and a detailed analytical index to the Constitution and amendments with references to articles, sections, and clauses.

512. Senate. **The Constitution of the United States of America: Analysis and Interpretation: Annotations of Cases Decided by the Supreme Court of the United States to July 2, 1982**. (S.Doc.99-16). GPO, 1987. Rev. and annotated. 2308p. LC 88-602051. KF4527.K55 1987. 342.73/023. OCLC 19573247. (Serial Set 13611). Y 1.1/3:99-16.

> ... **1990 Supplement ... to June 27, 1990**. (S.Doc.101-36). (Serial Set 13969). Y 1.1/3:101-36.

The "Annotated Constitution" supplements the Constitution with citations to key constitutional Supreme Court cases given clause by clause. It also lists federal, state, and local laws determined to be unconstitutional and Supreme Court decisions overruling previous decisions. Also known as the "Constitution Annotated," it is revised each decade, with cumulative supplements issued every two years. It includes a subject index and a table of cases.

COPYRIGHT

> Copyright Office: *URL http://marvel.loc.gov/* or
> *URL gopher://marvel.loc.gov:70* or
> *URL http://lcweb.loc.gov/copyright/.*

513. Library of Congress. Copyright Office. **Concordance—Title 17, Copyright Law, Keyword-in-Context Index**. NTIS (PB82-166992/HDM), 1979. 344p. LC 79-65087. OCLC 5278535. LC 3.2:C 74.

This alphabetical word list shows the words immediately before and after each term in the text of the law.

514. Library of Congress. Copyright Office. **Copyright Law of the United States of America: Contained in Title 17 of the United States Code**. GPO, 1995. Rev. to Sept. 30, 1994. 140p. OCLC 32378310. LC 3.4/2:92/994.

The text of Title 17 *U.S. Code*, chapters 1-8 and 10, is reproduced, along with amendments to the Copyright Act of 1976 through 1994. An appendix includes sections of the Berne Convention Implementation Act of 1988.

515. Library of Congress. Copyright Office. **Decisions of the United States Courts Involving Copyright**. GPO, 1914- . Irregular. LC 72-625239. KF2994.A1C63. 346/.73/04820264. OCLC 975912. LC 3.3/3: .

This is a compilation of citations to federal and state copyright and intellectual property cases since 1789. Most citations are to West Publishing Company's National Reporter System and the Bureau of National Affairs, Inc.'s *United States Patents Quarterly*.

Volumes include tables of cases, supplemental cases, and works involved in the cases, plus a subject index. Volumes are cited in this format: 49 C. O. Bull. (Copyright Office Bulletin no. 49). There is considerable time lag: Volume 49, covering decisions in 1989, was issued in 1992. Updates *Decisions of the United States Courts Involving Copyright and Literary Property, 1789-1909, with an Analytical Index* (LC 3.3/3:13-16) and *Decisions of the United States Courts Involving Copyright, Cumulative Index, 1909-1970* (LC 3.3:17-37/ind.).

516. Library of Congress. Copyright Office. **General Guide to the Copyright Act of 1976** by Marybeth Peters. NTIS (PB82-171968/HDM), 1977. 144p. LC 77-604835. KF2994.A334. 346/.73/0482. OCLC 3891939. LC 3.7/2:C 79.
This training manual is a plain-English overview of the Copyright Act of 1976. It covers history, subject matter, legalities, fair use, copyright notice, infringement, and administration. Appendixes provide an outline of the law, comparison between the 1909 and 1976 laws, and official source materials.

DIGEST

517. Department of State. Office of the Legal Advisor. **Cumulative Digest of United States Practice in International Law**. GPO, 1988- . LC 95-645613. JX21 .R68. 341/.0973. OCLC 30489374. S 7.12/3: .
This digest offers an overview of background, interpretation, and trends related to international law, state representation, and the law of treaties and other international agreements, along with material originally published under "Contemporary Practice of the United States Relating to International Law" by the *American Journal of International Law*. It can be consulted in conjunction with the contemporary foreign policy materials in *American Foreign Policy: Current Documents* (entry 603). Coverage began in 1981, continuing the *Digest of United States Practice in International Law* series, issued annually during the period 1973-80, with a consolidated *Cumulative Index, 1973-1980* (S 7.12/3:).

FREEDOM OF INFORMATION AND PRIVACY ACTS

518. Department of Justice. Office of Information and Privacy. **Freedom of Information Act Guide & Privacy Act Overview**. GPO, 1992- . Annual. LC 93-648754. KF5753.A29F74. 342.73/0662. OCLC 27055241. J 1.8:F 87.
The "Guide and Overview" includes an overview of the Privacy Act of 1974, plus the "Justice Department Guide to the Freedom of Information Act," an overview of FOIA exemptions, FOIA law enforcement record exclusions, and key procedures. Cited cases can be referenced in *Freedom of Information Case List* (entry 519). Also included are recent presidential and U.S. attorney policy statements.

519. Department of Justice. Office of Information Law and Policy. **Freedom of Information Case List**. GPO, 19??- . Annual. LC 79-644034. KF5753.A58D46. 342.73/0853. OCLC 5003799. J 1.56: .
This is a subject compilation of published and unpublished judicial decisions related to FOIA and Privacy Act access issues, including "reverse" FOIA cases and an "overview" list of selected FOIA decisions. Also included are Government in the Sunshine Act and Federal Advisory Committee Act cases. Cases can be identified by topics and case name. Entries note official and unofficial case citations. The text of the laws is included, along with a bibliography of related law review articles.

520. National Archives and Records Administration. **Compilation, Privacy Act Issuances [computer file]**. GPO, 1993- . Biennial. CD-ROM. LC sn95-27140. OCLC 31961393. AE 2.106/4-2: .

Also available on the Internet *URL http://wais.access.gpo.gov*.

Federal agency files kept on individuals are described, along with agency rules for requesting information from them and tips on how the records may be used.

INTERNATIONAL LAW

521. Law Library of Congress. **Introductions to Research in Foreign Law**. LLC, 1991- . OCLC 25957653. LC 42.15: .

No. 1. **Japan** compiled by Sung Yoon Cho. 1991.

No. 2. **Israel** compiled by Ruth Levush. 1992.

Each booklet focuses on the law of a particular nation, offering an introduction to legal research with an overview of the nation's government, constitution and statutes, treaties, and judicial and administrative materials.

522. Library of Congress. European Law Division. **The Coutumes of France in the Library of Congress: An Annotated Bibliography** by Jean Caswell and Ivan Sipkov. LC, 1977. Free to U.S. Libraries and Institutions: Office Systems Services, Printing and Processing Section, Washington, DC 20540-5446. 80p. LC 76-608412. 016.34/00944. OCLC 2819192. LC 1.12/2:C 83.

This is a list of materials related to French "coutumes," which are comparable to English common law.

523. Library of Congress. Far Eastern Law Division. **Law and Legal Literature of North Korea: A Guide** by Sung Yoon Cho. GPO, 1988. 256p. LC 88-600053. KPC47.C46 1988. 349.519/3. OCLC 17550293. LC 42.9:L 41/3.

This is an annotated guide to legal material published between 1945 and 1983 in North Korea, South Korea, Japan, and the U.S. and written in Korean, Japanese, or English. Includes a name index.

524. Library of Congress. Law Library. Far Eastern Law Division. **Chinese Law: A Bibliography of Selected English-Language Materials** compiled by Constance A. Johnson. LC, 1990. Free: Washington, DC 20540-5446. 138p. LC 91-600265. KNQ3.J64 1990. 016.34951. OCLC 23362157. LC 42.9:C 44.

This is an unannotated list of Library of Congress holdings of journal articles, books, and translated news reports about the laws of the People's Republic of China, covering the years 1985-89. It is arranged by subjects and updates *The People's Republic of China: A Bibliography of Selected English-Language Legal Materials* (LC 42.9:C 44/2).

525. Library of Congress. **Nomenclature & Hierarchy—Basic Latin American Legal Sources** by Rubens Medina and Cecilia Medina-Quiroga. LC, 1979. Free to U.S. Libraries and Institutions: Office Systems Services, Printing and Processing Section, Washington, DC 20540-5446. 123p. LC 79-14005. 016.34/0098. OCLC 5007223. LC 24.2:N 72.

This is a guide to statutory and regulatory texts in the Hispanic nations of Latin America, Brazil, and Haiti.

PATENT LAW

526. Federal Judicial Center. **Patent Law and Practice** by Herbert F. Schwartz. FJC, 1988. 119p. LC 88-602604. KF3120.S38 1988. 346.7304/86. OCLC 18348188. Ju 13.9:88-1.
This introduction explains the patent application process, procedures in patent disputes, valid patents, and infringement. Includes a table of cases and a bibliography.

527. Patent and Trademark Office. **Attorneys and Agents Registered to Practice Before the U.S. Patent and Trademark Office**. GPO, 197?- . Irregular. LC 75-648024. KF3165.A3A8. 346/.73/0486025. OCLC 2246063. C 21.9/2: .
Gives names and addresses of people authorized to represent inventors before the PTO, by name and in a geographical listing.

REGULATIONS

528. Administrative Conference of the United States. Office of the Chairman. **A Guide to Federal Agency Rulemaking** prepared by Benjamin W. Mintz and Nancy G. Miller. GPO, 1991. 2d ed. 429p. LC 91-600991. KF5407.A616 1991. OCLC 23675832. Y 3.AD 6:8 R 86/991.
This introduction provides an overview of agency rulemaking, its legal basis, the informal rulemaking process, and judicial review.

529. Office of the Federal Register. **Code of Federal Regulations**. GPO, 1938- . Annual. OCLC 2786662. AE 2.106/3: .
The CFR is a codification of general and permanent rules issued by executive departments and federal regulatory agencies, plus presidential executive orders and proclamations. The CFR is divided into 50 subject titles, which are revised annually at staggered intervals. It is updated by the *Federal Register* (entry 532). Several commercial vendors provide the full text online.

530. Office of the Federal Register. **Code of Federal Regulations. CFR Index and Finding Aids**. GPO, 1977- . Annual. LC sn81-3304. 342. OCLC 4828101. AE 2.106/3-2: .
This CFR volume includes a subject/agency index to regulations codified in the CFR. The subject/agency index refers users to CFR parts rather than to the section level, and is current to January 1 each year. An index to the text of Title 3 of the CFR, The President, is included in Title 3. The index also includes a list of agency-prepared indexes in CFR volumes; acts requiring publication in the *Federal Register*; CFR titles broken down into chapters, subchapters, and parts; a list of agencies appearing in the CFR (also found in every CFR volume); plus tables of laws and presidential documents cited as authority for regulations in the CFR.

531. Office of the Federal Register. **Code of Federal Regulations. LSA, List of CFR Sections Affected**. GPO, 1977- . Monthly. LC sn85-10253. OCLC 4509194. AE 2.106/2: .
Also known as the "List of Sections Affected" indexes amendments and proposed rules published in the *Federal Register* since the last CFR revision. LSA may be searched by CFR title, chapter, part, and section. Also included is a table translating FR volume and page citations into FR issue dates, and a table of statutory authorities for regulations that updates the authority table in the *CFR Index*. LSA issues cumulate quarterly: Four permanent issues of LSA must be saved until the next CFR revision. Using the cumulative

list of parts affected during the current month published in the daily *Federal Register* along with the most recent LSA allows researchers to identify the latest version of a rule.

> **Code of Federal Regulations: List of CFR Sections Affected, 1973-1985** AE 2.106/2-2: .

> **Code of Federal Regulations: List of CFR Sections Affected, 1964-1972** GS 4.108:List/964-72/vol.

> **Code of Federal Regulations: List of CFR Sections Affected, 1949-1963** GS 4.108:List/949-63.

> These historical research tools for locating changes to the CFR published in issues of the *Federal Register* are compilations of *LSA: List of CFR Sections Affected* volumes.

532. Office of the Federal Register. **Federal Register**. GPO, 1936- . Daily (except Saturday, Sunday, and official federal holidays). LC 36-26246. KF70.A2. 353.005. OCLC 1768512. AE 2.106: .

This is the official publication for public regulations and legal notices issued by federal executive agencies and independent agencies, including presidential proclamations and executive orders, rules and regulations, proposed rules, notices, and Sunshine Act meetings. Final rules published in the *Federal Register* update the most recently published CFR (entry 531). Several commercial vendors sell online or CD-ROM access to the full text of the *Federal Register*. The file since January 2, 1994 (volume 59) is also available for a fee from the GPO through GPO Access. To subscribe through the Internet *URL telnet://wais. access.gpo.gov*, login as *newuser*, no password. Modem: Call (202) 512-1661, login as *wais*, no password, at the second login as *newuser*, no password. GPO Access is available free in depository libraries and through Internet depository "gateways." The table of contents and depository gateways can be accessed free through the Superintendent of Documents Home Page *URL http://www.access.gpo.gov/su_docs* or through the National Archives *URL http://gopher.nara.gov/*.

533. Office of the Federal Register. **Federal Register Index**. GPO, 19??- . Monthly. AE 2.106: .

This cumulative, monthly index is a consolidation of *Federal Register* tables of contents, supplemented with general subject headings. The index also lists Privacy Act publications, a table of pages and dates referring from page numbers to *Federal Register* issues, and a quarterly Guide to Freedom of Information Indexes. The December issue is the annual cumulative index.

534. Office of the Federal Register. **The Federal Register: What It Is and How to Use It: A Guide for the User of the Federal Register-Code of Federal Regulations System** edited by Jim Wickliffe and Ernie Sowada. GPO, 1992. 123p. OCLC 27335858. AE 2.108:F 31/992.

This guide to using publications in the *Federal Register* system provides an introduction to locating regulations in the *Federal Register* and *Code of Federal Regulations* and to the federal rulemaking process.

STATUTES

535. House. Office of the Law Revision Counsel of the House of Representatives. **United States Code**. GPO, 1940- . Sexennial. LC sn88-40171. OCLC 2368380. Y 1.2/5: .

> Annual Supplement. Y 1.2/5: .

This consolidation and codification of the general and permanent laws of the United States is arranged by subject under 50 titles. The U.S.C.—the official compilation of public laws in force—gives the current status of laws as amended. The *Code* contains an index of popular names of acts and an index of subjects, official names of acts, and agency names (citing *U.S. Code* title and section), along with conversion tables to translate *Statutes at Large*, revised statutes, executive orders, proclamations, and reorganization plan citations into *U.S. Code* citations. Also includes tables to translate *U.S. Code* citations into sections of the District of Columbia Code, and vice versa. New editions have been published every six years since 1926, with annual cumulative supplements published after each session of Congress. See SB 197 for prices of individual volumes. The full text of the *U.S. Code* is available on CD-ROM from the GPO, on GPO Access (entry 104), and through several commercial online database vendors.

536. Office of the Federal Register. **United States Statutes at Large**. GPO, 1789- . Annual. LC sc79-3701. 349. OCLC 1768474. AE 2.111: .

Following each congressional session, laws initially published individually as "slip laws" are compiled in the *Statutes at Large* (cited in this manner: volume Stat. page). It contains the full text of all public and private laws and concurrent resolutions passed during the congressional session, arranged chronologically by enactment date, along with reorganization plans, proposed and ratified Constitutional amendments, and presidential proclamations. Treaties, included until 1949, are now published in *United States Treaties and Other International Agreements* (entry 540). Each volume is indexed by popular name of the law, personal name, and subject. There are also lists of public and private bills enacted (noting law number), plus lists of public and private laws, concurrent resolutions, and proclamations. The laws published in *Statutes at Large* are codified in the *United States Code* (entry 535). Volumes 1-17 (1789-1873) were published by Little, Brown.

TREATIES

537. Department of State. Office of the Legal Adviser. **Treaties in Force; A List of Treaties and Other International Agreements of the United States**. GPO, 1929- . Annual. LC 56-61604. JX236.1929c. 341.273. OCLC 3500023. S 9.14: .

TIF lists all U.S. treaties and international agreements in force as of January 1 each year.

538. Department of State. **Treaties and Other International Acts Series**. GPO, 1946- . Irregular. LC 46-6169. JX235.9.A32. 341.273. OCLC 1774183. S 9.10: .

TIAS contains the text of treaties and international agreements entered into by the United States and other countries. Each individually numbered volume contains the text of a single treaty or agreement. The series began with number 1501, 1946. Treaties originally published in TIAS are later bound and cumulated in UST, *United States Treaties and Other International Agreements* (entry 540).

539. Department of State. **Treaties and Other International Agreements of the United States of America, 1776-1949** compiled under the direction of Charles I. Bevans. 13v. GPO, 1968-76. LC 70-600742. JX236 1968 .A5. 341/.0264/73. OCLC 6940. S 9.12/2:2:v.1-13.

"Bevans" (after its compiler, Charles I. Bevans) contains the text of all U.S. treaties and international agreements entered into prior to the current *United States Treaties and Other International Agreements* series (entry 540). Volume 13 is a general index. This series supersedes earlier compilations by William M. Malloy, C. F. Redmond, Edward J. Trenwith, and Hunter Miller.

540. Department of State. **United States Treaties and Other International Agreements**. GPO, 1950- . Annual. LC sn86-47004. JX231.A34. 341.273. OCLC 1307767. S 9.12: .
UST contains the official text of treaties and other international agreements entered into by the United States beginning in 1950 (when treaties ceased to be published in the *Statutes at Large*) with TIAS 2010. It cumulates in bound volumes the slip treaties originally published in TIAS. UST arranges treaties chronologically, with country and subject indexes.

UNITED STATES COURTS

541. Administrative Office of the United States Courts. **United States Court Directory**. GPO, 19??- . Annual. LC 78-645528. KF8700.A19U55. 347/.73/1025. OCLC 4010539. Ju 10.17: .
Gives telephone numbers and addresses for U.S. Court judges, clerks, and staff, including those in district courts, tax court, courts of appeals, and supreme courts. Includes a directory for the Administrative Office of the U.S. Courts and the Federal Judicial Center, along with a name index.

542. Administrative Office of the United States Courts. **United States Courts: Selected Reports**. AO, 1993- . Annual. LC sn94-28450. OCLC 31091324. JU 10.1/2: .
These are proceedings of the annual Judicial Conference which surveys the condition of the U.S. courts and is attended by the Chief Justice of the United States, the chief judges and a district judge from each of the judicial circuits, and the chief judge of the Court of International Trade. Formerly titled *Reports of the Proceedings of the Judicial Conference of the United States and Annual Report to the Director of the Administrative Office of the U.S. Courts.*

543. Bureau of Justice Statistics. **Compendium of Federal Justice Statistics**. BJS, 1984- . Annual. LC 89-646324. HV9950.C65. 364.973/05. OCLC 20590663. J 29.20: .
Data for the national and federal districts describe the processing of felony and misdemeanor suspects from case screening and prosecution through adjudication, sentencing, and corrections. Includes a glossary.

544. Court of Appeals (Federal Circuit). **Cases Decided in United States Court of Appeals for the Federal Circuit: Customs Cases Adjudged in the Court of Appeals for the Federal Circuit**. GPO, 1983- . Annual. LC 86-642490. KF6655.A2U539. 343.7305/6/02643. OCLC 12924363. Ju 7.5/2: .
Includes a listing of judges and officers of the court; designation of judges to serve on the court; summary of action in appealed cases; court opinions; dismissals; cited statutes; and indexes to subjects, cases reported, cases cited, and appeals decisions. Coverage began in October 1982.

545. Department of Justice. **Department of Justice (DOJ) Telephone Directory**. GPO, 1993- . Irregular. Microform. LC sn94-27652. OCLC 29863250. J 1.89: .
Lists all departmental offices, with fax numbers and personnel and their telephone numbers. Staff are also listed alphabetically, with telephone number and location. Includes a list of U.S. Attorneys by state and district and an index.

546. Department of Justice. **Register of the U.S. Department of Justice and the Federal Courts**. GPO, 1978- . Irregular. LC 89-645459. KF8700.A19J85. 353.5/025. OCLC 4179076. J 1.7: .
This is a directory of principal officers of the Department of Justice, the Administrative Office of the United States Courts and Federal Judicial Center, and the federal courts. U.S. attorneys and marshals, and officers of federal corrections institutions, are also included.

Entries provide address, telephone number, office, date of appointment, and state. Includes a list of former Department of Justice officers and Supreme Court justices.

547. Federal Judicial Center. Federal Judicial History Office. **A Directory of Oral History Interviews Related to the Federal Courts** compiled and edited by Anthony Champagne, Cynthia Harrison, and Adam Land. FJC, 1992. 73p. LC 92-234223. KF352.D54 1992. 347.73/2. OCLC 26268789. Ju 13.14:H 62.

This is a directory of interviews with federal judges and others involved with federal litigation or the federal courts that are held in the collections of universities, presidential libraries, and historical societies. Includes name and position indexes. A related title is *Federal Court Records: A Select Catalog of National Archives Microfilm Publications* (nondepository, 1987).

548. Judicial Conference of the United States. Committee on the Bicentennial of the Constitution. **The United States Court of Appeals for the Federal Circuit: A History, 1982-1990**. JCUS, 1991. 369p. LC 91-601231. KF8751.U55 1991. 347.73/24/03. OCLC 24031894. Ju 7.2:H 62/2.

This history of the court's first eight years describes its origins, organization, and operations; provides a directory of judges (with photographs) and their staffs; discusses jurisdiction and highlighted cases; and contains appendixes listing judges' appointments, birth and death dates, lines of succession, court composition, and visiting judges.

UNITED STATES SUPREME COURT

549. Commission on the Bicentennial of the United States Constitution. **The Supreme Court of the United States: Its Beginnings & Its Justices, 1790-1991**. CBUSC, 1992. 300p. LC 92-10459. KF8744.S87 1992. 347.73/26/09. OCLC 25546099. Y 3.B 47/2:2 Su 7.

Biographical sketches and color portraits of all 106 Supreme Court justices are augmented by historical background, a succession table, and a bibliography.

550. Senate. Committee on the Judiciary. **Nomination of Judge Clarence Thomas to Be Associate Justice of the Supreme Court of the United States: Hearings Before the Committee on the Judiciary, United States Senate, First Session. . . .** (S.Hrg.102-1084). GPO, 1993. 4v. LC 93-200920. KF26.J8 1991n. 347.73/2634. OCLC 29600467. Y 4.J 89/2:S.Hrg.102-1084/Pt.1-4.

Contains the text of hearings to consider the Supreme Court nomination of Clarence Thomas, along with supplementary material appended to the record. Part 4 includes testimony by Anita Hill.

551. Supreme Court. **United States Reports. Cases Adjudged in the Supreme Court**. GPO, 1754- . LC 1-26074. OCLC 1768670. Ju 6.8: .

This final, bound cumulation of Supreme Court opinions lists justices on the bench and includes an index, a table of cases, a list of cases adjudged with dates of argument and decision and names of counsel, the opinion and the justice who delivered it, a list of orders on cases adjudged, and rules of civil and appellate procedure and bankruptcy rule. Updated by individually numbered slip opinions (Ju 6.8/b:), which are accumulated throughout the term in *Preliminary Prints* (Ju 6.8/a:). The daily *Journal - Supreme Court of the United States* (Ju 6.5:) summarizes Court proceedings. *Rules of the Supreme Court of the United States* (Ju 6.9:) lists rules and procedures governing the Court (also included in Title 28 of the *U.S. Code*). Supreme Court opinions since 1990 (with selected pre-1990 decisions) are available on the Internet *URL http://www.law.cornell.edu/supct/supct.table.html.*

Political Science

COMMUNISM

552. Department of State. International Information Administration. Documentary Studies Section. **Problems of Communism**. 41v. DS, 1952-1992. Bimonthly. LC 54-61675. HX1.P75. 335.43/05. OCLC 1762908. IA 1.8: .

These analyses and background discussions on world communism are now published commercially.

CONGRESS

General Works

553. Congress. **Congressional Record: Proceedings and Debates of the . . . Congress**. GPO, 1873- . Daily (when Congress is in session). LC 80-646573. KF35. 328.73/02. OCLC 2437919. X/a.

> Also available through THOMAS (entry 632), and online through GPO Access (entry 104). To subscribe through the Internet *URL telnet://wais.access. gpo.gov,* login as *newuser,* no password. Modem: Call (202) 512-1661, login as *wais,* no password, at the second login as *newuser,* no password.

This is a record of congressional debates and proceedings, messages to Congress, and voting records. Speeches and debates do not necessarily appear verbatim, however. Daily issues are cumulated annually into a permanent, bound, final edition for each session of Congress, creating differences in page numbering and indexing between the daily and bound editions. The daily editions contain four sections: H (House proceedings), S (Senate proceedings), E (Extensions of Remarks), and D (Daily Digest, a summary of daily activities). Pages in the bound volume are numbered in a single sequence. At session's end, the Daily Digest is issued as a separate part, with a subject index and a table of bills enacted into public law. There is a separate index to the permanent, bound *Congressional Record* which includes Daily Digest volumes. In the bound annual edition, Extensions of Remarks are integrated into the body of the text. Earlier titles of the *Congressional Record* were *Annals of Congress, Register of Debates,* and *Congressional Globe.*

Since 1983, the "bound" edition has been distributed in microfiche, except for the Index and Daily Digest volumes, which depositories can select in either paper or microfiche. The full text of the 1985 annual *Congressional Record*, its Index, and the Daily Digest was sent to depositories on CD-ROM. The *Congressional Record* is available through several commercial vendors.

554. Congress. **Congressional Record Index: Proceedings and Debates of the . . . Congress.** GPO, 1873- . Semimonthly. LC sn85-8544. OCLC 2428236. X/a.

Also available through THOMAS (entry 632), and online through GPO Access (entry 104). To subscribe through the Internet *URL telnet://wais.access. gpo.gov,* login as *newuser,* no password. Modem: Call (202) 512-1661, login as *wais,* no password, at the second login as *newuser,* no password.

CRI is a subject and name index providing biweekly access to the contents of the daily *Congressional Record,* plus a "History of Bills and Resolutions" with legislative histories of legislation acted upon during the previous two weeks. The "History of Bills and Resolutions" does not cumulate until the bound end-of-session editions. In the cumulated, bound, annual *Congressional Record Index,* page numbers are changed to reflect the single numbering sequence of the bound volumes.

555. Congress. DPC Vote Information Staff. **DPC Issue Book: Nominations, 97th Congress-102nd Congress (1981-1992).** v.1-. GPO, 1993. LC 93-215651. JK736.D64 1993. OCLC 28101001. Y 1.3:S.PRT.103-2/vol.

Senate actions on presidential nominations are listed by cabinet-level department/agency names, ambassadorships, or judgeships. Entries note nominee's name and position, vote number, Congress and session, date and time, committee action, floor vote, and summary of floor debate. Includes an index.

556. Congress. Joint Committee on Printing. **The Capitol: A Pictorial History of the Capitol and of the Congress.** (S.Doc.v 99-17). GPO, 1988. 9th ed. 192p. OCLC 18555601. (Serial Set 13612). Y 1.1/3:99-17.

This collection of facts and photos related to Congress and its support agencies includes a history of Congress, a list of people laid in state in the Rotunda, photos of the busts of vice presidents, a map of memorial and historic trees, biographical sketches, and a list of speakers of the House, Senate majority leaders, and architects of the Capitol through the 100th Congress.

557. House. **Calendars of the United States House of Representatives and History of Legislation.** GPO, 1???- . Weekly when House is in session. LC 52-63188. J47.A3. 328.73. OCLC 1768279. Y 1.2/2: .

Available on GPO Access (since the 104th Congress).

The House Calendars is a cumulative legislative history of bills reported from committee in both the House and Senate. Legislative histories are arranged by bill number in the "History of Bills and Resolutions" section; information is given about bills in and through conference; and the history of major bills is summarized. A cumulative subject index is included in each Monday issue (or the first issue for the week). The first-session final issue is a permanent reference until the second-session final issue, which cumulates for the two-year Congress.

557a. House. Committee on House Administration. **History of the United States House of Representatives, 1789-1994.** (H.Doc.103-324). GPO, 1994. 424p. KF4990.H577 1994. OCLC 32751780. Y 1.1/2:103-324.

A detailed narrative history arranged according to topics, this tome includes a bibliography and tables of data about Congress, the House of Representatives, and members of both.

558. House. Committee on Ways and Means. **Background Material and Data on Major Programs Within the Jurisdiction of the Committee on Ways and Means.** GPO, 1981- . Annual. LC 87-644619. HC110.P63B29. 338.973/005. OCLC 15390378. Y 4.W 36:10-4/ .

Also available on CD-ROM. Y 4.W 36: 10-7/ .

This report, better known as the *"Green Book,"* gives an overview of entitlement programs within the Ways and Means Committee's legislative jurisdiction, including Social Security, Medicare, trade adjustment assistance, unemployment compensation, Aid to Families with Dependent Children, child support enforcement, Supplemental Security Income, the Title XX social services block grants, child welfare, foster care, and adoption assistance. Each program is described, with data on population served, analysis of interactions with other programs, and historical background. Also known as Overview of Entitlement Programs.

559. House. Office of the Clerk. **Reports to Be Made to Congress: Communication from the Clerk, U.S. House of Representatives, Transmitting a List of Reports Which It Is the Duty of Any Officer or Department to Make to Congress, Pursuant to Rule III, Clause 2, of the Rules of the House of Representatives**. GPO, 19??- . Annual. LC sn87-43547. OCLC 6128042. Y 1.1/7:nos. vary.
This list of reports required from the legislative, judicial, and executive branches; cabinet-level departments; and independent agencies, boards, commissions, and federally chartered private corporations notes the nature of the report, authority, date due, and committee referral. Includes an index.

560. House. **Origins of the House of Representatives: A Documentary Record** (H.Doc. 101-118) edited by Bruce A. Ragsdale. GPO, 1990. 166p. LC 89-600406. JK1316. O75 1990. 328.73/072/09. OCLC 20935410. (Serial Set 13948). Y 1.1/7:101-118.
A compilation of James Madison's notes of debate in the Federal Convention of 1787, letters and essays, and documents illuminating the early years of the House of Representatives.

561. House. **Telephone Directory**. GPO, 19??- . Annual. LC sc79-2621. OCLC 2662044. Y 1.2/7: .
Also available on the House of Representatives Web Internet
URL *http://www.house.gov/*.
The directory lists House officers, representatives, committees, and staff, along with committee members and staff for each committee. It also lists House Commissions, member organizations, Senate officers and members, and staff organizations.

562. Library of Congress. **Jefferson's Legacy: A Brief History of the Library of Congress** by John Y. Cole. LC, 1993. 103p. LC 92-30311. Z733.U6C567 1993. 027.573. OCLC 26502795. LC 1.2:J 35/8.
This narrative history of LC is embellished with color photographs and includes a chronology of its collection growth, a description of the buildings, a bibliography, and biographies (most with portraits) of the Librarians of Congress.

563. Library of Congress. **To Make All Laws: The Congress of the United States, 1789-1989** by James H. Hutson. GPO, 1989. 120p. LC 89-600098. JK1061.H86 1989. 328.73. OCLC 19589767. LC 1.2:C 76/11.
This illustrated history of Congress and its activities chronicles events and personalities that have molded Congress.

564. National Archives and Records Administration. **Guide to the Records of the United States House of Representatives at the National Archives, 1789-1989** (H.Doc.100-245) by Charles E. Schamel et al. GPO, 1989. Bicentennial ed. 466p. LC 88-607954. CD3042.H68U55 1989. 016.32873/072. OCLC 18987156. (Serial Set 13886). Y 1.1/7:100-245.
Internet URL *http://gopher.nara.gov:70/1/inform/dc/legislat.*

This guide to unpublished House records through the 100th Congress describes general records and those of standing, select, and joint congressional committees. It includes a discussion of published congressional records and research tools. Supplemental information includes lists of speakers and minority leaders, congressional beginning and ending dates, published and unpublished finding aids for House records, National Archives microfilm publications of House records, a glossary of legislative and archival terms, and a selected bibliography. A companion volume describes records of the Senate (entry 565). The guide updates National Archives Preliminary Inventory 113, *Records of the House of Representatives, 1789-1946*, published in 1959 and still available to researchers.

565. National Archives and Records Administration. **Guide to the Records of the United States Senate at the National Archives, 1789-1989** (S.Doc.100-42) by Robert W. Coren et al. GPO, 1989. Bicentennial ed. 356p. LC 88-36037. CD3042. S46U54 1989. 328.73/071. OCLC 19130533. (Serial Set 13853). Y 1.1/3:100-42.

Internet *URL http://gopher.nara.gov:70/1/inform/dc/legislat*.

This guide to noncurrent permanent Senate records held in the National Archives in Record Groups 46 and 128 describes records of standing, select, special, and joint congressional committees; executive proceedings; and noncommittee records such as Senate journals, legislation, presidential messages and executive documents, communications transmitted to the Senate, original Senate reports and documents, tabled petitions and memorials, records of the Secretary of the Senate, campaign expenditure and lobbying reports, and unpublished records related to legislation (especially from the years 1901-1946). The guide does not cover Senate records not in the National Archives or senators' personal papers. It includes a discussion of published congressional records and research tools. Supplemental information includes lists of majority and minority leaders, Secretaries of the Senate, congressional beginning and ending dates, finding aids for Senate records, National Archives microfilm publications of Senate records, a glossary of legislative and archival terms, and a selected bibliography. A companion volume describes records of the House (entry 564). The guide updates National Archives Preliminary Inventory 23, a guide to Record Group 46, published in 1950 and still available to researchers.

566. Senate. **Historical Almanac of the United States Senate: A Series of "Bicentennial Minutes" Presented to the Senate During the One Hundredth Congress** (S.Doc.100-35) by Robert J. Dole. GPO, 1989. 312p. LC 89-600234. JK1158.D65 1989. 328.73/071/09. OCLC 20167571. (Serial Set 13850). Y 1.1/3:100-35.

This is a collection of "bicentennial minutes," historical vignettes delivered by Senator Bob Dole during the 100th Congress. The vignettes describe the Senate during its first two centuries, focusing on people, unusual customs, and memorable events.

567. Senate. **Journal of the Senate of the United States of America**. GPO, 1789- . Annual. LC 55-52001. KF45.A22. 328.73/01. OCLC 7913890. XJS: .

568. House. **Journal of the House of Representatives of the United States**. GPO, 1789- . Annual. LC 31-5736. KF46.A22. 328.73/01. OCLC 8632633. XJH: .

The official records of congressional proceedings are compiled in these annual legislative logs for each chamber. The House and Senate Journals provide minutes of daily sessions and a record of legislative action, including motions and votes, in a "History of Bills and Resolutions" section arranged by bill number, with name, title, and subject indexes. Text of floor debates is not included.

569.   Senate. **Public Documents of the First Fourteen Congresses, 1789-1817: Papers Relating to Early Congressional Documents** (S.Doc.428) by Adolphus W. Greely. GPO, 1900. 903p. LC 01-20895. Z1223.A 1900. OCLC 581556. (Serial Set 3879). [no SuDocs number].

      Supplement. (H.Doc.745). (Serial Set 4735). [no SuDocs number].

This attempt to compile a complete list of early congressional journals, documents, and reports resulted in a chronological list of publications with descriptive notes. The library locations of the originals were noted.

569a.   Senate. **Senators of the United States: A Historical Bibliography: A Compilation of Works By and About Members of the United States Senate, 1789-1995** (S.Doc.103-34) compiled by Jo Anne McCormick Quatannens. GPO, 1995. 356p. LC 95-41039. Z1249.C67. 016.973. OCLC 33209210. Y 1.1/3:103-34.

This selected bibliography of writing by and about the men and women who served in the Senate between 1789 and 1995 includes biographies, books, articles, and dissertations. It is a companion to *Guide to Research Collections of Former United States Senators, 1789-1995* (entry 581).

570.   Senate. Subcommittee on Oversight of Government Management. **Compilation of Federal Ethics Laws.** GPO, 1993. 107p. LC 93-233792. KF4568.A25 1993. OCLC 28046453. Y 4.G 74/9:S.PRT.103-25.

The text of laws related to federal employee ethics are compiled from Title 18 *U.S. Code*, the Ethics in Government Act of 1978, and other laws pertaining to procurement, gifts and travel, employment conflicts, and taxes.

571.   Senate. **The Senate 1789-1989** (S.Doc.100-20) by Robert C. Byrd. 4v. GPO, 1988- . Bicentennial ed. LC 88-24545. JK1158.B97.1988. 328.73/071/09. OCLC 18442225.

      Volume 1. **Addresses on the History of the United States Senate** edited by Mary Sharon Hall. Y 1.1/2:SERIAL 13723.

      Volume 2. **Addresses on the History of the United States Senate** edited by Wendy Wolff. Y 1.1/2:SERIAL 13724.

      This, "the most ambitious study of the United States Senate," was delivered on the Senate floor in a series of bicentennial addresses by Senator Robert Byrd between 1981 and 1987. It is a chronological history of the institution, with topics ranging from the Library of Congress to the Senate press gallery.

      Volume 3. **Classic Speeches 1830-1993** edited by Wendy Wolff. Y 1.1/2: SERIAL 13725.

      This anthology of classic speeches delivered since 1830 is supplemented by portraits of the speakers. It includes an alphabetical list of orators, with the popular name of the speech and the date given.

      Volume 4. **Historical Statistics, 1789-1992** edited by Wendy Wolff. Y 1.1/2: SERIAL 13726.

      Tables of data on hundreds of topics summarize facts about the Senate, senators since 1789, Senate employees, nominations received by the Senate, treaties defeated, and impeachments. Includes an index.

572.   Senate. **United States Senate Telephone Directory.** GPO, 1983- . Irregular. LC sn85-20994. JK1154.U55. OCLC 9629120. Y 1.3/10: .

This alphabetical list of U.S. Senators (with office and telephone numbers) features lists of Senate staff, task forces, and committee membership. A Senate leadership chart, an alphabetical list of representatives (without phone numbers), a directory of executive branch personnel, and a map of congressional buildings round out this book.

573. Superintendent of Documents. **Final Cumulative Finding Aid, House and Senate Bills**. GPO, 1979- . Biennial. Microfiche. OCLC 6346120. GP 3.28: .

Bills, resolutions, and joint and concurrent resolutions are listed numerically on this microfiche index, issued after each Congress.

Biographical Sources

574. Congress. **Biographical Directory of the United States Congress, 1774-1989: The Continental Congress, September 5, 1774, to October 21, 1788, and the Congress of the United States, from the First Through the One Hundredth Congresses, March 4, 1789, to January 3, 1989, Inclusive**. (S.Doc.100-34). GPO, 1989. Bicentennial ed. 2104p. LC 88-600335. JK1010.A5 1989. 973.3/12/0922. OCLC 18497652. (Serial Set 13849). Y 1.1/3:100-34.

This bicentennial edition, the first revision since 1971, provides biographies of senators, representatives, delegates to the Continental Congress, resident commissioners, and vice presidents through the 100th Congress (complete through June 30, 1988). Also included are lists of state congressional delegations and delegates from American Samoa, Puerto Rico, the District of Columbia, Guam, and the Virgin Islands. Entries include nicknames, offices held, states represented, kinship to other members, birthplace and birth date, education, military service, other political offices held and nonpolitical careers, party affiliation, dates of service, leadership positions and committee chairmanships, disciplinary actions, unsuccessful bids for reelection, retirement, place and date of death, burial site, and references to *Dictionary of American Biography* and other biographical essays. This directory has been published irregularly since its private publication in 1859 as the *Dictionary of Congress*, by Charles Lanman (later updated by Benjamin Perley Poore and published by the GPO). It was first issued under its current title in 1928.

575. Congress. Joint Committee on Printing. **Congressional Pictorial Directory**. GPO, 1967- . Biennial. LC sc79-2635. OCLC 1239852. Y 4.P 93/1:1 P/cong.

This pocket-sized directory features small black-and-white photographs of the president, vice president, House and Senate officers and members (arranged by state, with political affiliation and number of terms served), and chaplains and officials of the Capitol. Includes lists of senators and representatives for the 50 states; delegates for Guam, the Virgin Islands, American Samoa, and Washington, D.C.; the resident commissioner for Puerto Rico; a name-state index; and the number of Democrats and Republicans representing each state. Formerly titled *Congressional Picture Directory* and *Pocket Congressional Directory*.

576. Congress. **Official Congressional Directory**. GPO, 1887- . Biennial. LC 06-35330. JK1011. 328.73/073/025. OCLC 1239877. Y 4.P 93/1:1/cong.

Also available on GPO Access (entry 104).

Contains short biographies of members of the Senate and House of Representatives, arranged by states and districts, respectively. Additional data includes committee memberships, term of service, name of administrative assistant/secretary, room, telephone number, and zip code for each congressperson's district. The directory also lists officials of the federal courts, the military, and other federal departments and agencies including the District of Columbia government; state and territorial governors; foreign diplomats; and representatives of the media. A description of the Capitol building, its grounds and floor plans, is included, as are maps of congressional districts.

577. House. Commission on the Bicentenary of the U.S. House of Representatives. **Women in Congress, 1917-1990**. (H.Doc.101-238, 101/2). GPO, 1991. 266p. LC 91-600757. JK1013.W66 1991. 328.73/092/2. OCLC 23864788. Y 1.1/2:SERIAL 14004.
Presents biographical sketches and photographs of women serving in the House and Senate between 1917 and 1990. Each profile includes state, party, branch of Congress, and dates served.

578. House. Office for the Bicentennial of the House of Representatives. **A Guide to Research Collections of Former Members of the United States House of Representatives, 1789-1987** (H.Doc.100-171) editor-in-chief Cynthia Pease Miller. H, 1988. Bicentennial ed. 504p. LC 89-602291. CD3043.G84 1988. OCLC 19000791. (Serial Set 13874). Y 1.1/7:100-171.
This is a nationwide directory of repositories of manuscript collections, papers, and oral histories relating to former House representatives. Under each representative's name are given birth and death dates, state or territory represented, and repositories of histories. Also included are dates and size of the research collection, along with a brief description. The volume lists representatives for whom papers remain unlocated or privately held, addresses of repositories, documentary publication projects, and a chronological table of congressional sessions.

579. House. Office of the Historian. **Black Americans in Congress, 1870-1989** (H.Doc.101-117) by Bruce A. Ragsdale and Joel D. Treese. GPO, 1990. 164p. LC 89-600409. E185.96.R25 1990. 328.73/092/2. OCLC 20935421. (Serial Set 13947). Y 1.1/7:101-117.
Biographical essays about Black men and women serving in the House and Senate since 1870 include portraits and references for further reading.

580. Library of Congress. Manuscript Division. **Members of Congress: A Checklist of Their Papers in the Manuscript Division, Library of Congress** compiled by John J. McDonough. LC, 1980. Free: Office Systems Services, Printing and Processing Section, Washington, DC 20540-5446. 217p. LC 78-606102. Z1236.U613 1980. 016.32873/092/2. OCLC 4131493. LC 4.2:C 76/2.
This is a list of collections of personal papers of senators, representatives, and delegates to the Continental Congress held in LC's Manuscript Division. Entries feature members who served between 1774 and 1979 (the first Continental Congress to the 95th Congress), providing biographical sketches and descriptions of the papers. Appendixes list members by state and by Congress.

581. Senate. **Guide to Research Collections of Former United States Senators, 1789-1995: A Listing of Archival Repositories Housing the Papers of Former Senators, Related Collections, and Oral History Interviews** (S.Doc.103-35) compiled by Karen Dawley Paul. GPO, 1995. 743p. LC 95-41409. CD3043.P39 1995. 016.32873/092/2. OCLC 33132717. Y 1.1/3:103-35.
This is an inventory of locations and contents of collections relating to former senators housed in publicly accessible repositories in the U.S. The collections include personal papers, portraits, photos, oral histories, and memorabilia. Entries describe holdings and oral histories, dates of coverage, finding aids, and user restrictions. Includes a list of repositories and a state-by-state list of all former senators, noting party, dates of service, offices held, and birth and death dates.

Congressional Districts

582. Bureau of the Census. **Congressional District Atlas**. GPO, 1964- . Biennial. LC 84-643174. G1201.F7U45. 912/.13287307345. OCLC 1768235. C 3.62/5: .

The atlas provides maps of congressional district boundaries and listings for multi-congressional districts, covering the 50 states, District of Columbia, American Samoa, Guam, Puerto Rico, and the Virgin Islands. The maps show counties and their statistical equivalents, county subdivisions, incorporated and census designated places, and American Indian reservations.

General Accounting Office

583. General Accounting Office. History Program. **GAO History, 1921-1991** by Roger R. Trask. GAO, 1991. 168p. LC 92-186992. HJ9802.T73 1991. 353.0072/3/09. OCLC 24895874. GA 1.13:OP-3-HP.

This history describes the terms of the six Comptroller Generals since 1921, with organization charts, personnel statistics, and information about appropriations and reports.

584. General Accounting Office. Office of Information Management and Communications. **Abstracts of Reports and Testimony**. GAO, 19??- . Free: Box 6015, Gaithersburg, MD 20884-6015. Annual. LC 93-642738. Z7164.P9555A27. OCLC 28226532. GA 1.16/3-3: .

Abstracts of GAO "blue books" of reports and testimony are listed alphabetically by GAO division and report number. Entries include title, abstract, GAO report number, and publication date.

585. General Accounting Office. Office of Information Management and Communications. **Indexes for Abstracts of Reports and Testimony**. GAO, 19??- . Free: Box 6015, Gaithersburg, MD 20884-6015. Annual. LC 93-642737. Z7164.P9555I53. OCLC 28226441. GA 1.16/3-3:[year]/IND.

GAO reports and testimony are indexed by subject, category, title, and GAO witness, citing GAO report numbers.

586. General Accounting Office. Office of Public Affairs. **Reports and Testimony**. GAO, 1989- . Free: Box 6015, Gaithersburg, MD 20884-6015. Monthly. LC sn90-14043. OCLC 20707570. GA 1.16/3: .

> Also available on GPO Access (entry 104) and as ASCII full text files for a fee from *URL http://federal.bbs.gpo.gov:3001/*, type "new" for first-time user; select *Congressional Information - B/, GAO - #4/.*

This is a monthly subject list of GAO "blue cover" reports describing GAO audits, congressional testimony, and governmental oversight. Blue cover reports are indexed using the *GAO Thesaurus* (GA 1.2:T 34), and are annotated, noting GAO report number, length, date, and instructions for ordering free single copies. Cumulated in the annual index and abstract volumes described below.

587. General Accounting Office. **Status of Open Recommendations**. GPO, 19??- . Annual. LC 86-642638. JK404.U55a. 353.07/6. OCLC 13778046. GA 1.13/18: .

GAO recommendations not yet implemented are arranged by publication date. Some recommendations are closed because the agency won't act or because they are no longer valid.

Legislative Procedure

588. House. Committee on Standards of Official Conduct. **Ethics Manual for Members, Officers, and Employees of the U.S. House of Representatives**. GPO, 1992. 493p. LC 94-122278. KF4990.A359U55 1992. 172/.2/0973. OCLC 26251641. Y 4.St 2/3:Et 3/992.
Describes ethical standards, conduct, and rules related to: Accepting gifts, travel, entertainment, and favors; outside employment and income of members, employees, and spouses; financial disclosure; staff rights and duties; official allowances and franking; casework; campaign funds and practices; and involvement with organizations. Appendixes provide the text of selected rules and laws.

589. House. **Constitution, Jefferson's Manual, and Rules of the House of Representatives of the United States**. GPO, 19??- . Biennial. LC 79-641093. KF4992.U54. 328.73/05. OCLC 3163759. Y 1.1/7:nos. vary.
These House parliamentary rules, developed by Vice President Thomas Jefferson, are collectively known as the House Manual. The manual contains the texts of the Constitution and Jefferson's Manual, plus the rules of the House of Representatives annotated with notes on their history and interpretation. This fundamental guide to House parliamentary procedures is reissued for each two-year Congress. A related title is *Rules Adopted by Committees of the House of Representatives* (1993 edition is Y4.R 86/1-12:993-94), with rules for standing, select, and joint committees. Also available on GPO Access (entry 104) as "House Rules Manual."

590. Senate. Committee on Rules and Administration. **Authority and Rules of Senate Committees: A Compilation of the Authority of Senate Committees and Joint Committees, and Related Materials**. GPO, 1990- . Biennial. LC 95-647634. KF4986.A329U55. 328.73/07653/05. OCLC 29924479. Y 1.1/3: .
This text of legal authorizations for Senate and joint committees and their rules extends coverage as far back as 1989.

591. Senate. **Procedure and Guidelines for Impeachment Trials in the United States Senate: Prepared Pursuant to Senate Resolution 439, 99th Congress, 2d Session** (S.Doc.v 99-33) submitted by Senator Robert C. Byrd and Senator Robert Dole; by Floyd M. Riddick and Robert B. Dove. GPO, 1986. rev. ed. 101p. LC 86-603142. KF4958.A25 1986. 328.73/07453. OCLC 14479984. (Serial Set 13666). Y 1.1/3:99-33.
Senate rules of impeachment trial procedure and practice and precedents are described, with opening and closing events enumerated.

592. Senate. Select Committee on Ethics. **Interpretative Rulings of the Select Committee on Ethics**. GPO, 1993. 292p. LC 94-131861. KF4970.A25 1993. OCLC 28492323. Y 4.ET 3/4:S.PRT.103-35.
This text of interpretative rules issued for the years 1977-92 notes issue date, applicable Senate rule, question considered, and ruling. It also includes rules 34 and 43 of the *Standing Rules of the Senate*, known as the Senate Code of Official Conduct. A related title is *The Ethics CD-ROM* (Y 3.ET 3:16/), available from the GPO.

593. Senate. **Senate Manual Containing the Standing Rules, Orders, Laws, and Resolutions Affecting the Business of the United States Senate;. . . .** GPO, 18??- . Biennial. LC sn90-20245. OCLC 22093647. Y 1.1/3:nos. vary.
The Senate Manual contains standing rules, orders, laws, and resolutions; the Articles of Confederation; and the U.S. Constitution. Issued for each Congress, the manual also

contains Senate rules of conduct, lists of presidents pro tempore since the first Senate, presidential election electoral vote counts since 1789, and lists of senators and Supreme Court justices since 1789. A related title is *Standing Rules of the Senate* (1992 edition is Y 1.1/3:103-8).

DISARMAMENT

594. Arms Control and Disarmament Agency. **Documents on Disarmament**. GPO, 1959- . Irregular. LC sn85-19569. OCLC 1966148. AC 1.11/2: .
Documents on disarmament and arms control are arranged chronologically, augmented by chronological and topical title lists, a bibliography, and an index. Principal organizations, conferences, and experts are listed. Last issued in 1986, the 1987 volume is expected in 1996. Coverage goes back to 1945.

595. Arms Control and Disarmament Agency. Library-Technical Reference Center. **Current Articles of Interest. Cumulative Index**. ACDA, 1993- . Semiannual. LC sn94-20363. OCLC 30507813. AC 1.13/2-2:date-no.
This is an unannotated bibliography of articles from government and commercial journals on arms control and nonproliferation, arranged under general subjects.

IMMIGRATION

596. Department of State. Bureau for Refugee Programs. **World Refugee Report**. DS, 1985- . Annual. LC 88-645749. HV640.W65. 362.87/05. OCLC 14402442. S 1.1/7: .
Overseas refugee assistance is described for regions of the world and countries, with a statistical appendix.

597. Immigration and Naturalization Service. **Statistical Yearbook of the Immigration and Naturalization Service**. GPO, 1978- . Annual. LC 84-642496. JV6461.S8. 325.73. OCLC 7063193. J 21.2/10: .
Current and historical data on immigrants, refugees, asylees, nonimmigrant arrivals (tourists, students, etc.), naturalizations, and enforcement give a snapshot of legal and illegal aliens in the U.S. The title does not include emigration data. Includes a glossary.

598. National Institute of Mental Health. **An Annotated Bibliography on Refugee Mental Health** by Carolyn L. Williams. GPO, 1987. 335p. LC 87-601921. Z6665.6.W54 1987. OCLC 24065711. HE 20.8113:R 25.
This annotated bibliography covers the cultural backgrounds of various groups, research, policies, health and medical care, and assimilation, with information on the mental health of subgroups like children and victims of torture. Includes an author, subject, and ethnic group index and a bibliography.

599. Senate. Committee on the Judiciary. Subcommittee on Immigration and Refugee Affairs. **U.S. Immigration Law and Policy: 1952-1986: A Report Prepared for the Use of the Subcommittee on Immigration and Refugee Affairs, Committee on the Judiciary, United States Senate**. GPO, 1988. 138p. LC 88-601915. KF4805.5.U27 1988. 342.73/082. OCLC 17943290. Y 4.J 89/2:S.prt.100-100.
This is an overview and analysis of immigration issues since passage of the Immigration and Nationality Act of 1952, which includes discussion of legal aspects of refugees, illegal immigrants, and the Refugee Act and the Immigration Reform and Control Act of 1986. A related title is *U.S. Immigration Laws: General Information* (J 21.5/2:Im 6/989).

INTERNATIONAL RELATIONS

General Works

600. Department of State. Bureau of Public Affairs. **US Department of State Dispatch.** GPO, 1990- . Weekly. LC 90-660311. JX232.U83. 327.73. OCLC 22105966. S 1.3/5: .
This is the official compilation of State Department speeches, congressional testimony, policy statements, fact sheets, and other foreign policy information. *Dispatch* is indexed every six months. Available on *U.S. Foreign Affairs on CD-ROM* (entry 605) and online through CIDS, the State Department's electronic bulletin board, and through commercial vendors. *Dispatch* succeeded *Department of State Bulletin*, which ceased in 1989.

601. Department of State. Center for the Study of Foreign Affairs. **U.S.-Soviet Summitry: Roosevelt Through Carter** edited by John W. McDonald, Jr. GPO, 1987. 158p. LC 87-619871. E183.8.S65U74 1987. 327.73047. OCLC 18716434. S 1.114/3:So 8/2.
Consists of summaries of summit meetings for World War II, the Eisenhower years, Kennedy's meetings with Khrushchev, Glassboro, the Johnson summit, Nixon, Ford at Vladivostok and Helsinki, and the Carter summit.

602. Department of State. **Foreign Relations of the United States.** GPO, 1932- . Annual. LC 10-3793. JX233.A3. 327.73. OCLC 7809779. S 1.1: .
FRUS, the official record of U.S. foreign policy and diplomacy, is the most comprehensive and current publication of diplomatic papers in the world. This monumental series includes "all documents needed to give a comprehensive record of the major foreign policy decisions within the range of the Department of State's responsibilities, together with appropriate materials concerning the facts which contributed to the formulation of the policies." Included are diplomatic notes and communications, memoranda, and telegrams. Declassification requires at least a 25-year time lag before publication. Each volume covers only certain countries within a particular year, with documents arranged chronologically under each country. For a list of in-print volumes see SB 210. A general index covering the years 1861-99 was published in 1902, and one covering the years 1900-18 was published in 1940. Continues *Papers Relating to Foreign Affairs* (1861-69), *Papers Relating to the Foreign Relations of the United States* (1870-1931), *A Decade of American Foreign Policy: Basic Documents, 1941-49* (S 1.69:415), and *American Foreign Policy, 1950-1955, Basic Documents* (S 1.71:117). A related title is *Diplomatic Records: A Select Catalog of National Archives Microfilm Publications* (nondepository, 1984).

603. Department of State. Office of the Historian. **American Foreign Policy: Current Documents.** GPO, 1981- . Annual. LC 85-641230. JX1417.A33. 327.73. OCLC 11577599. S 1.71/2: .
 American Foreign Policy: Foreign Affairs Press Briefings and Treaties. Supplement. Annual. Microform. LC 91-660975. OCLC 22488099. S 1.71/2-2: .
Unlike *Foreign Relations of the United States* (entry 602), which requires a 25-year time lag before publication, *American Foreign Policy: Current Documents* contains contemporary foreign policy materials, indexed and arranged by subject and geography. Included are foreign policy messages, addresses, statements, interviews, press conference transcripts, and presidential and executive branch congressional testimony. It has been published under several titles since 1950. Suspended after the 1967 volume, it resumed

publication in 1981. The annual microfiche supplement provides the only published full text of State Department Daily Press Briefings, State Department and White House special press briefings, and treaties, conventions, and protocols subject to ratification. Extracts of some were published previously in *American Foreign Policy: Current Documents*.

604. Department of State. Office of the Historian. **Foreign Travels of the Secretaries of State, 1866-1990** by Evan M. Duncan. DS, 1990. 187p. LC 91-600275. E183.7.D79 1990. 327.73/0092/2. OCLC 25876574. S 1.2:Se 2/9.

This list of all official and nonofficial foreign visits (except to U.S. territories) covers from William Henry Steward to James Baker. Trips are listed chronologically by secretary of state and by host country, noting dates and highlights.

605. Department of State. **U.S. Foreign Affairs on CD-ROM [computer file]: USFAC**. GPO, 1993- . Quarterly. CD-ROM. LC 94-660673. JX232. 351. OCLC 29818158. S 1.142/2: .

Contains the full text of presidential, secretary of state, and senior administrators' official speeches, statements, testimony, briefings, and policy overviews since 1990. Includes the full text of Daily Press Briefing Transcripts, country *Background Notes* (entry 395), *Dispatch* (entry 600), *Key Officers of Foreign Service Posts* (entry 196), current issue briefs, and titles from the *Tips for Travelers* series.

606. House. Committee on Foreign Affairs. **Required Reports to Congress on Foreign Policy**. GPO, 1988. 402p. LC 88-602430. JX1706.A4 1988a. 353.0089. OCLC 18436559. Y 4.F 76/1:C 76/20.

Reports that the executive branch must submit to Congress are listed by law number, with summary, citation, submitting source and recipient, frequency, date received, and status. Includes a bibliography.

607. Library of Congress. Manuscript Division. **W. Averell Harriman: A Register of His Papers in the Library of Congress**. LC, 1991. 154p. LC 91-24696. Z6616.H26L53 1991. 018. OCLC 24066591. LC 4.10:62.

This register of Averell Harriman materials in LC's Manuscript Division includes a biographical chronology, scope note and description, and a container list of file folders in each box.

Dictionaries

608. Department of State. Library. **Dictionary of International Relations Terms**. GPO, 1987. 2d rev. 115p. LC 87-600829. JX1226.D49 1987. 327/.014. OCLC 15160631. S 1.2:In 8/30/987.

Terms, phrases, acronyms, catchwords, and abbreviations used in conducting foreign affairs are defined, with documentation for some terms.

609. Library of Congress. African and Middle Eastern Division. **Diplomatic Hebrew: A Glossary of Current Terminology** compiled by Lawrence Marwick. LC, 1980. Free to U.S. Libraries and Institutions: Office Systems Services, Printing and Processing Section, Washington, DC 20540-5446. 188p. LC 79-12383. JX1226.M3. 327/.2/03. OCLC 4857847. LC 41.2:H 35.

A glossary of Hebrew-English vocabulary, with an acronyms list and a bilingual listing of international associations, bureaus, institutes, councils, and treaties.

Directories

610. Army. Directorate of Foreign Liaison. Office of the Deputy Chief of Staff for Intelligence. **Directory of Foreign Military Attaches**. A, 1989. 174 leaves. OCLC 19560486. D 101.120:F 76.
Biographical sketches of military attachés accredited to the Department of the Army in foreign countries, for senior officers of the Office of the Deputy Chief of Staff for Intelligence, and for the Directorate of Foreign Liaison provide title, service, rank and date of rank, date of accreditation, office address and telephone number, home address and telephone number, family, and interests and hobbies. Photographs of most attachés and some spouses are included.

611. Central Intelligence Agency. Directorate of Intelligence. **Chiefs of State and Cabinet Members of Foreign Governments**. Document Expediting (DOCEX) Project, Exchange and Gift Division, Library of Congress, 19??- . Bimonthly. LC 78-645126. JF37.U5. 351.003/13/05. OCLC 4124278. PREX 3.11/2: .
Country listings give position title and officeholder's name. The country's head of the central bank and ambassadors to the United States are also listed. Indexed by personal name.

612. Department of State. Center for the Study of Foreign Affairs. **America's Diplomats and Consuls of 1776-1865: A Geographic and Biographic Directory of the Foreign Service from the Declaration of Independence to the End of the Civil War** by Walter B. Smith II. GPO, 1986. 365p. LC 86-600515. E302.5.S62 1986. 353.008/92/0922. OCLC 16648189. S 1.114/3:D 62/2/776-865.
Diplomatic and consular commissioned officers, U.S. citizen noncommissioned staff, appointees who failed to reach their posts or died abroad, and foreigners in the U.S. service are listed by geographic location and name. Includes name and place indexes.

613. Department of State. **Diplomatic List**. GPO, 1893?- . Quarterly. LC 10-16292. JX1705.A22. 353. OCLC 1768336. S 1.8: .
This is a directory of diplomatic staffs stationed in the United States. Information includes Washington, D.C. address and telephone number, along with the names of relatives living in Washington. Ambassadors are listed by order of precedence with their credentials presentation date. Included is the dean of the diplomatic corps for each country. Featured is a special list of countries with temporary chancery addresses. National holidays are also listed for each country. A related title is *Guidance for Law Enforcement Officers: Personal Rights and Immunities of Foreign Diplomatic and Consular Personnel* (S 1.2:G 94).

614. Department of State. **Foreign Consular Offices in the United States**. GPO, 1932- . Semiannual. LC 32-26478. JX1705.A28. 351/.892. OCLC 1241455. S 1.69/2: .
This is the complete, official listing of the foreign consular offices and their officers working in the United States, including officer rank, address, telephone number, and date of recognition.

615. Department of State. Office of the Historian. **Principal Officers of the Department of State and United States Chiefs of Mission, 1778-1990**. GPO, 1991. 219p. OCLC 23251219. S 1.2:Of 2/778-990.
Lists the secretary of state, under secretaries, ambassadors at large, and other principal Department of State officers since 1778. Information on the terms of service of heads of U.S. foreign assistance agencies, the U.S. Information Agency, and Arms Control and Disarmament Agency, along with those of U.S. trade representatives, is given. Includes a country list of chiefs of mission at foreign embassies and chanceries.

616. Department of State. **Telephone Directory**. GPO, 1980- . Irregular. OCLC 6411112. S 1.21: .

The directory includes Department of State and Arms Control and Disarmament Agency personnel, with an organizational directory for the Department of State, Arms Control and Disarmament Agency, Agency for International Development, Overseas Private Investment Corporation, Trade and Development Agency, and the United States Information Agency.

Texts

617. Congress. House. Committee on Foreign Affairs [and] Senate. Committee on Foreign Relations. **Legislation on Foreign Relations Through [year]**. GPO, 1977- . Vols.1-4, Annual; vol. 5, irregular. LC 83-640253. KF4650.A29F67. 342.73/0412. OCLC 3700343. Y 4.F 76/2-10:yr./vol.

This congressional committee print is a compilation of full and partial texts of foreign relations legislation, Executive Orders, and State Department delegations of authority. It includes a subject index and appendixes listing foreign relations legislation by Public Law number, short title, and popular name. Volumes 1-4 are republished with amendments and additions after each session of Congress. Volume 5, containing text of treaties and international agreements, along with a subject index, is revised only as necessary.

618. Court of Appeals for the District of Columbia Circuit. **Final Report of the Independent Counsel for Iran/Contra Matters** by Lawrence E. Walsh, Independent Counsel. 3v. GPO, 1993. LC 94-126170. KF221.P6W35 1993. 345.73/02. OCLC 29664682. Ju 2.2:IR 5/v.1-3.

Also available on the *Federal Bulletin Board* (entry 35).

This legal and factual compendium includes background on the investigation, legal details, and supporting documents, with charts, tables, photographs, and an index.

619. Department of State. Office of the Historian. **Documents on Germany 1944-1985**. DS, 1985. 4th ed., rev. 1421p. LC 86-600826. E183.8.G3D62 1985. 327.73043. OCLC 13526453. S 1.2:G 31/5/944-85.

This official documentary volume contains the text of agreements, exchanges, statements, speeches, and other public papers representing U.S. foreign policy related to Germany since World War II, arranged chronologically.

620. House. Committee on Foreign Affairs. **Selected Executive Session Hearings of the Committee**. GPO, 1950- . Irregular. LC 86-640435. KF27.F6 1943. OCLC 13166566. Y 4.In 8/16:H 62/v.1-8; Y 4.F 76/1:H 62/v.9-18.

The Historical Series comprises previously unpublished executive session transcripts since 1943 on key policy issues.

621. House. Committee on Foreign Affairs. Subcommittee on Arms Control, International Security, and Science. **The Persian Gulf Crisis: Relevant Documents, Correspondence, Reports: Report**. GPO, 1991. 259p. LC 91-601655. JX1428.P38P47 1991. OCLC 24018150. Y 4.F 76/1:P 43/16.

Presents the full text of laws, reports, presidential statements, correspondence, and United Nations Security Council Resolutions from August 2, 1990 to March 7, 1991, with a chronology of events.

622. House. Committee on Foreign Affairs. Subcommittee on International Security, International Organizations, and Human Rights. **The War Powers Resolution: Relevant Documents, Reports, Correspondence.** GPO, 1994. May 1994 ed. 267p. LC 94-190867. KF5060.A25 1994. OCLC 30740591. Y 4.F 76/1:W 19/10/994.

The texts of documents, correspondence, and reports submitted to Congress by the president in compliance with the War Powers Resolution of 1973, requiring the president to consult Congress before introducing U.S. armed forces into hostile actions, is provided. Documents included relate to actions in Southeast Asia, Iran, El Salvador, the Sinai, Lebanon, Chad, and Grenada.

623. President's Special Review Board. **Report of the President's Special Review Board.** GPO, 1987. 1v. LC 87-601049. E876.U55 1987. 353.0089. OCLC 15243889. PR 40.8:Sp 3/R 29.

The Tower Commission report analyzed the impact of the National Security Council on foreign and national policy, including the sale of weapons to Iran. Appendixes contain excerpts of witness testimony. Related congressional hearings are compiled in *Report of the Congressional Committees Investigating the Iran-Contra Affair: With Supplemental, Minority, and Additional Views* (Y 1.1/5:100-216 and Y 1.1/8:100-433).

624. Senate. Committee on Foreign Relations. **Executive Sessions of the Senate Foreign Relations Committee.** GPO, 1948- . Irregular. LC 88-652164. KF25.8.F6E9. 327.73. OCLC 3512291. Y 4.F 76/2:EX 3/2/vol.

The Historical Series includes selected, previously unpublished transcripts of Senate Foreign Relations Committee hearings and meetings since 1947, along with minutes for less important executive sessions. The volumes are supplemented by letters, a publications list (for 1965), and a list of volumes in the series.

UNITED STATES GOVERNMENT

General Works

625. Bureau of the Census. **Census of Governments.** C 3.145/ : .

The 1987 *Census of Governments* depicts the organization, taxable property values, public employment, and finances of state and local governments. Volumes in the 1987 census are: *Preliminary Report, Number 1. Governmental Units in 1987* (number of governments by type); *Volume 1. Government Organization* (data on governmental units, public school systems, and elected officials); *Volume 2. Taxable Property Values* (real estate parcels and assessed values); *Volume 3. Public Employment* (employment, payrolls, unions, and benefits); *Volume 4. Government Finances* (governmental units, school systems, and retirement systems); *Volume 5. Topical Studies* (historical financial and employment statistics, state payments to local governments, statistics for Puerto Rico, and graphic summary for all reports in the series); *Volume 6. Guide to the 1987 Census of Governments* (a compilation of sample tables).

626. Bureau of the Census. **Census of Governments, Graphic Summary.** C 3.145/4: .

Charts, graphs, and maps depict historical and current national, state, and local statistics about government organization, elected officials, taxable property values, public employment and retirement systems, and government financing, with references to the source documents.

627. Bureau of the Census. **Guide to the [year] Census of Governments**. GPO, 1957- . Quinquennial. C 3.145/4: .

A compilation of sample tables from the five other volumes in the *Census of Governments*.

628. Congress. Joint Committee on Printing. **Our American Government** (H.Doc.102-192) edited by Ann B. Chambers. GPO, 1993. 1993 ed. 124p. LC 93-242853. JK38.O97 1993. 320.473. OCLC 28308652. [Serial Set number not available]. Y 1.1/7:102-192.

This introduction to the legislative, executive, and judicial branches of government; the electoral process; and political parties appears in question-and-answer format. It includes a glossary, bibliography, texts of the Declaration of Independence and Constitution, state population and House apportionment, and House and Senate political divisions.

629. Congress. Office of Technology Assessment. **Informing the Nation: Federal Information Dissemination in an Electronic Age**. GPO, 1988. 333p. LC 88-600567. Z286.E43I55 1988. 070.5/0285. OCLC 18595428. Y 3.T 22/2:2 In 3/9.

OTA's analysis of the nation's information collection, processing, and dissemination provides an overview of the implications of electronic technology for the GPO, the Superintendent of Documents, NTIS, and depository libraries. The report discusses equity of access and government and private-sector information dissemination roles. A summary of the report (Y 3.T 22/2:2 In 3/9/sum) is free from Congressional and Public Affairs Office, Office of Technology Assessment, U.S. Congress, Washington, DC 20510-8025.

630. General Accounting Office. **Decisions of the Comptroller General of the United States**. GPO, 1922- . Annual. LC sn89-26460. OCLC 9594189. GA 1.5: .

This is the full text of selected decisions (about 10 percent of the annual total) rendered to department and establishment heads and disbursing and certifying officers, plus decisions on the validity of awarded contracts. The annual compilation is a consolidation of the Advance Sheets (GA 1.5/2:vol./Adv.Shs.) and, formerly, of monthly pamphlets of the same name (GA 1.5/A:71/P. nos.; with the number range representing the paging in that issue). Page numbers in the monthly issues were identical to those in the permanent bound volume. Coverage began in 1921. The annual bound volume (and the former monthly issues) include citation tables and a cumulative index digest, *Index Digest of the Published Decisions of the Comptroller General of the United States*. The Index Digests, published since 1984, were discontinued with volume 71, September 1992 (GA 1.5/3:981-86). Decisions are cited as 70 Comp. Gen. 4 (1990), which means volume 70, page 4, publication date. Unpublished decisions are cited as B-239800, September 28, 1990, which means file number and date.

631. House. Committee on Government Operations. **Profiles of Existing Government Corporations: A Study**. GPO, 1989. 301p. LC 89-601371. HD3885.P75 1989. 353.09/2. OCLC 19079700. Y 4.G 74/7:P 94/19.

Describes government corporations such as Amtrak, the Federal Deposit Insurance Corporation, and the Tennessee Valley Authority, giving legal authority and status, creation date, legislated termination date, agency status, board of directors, advisory board members, parent agency, budget, treasury status, reporting status, litigation status, and finances.

632. Library of Congress. **THOMAS.** Internet *URL http://thomas.loc.gov/*.

Named after Thomas Jefferson, LC's World Wide Web server is a single gateway to congressional information. It includes the full text of bills since the 103rd Congress (1993-94), the *Congressional Record* and its index, legislation in the news, *How Our Laws Are Made* (Y 1.1/7:101-139); the Senate, House, and C-Span Gophers; and congressional E-mail addresses.

633. National Performance Review. **From Red Tape to Results: Creating a Government That Works Better & Costs Less: Report.** GPO, 1993. 168p. LC 93-211405. JK469 1993b. 353.07/5. OCLC 28768502. PRVP 42.2:G 74.
Also available on the *Federal Bulletin Board* (entry 35).

Better known as Report of the National Performance Review, this work discusses the federal budget, personnel, procurement, financial management, accountability, and management systems, with emphasis on reducing waste and red tape. An executive summary, *Creating a Government That Works Better and Costs Less*, is also available (PrVp 42.2:G 74/Exec.Sum.).

634. Senate. Committee on Post Office and Civil Service. **United States Government Policy and Supporting Positions.** GPO, 1960- . Quadrennial. LC 89-643528. JK661.U55. OCLC 7111837. Y 4.G 74/9: .

Published after each presidential election, the "Plum Book" lists federal legislative and executive branch civil service positions subject to noncompetitive appointments. Brief position descriptions are arranged by federal departments and note location; title; incumbent; pay plan; appointment type, level, grade, or pay; tenure; and expiration date. Includes tables of federal salary schedules. Issued alternately by the House Committee on Post Office and Civil Service and by the Senate Committee on Governmental Affairs. [Note: *The Prune Book: The 100 Toughest Management and Policy-Making Jobs in Washington* is commercially published.]

Armed Forces

General Works

635. Army. Center of Military History. **Integration of the Armed Forces, 1940-1965** by Morris J. MacGregor, Jr. GPO, 1981. 647p. LC 80-607077. UB418.A47M33. 355.5/3. OCLC 7501802. D 114.2:In 8/940-65.

This narrative history of Black American military participation since World War II includes photographs and an index.

636. Defense Logistics Agency. **DLAPS [computer file]: Defense Logistics Agency Publishing System: Regulations, Manuals, and Handbooks.** GPO, 19??- . Quarterly. CD-ROM. LC 94-660797. U168. 355. OCLC 28089991. D 7.41: .

DLAPS is a compilation of DLA (and some Department of Defense) internal and administrative manuals, handbooks, regulations, directives, and instructions, with publication number and date. It includes a list of publications added, revised, or deleted since the last CD-ROM issue.

637. Defense Technical Information Center. **How to Get It: A Guide to Defense-Related Information Resources.** DTIC, 1992. 532p. LC 93-124043. Z1361.D4H68 1992. 616.355/00973. OCLC 26936553. D 7.15/2:92/5.

This is a list of government-sponsored technical documents and information sources, maps, patents, standards and specifications, numerical titles, and other resources of interest to the defense community. Entries provide ordering information and price, distribution restrictions, source of indexing, and notes. Includes a glossary and a bibliography of government information sources.

638. Department of Defense. Directorate for Information Operations and Reports. **Military Manpower Statistics.** GPO, 1979- . Quarterly. LC 83-646818. UB23.M5. 355.2/2/0973. OCLC 7952852. D 1.61: .

Tables of data on active duty, civilian, reserve, and retired personnel provide a snapshot of DoD manpower and turnover. Data for officers, enlisted military, and cadets and midshipmen show percentages of personnel and personnel grades in military branches, reenlistments, and women. Excluded are full-time personnel paid as reserves. Data are issued annually in *Selected Manpower Statistics* (D 1.61/4:). Related titles are *Official Guard and Reserve Manpower Strengths and Statistics* (D 1.61/7:), *Health Manpower Statistics* (D 1.61/2:), and *Civilian Manpower Statistics* (D 1.62/2:).

639. Department of Defense. Directorate for Information Operations and Reports. **Prime Contract Awards**. GPO, 1980- . Semiannual. LC sn89-23382. 355. OCLC 7261843. D 1.57/3: .

The net value of DoD prime military weapon and equipment, service, and construction contracts of more than $25,000 for the year are summarized in charts and tables, with narrative commentary. Retrospective data go back a decade. Includes a glossary. Related titles are *100 Companies Receiving the Largest Dollar Volume of Prime Contract Awards* (D 1.57:), *500 Contractors Receiving the Largest Dollar Volume of Prime Contract Awards for Research, Development, Test, and Evaluation, [fiscal year]* (D 1.57/2:), and *Prime Contract Awards by State* (D 1.57/6:).

640. Department of Defense. Office of the Deputy Assistant Secretary of Defense for Civilian Personnel Policy/Equal Opportunity. **Black Americans in Defense of Our Nation**. GPO, 1991. 300p. LC 91-601250. UB418.A47B54 1991. 355/.0089/96073. OCLC 24145850. D 1.2:B 56/991.

This is a "pictorial documentary" of the military role of Black American men and women in peace and war since colonial times. It includes a brief statistical profile; pictures of many generals, flag officers, and recipients of medals of honor; and a roster of Black graduates of military service academies.

641. Department of Defense. Office of the Deputy Assistant Secretary of Defense for Military Manpower and Personnel Policy. **Hispanics in America's Defense**. GPO, 1990. 237p. LC 90-600757. UB418.H57H57 1990. 355/.0089/68073. OCLC 21889022. D 1.2:H 62/2/989.

This history of Hispanic military contributions since the Hispanic exploration of North America (1492-1541) includes photographs of civilian employees in the DoD senior executive service; biographies of generals and flag officers; a list of recipients of medals of honor; and a roster of Hispanic graduates of military service academies, 1966-89.

642. Department of Defense. Office of the Secretary of Defense. **Military Women in the Department of Defense**. DD, 1983- . Annual. LC 88-640585. UB418.W65M53. 355/.0088/042. OCLC 14556859. D 1.90: .

This chartbook on the status of officers and enlisted women in the military, including the Coast Guard, summarizes percentage of total strength, grade and years of service, military occupation group, civilian education, retention and reenlistments, and time in service at promotion.

643. Department of Defense. Washington Headquarters Services. Directorate for Information Operations and Reports. **Atlas/Data Abstract for the United States and Selected Areas**. GPO, 1986- . Annual. LC 88-646330. UC267.D46. OCLC 15788265. D 1.58/4: .

Maps show military installations and plants in states, major cities, and countries. Tables show active duty, reserve, and civilian personnel; payroll; and prime contracts exceeding $25,000, for the nation, states, and outlying areas.

644. Department of Veterans Affairs. Office of Administration. **Publications Catalog, LOG 1.** VA Forms and Publications Depot, 1990- . Annual. LC sn91-23425. OCLC 23761475. VA 1.20/4:1-P/yr.

LOG 1 is a numerical list of publications in series stocked in the Department of Veterans Affairs Forms and Publications Depot, with availability information. The list includes books, bulletins (by number), maps, operating manuals, posters, regulations, and VA specifications, with VA stock numbers. Includes a stock number index. A related title, *VA Catalog of Recurring Publications Code Numbers* (VA 1.20/4:2/yr.) lists publication series with short title and recurring publication code number (RPC).

645. Department of Veterans Affairs. Publications Service. **Department of Veterans Affairs Publications Index.** DVA, 1989- . Annual. LC 89-657085. Z1223.V42a. OCLC 19387997. VA 1.20: .

This numerical list of VA directives includes a rescinded directives listing. Also includes a subject index.

646. Joint Chiefs of Staff. **Department of Defense Dictionary of Military and Associated Terms.** GPO, 1972- . Irregular. LC 90-657655. U24.U55. 355/.0014. OCLC 4381101. D 5.12: .

Also available from the GPO on CD-ROM D 5.12/3: .

This guide to DoD terminology defines unclassified military terms inadequately covered in standard dictionaries. Entries include a code indicating the agencies using them. Weapons terms are for modern weapons only. A related source, *Glossary: Defense Acquisition Acronyms & Terms* (D 1.2:G 51/2/991), contains terms used in weapons acquisition.

647. Joint Chiefs of Staff. **Joint Electronic Library [computer file]: Approved Joint Publications, Selected Service Publications, Research Papers.** GPO, 1993- . Annual. CD-ROM. LC sn94-20541. UA23.7.J65. OCLC 30854857. D 5.21: .

JEL CD-ROM contains unclassified text and images including Army, Marine, and Air Force publications, Joint Publications, Selected Service Publications, memoranda of policy, terminology, the U.S. Marine Corps supplement to the *DoD Dictionary* (entry 646), and military indexes, papers, articles, and research papers.

648. Secretary of Defense. Historical Office. **The Secretaries of Defense: A Brief History, 1947-1985** by Roger R. Trask. SD, 1985. 75p. LC 85-602288. UA23.6.T73 1985. 353.6/09. OCLC 13360260. D 1.2:H 62/4/947-85.

Biographies and black-and-white photographs of defense secretaries describe tenure, accomplishments, philosophy, management style, and policies. Includes a list of U.S. presidents served under and Department of Defense organizational charts for the years 1948-84.

649. Smithsonian Institution. **United States Women in Aviation, 1940-1985** by Deborah G. Douglas. SI Press, 1991. 142p. LC 89-600095. TL521.D68 1990. 629.13/0082. OCLC 19589756. SI 1.42:7.

This history of women in aviation since World War II describes pilots, flight engineers, aircraft industry workers, and flight attendants. Includes an index, a glossary, and references.

Air Force

650. Air Force. **Numerical Index of Standard and Recurring Air Force Publications.** AF, 19??- . Semiannual. LC sn87-33160. OCLC 15621362. D 301.6:0-2/ .
This numerical list of periodicals, AV materials, regulations (AFRs), manuals (AFMs), and pamphlets (AFPs) provides title, date, issuing agency, number of pages, and distribution information.

651. Air Force. Office of Air Force History. **Publications.** AF, 1989. 36p. OCLC 19038518. D 301.62/2:P 96/989.
This bibliography of current, forthcoming, and out-of-print titles from the Office of Air Force History and the USAF Naval Research Center includes histories, special studies, reference titles, proceedings of symposia, and titles in the Southeast Asia Monograph Series. Includes an order form and title index.

652. Air Force. Office of Air Force History. **The United States Air Force: Basic Documents on Roles and Missions** compiled and edited by Richard I. Wolf. AF, 1988. 455p. LC 88-19530. UG633.U625 1987. 358.4/00973. OCLC 18134600. D 301.82/6:D 65.
This compilation of the text of official documents that have defined the Air Force since World War II includes an index and bibliography.

Army

653. Army. Center of Military History. **Aviation** compiled by Wayne M. Dzwonchyk. GPO, 1986. 155p. LC 85-600241. UG633.D98 1986. 358.4/00973. OCLC 12665063. D 114.11:Av 5.
Lineages and honors information for Army aviation units provide campaign participation credit, decorations, and unit bibliographies; heraldic data include descriptions of shoulder insignia, badge, and flag device.

654. Army. **Consolidated Index of Army Publications and Blank Forms [computer file].** Army Publications and Printing Command, 19??- . Annual. CD-ROM. LC sn93-27763. OCLC 28096005. D 101.22:25-30.
Also known as DA PAM 25-30, this lists all Army publications and forms, including current and obsolete titles; those that are new, revised, changed, rescinded, or superseded; and those rescinded from active Army use but still used by the National Guard, Army Reserves, or foreign military sales (known as P-88 publications). It includes subject, National Stock Number (NSN), and Line Item Number (LIN) indexes, along with all of the data in the full microfiche edition.

655. Army. Research Institute for the Behavioral and Social Sciences. **List of U.S. Army Research Institute Research and Technical Publications: October 1, 1990, to September 30, 1991 with Author and Subject Index.** ARI, 1992. 80p. OCLC 26016041. D 101.56:R 31/990-91.
This annotated list of reports from the Army's agency for behavioral and social science research includes research notes (final reports filed with the Defense Technical Information Center but not printed), handbooks and manuals, and research and technical reports. Entries include DTIC accession numbers. This volume supplements earlier Army Research Institute lists covering periods from 1 to 44 years.

Marines

656. Marine Corps. **Catalog of Publications**. MC, 1990- . Quarterly. LC sn91-23591. OCLC 22760897. D 214.28: .
An unannotated bibliography of nontechnical publications used by the Marine Corps, including directives, books, manuals, and training visual aids, arranged by topic. Appendixes include lists of publication symbols and control number prefixes. A related title is *Marine Corps Historical Publications Catalog: Available Publications List and Chronological Bibliography* (D 214.13:P 96/988).

Navy

657. Naval Military Personnel Command. Personnel Statistics Office. **Navy Military Personnel Statistics**. NMPC, 19??- . Quarterly. LC sn87-42729. OCLC 13153284. D 208.25: .
Provides information related to Navy and naval reserve officers and enlisted personnel on active duty (with age, sex, education, and home state), reenlistments, and attrition. Data are categorized by grade, sex, education, and occupational and command eligibility. The fourth quarterly issue is cumulative.

Directories

658. Bureau of the Census. **Official Register of the United States: Persons in the Civil, Military, and Naval Service**. GPO, 1913-1959. Biennial, then Annual. LC sn91-34226. OCLC 1242149. CS 1.31: .
The "Blue Book" is a source of historical information about government personnel, listing agency employees, with birthplace, official title, place employed, and salary. Before 1925 it included all federal officers, agents, clerks, and other employees of bureaus, offices, commissions, and institutions. From 1925 until its demise in 1959, only principal administrators were listed. A complete name index appears in each volume.

659. Congressional Budget Office. **List of Publications**. CBO, 1979- . Free: Publications Office, Office of Intergovernmental Relations, Ford House Office Bldg., Second and D Streets, SW, Washington, DC 20515. Annual. LC 81-645023. Z7164.F5U465a. 016.3530072/2. OCLC 5849612. Y 10.14: .
CBO studies are listed chronologically and by subject, noting title, issue date, and availability. All CBO studies are available free. Updated by a supplement sheet available from the CBO's Publications Office.

660. Office of Management and Budget. **Budget of the United States Government**. GPO, 1922- . Annual. Dept.Ed. LC 70-611049. HJ2051.A59. 353.007/22. OCLC 932137. PREX 2.8: .
> Also available from the GPO on CD-ROM PREX 2.8/1: ; on the Internet *URL http://www.doc.gov/inquery/BudgetFY96/*; on the *National Economic, Social & Environmental Data Bank* (entry 172); on the Superintendent of Documents Home Page: *http://www.access.gpo.gov/su_docs/.* ; and on the Superintendent of Documents Home Page *URL http://www.access.gpo.gov/su_docs/*.

Contains the president's proposed budget and the Office of Management and Budget's introduction to the new budget; receipts; federal programs by function, agency, and account; Budget Enforcement Act preview report and current services estimates; alternative budget presentation; historical tables; and a glossary of budget terms. Supplemental volumes include: *Appendix* (PrEx 2.8:yr/APP), *Analytical Perspectives* (PrEx 2.8:yr/ ANALYT.), *Historical Tables* (PrEx 2.8/8:), and *Citizen's Guide to the Federal Budget* (PrEx 2.8:yr/CITIZE). Related titles are *The Budget System and Concepts of the United States* (PrEx 2.2:B 85/5/993), an introduction, and *Budget Process Law Annotated* (Y 4.B 85/2:S.prt.103-49), with annotated text of laws and rules related to the budget cycle.

661.   Office of the Federal Register. National Archives and Records Administration. **United States Government Manual**. GPO, 1974- . Annual. LC 73-646537. JK421.A3. 353. OCLC 1788884. AE 2.108/2: .

Also available on the *Federal Bulletin Board* (entry 35) and GPO Access (entry 104).

This directory of the legislative, judicial, and executive branches summarizes agency programs, activities, and responsibilities, and includes organization charts, names of principal officials, addresses, and telephone numbers. It also provides information on quasi-official agencies, international organizations, boards, committees, and commissions, plus the texts of the Declaration of Independence and the U.S. Constitution. Appendixes cover standard federal regions, terminated and transferred agencies, abbreviations and acronyms, and agencies appearing in the *Code of Federal Regulations*. Includes name and agency/subject indexes. Coverage for the series began in 1973.

Elections

662.   Bureau of the Census. **Voting and Registration in the Election of. . . .** GPO, 19??- . Biennial. LC sn88-40227. OCLC 8619987. C 3.186/3-2: .
Demographic data for the nation, regions, and states show voter turnout and registration, cross-classifying voters and nonvoters by race, Hispanic origin, socioeconomic characteristics, sex, and age.

663.   Federal Election Commission. **Combined Federal/State Disclosure Directory**. FEC, 1987- . Annual. LC 88-656028. JK1991.C645. 324.7/8/02593. OCLC 15713385. Y 3.EL 2/3:14-2/ .
This is a directory of organizations and individuals responsible for political financial disclosure, including campaign and personal finances, lobbying, corporate registration, public financing, state initiative and referendum spending, candidates on ballot, and election results. A related title is *Campaign Finance Law* (Y 3.El 2/3:2-10/yr), which summarizes state campaign finance laws.

664.   Federal Election Commission. **Election Directory**. GPO, 19??- . Annual. LC 78-648244. JK2021.E43. 329/.0025/73. OCLC 4394207. Y 3.El 2/3:14/yr.
The directory describes the composition, functions, and duties of state agencies responsible for voter registration, election administration, campaign finance oversight, and campaign disclosure regulation. It also gives addresses and telephone numbers for federal and state officials with election-related duties, and lists chairpersons of election committees in state legislatures, state legislative reference services, and officers of associations of election officials.

665.   House. **Statistics of the Presidential and Congressional Election of. . . .** GPO, 1940- . Quadrennial. LC sn85-17151. OCLC 11573029. Y 1.2:El 2/ .
State and summary statistics show the number of votes for presidential electors, political parties, and Senate, House of Representatives, Resident Commissioner, and delegate nominees in Washington, D.C., American Samoa, Guam, and the Virgin Islands. Includes

a table showing the number of congressional seats held by political parties since the 34th Congress (1855-57). The title in years without a presidential election is *Statistics of the Congressional Election*.

666. Senate. Committee on Rules and Administration. **Nomination and Election of the President and Vice President of the United States, Including the Manner of Selecting Delegates to National Political Conventions.** GPO, 19??- . Quadrennial. LC 89-659158. KF4910.A246. 342.73/07. OCLC 3561678. Y 1.1/3: .

This compilation of constitutional provisions, federal and state requirements, and rules of the Democratic and Republican parties governing the nomination and election of the president and vice president of the United States is based on federal and state laws. It lists states holding presidential primaries and their dates and describes delegate selection for the national conventions, noting dates and number of delegates. It also includes surveys of political party rules and state election laws, and abstracts of laws related to minor and new parties and independent candidates.

Presidential Libraries

667. John F. Kennedy Library. **Historical Materials in the John Fitzgerald Kennedy Library** compiled and edited by Ronald E. Whealan. JFKL, 1993. 154p. LC 93-228879. E838.5.K49J6 1993. OCLC 28705009. AE 1.102:H 62/2/993.

This introductory guide to the library's holdings describes the papers, memorabilia, recordings, photographs, films, and oral history interviews of John F. Kennedy, Robert F. Kennedy, and many of their contemporaries. Includes an index.

Presidents

668. Congress. Joint Congressional Committee on Inaugural Ceremonies. **Inaugural Addresses of the Presidents of the United States from George Washington 1789 to George Bush 1989.** (S.Doc.101-10). GPO, 1989. Bicentennial ed. 350p. LC 89-603540. OCLC 20802697. (Serial Set 13914). Y 1.1/3:101-10.

This compilation of texts of inaugural addresses includes black-and-white drawings of each president and a description of Inauguration Day events. Vice presidents who succeeded to the presidency without formal inaugurations are briefly introduced, with portraits.

669. Department of State. Bureau of Public Affairs. **Visits Abroad of the Presidents of the United States, 1906-1989** by Evan M. Duncan. DS, 1990. 58p. LC 90-600926. E176.1.D84 1990. OCLC 21362817. S 1.2:V 82/4/906-89.

This list of official visits to foreign countries by U.S. presidents or presidents-elect from Theodore Roosevelt to George Bush, along with unofficial foreign vacations, can be searched by president and by host country. Omitted are trips to U.S. territories overseas.

670. House. **A Compilation of the Messages and Papers of the Presidents, 1789-1897** (H.Misc.Doc.210) by James D. Richardson. 10v. GPO, 1896-1899. LC 01-2728. J81.B96. OCLC 2016530. (Serial Set 3265/V.1-10). Y 4.P 93/1:3/1-10.

This, the first compilation of presidential messages and papers, covered Presidents Washington through McKinley. Richardson compiled updates covering through 1905, which were published privately.

671. Library of Congress. Bibliography and Reference Correspondence Section. **Presidential Inaugurations: A Selected List of References** compiled by Ruth S. Freitag. LC, 1969. Free: Office Systems Services, Printing and Processing Section, Washington, DC 20540-5446. 3d ed., rev. and enl. 230p. LC 76-602825. Z1249.P7F7 1969. 016.394/4. OCLC 58014. LC 2.2:P 92/3/969.

This is a selected list of references to inaugural ceremonies and festivities from 1789 to the late 1960s.

672. Library of Congress. Manuscript Division. **Presidents' Papers Index Series**. LC, 19??- . Photoduplication Service, Washington, DC 20540-5230. Microfilm or electrostatic print. LC 4.7: .

> **Index to the Abraham Lincoln Papers.**
>
> **Index to the Andrew Jackson Papers.**
>
> **Index to the Andrew Johnson Papers.**
>
> **Index to the Benjamin Harrison Papers.**
>
> **Index to the Calvin Coolidge Papers.**
>
> **Index to the Chester A. Arthur Papers.**
>
> **Index to the Franklin Pierce Papers.**
>
> **Index to the George Washington Papers.**
>
> **Index to the Grover Cleveland Papers.**
>
> **Index to the James A. Garfield Papers.**
>
> **Index to the James K. Polk Papers.**
>
> **Index to the James Madison Papers.**
>
> **Index to the James Monroe Papers.**
>
> **Index to the John Tyler Papers.**
>
> **Index to the Theodore Roosevelt Papers.**
>
> **Index to the Thomas Jefferson Papers.**
>
> **Index to the Ulysses S. Grant Papers.**
>
> **Index to the William H. Harrison Papers.**
>
> **Index to the William Howard Taft Papers.**
>
> **Index to the William McKinley Papers.**
>
> **Index to the Woodrow Wilson Papers.**
>
> **Index to the Zachary Taylor Papers.**

The Library of Congress's Presidential Papers Collection includes letters, financial records, speeches, notes, and writings of most of the presidents from Washington to Coolidge—all for sale on microfilm. The indexes are guides to each president's collection, with content descriptions and an index to the microfilm. An index accompanies each purchase of a microfilmed presidential collection; it may be bought separately from the Photoduplication Service, Library of Congress, Washington, DC 20540.

673. Library of Congress. Motion Picture, Broadcasting, and Recorded Sound Division. **The Theodore Roosevelt Association Film Collection: A Catalog** prepared by Wendy White-Henson and Veronica M. Gillespie with the assistance of Harriet Harrison. LC, 1986. Free to U.S. Libraries and Institutions: Office Systems Services, Printing and Processing Section, Washington, DC 20540-5446. 263p. LC 84-600384. E757.L76 1986. 016.97391/092/4. OCLC 11549503. LC 40.2:R 67.

This catalog of films about Roosevelt's career and contemporary politics during the years 1897-1934 provides information on production, copyright, series, LC location, and genre.

It includes physical descriptions, summaries, credits, notes and review citations, subject headings, and added entries. Also features chronological and title/subject/name indexes.

674. Library of Congress. **The Presidents of the United States: The First Twenty Years** compiled by John Guidas and Marilyn K. Parr. GPO, 1993. 66p. LC 92-18145. Z1239.G84 1993. 016.973/099. OCLC 26395762. LC 1.2:P 92/3.

An annotated bibliography of general and scholarly information by and about the first three presidents: George Washington, John Adams, and Thomas Jefferson. Includes a name and title index.

675. National Park Service. **The Presidents: From the Inauguration of George Washington to the Inauguration of Jimmy Carter: Historic Places Commemorating the Chief Executives of the United States**. GPO, 1977. rev. ed. 606p. LC 77-608061. E159.U55 1977. 973/.0922. OCLC 2893027. I 29.2:H 62/9/v.20/977.

This is a source of presidential biographical sketches, with portraits, other illustrations, and descriptions of historical sites commemorating presidents.

676. Office of the Federal Register. **Codification of Presidential Proclamations and Executive Orders**. GPO, 1977- . Irregular. LC 79-642776. KF70.A473. 348/.73/1. OCLC 4826797. AE 2.113: .

The text of active proclamations and executive orders issued from the Truman through the Reagan administrations is arranged in 50 subject chapters, with amendments incorporated. The cumulative codification allows referral from statutes, title, and the *U.S. Code* to presidential document number and includes a table that lists each proclamation and executive order issued during the years 1945-89. It can be searched by subject, and by executive order and proclamation numbers. Updated every four years, this is an editorial codification, not a definitive legal authority. Temporarily suspended: The last volume issued was 1945-1989.

677. Office of the Federal Register. **Herbert Hoover: Proclamations and Executive Orders, March 4, 1929 to March 4, 1933**. 2v. GPO, 1974. LC 74-602466. J82.D5 1974. 353.03/5. OCLC 1104888. GS 4.113/2:H 76/v.1,2.

This is a compilation of Herbert Hoover's proclamations and orders that predate the publication of presidential proclamations and executive orders in the *Federal Register* and the *Code of Federal Regulations*. This companion to the *Public Papers of the Presidents* series for the Hoover administration is the first official compilation of Hoover documents that originally appeared in the *Statutes at Large*. Includes a subject index.

678. Office of the Federal Register. National Archives and Records Administration. **Weekly Compilation of Presidential Documents**. GPO, 1965- . Weekly with quarterly, semiannual, and annual indexes. LC 65-9929. J80.A284. 353. OCLC 1769543. AE 2.109: .

Includes the text of public speeches and statements, messages to Congress, transcripts of news conferences, and other presidential materials released by the White House each week, plus lists of laws approved by the president, nominations submitted to the Senate, a monthly dateline, and a checklist of White House releases. Each weekly issue includes a cumulative index for the year, with separate indexes published quarterly, semiannually, and annually.

679. Office of the Federal Register. **Public Papers of the Presidents of the United States**. GPO, 1957- . Annual. LC 58-61050. J80.A283. 353.03/5. OCLC 1198154. AE 2.114: .

This series includes retrospective volumes back to 1945 (Harry S. Truman) plus volumes for the Hoover administration (1929-33). It was the first official publication of presidential papers since *A Compilation of the Messages and Papers of the Presidents, 1789-1897* (entry 670). Volumes provide the full text of presidential papers and speeches, including messages to Congress, news conferences, selected press releases, statements, executive orders, proclamations, nominations, and appointments. Since 1977, *Public Papers* has incorporated all of the material originally released in the *Weekly Compilation of Presidential Documents* (entry 678). Volumes include subject and name indexes, with appendixes of supplementary material such as the president's public schedule, White House announcements, and a list of public and private laws. Prices and availability vary for individual volumes.

680. President. **Economic Report of the President Transmitted to the Congress**. GPO, 1947- . Annual. Dept.Ed. LC 47-32975. HC106.5.A272. 330.973. OCLC 1193149. PR_.9: .[numbered individually for each president].

This is the U.S. president's report to Congress on the nation's economic health, including the Annual Report of the Council of Economic Advisors, which reviews the economy and proposed spending. The SuDocs number stem denotes individual presidents (e.g., Pr 42.9: for President Clinton, the 42nd U.S. president).

681. Senate. Library. **Presidential Vetoes, 1789-1968**. GPO, 1969. 252p. LC 70-602991. KF42.2 1969. 348/.73/1. OCLC 25757. Y 1.3:V 64/2/789-968.

    Presidential Vetoes, 1789-1976. Y 1.3:V 64/2/789-976.

    Presidential Vetoes, 1789-1988. Y 1.3:S.pub.102-12.

    Presidential Vetoes, 1977-1984. Y 1.3:S.pub.99-5.

    Presidential Vetoes, 1989-1991. Y 1.3:S.pub.102-13.

    Presidential Vetoes, 1989-1994. Y 1.3:S.pub.103-13.

Legislative histories of regular and pocket vetoes since the first Congress are arranged chronologically by Congress and bill number, with name and subject indexes, notes on any congressional action following the veto, and citations to the *Congressional Record* (daily issues). Recent editions include a "Numerical Summary of Bills Vetoed, 1789-1984" and "Dates of Sessions of the Congress."

Recreation and Hobbies

COINS AND MEDALS

682. Mint. **World Coinage Report**. GPO, 19??- . Annual. LC 93-648195. HG327.W67. 737.4/05. OCLC 27831122. T 28.14: .
Production of coins is shown in tables for each nation, with denomination, metallic composition, weight, diameter, thickness, edge type, and number produced.

OUTDOOR RECREATION

683. Fish and Wildlife Service. **National Survey of Fishing, Hunting, and Wildlife-Associated Recreation**. FWS, 19??- . Quinquennial. I 49.98/2-no: .
Also available on CD-ROM I 49.98/4: .
National survey data portray demographic characteristics of sportsmen, along with trips, distance traveled, location, and time spent. Covers hunting, fishing, observation, photography, feeding of wildlife, and home wildlife landscaping. This survey has been conducted quinquennially since 1955.

684. National Park Service. History Division. **National Park Service Administrative History: A Guide**. NPS, 1991. 144p. LC 92-201331. SB482.A4N3737 1991. 016.3530086/32. OCLC 25562542. I 29.9/2:H 62/4.
The guide includes an annotated bibliography of administrative histories of NPS parks and other units; a selected list of historical works; a guide to materials in the NPS History Collection in Harpers Ferry, West Virginia; the National Archives Preliminary Inventory of the Records of the National Park Service (Record Group 79); a guide to NPS research; and a list of NPS records and correspondence file codes.

685. National Park Service. National Natural Landmarks Program. Wildlife and Vegetation Division. **National Registry of Natural Landmarks**. NPS, 1989. 128p. LC 90-600102. QH76.N263 1989. 333.7/2/0973. OCLC 20743638. I 29.2:R 26/4.
Descriptions of ecological and geological features on the National Registry of Natural Landmarks are arranged by state and county, or by territory. Entries note location, natural values, designation date, and ownership.

686. National Park Service. **National Recreation Trails Guide**. NPS, 1988. 108p. OCLC 18728755. I 29.9/2:T 68/2/988.

This state-by-state directory describes trail uses, surface, length, and open times, with addresses for further information.

687. National Park Service. Office of Public Affairs. **The National Parks: Index**. GPO, 1985- . Biennial. LC 86-641558. E160.N25. 917.3/0025. OCLC 13301877. I 29.103: .

This state-by-state directory of U.S. national parks, monuments, preserves, lakeshores, seashores, rivers, battlefields, and historic sites gives address, description, acreage and land area, and establishment date. There is also information about affiliated areas, wild and scenic rivers, and national trails. *National Parks: Lesser-Known Areas* (I 29.9/2:P 21/985) is a smaller pamphlet focusing on sites less frequented by visitors.

688. National Park Service. **The National Parks: Camping Guide**. GPO, 1987- . Annual. LC 86-641561. GV191.35.N34. 647/.9473. OCLC 13738875. I 29.71: .

This state-by-state directory gives mailing address and descriptions of park setting, camping facilities, and special notes. Indexed by park name.

STAMP COLLECTING

689. Fish and Wildlife Service. **The Duck Stamp Collection**. 1v. GPO, 1988. LC 89-601288. HE6183.B53D83 1988. OCLC 19225624. I 49.93:934-89.

Provides a photograph, enlargement, and information about the designer, engraver, plates issued, first day of sale, and number sold for each annual migratory bird hunting stamp issued since 1934. Formerly *Duck Stamp Data*.

Sociology

GENERAL WORKS

690. Attorney General's Commission on Pornography. **Attorney General's Commission on Pornography: Final Report**. GPO, 1986. 1960p. LC 86-602212. KF9444.A822 1986. 363.4/7/0973. OCLC 13864307. J 1.2:P 82/v.1-2.

The Meese Commission report examines pornography's relationship to antisocial sexual behavior, including a history and overview of pornography, antipornography laws, and law enforcement. It includes witness testimony and a bibliography.

691. Bureau of Justice Statistics. Office of Justice Programs. **Criminal History Record Information: Compendium of State Privacy and Security Legislation, 1992**. BJS, 1992. 153p. OCLC 27242352. 29.10:ST 2/992/SUM.

State laws and regulations related to collection, maintenance, use, and audit of criminal records are cited, described, and classified under categories such as inspection, sealing records, and transaction logs. Includes a glossary.

692. Department of Defense. **Terrorist Group Profiles**. GPO, 1988. 131p. LC 89-601202. HV6431.T53 1988. OCLC 19016220. D 1.2:T 27.

Profiles of terrorist groups are organized by world region and include establishment date, membership, headquarters, area of operation, leadership, sponsors, political objectives, background, and incidents.

693. House. Committee on Foreign Affairs. **International Terrorism: A Compilation of Major Laws, Treaties, Agreements, and Executive Documents: Report**. GPO, 1995. 1155p. OCLC 31994560. Y 4.F 76/1:T 27/2/994.

Gives the text of presidential determinations, proclamations and executive orders; messages to Congress; economic summit conference statements; bilateral agreements; and multilateral treaties related to combating terrorism, hostage relief, and air safety.

694. National Institute of Justice. **Data Resources of the National Institute of Justice**. National Criminal Justice Reference Service, 1985- . Free: Justice Statistics Clearinghouse, NCJRS, U.S. Department of Justice, Box 6000, Rockville, MD 20850. Annual. LC 93-640776. HV7419.5.N38a. 364.973/05. OCLC 27245313. J 28.2:D 26/2/ .

Abstracts of data files of NIJ-sponsored research deposited at the Inter-University Consortium for Political and Social Research (ICPSR) at the University of Michigan describe purpose, methodology, unit of observation, number of records, number of variables, time and location of the research, and related publications.

CRIMINAL JUSTICE

Bibliographies

695. Bureau of Justice Assistance. **Bureau of Justice Assistance Publications List**. BJA, 19??- . Free: National Institute of Justice/NCJRS, Box 6000, Rockville, MD 20850. Quarterly. LC 94-643177. Z5703.4.C73U55A. 016.364973. OCLC 28734228. J 26.9/2: .

This bibliography of BJA drug abuse prevention documents published since 1984 for criminal justice professions includes many free titles; others note source, cost, and order number.

696. Bureau of Justice Statistics. **Bureau of Justice Statistics Publications Catalog**. BJS, 19??- . Free: BJS Clearinghouse, Box 179, Dept. BJS C-1, Annapolis Junction, MD 20701-0179. Annual. LC sn94-28481. OCLC 31332418. J 29.14/2: .

An annotated list of published and forthcoming BJS reports on crime victims, law enforcement, state felony courts, corrections, statistics, expenditures, employment, and drugs, many of which are free.

697. Department of Justice. Office of Juvenile Justice and Delinquency Prevention. **OJJDP Publications List**. OJJDP, 1994. Free: Juvenile Justice Clearinghouse, Box 6000, Rockville, MD 20850. 23p. [SuDocs number not available].

This is an annotated list of publications produced under the auspices of OJJDP, the primary federal source of information on juvenile crime and victimization and missing children. Many of the cited documents are free.

698. National Criminal Justice Reference Service. **NCJRS**. Database. 1972- .

This international bibliographic database contains citations to books, research reports, journal articles, government documents, program descriptions, and evaluations related to law enforcement, crime, and juvenile justice. All are held by NCJRS and indexed according to the *National Criminal Justice Thesaurus* (entry 701). Custom literature searches of the database are available through the Bureau of Justice Statistics Clearinghouse (entry 706). Also available from commercial vendors and on CD-ROM from the GPO.

699. National Institute of Justice. **The NIJ Publications Catalog**. National Criminal Justice Reference Service, 198?- . Free: Publications Catalog, Dept. F, Box 6000, Rockville, MD 20850. Irregular. LC sn94-28541. OCLC 30148600. J 28.11:P 96/3/ .

This is an unannotated bibliography of free and inexpensive publications and videotapes produced by NIJ since 1985. Entries are arranged by subject and include title, author, date, paging, NCJ number, and availability. The catalog includes an order form. The bimonthly *NIJ Catalog* (J 28.14/2:) is an announcement journal for NIJ, NCJRS, and other agency publications, also free from NCJRS.

Dictionaries and Thesauri

700. Bureau of Justice Statistics. **Dictionary of Criminal Justice Data Terminology: Terms and Definitions Proposed for Interstate and National Data Collection and Exchange: Report of Work Performed by Search Group, Inc.** GPO, 1981. 2d ed. 257p. LC 82-601585. HV6017.S4 1982. 364/.03/21. OCLC 8420972. J 29.9:NCJ-76939.

Definitions are given for terminology related to crime, criminal justice, and statistics. The volume includes the Uniform Crime Reports offense category lists, the National Crime Information Center's Uniform Offense Classifications code structure outline, state court model caseload reporting terminology, and a bibliography.

701. National Institute of Justice. National Criminal Justice Reference Service. **National Criminal Justice Thesaurus**. NIJ, 19??- . Annual. LC 80-640746. Z695.1.C84. 025.4/9364. OCLC 5174157. J 28.28: .
Lists terms used to index the National Criminal Justice Reference Service (NCJRS) database of criminal justice literature. It is divided into sections listing subject, geographical, and organizational descriptors.

Directories

702. Administrative Office of the United States Courts. Probation and Pretrial Services Division. **Directory of United States Probation and Pretrial Services Officers**. AOUSC, 198?- . Annual. LC 90-660155. HV9304.D57. 364.6/3/02573. OCLC 20654959. JU 10.15: .
Lists federal offices in states and state districts, with address, telephone, and fax numbers; staff; counties served; and any special instructions on travel to the district. Offices and staff in the Administrative Office of the U.S. Courts, U.S. Parole Commission, U.S. Sentencing Commission, and the Federal Bureau of Prisons are also listed.

703. Bureau of Justice Statistics. **State Drug Resources, [year] National Directory**. Drugs & Crime Data Center & Clearinghouse, 1990- . Biennial. LC 92-660680. HV5825.S66. 362.29/18/02573. OCLC 22250455. J 29.2:D 84/2/yr.
This directory of state agencies addressing drug abuse provides addresses and telephone numbers, with appendixes listing federally sponsored drug control offices, national clearinghouses and associations, national drug abuse or criminal justice resources, and state drug control or statistical agencies.

704. Department of Justice. Law Enforcement Assistance Administration. **Directory of Automated Criminal Justice Information Systems**. Justice Statistics Clearinghouse, 1972- . Irregular. LC 85-645296. HV9950.D57. 025/.06364. OCLC 4710026. J 29.8/2: .
The directory profiles automated criminal justice information systems used by police, courts, corrections, and other justice agencies, describing the system, its status, and contact people. The five volumes (Corrections; Courts; Law Enforcement; Probation and Parole; Prosecution) are each divided into four parts: Agency descriptions, system descriptions, agency and system indexes, and appendixes.

705. National Institute of Justice. **Directory of Criminal Justice Information Sources**. Justice Statistics Clearinghouse, 19?? - . Biennial. LC 93-642453. HV9950.D59. 364/.025/73. OCLC 26296149. J 28.20: .
National and regional organizations providing criminal justice-related information are described. Entries include address, telephone number, user restrictions, staff, contact person, objectives, services, collection, and publications. Features subject, geographic, and organizational indexes, plus appendixes listing Criminal Justice Information Exchange group members, state criminal justice system representatives, and organizational charts for the Department of Justice and the National Institute of Justice.

Information Centers

706. Bureau of Justice Statistics. **Bureau of Justice Statistics Clearinghouse**. Box 6000, Rockville, MD 20850; (800) 732-3277, (301) 251-5500.
The Clearinghouse offers referral, provides access to BJS statistics and reports, and performs custom literature searches of the National Criminal Justice Reference Service Database.

707. Bureau of Justice Statistics. **Drugs & Crime Data Center & Clearinghouse**. 1600 Research Blvd., Rockville, MD 20850; (800) 666-3332.
The Center provides reference, referral, and free publications about drugs and crime.

708. Department of Justice. Office of Justice Programs. Office of Juvenile Justice and Delinquency Prevention. **Juvenile Justice Clearinghouse**. Box 6000, Rockville, MD 20850; (800) 638-8736.
The JJC maintains a juvenile justice library, distributes Office of Juvenile Justice and Delinquency Prevention publications, operates an electronic bulletin board, provides referral, and disseminates information about research, training, and programs. *Juvenile Court Statistics* (J 32.15:) is an annual report of delinquency cases handled by juvenile courts.

709. Health and Human Services. **Federal Drug, Alcohol and Crime Clearinghouse Network**. 1600 Research Blvd., Rockville, MD 20850; (800) 788-2800.
The Network is a source of information and referral to all federal alcohol and drug clearinghouses. Its free *Catalog of Selected Federal Publications on Illegal Drug and Alcohol Abuse* (PrEx 1.2:P 96/) lists publications of the CDC National AIDS Clearinghouse, the Drug Information and Strategy Clearinghouse, the Drugs & Crime Data Center & Clearinghouse, the National Clearinghouse for Alcohol and Drug Information, the National Criminal Justice Reference Service, the National Institute on Drug Abuse, and the Department of Education.

710. National Criminal Justice Reference Service. **Bureau of Justice Assistance Clearinghouse**. National Institute of Justice/NCJRS, Box 6000, Rockville, MD 20850; (800) 688-4252.
The BJA provides criminal justice professionals with free publications, information, and referral about drug abuse and crime, and operates an electronic bulletin board.

711. National Institute of Justice. National Criminal Justice Reference Service. **NCJRS Gopher**. Internet *URL http://ncjrs.aspensys.com/* or *URL http://198.77.70.104/*; for information about criminal justice send E-mail to *askncjrs@aspensys.com*.
The NCJRS, the NIJ's clearinghouse, is the world's largest criminal justice information network. The gopher offers a wealth of information on law enforcement, crime, and juvenile justice, with connections to other Internet resources.

712. National Institutes of Health. Substance Abuse and Mental Health Services Administration. **National Clearinghouse for Alcohol and Drug Information**. Box 2345, Rockville, MD 20847-2345; (800) 729-6686, (301) 468-2600.
The NCADI is a central source of information on alcohol and drug education, prevention, and treatment. The NCADI's Prevention Materials Database (PMD), the most comprehensive source of materials on preventing drug and alcohol abuse, is available on computer diskettes from the Clearinghouse for a nominal fee. The *National Clearinghouse for Alcohol and Drug Information Publications Catalog* (HE 20.8012/2:) is free.

Manuals

713. Department of Justice. Office of Juvenile Justice and Delinquency Prevention. **Desktop Guide to Good Juvenile Probation Practice**. DJ, 1993. 132p. OCLC 28866033. J 32.8:P 94/993.
An overview of the juvenile justice system, probation, legal rights of offenders, and case processing, with recommended practices for probation officers.

714. Department of the Treasury. **Crime Scene and Evidence Collection Handbook**. GPO, 1986. 98p. OCLC 13556782. T 1.10/2:F 76/985.
This manual of procedures for collecting, preserving, and transmitting evidence describes types of crime scenes, with specifics for body fluids, explosives, fabrics and fibers, fingerprints, firearms, food and drugs, glass, hair, impressions, metals, paint, documents, and soil.

715. Drug Enforcement Administration. **Drug Enforcement Handbook**. DEA, 1987. 159p. OCLC 15716355. J 24.8:D 84/8.
This manual of investigative methods includes case preparation, the use of informants, interviews and interrogations, surveillance, undercover activities, raid and search operations, and handling of physical evidence.

716. Federal Bureau of Investigation. **Handbook of Forensic Science**. GPO, 1994. 121p. OCLC 31404410. J 1.14/16:F 76/994.
This manual of on-the-scene criminal investigation techniques includes information on services provided by the FBI.

717. National Institute of Justice. **Firearms Evidence Sourcebook (FES) [computer file]**. NIJ, 1994. 11 computer disks; 3 1/2 in. OCLC 30052934. J 28.31:F 51/FLOPPY.
FES is a manual for collecting evidence as it relates to ammunition, bullet and cartridge marks, examination protocol, matching, ballistics, and shotgun data. Includes a bibliography of reference works and a glossary.

718. National Institute of Justice. Office of Justice Programs. **Computer Crime: Criminal Justice Resource Manual** by Donn B. Parker. NIJ, 1989. 2d ed. 221p. LC 90-600001. HV6773.P36 1989. 364.1/68. OCLC 20716064. J 28.23:C 73/4.
This is an advanced training and reference manual for prosecuting computer crime. It includes a glossary, representative state computer crime laws, and sources of further information. Companion volumes are *Organizing for Computer Crime Investigation* (J 28.23:C 73/5) and *Prosecution and Dedicated Computer Crime Units* (J 28.23:C 73/3).

Statistics

719. Bureau of Justice Statistics. **Criminal Victimization in the United States...Trends**. GPO, 1978- . Irregular. LC 82-642902. HV6250.3.U5C67. 362.8/8. OCLC 7456257. J 29.9/2: .
This is the report of the National Crime Victimization Survey (NCVS), showing numbers of completed and attempted rapes, robberies, assaults, larcenies, burglaries, and thefts of motor vehicles, with coverage since 1973. Numerical tables focus on the frequency and impact of crimes, characteristics of victims and offenders, circumstances, and reporting patterns. Includes a glossary. A companion CD-ROM of NCVS data sets since 1973 is available for sale from the Bureau of Justice Statistics Clearinghouse.

720. Bureau of Justice Statistics. **Historical Corrections Statistics in the United States, 1850-1984** by Margaret Werner Cahalan with the assistance of Lee Anne Parsons. BJS, 1987. 248p. LC 87-601491. HV7415.C34 1987. 364.3/0973. OCLC 15728211. J 29.2:C 81/850-984.

Tables and narrative summarize correction data since national government reporting began in 1850 related to capital punishment, state and federal prisons, jails, juvenile centers, parole, and probation.

721. Bureau of Justice Statistics. National Judicial Reporting Program. **National Judicial Reporting Program: [Biennial Report]**. BJS, 198?- . Biennial. LC 94-657007. OCLC 30688017. J 29.2:J 89/ .

Presents data for the nation and large counties about felons convicted in state courts, with sentences, trial or guilty pleas, probation, type of crime, and demographic characteristics.

722. Bureau of Justice Statistics. **Sourcebook of Criminal Justice Statistics**. GPO, 1973- . Annual. LC 74-601963. HV7245.N37b. 364/.973. OCLC 2441090. J 29.9/6: .

This compendium has been characterized as the "Statistical Abstract" for criminal justice, with data from government and private agencies, universities, research institutions, and opinion polls. Data describe criminal justice systems, public attitudes, offenses, persons arrested, court processing of defendants, and persons under correctional supervision. Most data are national but are also depicted by regions, states, and cities. Consists largely of tables, with data sources noted.

723. Federal Bureau of Investigation. **Uniform Crime Reports for the United States**. GPO, 1930- . Annual. LC 30-27005. HV6787.A3. OCLC 2165904. J 1.14/7: .

Also known as Crime in the United States, this is a statistical compilation and analysis for the nation and smaller geographic areas of data on murder, rape, robbery, assault, burglary, theft, vehicle theft, and arson. Also includes statistics about law enforcement personnel, the two national crime measures, definitions, and a directory of Uniform Crime Reporting Programs.

ETHNIC GROUPS

724. Bureau of the Census. **The Black Population in the United States**. GPO, 19??- . Annual. LC 93-642496. HA195.A53 subser. 304.6/0973/021 s. OCLC 24622121. C 3.186:P-20/no.

Data on the demographic, social, and economic status of African-Americans are depicted largely in tables and graphs. Included are data on population growth, income, employment, earnings, education, family composition, and poverty status. Focusing on the current and previous year, with some comparative earlier data, the report highlights comparisons and changes in conditions. Data are also available through CENDATA (entry 758) and are summarized in the pamphlet *The Black Population in the United States: A Chartbook* (C 3.2:B 56/2), free from Census Customer Services, Washington, DC 20233-8300. Continues *Social and Economic Status of the Black Population of the United States: An Historical View, 1790-1978*.

725. Health Resources and Service Administration. Division of Disadvantaged Assistance. **Health Status of Minorities and Low-Income Groups**. GPO, 1991. 3d ed. 376p. LC 91-600779. RA448.4.H43 1991. 614.4/273/08693. OCLC 25413661. HE 20.9302:M 66/3/991.

Tables of data cover vital statistics, prevention, reproductive health, diseases, injuries, HIV, dental health, mental health, older Americans, use of services, and insurance and health care expenditures.

726. Library of Congress. American Folklife Center. **Ethnic Recordings in America: A Neglected Heritage**. LC, 1982. Free to U.S. Libraries and Institutions: Office Systems Services, Printing and Processing Section, Washington, DC 20540-5446. 269p. LC 80-607133. ML3551.E75 1982. 789.9/121773. OCLC 6357839. LC 39.11:1.
This is a guide to Irish, Mexican, Polish, and other ethnic recordings produced on commercial labels in the U.S. since 1900, with essays on subjects, individuals, and research tools. Includes indexes to subjects, people, performers, and performing groups.

727. Library of Congress. **The African-American Mosaic: A Library of Congress Resource Guide for the Study of Black History and Culture** edited by Debra Newman Ham. GPO, 1993. 300p. LC 93-21605. Z1361.N39L47 1993. 016.973/0496073. OCLC 28336627. LC 1.6/4:AF 8.
This bibliography of LC holdings by and about African-Americans lists bibliographies, guides, and finding aids related to Black history and culture. The LC collections include letters, documents, books, maps and atlases, photos, posters, architectural histories, sound recordings, films, manuscripts, plays, music, and reference materials. Related titles are *Black Studies: A Select Catalog of National Archives Microfilm Publications* (nondepository, 1984) and *Black History: A Guide to Civilian Records in the National Archives* (nondepository, 1984).

728. United States Information Agency. Collections Development Branch. **Afro-American Life, History and Culture**. USIA, 1985. 779p. OCLC 11879576. IA 1.27:Af 8.
This is an annotated bibliography of Afro-American writing and music from slavery to the 1980s. Titles for a core collection are noted.

SOCIAL CONDITIONS

729. Bureau of the Census. **Poverty in the United States [year]**. GPO, 19??- . Annual. LC sn88-40486. OCLC 17161277. C 3.186/22: .
Presents social and economic characteristics of the poor, including a discussion of the poverty threshold. A related title is *A Profile of the Working Poor* (L 2.71/20x:).

Aging

730. Bureau of the Census. **An Aging World II** by Kevin Kinsella and Cynthia M. Taeuber. GPO, 1993. 160p. OCLC 28055739. C 3.186:P 95/92-3.
Current and historical data on the world's elderly include demographics, life expectancy, health, urban/rural location, sex, marital status, living arrangements, family and social support, education and literacy, employment, and household economic trends. A related title is *Aging in Eastern Europe and the Former Soviet Union* (C 3.186:P-95/93-1).

731. Bureau of the Census. **Sixty-Five Plus in America** by Cynthia Taeuber. 1v. GPO, 1993. rev. ed. OCLC 28627239. C 3.186:P-23/178 RV.
Current and forecasted data on the elderly include growth in numbers, life expectancy, health, economic status, geographic distribution and migration patterns, and social characteristics.

732. National Center for Health Statistics. **Health Data on Older Americans: United States, 1992**. GPO, 1993. 309p. LC 92-48880. RA408.A3H4 1993. 362.1/9897/00973021. OCLC 26895266. HE 20.6209:3/27.

Health and use of health care during the years 1960-90 is portrayed by sex, age, and race. A companion title is *Chartbook on Health Data on Older Americans: U.S., 1992* (HE 20.6209:3/29).

733. National Center for Health Statistics. **The Longitudinal Study of Aging, 1984-90.** NCHS, 1992. 248p. LC 92-17525. RA409.U44 no.28. 362.1/0723. OCLC 25874353. HE 20.6209:1/28.

      Also available from the GPO on CD-ROM HE 20:7041:1.

The print volume describes data collection and the data tapes. The CD-ROM contains LSOA data from biennial surveys in three files: Interview and National Death Index, Medicare Hospital Record, and Medicare Use Record.

734. National Institute on Aging. Alzheimer's Disease Education & Referral Center. **Alzheimer's Disease: A Guide to Federal Programs.** NIH, 1993. 113p. OCLC 30082035. HE 20.3858:AL 9.

This is a directory of federally sponsored research, services, education and training of health and social service personnel, information sources, and data. Programs are described, including field centers, project sites, and regional and local resources, with address and telephone numbers given. Contains program, project, location, and subject indexes.

735. National Institutes of Health. National Institute on Aging. **National Institute on Aging Information Center.** Box 8057, Gaithersburg, MD 20898-8057; (800) 222-2225.

The Center is a source of NIA publications on health, Alzheimer's disease, independence, care, demographics, women and minorities, and international activities.

736. National Institutes of Health. National Institute on Aging. **Resource Directory for Older People.** NIH, 1993. 240p. LC 94-131829. HV1450.R47 1993. 362.6/3/02573. OCLC 28059602. HE 20.3868:R 31/993.

This is a directory of federal agencies, professional societies, and private and voluntary organizations that provide health information, self-help programming, legal aid, education, social services, consumer advice, and other assistance to the elderly.

737. Office of Personnel Management. **The Handbook of Child & Elder Care Resources.** GPO, 1993. 96p. 362.6. OCLC 29746889. PM 1.8:C 43.

A directory of organizations, publications, and other resources for dependent care of children, disabled adults, or the elderly.

738. Senate. Special Committee on Aging. **Aging America.** S, 1984- . Free: SD-G31, Washington, DC 20510-6400. Irregular. LC 92-658680. HQ1064.U5A63336. 305.26/0973/05. OCLC 22197875. Y 3.F 31/15:2 Ag 4/2/ .

This profile of the elderly depicts the size and growth of the older population, their economic status, work and retirement patterns, health, long-term care, social characteristics, federal outlays, number of elderly living alone, and international comparisons. Includes projections, charts, tables, and maps.

739. Senate. Special Committee on Aging. **Developments in Aging: A Report of the Special Committee on Aging, United States Senate.** GPO, 19??- . Annual. LC 82-644861. HQ1064.U5U53a. 305.2/6/0973. OCLC 3582309. Y 1.1/5: .

This annual committee report summarizes federal policies, programs, and legislative initiatives for the elderly, including Social Security, pensions, taxes and savings, employment, food stamps, health care, housing, the Older Americans Act, social services, and women's issues. An appendix includes the annual report of the Federal Council on Aging and federal agency reports on aid and benefit programs. Also included is a committee publications list of titles published since 1961.

740. Senate. Special Committee on Aging. **Publications List**. S, 19??- . Free: SD-G31, Washington, DC 20510-6400. Annual. LC 95-655038. OCLC 5036100. Y 4.Ag 4:P 96/ .

This is an unannotated, chronological list of the committee's reports, prints, and hearings, many of which are free.

Children and Youth

741. Children's Bureau. Adoption Opportunities Branch. **National Adoption Directory** prepared by Elizabeth S. Cole with the assistance of Victoria Lombardi. Office of Human Development Services, 1990. 261p. LC 89-602179. HV875.55.C67 1990. OCLC 21166020. HE 23.1215:Ad 7.

This state-by-state listing includes state adoption and licensing specialists, local agencies, private agencies, exchanges and photo listings, support groups, and attorney referral services. Includes a list of Immigration and Naturalization Service district offices and national adoption organizations.

742. Department of Justice. **PAVNET**. Internet *URL gopher:// cyfer.esusda.gov/*.

Partnerships Against Violence Network is an Internet clearinghouse for federal information about violence programs, funding, and at-risk youth. A cooperative initiative between numerous agencies, PAVNET links information from all at-risk-youth government clearinghouses and resource centers.

743. House. Select Committee on Children, Youth, and Families. **Federal Programs Affecting Children and Their Families, 1992: A Report of the Select Committee on Children, Youth, and Families, House of Representatives, One Hundred Second Congress, Second Session**. (H.Rep.102-1075). GPO, 1992. 194p. LC 94-149708. HV741.F424 1992. OCLC 27754554. [Serial Set number not available]. Y 1.1/8:102-1075.

Descriptions for income, nutrition, social service, education and training, health, and housing programs include information on services and benefits, funding, and participation. A related title is *Opportunities for Success: Cost-Effective Programs for Children* (Y 1.1/8:101-1000).

744. House. Select Committee on Children, Youth, and Families. **U.S. Children and Their Families: Current Conditions and Recent Trends, 1989: A Report Together with Additional Views of the Select Committee on Children, Youth, and Families, U.S. House of Representatives, One Hundred First Congress, First Session**. GPO, 1989. LC 89-603367. HQ792.U5U15 1989. 362.7/0973. OCLC 20607433. (Serial Set 13960). Y 4.C 43/2:C 43/989.

This review of the status of American children and families uses text and tables to summarize social, demographic, and economic changes during the past 20 years. Topics include population and residence, families, parental employment and child care, economic status, education, health, behavior and attitudes, and selected government programs.

745. National Agricultural Library. **Youth Development Information Center**. 10301 Baltimore Blvd., Room 304, Beltsville, MD 20705-2351; E-mail *ydic@nalusda.gov*; Internet *URL gopher:// cyfer.esusda.gov/*.

YDIC's library, information services, referral, literature searches, and bibliographies serve 4-H professionals doing youth programming. Materials in YDIC's library, earmarked

4hprk in AGRICOLA, relate to communication, educational design, youth development, youth program management, and volunteerism.

746. National Agricultural Library. Youth Development Information Center. **CYFERNET**. Internet *URL gopher://cyfer.esusda.gov/*.
The Child, Youth, and Family Education and Research Network is an Internet-based system of child, youth, and family information containing current resources and research, curricula, program support material, online bulletin boards, discussion groups, and electronic newsletters. Includes PAVNET (entry 742).

747. National Center for Education Statistics. **Youth Indicators**. GPO, 1988- . Irregular. LC 89-649463. OCLC 18436512. ED 1.327: .
This statistical compendium uses charts and tables to show current and historical demographics, family structure, economic factors, jobs, health, extracurricular activities, school achievement, and values of children and teens. Also available on diskette as Digest-on-Disk or *EDSearch, Education Statistics on Disk [computer file]* (entry 346). A related title is *Children's Well-Being: An International Comparison* (Y 1.1/8:101-628; also C 3.186:P-95/80).

748. National Institute for Child Support Enforcement. **History and Fundamentals of Child Support Enforcement**. NICSE, 1986. 146p. OCLC 14869146. HE 24.8:H 62.
This is an overview of federal and state enforcement, cases, methods for locating absent parents and establishing paternity, assessment of financial obligations, court orders, and payments. Includes a glossary. Related titles are *A Guide for Designing and Implementing a Case Processing System for Child Support Enforcement* (HE 24.8:C 26) and *A Guide for Judges in Child Support Enforcement* (HE 24.8:J 89/987).

Child Abuse

749. Department of Health and Human Services. Administration for Children and Families. **National Clearinghouse on Child Abuse and Neglect Information**. Box 1182, Washington, DC 20013-1182; (800) 394-3366, (703) 385-7565, fax (703) 385-3206.
Provides publications, annotated bibliographies, fact sheets, database searches, reference and referral, and a reading room open to the public.

750. National Center on Child Abuse and Neglect. **NCCAN's National Clearinghouse on Child Abuse and Neglect Information: Catalog of Services and Publications**. NCCAN, 1994. Free: P.O. Box 1182, Washington, DC 20013-1182. 17p. [SuDocs number not available].
This is a bibliography of materials associated with training, networking, legislation, programs, public awareness, data collection and analysis, and databases related to the medical, legal, mental health, social welfare, and educational aspects of child abuse and neglect.

751. U.S. National Center on Child Abuse and Neglect. Clearinghouse on Child Abuse and Neglect Information. **Child Abuse and Neglect and Family Violence**. Database. 1967- .
This computerized database contains citations and abstracts for published literature and audiovisual materials, descriptions of programs and ongoing research projects, and excerpts from state laws. Searches may be requested by mail or telephone: NCCAN, U.S. Children's Bureau, P.O. Box 1182, Washington, DC 20013; (703) 558-8222.

Native Americans

752. Indian Health Service. Division of Program Statistics. **Trends in Indian Health.**
GPO, 1989- . Annual. LC 90-641173. RA448.5.I5I535. 362.1/089/97073. OCLC
20789041. HE 20.316: .
Charts and tables depict births and infant mortality, deaths, patient care, and community
health of American Indians and Alaska Natives, with comparisons to other populations.
Data on the Indian Health Service are also included. Includes a glossary and contacts for
additional information. Related titles are *Regional Differences in Indian Health, 1994* (HE
20.9422:994) and *Indian Health Service Directory* (HE 20.310/2:).

753. Senate. Select Committee on Indian Affairs. **Federal Programs of Assistance to
Native Americans: A Report** by Roger Walke. GPO, 1991. 331p. LC 94-122261.
E93.W16 1991. OCLC 25416011. Y 4.In 2/11:S.prt.102-62.
Programs benefiting American Indians, Hawaiian Native and homesteader associations,
and Alaska Natives are described. A related title is *Guide to USDA Programs for Native
Americans* (A 1.11/3:N 19).

Veterans

754. Department of Veterans Affairs. **Federal Benefits for Veterans and Dependents.**
GPO, 19??- . Annual. LC 85-641702. UB357.F43. 355.1/15/0973. OCLC
6433912. VA 1.19: .
VA and other federal benefits are summarized, with a state directory of VA facilities.

755. House. Committee on Veterans' Affairs. **State Veterans' Laws: Digests of State
Laws Regarding Rights, Benefits, and Privileges of Veterans and Their Dependents, Revised to December 13, 1991.** GPO, 1992. 351p. LC 92-168029.
KF7710.Z95S7 1992. 343.73/011/02638. OCLC 25566986. Y 4.V 64/3:L
41/2/991.
Tables summarize state benefits and privileges for veterans, their dependents, and their
organizations, showing type of law and benefit, law digest, and a legal citation. Included
are summaries of state expenditures for veterans' services and a list of states with the status
of bonus payments to veterans of World War II, Korea, Vietnam, and the Persian Gulf War.
A related title is *Title 38-United States Code: Veterans' Benefits As Amended Through
January 3, 1993 and Related Material* (Y 4.V 64/3:B 43/6/993).

Statistics and Demography

GENERAL WORKS

Bureau of the Census: *URL http://gopher.census.gov/;*
URL http://ftp.census.gov/; URL http://www.census.gov/.

756. Bureau of the Census. **A Guide to State and Local Census Geography**. GPO,
      1993. 119p. LC 93-232202. HA201.1990ah. OCLC 28646784. C 3.6/2:G 29.
State-by-state geographical summaries provide basic information (land area, population,
density, capital, nickname, originating date, highest and lowest points, bordering states)
and descriptions of American Indian areas, metropolitan areas, counties, county subdivi-
sions, places, census tracts, and block numbering areas. Similar information is given for
American Samoa, Guam, the Northern Marianas, Palau, Puerto Rico, and the Virgin
Islands. Includes a glossary. A related title is *Population and Housing Characteristics for
Census Tracts and Block Numbering Areas: Finders Guide to Census Tract Reports*
(C 3.223/11-2:F 49).

757. Bureau of the Census. **Bureau of the Census Catalog of Publications, 1790-
      1972**. GPO, 1974. 911p. LC 74-600076. Z7554.U5U58 1974. 016.3173. OCLC
      1232904. C 56.222/2-2:790-972.
This is a comprehensive historical bibliography of Census Bureau publications from the
first census in 1790 through 1972. It comprises two catalogs: The *Catalog of United States
Census 1790-1945*, which lists all materials issued by the Bureau and its predecessor
organizations during that period, and *Catalog of Publications, 1946-1972*. Annual guides
were issued throughout the balance of the 1970s. Information between 1980 and 1988 is
cumulated in the *Census Catalog and Guide: 1989* (entry 760), which is kept as a
permanent reference.

758. Bureau of the Census. **CENDATA**. Database. Data User Services Division, 19??- .
      Updated daily. OCLC 26981830.
This is the Census Bureau's online database of current statistics, news releases, and
ordering information. Most statistics are for the nation as a whole; many are for states,
and a few cover counties, metropolitan areas, and cities. CENDATA is available through
commercial vendors.

759. Bureau of the Census. **Census and You: Monthly News from the U.S. Bureau of the Census.** GPO, 1988- . Monthly. LC 88-645279. HA203.B8b. 001.4/22/0973. OCLC 18054335. C 3.238: .

This current awareness publication features articles about new products, data collection, and information sources. Emphasis is on social, demographic, housing, and economic data for states and smaller areas. Key economic indicators are included. Substantial excerpts are available on CENDATA (entry 758). Formerly *Data User News*.

760. Bureau of the Census. **Census Catalog and Guide.** GPO, 1985- . Annual. LC 85-644573. Z7554.U5U32. 016.3173. OCLC 12630855. C 3.163/3: .

Summaries of Census Bureau data products describe contents, scope, geographic coverage, format, and ordering information, along with overviews of Census Bureau programs and services. The catalog includes a directory of Bureau specialists and regional offices, State Data Centers, Census Depository Libraries, and other service centers. Some information is duplicated in CENDATA (entry 758). The editions for 1989 (covering the years 1980-88) and 1994 (covering mid-1980 through 1993) are cumulative and should be kept. The 1995 edition began a new cumulation, omitting many products listed in the 1994 edition.

761. Bureau of the Census. Data User Services Division. **1990 Census of Population and Housing. Public Use Microdata [computer file].** BC, 1990. CD-ROM. C 3.285: .

Data from a population sample of housing units include information on each unit and the people in it. These microdata files allow users to create their own special tabulations. A user guide to the file is *Reference Materials—1990 Census of Population and Housing: Public Use Microdata Samples: United States Technical Documentation* (C 3.285:P 96/DOC.).

762. Bureau of the Census. Data User Services Division. **1990 Census of Population and Housing. Summary Tape File [no.] [computer file].** BC, 1992. CD-ROM. C 3:282: .

Summary Tape Files 1A, 1C, 3A, and 3C are available individually in CD-ROM format.

763. Bureau of the Census. Data User Services Division. **TIGER/Line Census Files [computer file].** BC, 1990- . CD-ROM. C 3.279: .

TIGER/Line files cover all counties and statistical equivalents, urbanized areas, congressional districts, school districts, corporate limits, American Samoa, Guam, Puerto Rico, the Virgin Islands, the Northern Marianas, and Palau. The files consist of line segments representing physical, governmental, and statistical boundaries that can be used to prepare maps.

764. Bureau of the Census. **Factfinder for the Nation.** BC, 19??- . Irregular. LC sc79-2977. OCLC 4026191. C 3.252: .

These concise booklets give an overview of Census Bureau data gathering on specific topics and cite key references. All are revised periodically.

     No. 1. Statistics on Race and Ethnicity.

     No. 2. Availability of Census Records About Individuals.

     No. 3. Agriculture Statistics.

     No. 4. History and Organization.

     No. 5. Reference Sources.

     No. 6. Housing Statistics.

No. 7. Population Statistics.

No. 8. Census Geography Concepts and Products.

No. 8a. 1990 Census Geography.

No. 9. Construction Statistics.

No. 10. Retail Trade Statistics.

No. 11. Wholesale Trade Statistics.

No. 12. Statistics on Service Industries.

No. 13. Transportation Statistics.

No. 14. Foreign Trade Statistics.

No. 15. Statistics on Manufactures.

No. 16. Statistics on Mineral Industries.

No. 17. Statistics on Governments.

No. 18. Census Bureau Programs and Products.

No. 19. Enterprise Statistics.

No. 20. Energy and Conservation Statistics.

No. 21. International Programs.

No. 22. Data for Communities.

765. Bureau of the Census. **Household and Family Characteristics**. GPO, 1953- . Annual. LC sn87-42093. OCLC 8620642. C 3.186/17: .
Data on social and economic characteristics of households and families include age, sex, race, Hispanic origin of householder; age and sex of family members; age of children; married family income and race, Spanish origin, and labor force status; and type of household by region, residence, and tenure. Data are presented at the national and regional levels.

766. Bureau of the Census. **Monthly Product Announcement**. BC, 1981- . Free: Customer Services, Washington, DC 20233. Monthly. LC sn83-11578. OCLC 7372650. C 3.163/7: .
MPA announces data products released during the month by the Bureau of the Census and the GPO, including publications, data files, maps, and microfiche. One or two new data products are described in each issue, with brief overviews of several others. Issues include order forms. Each year's MPAs are superseded by the publication of the annual *Census Catalog and Guide* (entry 760). New data products are also announced on CENDATA (entry 758). The *Daily List* (not free) announces new products in four or five issues each week.

767. Bureau of the Census. **1990 Census of Population and Housing. Guide**. Part A. Text; Part B. Glossary; Part C. Index to Summary Tape Files 1 to 4. GPO, 1992-199?. LC 93-104159. HA201.1990f. 304.6/0723. OCLC 27429004. C 3.223/22:1990 CPH-R 1.
This is a three-volume guide to locating and using 1990 Census data. *Part A. Text* (C 3.223/22:1990 CPH-R 1 A) describes fundamentals, the questionnaire, geography, data products, the statistics, and sources of assistance. *Part B. Glossary* (C 3.223/22:1990 CPH-R 1 B) defines population, housing, geographic, and technical terms. *Part C. Index to Summary Tape Files 1 to 4* will be an index to data in the Census STFs. The guide to the 1980 Census was *User's Guide, 1980 Census of Population and Housing* (C 3.223/22: PHC80-R1-A-). A related title is *Subject Index to Current Population Reports* (C 3.186:P-23/174), a subject index to Series P-20, P-23, P-25, P-26, P-60, and P-70.

768. Bureau of the Census. **1990 Census of Population and Housing. Reference Reports. 1990 Census Questionnaires and Other Public-Use Forms.** 1v. GPO, 1993. OCLC 29253056. C 3.223/22:90-R-5.

Facsimiles of Census 1990 questionnaires and forms are accompanied by descriptions of their use. Includes a glossary.

769. Bureau of the Census. **Population and Housing Characteristics for Congressional Districts of the [number] Congress [name of state].** GPO, 1???- . C 3.223/20: .

   Also available on CD-ROM. C 3.282:CD90-1D-3D.

Also known as Congressional Districts of the U.S., this is a compilation of data from the decennial Census of Population and Housing, with 100-percent data on age, family, persons in group quarters, Hispanic origin, household relationship, race and sex; and sample data for ancestry, disability, education, fertility, language, migration, birthplace, citizenship, and year of entry into the area. The report also includes data on employment, occupation, industry, income, rooms in housing unit, tenure, number of units, rent or home value, vacancy, and other housing aspects. Each item appears by race and Hispanic origin. Data are presented for states, congressional districts, county subdivisions of 10,000 or more in some states, places of 10,000 or more, and American Indian and Alaska Native areas. CPH-4 is also available on CD-ROM as Summary Tape Files (STF) 1D and 3D, *Congressional Districts of the United States.* The paper version was formerly *Congressional District Data Book.*

770. Bureau of the Census. **200 Years of U.S. Census Taking: Population and Housing Questions, 1790-1990.** GPO, 1989. 109p. LC 90-600122. HA37.U55B63 1989. 304.6/0723. OCLC 22808274. C 3.2:T 93.

This compilation of Census questionnaires and instructions also includes a historical overview, guide to information sources and schedules, and selected editorial cartoons.

771. National Center for Health Statistics. **Where to Write for Vital Records.** GPO, 1982- . Triennial. LC 83-643623. HA38.A493. 929/.1/02573. OCLC 8738425. HE 20.6210/2: .

This directory of marriage, birth, death, and divorce records filed in state or local vital statistics offices tells how and where to obtain certified copies, gives addresses, presents descriptive remarks, and lists fees.

772. National Institutes of Health. **Inventory and Analysis of Federal Population Research.** NIH, 1976- . Annual. LC 77-644281. HB850.5.U5U54b. 301.32/07/2073. OCLC 3393233. HE 20.3362/2: .

This is an annual directory of federally sponsored research related to population, biology, medicine, and social and behavioral sciences. Project descriptions note title, principal investigator and organization, funding, project number, and time span. The directory, prepared by the Interagency Committee on Population Research (ICPR), includes an analysis of trends in supported population research, an investigator index, a list of projects by topic, and a list of ICPR members and staff.

773. Public Health Service. Centers for Disease Control. **National Center for Health Statistics.** Scientific and Technical Information Branch, National Center for Health Statistics, 6525 Belcrest Rd., Room 1064, Hyattsville, MD 20782; (301) 436-8500.

NCHS is the nation's principal source of vital and health statistics, gathering data on overall health, lifestyle, exposure to unhealthy influences, illness and disability, and use of health care. NCHS disseminates information through publications, data files, and unpublished tabulations. NCHS publications are described in the annual *Catalog of Publications* (HE 20.6216/4:) and in the quarterly *Publication Note* (HE 20.6216/3:). Data files are described in *Catalog of Electronic Data Products* and *Catalog of Electronic Data Products Update.*

CENSUS SCHEDULES

774.   National Archives and Records Administration. **The 1790-1890 Federal Population Censuses: Catalog of National Archives Microfilm.** National Archives
Trust Fund Board, 1993. LC 93-17537. Z5313.U5U53 1993. 016.929/373. OCLC
28220572. GS 4.2:P 81/2/790-890.

   Also available on the Internet *URL http://gopher.nara.gov/* or *URL
http://www.nara.gov/.*

This catalog of microfilm copies of Census schedules lists rolls of Census microfilm, with
reproduced Census schedules and an enumeration district map. Listings are chronological
under states and counties. Each entry gives information on the number of rolls, contents,
and price for ordering copies of the population schedules for the years 1790-1890,
including the 1880 Soundex (phonetically coded indexes of surnames). This revised
catalog features an expanded introduction to Soundex, with facsimiles of Soundex cards.
The pamphlet "Using the Soundex System" (GIL 55) is free from Publications Distribution
(NECD), National Archives, Room G9, 7th and Pennsylvania Ave., N.W., Washington, DC
20408.

775.   National Archives and Records Service. National Archives Trust Fund Board. **The
1900 Federal Population Census: A Catalog of Microfilm Copies of the Schedules.** NARS, 1978. 84p. LC 72-610891. OCLC 4525931. GS 4.2:P 81/2/900.

   Also available on the Internet *URL http://gopher.nara.gov/* or *URL
http://www.nara.gov/.*

This catalog lists the 1900 microfilm Census schedules and the 1900 Soundex system
(reproduced as a separate microfilm publication for each state and territory). Soundex
microfilm rolls are phonetically coded indexes. Census schedules are arranged by state or
territory, then by county. The 50 states, military and naval, and Indian territories are
included. The pamphlet "Using the Soundex System" (GIL 55) is free from Publications
Distribution (NECD), National Archives, Room G9, 7th and Pennsylvania Ave., N.W.,
Washington, DC 20408.

776.   National Archives and Records Service. National Archives Trust Fund Board. **The
1910 Federal Population Census: A Catalog of Microfilm Copies of the Schedules.** NARS, 1982. 44p. LC 84-603452. Z7553.C3N37 1982. 016.3046/0973/021.
OCLC 8435642. GS 4.2:P 81/2/910.

   Also available on the Internet *URL http://gopher.nara.gov/* or *URL
http://www.nara.gov/.*

This catalog is a finding aid for ordering copies of the 1910 Census schedules. Schedules
are listed for all 50 states (under counties), Puerto Rico, and military and naval areas. A
Soundex index to the schedules is included. The pamphlet "Using the Soundex System"
(GIL 55) is free from Publications Distribution (NECD), National Archives, Room G9,
7th and Pennsylvania Ave., N.W., Washington, DC 20408.

777. National Archives and Records Administration. National Archives Trust Fund Board. **The 1920 Federal Population Census: Catalog of National Archives Microfilm**. NARA, 1992. 2d ed. 77p. LC 92-29412. Z7553.C3A17 1992. 016.3046/0973/09042. OCLC 26504643. GS 4.2:P81/2/920.

> Also available on the Internet *URL http://gopher.nara.gov/* or *URL http://www.nara.gov/*.

The 1920 Census of population was opened to researchers in March 1992. This is a guide to identifying Census microfilm rolls, with lists of contents of Census schedules and the Soundex for each state and territory. The pamphlet "Using the Soundex System" (GIL 55) is free from Publications Distribution (NECD), National Archives, Room G9, 7th and Pennsylvania Ave., N.W., Washington, DC 20408.

778. National Archives and Records Administration. **Federal Population and Mortality Schedules, 1790-1910, in the National Archives and the States**. NARA, 1986. LC 86-8555. Z7554.U5U724 1986. 016.3046/0973/021. OCLC 13560292. AE 1.115:24.

This checklist of microfilmed Census and mortality schedules from the decennial censuses for the years 1790-1880 and 1900-10 (most of the 1890 Census schedules were destroyed by fire) is arranged by state, then by city, institution, years, and holdings.

COMPENDIUMS

779. Bureau of the Census. **Country Demographic Profiles**. GPO, 1973- . LC 75-649550. HB848.C68. 312. OCLC 1245673. C 3.205/3:DP-nos.

Also known as ISP-DP reports, these present demographic data on age, sex, fertility, mortality, migration, and social and economic status for selected countries.

780. Bureau of the Census. **County and City Data Book**. GPO, 1949- . Irregular. LC 52-4576. HA202.A36. 317.3. OCLC 1184940. C 3.134/2:C 83/2/yr.

This *Statistical Abstract* supplement gives social and economic data for states, counties, cities, and Census regions and divisions. It is available on CD-ROM, microfiche, floppy disk, and computer tape. Excerpts are included in CENDATA (entry 758). County data are also cumulated in *USA Counties* (entry 781).

781. Bureau of the Census. Data User Services Division. **USA Counties [computer file]**. BC, 1992- . Annual. CD-ROM. LC sn94-37060. OCLC 26605381. C 3.134/6: .

This *Statistical Abstract* supplement includes county data files published in the 1991, 1986, and 1982 editions of the *State and Metropolitan Area Data Book* (entry 783) and the 1988 and 1983 editions of the *County and City Data Book* (entry 780), plus unpublished data.

782. Bureau of the Census. **Historical Statistics of the United States, Colonial Times to 1970**. (H.Doc.93-78). 2v. GPO, 1975. LC 75-38832. HA202.B87 1975. 317.3. OCLC 2103868. (Serial Set 13051-2). C 3.134/2:H 62/970/pt.1-2.

This *Statistical Abstract* supplement contains data on the nation's social, economic, political, and geographic development from 1610 to 1970, including population, vital statistics, health, labor, prices, income, welfare, climate, agriculture, forestry, fisheries, minerals, construction, housing, manufactures, transportation, communications, energy, commerce, banking, and government. It is continued by the *Statistical Abstract of the United States* (entry 784). A summary, "Historical Statistics at a Glance," is included in CENDATA (entry 758).

783. Bureau of the Census. **State and Metropolitan Area Data Book**. GPO, 1979- .
Irregular. LC 80-600018. HA202.S84. 317.3. OCLC 7113217. C 3.134/5: .
This *Statistical Abstract* supplement includes data on states, metropolitan areas, counties,
and cities. It is available in print, on floppy disk, and on computer tape. Excerpts are
included in CENDATA (entry 758). County data are also cumulated in *USA Counties* (entry
781).

784. Bureau of the Census. **Statistical Abstract of the United States**. GPO, 1878- .
Annual. LC 04-18089. HA202. 317.3. OCLC 1193890. C 3.134: .
Also available on CD-ROM. C 3.134/7: .
This statistical compendium of data on U.S. social, political, and economic trends is
derived from government and private statistical sources. National data are emphasized,
but many tables give data for states, census regions, cities, or metropolitan statistical areas
(MSAs). Appendixes list key statistical sources for the nation, states, and foreign governments, including "Guide to Sources of Statistics," a subject index to Census Bureau
publications. Available in paper, microfiche, CD-ROM, and magnetic tape, and excerpted
in CENDATA (entry 758). The pocket-sized *USA Statistics in Brief* (C 3.134/2-2:) is
included as an insert, or can be purchased separately.

785. Bureau of the Census. **Statistical Brief from the Bureau of the Census**. BC,
19??- . Irregular. LC sn87-16763. OCLC 17154293. C 3.205/8: .
Fact sheets summarize population and housing data and policy issues from Census Bureau
statistical programs with an overview; tables, graphs, or charts; and references for further
information. Most are also available through CENDATA (entry 758). A list of topics is
provided in the *Census Catalog and Guide* (entry 760).

786. Bureau of the Census. **World Population Profile**. GPO, 1985- . Biennial. LC
87-647922. HA154.W65. 304.6/021. OCLC 15207459. C 3.205/3:WP-yr.
WP provides demographic, economic, and social data for continents, regions, countries,
and territories with populations exceeding 5,000, including population growth rate and
density, birth and death rates, life expectancy, contraception methods, and infant mortality.
Focus is on the current year, with some comparative data since 1950 and selected
projections to 2020. New editions, issued about every two years, are cited in this manner:
WP-91 (1991 edition). The profile's computerized counterpart is the *International Data
Base* (IDB), also from the Census Bureau's Center for International Research, a tape file
covering more years than the print version. The file includes statistics on population
estimates; births and deaths; rate of growth; life expectancy; infant deaths; urban, agricultural, and literate population; and birth projections. IDB is also available through
CENDATA (entry 758).

787. National Center for Health Statistics. **Vital Statistics of the United States**. GPO,
1937- . Annual. LC 40-26272. HA203.A22. 312/.0973. OCLC 1168068. HE
20.6210:yr./v.1-3.
Three annual sections are published: (1) Natality, covering births, birth and fertility rates,
and conditions of birth; (2) Mortality (covering deaths, death rates, infant and fetal deaths,
fatal accidents) which includes Lifetables; and (3) Marriage and Divorce. Provisional data
are released in *Monthly Vital Statistics Report Provisional Data* and *Monthly Vital
Statistics Report, Annual Summary of Births, Marriages, Divorces, and Deaths: U.S.
[year]* (HE 20.6217:), while advance final data are issued in *Monthly Vital Statistics
Report Supplement* (HE 20.6217:(vol.nos & nos.)/supp.).

Urbanology

BIBLIOGRAPHY

788. Housing and Urban Development. Office of Fair Housing and Equal Opportunity. **Fair Housing Catalog: Materials Developed with Funds Provided by HUD's Office of Fair Housing and Equal Opportunity**. HUD, 1993. 51p. OCLC 29432687. HH 1.2:F 15/25.

Information from public and private fair housing groups pertains to education and outreach, public service announcements, research and reference, housing finance and insurance, enforcement, and conference materials. Order information is provided for reports, AV materials, posters, brochures, and training manuals.

DIRECTORY

789. National Park Service. Preservation Assistance Division. **Preserving and Revitalizing Older Communities: Sources of Federal Assistance** by Lesley Slavitt; edited by Susan Escherich. GPO, 1993. 146p. LC 94-143459. E159.S63 1993. OCLC 29569420. I 29.2:P 92/12.

This is a directory of federal programs designed to aid in revitalizing declining historic neighborhoods. Entries, organized by *Catalog of Federal Domestic Assistance* program numbers, list agency, objectives, types of assistance, uses and restrictions, eligibility, contacts, and other background information. There are indexes to recipient eligibility, type of assistance, and subjects, along with a glossary and a summary of major federal preservation programs.

INFORMATION CENTER

790. Housing and Urban Development. **HUD USER**. Box 6091, Rockville, MD 20850; (800) 245-2691; in Maryland and Washington, DC (301) 251-5154; Internet *URL http://huduser.aspensys.com:73/*; *URL http://ftp.aspensys.com/*; *URL http://huduser. aspensys.com:84/huduser.html*.

This is an information service for housing and urban development research, publications, referral, resource guides, AV materials, and blueprints of affordable and energy-saving housing. *HUD USER: A Guide to Publications and Services* is free. *Directory of Information Resources in Housing and Urban Development* (HUD USER, 1993) is nondepository.

MANUAL

791. Housing and Urban Development. Office of Policy Development and Research. Innovative Technology Division. **Affordable Housing Development Guidelines for State and Local Government.** HUD, 1992. 166p. LC 92-202351. HD7287.F54 1992. 363.5/8/0973. OCLC 25692761. HH 1.6/3:Af 2/3.

This manual of practices discusses land development, construction, building codes, zoning, and subdivision requirements for delivery of affordable housing. Model ordinances and code language are included, along with a bibliography. A related title is *Affordable Community Housing* (A 17.29:34), an annotated bibliography.

STATISTICS

792. Bureau of the Census. **American Housing Survey for the United States in. . . .** GPO, 1985- . Biennial. LC 89-646270. HD7293.A1C862. 363.5/1/0973021. OCLC 19600672. C 3.215:H-150- .

    Also available on CD-ROM. C 3.215/19: .

AHS, the largest regular survey of U.S. housing stock, is sponsored by the Department of Housing and Urban Development and provides data on housing and households for the nation and its regions, distinguishing rural from urban data and metropolitan from nonmetropolitan data. AHS has been conducted since 1974 by the Census Bureau, which publishes it as part of Current Housing Reports. Data are provided on vacant units, occupied units, owner-occupied units, rented units, Black or Hispanic householders, elderly householders, central city and suburban units, and units outside metropolitan areas. Also given are family income and monthly housing costs, type of structure and condition, utility and fuel costs, type of mortgage, and condominium or cooperative fees. Supplemental data are presented in *Supplement to the American Housing Survey for the United States in 1991* (C 3.215:H 151/91). The 1985, 1987, and 1989 data sets are available on CD-ROM. An overview and guide is provided in *The American Housing Survey: Housing Data Between the Censuses* (C 1.2:H 81/3). Summaries are presented in *American Housing Briefs* (C 3.215/20:), a series of fact sheets focusing on individual metropolitan statistic areas (MSAs). Additional housing data are available in the decennial and economic censuses and current housing and construction reports. A related title is *Construction Statistics Data Finder* (C 3.163/6:C 76/986).

793. Bureau of the Census. **Current Housing Reports. H171. Supplement to the American Housing Survey for Selected Metropolitan Areas in. . . .** GPO, 1984- . Annual. LC sn91-17849. 301.5/4/0973. OCLC 24579595. C 3.215/16: .

Data for 11 metropolitan areas include demographics, housing details, neighborhood educational opportunities, shopping facilities, noise levels, and crime statistics. Includes subject and table number indexes.

794. Housing and Urban Development. Office of Policy Development and Research. **U.S. Housing Market Conditions.** HUD, 1993- . Quarterly. LC 94-646361. HD7293.A1U16. 381/.456908/0973021. OCLC 30901064. HH 1.120/2: .

This report on trends in housing supply, sales, prices, and financing for the nation and for HUD regions includes data for age of homeowners, rentals, rental vacancies, U.S. housing stock, home and housing unit starts, mobile homes, and single-family homes.

PART THREE

Science and Technology

Science and Technology

GENERAL WORKS

National Technical Information Service: *URL http://www.fedworld.gov/ntis/ntishome.html.*

795. Library of Congress. **The Tradition of Science: Landmarks of Western Science in the Collections of the Library of Congress** by Leonard C. Bruno. GPO, 1987. 351p. LC 86-600088. Q125.B87 1987. 509. OCLC 12534345. LC 1.2:Sci 2/4.

In this review of selected Western scientific treasures in LC's collection, discussion of Library holdings is interwoven with the history of astronomy, botany, zoology, medicine, chemistry, geology, math, and physics. It includes a bibliography and an index. Also published by Facts on File as *Landmarks of Science: From the Collections of the Library of Congress.*

796. National Science Board. **Science & Engineering Indicators**. GPO, 1987- . Biennial. LC 89-648281. Q172.5.S34S34. 509.73. OCLC 17847129. NS 1.28/2: .

Data reflect the status of American science and technology since 1960, with international comparisons. Included are statistics on the workforce in medicine, chemistry, physics, environmental sciences, agriculture, physical sciences, and biology; math and science education, minority student population, and teachers; higher education; R&D funding; patents and technology; and public attitudes.

797. National Science Foundation. **Guide to Programs**. GPO, 19??- . Annual. LC sn86-20228. Q180.U5A549. 507/.2073. OCLC 1142423. NS 1.47: .

Also available on the Internet *URL http://www.nsf.gov/.*

Provides information about all NSF research and education projects and grants, with notes on program purpose and characteristics, eligibility, deadlines, and sources of additional information.

ABSTRACT JOURNALS

798. National Technical Information Service. **Government Reports Announcements & Index**. NTIS, 1975- . Semimonthly. LC 75-645021. Z7916.G78. 016.6. OCLC 2242215. C 51.9/3: .

GRA&I is the nation's primary index to unclassified technical reports, indexing and abstracting U.S. and foreign government-sponsored research and development, engineering reports, and other analyses prepared by federal agencies, their contractors, or grantees. GRA&I covers behavioral and social sciences along with the hard sciences, with emphasis on materials from the Department of Energy, Department of Defense, and National Aeronautics and Space Administration. It also indexes unpublished foreign material, periodicals, government patents and patent applications, federally generated data files and databases, and software programs. Entries are arranged under subject categories and subcategories. Both the biweekly and annual GRA&Is index by subject, personal and corporate authors, contract/grant numbers, and NTIS order/accession number. Its electronic equivalent is NTIS Bibliographic Database (entry 799), available from the NTIS and through commercial vendors.

799. National Technical Information Service. **NTIS Bibliographic Database**. 1964- .

A companion to the print *Government Reports Announcements & Index* (entry 798), this database cites and abstracts U.S. and foreign technical reports, periodicals, government patents and patent applications, federal data files and databases, and software programs, with an increasing representation of unpublished foreign material. Although it covers numerous disciplines and subject areas, documents listed are primarily from three agencies: Department of Energy, Department of Defense, and National Aeronautics and Space Administration. The database is accessible through commercial vendors or through lease from NTIS.

BIBLIOGRAPHIES

800. Library of Congress. Science and Technology Division. **LC Science Tracer Bullet**. LC, 1972- . Free: Reference Section, Science and Technology Division, Washington, DC 20540-5581. Irregular. LC 77-647422. Z7401.L14. 016.5. OCLC 3315419. LC 33.10:nos.

These brief literature guides to materials in the Library of Congress are in pathfinder format. Basic materials (subject headings, basic texts) are presented first, building up to more sophisticated sources (abstracts, conference proceedings). New Tracer Bullets are announced in *Library of Congress Information Bulletin* (LC 1.18:). A free list of titles is available from LC's Science and Technology Division.

801. National Science Foundation. **Film & Video Catalog**. NSF, 1989. Free: Washington, DC 20550. 23p. OCLC 20149864. NS 1.13:F 48.

This annotated brochure of films and videos on scientific topics notes distributor sources. A new edition is expected in 1996.

802. National Science Foundation. **Publications of the National Science Foundation**. NSF, 19??- . Free: Arlington, VA 22230, or E-mail request to *pubs@nsf.gov*. Annual. LC sn87-43004. OCLC 4048280. NS 1.13/5: .

This is an unannotated list of NSF publications sold by GPO or NTIS or free from NSF.

803. National Science Foundation. **STIS (Science and Technology Information System)**. Database. Internet *URL ftp://stis.nsf.gov/*. Also available through FedWorld (entry 39).

This is an electronic dissemination system for accessing NSF publications, including the *NSF Bulletin, Guide to Programs, Grant Proposal Guide,* program announcements, general publications and reports, press releases, NSF telephone directory, and award abstracts.

804. National Technical Information Service. **Directory of Japanese Technical Reports**. NTIS, 1990- . Annual. LC 91-649885. Z7915.J3D56. 016.6. OCLC 22255319. C 51.19:J 27/3/ .

This is a bibliography of Japanese information sources available from NTIS; some are in English, others are in Japanese only. Entries have also appeared since 1989 in *Government Reports Announcements & Index* (entry 798) and are arranged in a similar format, including NTIS order number and abstracts. There are indexes to keywords; personal and corporate authors; report, contract, or grant numbers; and NTIS order numbers.

805. National Technical Information Service. **Directory of Japanese Technical Resources in the United States**. NTIS, 1988- . Annual. LC 89-649596. T10.63.A1N37. 609/.52. OCLC 18737273. C 51.19:J 27/.

Prepared in response to the Japanese Technical Literature Act of 1986, the directory provides names and addresses of government, commercial, nonprofit, professional and trade associations, and libraries that collect, abstract, translate, or disseminate Japanese technical literature; cites translations of Japanese technical documents available through NTIS or the National Translations Center; and describes university programs in technical Japanese.

806. National Technical Information Service. **NTIS Catalog of Products and Services**. NTIS, 1991- . Free: 5285 Port Royal Rd., Springfield, VA 22161: Request PR-827. Annual. LC sn91-23494. OCLC 24222079. C 51.11/8: .

Also available for downloading through FedWorld (entry 39).

This is a selected, annotated catalog of NTIS publications, software, electronic data, and periodicals. Also free is *Published Search Master Catalog* (C 51.13:), a list of annotated subject bibliographies for sale from NTIS.

CHEMISTRY

807. National Bureau of Standards. **Basic Tables for Chemical Analysis** by Thomas J. Bruno and Paris D. N. Svoronos. GPO, 1986. 233p. OCLC 14524794. C 13.46:1096.

Presents data tables for gas chromatography, liquid chromatography, infrared and ultraviolet spectrophotometry, mass spectrometry, and wet chemical techniques used in the analytical chemistry laboratory.

808. National Library of Medicine. **CHEMLINE (Chemical Dictionary Online)**. 1965- . Available through MEDLARS.

This data file of chemical substances cited in NLM databases and in EPA's Toxic Substances Control Act Inventory was created by NLM in collaboration with Chemical Abstracts Service (CAS). The file contains CAS registry numbers, molecular formulas, preferred chemical nomenclature, classification codes, generic and trivial names, and, when applicable, ring information and component line formula.

DICTIONARIES

809. General Services Administration. Office of Information Resources Management. **Telecommunications: Glossary of Telecommunication Terms**. 1v. GSA, 1991. OCLC 25047311. GS 2.8/3:1037 B/1991.
Terms used nationally and internationally are defined as a standard for federal agencies. Includes a list of acronyms and abbreviations.

810. National Bureau of Standards. **Color: Universal Language and Dictionary of Names** by Kenneth L. Kelly and Deane B. Judd. GPO, 1976. 158p. LC 76-600071. QC100.U57 no.440. 602/.1s. OCLC 2935667. C 13.10:440.
This is a combined issue of *Color Names Dictionary* and its supplement, *The Universal Color Language*. The dictionary relates color-order systems and methods of designating color in six levels of fineness, and explains the selection of the Inter-Society Color Council-National Bureau of Standards hue names and modifiers describing lightness and saturation of color.

MACHINE-READABLE DATA

811. National Technical Information Service. **Directory of U.S. Government Datafiles for Mainframes and Microcomputers**. NTIS, 1991- . Annual. LC 91-649919. QA76.D567. 001.64/25/029473. OCLC 24386274. C 51.19/4: .
This directory of numeric and textual data collected by federal agencies and sold by NTIS notes order number, description, and availability. Includes subject and agency indexes. Depositories receive it in microfiche; it can be purchased in paper from NTIS. Formerly titled *Directory of Computerized Data Files*.

812. National Technical Information Service. **Directory of U.S. Government Software for Mainframes and Microcomputers**. NTIS, 1992- . Annual. LC 92-649952. QA76.6.D574. 001.64/25/029473. OCLC 25473394. C 51.19/5: .
This list of computer programs developed by federal agencies and sold by NTIS notes function, type, and availability. Indexed by order number, subject, issuing agency or contractor, hardware compatibility, and computer language. Continues *Directory of Computerized Data Files and Related Technical Reports*, *A Directory of Computerized Data Files*, and *A Directory of Computer Software*. A related pamphlet, *U.S. Government Software for Microcomputers*, is free from NTIS (PR-815).

813. National Technical Information Service. **FEDRIP. (Federal Research in Progress)**. Database.
Summaries of federally funded research in the physical, life, social, and behavioral sciences and engineering emanate from the Environmental Protection Agency, the National Science Foundation, Department of Energy, Department of Agriculture (the CRIS database), Transportation Research Board, Small Business Innovation Research, NASA, National Institute for Occupational Safety and Health, National Institutes of Health (the CRISP database), National Institute for Standards and Technology, U.S. Geological Survey, and the Department of Veterans Affairs. Entries note title, investigator, and performing and sponsoring organizations. Available through commercial vendors.

MATHEMATICS

814. National Bureau of Standards. **Handbook of Mathematical Functions with Formulas, Graphs, and Mathematical Tables** edited by Milton Abramowitz and Irene A. Stegun. GPO, 1981. 1046p. C 13.32:55/2.

This handbook of numerical tables, graphs, polynomial and rational approximations for computers, and statements of the principal mathematical properties of mathematical functions is based on Jahnke and Emde's *Tables of Functions.* Includes bibliographies.

815. Naval Research Laboratory. **Table of All Primitive Roots for Primes Less Than 5000** by Herbert Hauptman, Emanuel Vegh, and Janet Fisher. GPO, 1970. 590p. OCLC 295323. D 210.8:7070.

This is a table of all of the primitive roots of the primes less than 5000, with a description of its construction and a brief historical account of conjectures and results.

PATENTS

Patent and Trademark Office: *URL*
http://www.uspto.gov/.

816. National Aeronautics and Space Administration. Scientific and Technical Information Program. **NASA Patent Abstracts Bibliography**. NTIS, 1991- . Semiannual. LC sn91-23674. OCLC 24342715. NAS 1.21:7039(45)SEC.2.

NASA PAB provides abstracts and patent drawings for NASA-owned U.S. patents, along with abstracts of patent applications. The Abstract Section covers NASA-owned inventions cited in *Scientific and Technical Aerospace Reports* (STAR) during the last six months, while the Index Section lists STAR entries since 1969. Entries include NASA accession and case number, inventor, patent number or application serial number, and patent classification number. Patents may be searched by subject, inventor, inventing organization, or number.

817. Patent and Trademark Office. **Attorneys and Agents Registered to Practice Before the U.S. Patent and Trademark Office**. GPO, 197?- . Irregular. LC 75-648024. KF3165.A3A8. 346/.73/0486025. OCLC 2246063. C 21.9/2: .

This is a worldwide directory of names, addresses, and telephone numbers of attorneys and agents authorized to represent inventors before the PTO. Part 1 is an alphabetical listing by name; part 2 is a geographical list by state and zip code, and by foreign country.

818. Patent and Trademark Office. **CASSIS/CD-ROM [computer file]**. PTO, 19??- . CD-ROM. LC sn93-43538. OCLC 29540769. C 21.2-2:C 56/3.

> Not available for sale. Available for public use at U.S. Patent Depository Libraries.

This electronic index to patents is searchable by patent number, patent class/subclass (listing patent numbers since 1790 in each class), assignee, keywords in titles or abstracts, and by date, status, or inventor's residence. It does not include patent drawings. It includes *Index to the U.S. Patent Classification* (entry 822) and *Manual of Classification* (entry 823).

819.   Patent and Trademark Office. **Concordance, United States Patent Classification to International Patent Classification**. PTO, 1990. 184p. LC 90-601172. T223.F4U543 1990. 608.773. OCLC 21544806. C 21.14/2:C 74/990.

This is a guide for relating the U.S. Patent Classification System (as revised through June 1989) to the 5th edition of the *International Patent Classification System* (IPC) from the World Intellectual Property Organization.

820.   Patent and Trademark Office. **Consolidated Listing of Official Gazette Notices Re Patent and Trademark Office Practices and Procedures. Patent Notices**. GPO, 198?- . Annual. LC 87-640453. KF3120.A39C66. 353.0082/4. OCLC 11986828. C 21.5/5: .

This is a compilation of key PTO notices and rule changes published in the *Official Gazette* since July 1, 1964, with source citations (for example, 860 OG 662). It is arranged by broad subjects and includes an index, the "Classification of Patents," a list of patents facing expiration, a directory of Patent Depository Libraries, plus the PTO telephone directory and organization chart. Updated by the *Patent and Trademark Office Notices* (weekly: C 21.5/4 A: ; annual: C 21.5/4-2:).

821.   Patent and Trademark Office. **Index of Patents Issued from the United States Patent and Trademark Office**. GPO, 1974- . Annual. LC 76-643074. T223.D3. 608/.7/73. OCLC 2441502. C 21.5/2: .

This index to the Patent Gazette (entry 824) is issued in two parts. Part I, List of Patentees, lists patent numbers for persons or companies granted new or reissued patents. The patentee lists include design and plant patents, reexamination certificates, and Statutory Invention registrations. There is also a statistical profile of patents, reexamination certificates, and Statutory Invention registrations issued during the year. Part II, Index to Subjects of Inventions, lists patent numbers under patent class and subclasses. There is a list of class titles in class number order and an alphabetic list of class titles for patents on particular subjects. The index includes supplementary lists of libraries receiving current patents and the *Official Gazette,* and a summary of the number of patents issued annually since 1836.

822.   Patent and Trademark Office. **Index to the U.S. Patent Classification System**. GPO, 1977- . Annual. LC 78-643766. T223.A25. 608/.7/012. OCLC 4010459. C 21.12/2: .

This alphabetical keyword list refers from popular terminology to patent classes and subclasses, and serves as an index to the *Manual of Classification*. It can be searched in hard copy or on CASSIS (entry 818). The Index includes lists of utility and design patent class titles.

823.   Patent and Trademark Office. **Manual of Classification**. GPO, 197?- . Biennial. LC sn93-27534. OCLC 3455607. C 21.12: .

This is a list of all patent class and subclass numbers with their brief, descriptive titles. The Manual can be searched in print or scanned using CASSIS (entry 818).

824.   Patent and Trademark Office. **Official Gazette of the United States Patent and Trademark Office. Patents**. GPO, 1975- . Weekly. LC 75-641794. T223.A23. 608/.7/73. OCLC 2240595. C 21.5: .

OG contains summaries (patent abstracts) and drawings (except for plant patents) for utility, plant, and design patents issued during the previous week. Patent abstracts are arranged in patent number sequence and indexed by class and subclass numbers and by patentee (with separate indexes for utility, design, and plant patents). OG can be searched online or on CD-ROM in several commercial packages. The *Index of Patents* (entry 821) is a separately issued annual index.

825. Patent and Trademark Office. **Patent Abstracts of Japan [computer file]**. PTO, 19??- . Annual. CD-ROM. OCLC 25694710. C 21.2-2:P 27.

> Not available for sale. Available for public use at U.S. Patent Depository Libraries.

Contains English abstracts from "Published Unexamined Patent Applications" (Kokai tokkyo koho) issued by the Japanese Patent Agency. Each CD-ROM covers one year's patents.

826. Patent and Trademark Office. Patent Documentation Organizations. **Classification Definitions**. GPO, 1975- . Microform. OCLC 9023722. C 21.3/2: .

Detailed definitions and illustrations of inclusions and exclusions from each patent class and subclass serve as a supplement to the *Manual of Classification*. Distinctions are made between similar classes and subclasses, with references to those that include related subject matter.

STANDARDS

827. Federal Supply Service. **Index of Federal Specifications, Standards and Commercial Item Descriptions**. GPO, 1979- . Annual with 5 cumulative supplements. LC 80-643534. JK1679.I53. 353.0082/1. OCLC 5730039. GS 2.8/2: .

This is an index to alphabetic, numeric, and federal supply classification (FSC) listings of federal and interim federal specifications and standards, federal handbooks, and qualified products lists used by the federal government and described in *Federal Specifications* (GS 2.8:), *Federal Standards* (GS 2.8/3:), and *Commercial Item Descriptions* (nondepository).

828. National Institute of Standards and Technology. **Directory . . . Weights and Measures Officials in the U.S. and All Members of the National Conference on Weights and Measures**. National Conference on Weights and Measures, 1990- Annual. LC sn90-15006. OCLC 22840520. C 13.66: .

Names, addresses and telephone numbers for members of the National Conference on Weights and Measures (NCWM) are given, along with state weights and measures directors and staff. Includes a name index. This title merges the former Publication 2, *Weights and Measures Directory*, with Publication 9, *Directory of Associate Members*.

829. National Institute of Standards and Technology. Office of Information Services. **Publications of the National Institute of Standards and Technology [year] Catalog**. GPO, 1988- . Annual. LC 89-645693. QC100.U57 subser. 016.602/18. OCLC 20283563. C 13.10:305/supp.no.

This annotated bibliography of all NIST publications for the year is arranged by subject and abstract number. Entries include availability and ordering information. Indexed by author, subject, title and report number.

830. National Institute of Standards and Technology. Office of Physical Measurement Services. **NIST Calibration Services Users Guide**. GPO, 1989- . Irregular. LC 89-659238. QC100.U57. 602/.18. OCLC 19904603. C 13.10:250/yr.

This is a detailed listing of NIST calibration services, measurement assurance programs, and special-test services, including fees and contacts. It includes dimensional, mechanical, thermodynamic, optical radiation, ionizing radiation, and electromagnetic measurements.

831. National Institute of Standards and Technology. Standard Reference Materials
      Program. **NIST Standard Reference Materials Catalog**. GPO, 1991- . Biennial.
      LC sn92-40891. OCLC 22297567. C 13.10:260/yr.

This list of Standard Reference Materials (SRMs) and Reference Materials (RMs) available from the NIST provides ordering information. SRMs listed are for chemical composition, physical properties, and engineering materials. Includes subject, numerical/
certificate, and technical category indexes.

Agriculture

Department of Agriculture Gopher *URL*
http://sarah.nalusda.gov/ or
URL gopher://gopher.nalusda.gov:70/.

GENERAL WORKS

832. Bureau of Reclamation. **Drainage Manual: A Guide to Integrating Plant, Soil, and Water Relationships for Drainage of Irrigated Lands**. GPO, 1993. rev. reprint 1993. 321p. OCLC 28452144. I 27.19/2:D 78/993.
This is a guide to methods for artificial and natural draining of lands, with tips on gathering and analysis of data, references, and an index.

833. Department of Agriculture. **Agriculture Decisions: Decisions of the Secretary of Agriculture Under the Regulatory Laws Administered in the United States Department of Agriculture**. GPO, 1942- . Semiannual. LC agr42-262. 343/. 73/07602636. OCLC 1768305. A 1.58/A: .
Regulatory decisions and orders and selected court decisions are searchable by statute and name, with full text provided. Each issue includes a cumulative subject index, with the December issue containing an annual cumulation of decisions and subject index. Citations in the format *1 Agric. Dec 472 (1942)* refer to volume, page, and year.

834. Department of Agriculture. Soil Conservation Service. **Agricultural Waste Management Field Handbook**. 1v. SCS, 1992. OCLC 26655379. A 57.6/2:En 3/4.
This guide to planning, designing, and managing animal wastes, water, pesticides, and food processing includes a glossary and index.

835. Department of Agriculture. Soil Conservation Service. **List of Published Soil Surveys**. DA, 19??- . Annual. LC 87-642772. Z5074.S7L57. 016.6314/7/73. OCLC 4253590. A 57.38:LIST/ .
Soil Surveys are listed by state and identified by survey date and county name, with addresses of State Conservationists from whom updated information can be obtained. The surveys contain soil maps, background on area agriculture and climate, and descriptions

of soil types, with estimated crop yields and land capacity, soil-woodland and range interpretations, engineering uses of soils, and suitability for drainage, irrigation, wildlife, and recreation.

BIBLIOGRAPHIES

836. Department of Agriculture. Office of Publishing and Visual Communication. **List of Available Publications of the United States Department of Agriculture.** DA, 19??- . Irregular. LC 93-656194. Z5075.U5U572. OCLC 27869214. A 107.12:11/nos.
Prices and order numbers are provided for publications on agriculture, animal science, civil defense, conservation, entomology, extension work, forestry, home economics, safety, fire prevention, teaching aids, and visual aids.

837. National Agricultural Library. **AGRICOLA.** Database. 1970- .
This bibliographic database comprehensively covers world agriculture literature and allied subjects represented in the National Agricultural Library. AGRICOLA (formerly CAIN) contains citations to journal articles, monographs, proceedings, theses, patents, computer software, audiovisuals, technical reports, maps, manuscripts, microforms, and translations. The companion print index, *Bibliography of Agriculture*, is published commercially. Available online through NTIS and numerous commercial vendors, and on CD-ROM.

838. National Agricultural Library. **Bibliographies and Literature of Agriculture.** NAL, 1978- . LC sf80-592. OCLC 4286110. A 1.60/3: .
Titles in the BLA series list bibliographies in AGRICOLA since 1977. A title list is available on the NAL gopher *URL gopher://gopher.nalusda.gov:70/.*

839. National Agricultural Library. **Quick Bibliography Series.** NAL, 19??- . Free (include a self-addressed label): Reference and User Services Branch, Room 111, NAL Bldg., 10301 Baltimore Blvd., Beltsville, MD 20705-2351. LC 84-716344. A 17.18/4: .
Q.B.'s on current topics are compiled from AGRICOLA and include search strategies. Each Q.B. is numbered, with the year as prefix (example: Q.B.—94-07.). Some may be downloaded from ALF (entry 852). A cumulative list of titles is available in *Bibliographic Series, Current Titles Listing* (A 17.18/7:), free from NAL's Reference and User Services Branch, or through the NAL gopher *URL gopher://gopher.nalusda.gov:70/. Quick Bibliographies: Keyword Index* is free (include a self-addressed label) from National Agricultural Library, Reference and User Services Branch, Room 111, 10301 Baltimore Blvd., Beltsville, MD 20705-2351.

840. National Agricultural Library. Reference Section. **Special Reference Briefs.** NAL, 1983- . Free (include a self-addressed label): Reference and User Services Branch, Room 111, NAL Bldg., 10301 Baltimore Blvd., Beltsville, MD 20705-2351. Irregular. LC sc85-2173. 630. OCLC 11739950. A 17.24: .

Also available on the NAL gopher *URL gopher://gopher.nalusda.gov:70/.*

SRB's are numbered bibliographies, each with the year as prefix (example: SRB—94-01.). Some may be downloaded from ALF (entry 852). New titles are announced in *Agricultural Libraries Information Notes, ALIN* (A 17.23:). A cumulative title list is available in *Bibliographic Series, Current Titles Listing* (A 17.18/7:), free from National Agricultural Library, Public Services Division, 10301 Baltimore Blvd., Beltsville, MD 20705-2351.

841. National Agricultural Library. Technical Services Division. **List of Journals Indexed in AGRICOLA**. NAL, 1989- . Free: Attn: LJI, Indexing Branch, Room 011, USDA, ARS, 10301 Baltimore Blvd., Beltsville, MD 20705-2351. Annual. LC 89-644847. S493.L57. 630. OCLC 20026919. A 17.18/5: .

> Also available on the Internet *URL gopher://gopher.nalusda.gov/NAL Publications and Resources/List of Journals Indexed in AGRICOLA*, and ALF (entry 852).

LJI entries list title, abbreviated title, NAL call number, ISSN, imprint, indexing coverage, and availability of abstracts in AGRICOLA. Separate sections are included for new titles, deleted titles, alphabetical and abbreviated titles, subject categories, and a list of abstracted journals.

Department of Agriculture Publications Indexes

842. National Agricultural Library. **Index to USDA Agricultural Information Bulletins, Numbers 1-649** by Ellen Kay Miller. NAL, 1992. Free (include a self-addressed label): Reference and User Services Branch, Room 100, 10301 Baltimore Blvd., Beltsville, MD 20705-2351. 50p. LC 93-228387. S21.A74 Suppl. 016.63. OCLC 28369248. A 1.75:1-649/IND.

Bulletins issued during the years 1949-92 are listed by title and bulletin number (for example, AIB229) in unannotated entries that give publication date. Includes a subject index.

843. National Agricultural Library. **Index to USDA Miscellaneous Publications: Numbers 1-1479** by Ellen Kay Miller. NAL, 1992. Free (include a self-addressed label): Reference and User Services Branch, Room 100, 10301 Baltimore Blvd., Beltsville, MD 20705-2351. 109p. OCLC 26329178. A 17.18/2:M 68.

Miscellaneous Publications issued during the years 1927-91 are listed by title and document number (for example, MP#1150) in unannotated entries that give publication date. Includes a subject index.

844. National Agricultural Library. **Index to USDA Technical Bulletins, Numbers 1-1802** by Ellen Kay Miller. NAL, 1993. Free (include a self-addressed label): Reference and User Services Branch, Room 100, 10301 Baltimore Blvd., Beltsville, MD 20705-2351. 120p. OCLC 27752957. A 1.36:1-1802/INDEX.

Technical Bulletins issued during the years 1927-92 are listed by title and technical bulletin number (for example, TB#1725) in unannotated entries that give publication date. Includes a subject index.

DIRECTORIES

845. Department of Agriculture. Foreign Agricultural Service. **Food and Agricultural Export Directory**. FAS, 1981- . Free: Room 5920-S, Information Division, Washington, DC 20250-1000. Irregular. LC sn92-23660. OCLC 7533306. A 1.38: .

This listing of organizations offering advice and services for exporting food and agricultural products includes federal, regional, and state agencies; trade associations; and foreign embassies in the U.S. Entries describe services, publications, and contacts.

846. Department of Agriculture. Office of Information Resources Management. **Telephone Directory**. DA, 19??- . Annual. LC sn95-17115. OCLC 9010075. A 1.89/4: .
Building, room, and telephone numbers are provided for USDA personnel. USDA organizations are also listed, with personnel, address, and telephone number.

847. Department of Education. Office of Migrant Education. **Directory of Services for Migrant and Seasonal Farmworkers and Their Families**. DE, 1992. 148p. OCLC 28137588. ED 1.8:M 58/4.
Federal and nonfederal agencies offering health, education, early childhood, housing, employment, environmental, community service, or legal expertise are described. An appendix lists agency publications and directories related to migrants and farmworkers.

848. Science and Education Administration. Cooperative State Research Service. **Directory of Professional Workers in State Agricultural Experiment Stations and Other Cooperating State Institutions**. GPO, 1981- . Annual. LC 85-641585. S21.A37. 630. OCLC 7537305. A 1.76:305/yr.
Provides addresses and telephone numbers of federal agricultural personnel, university personnel, and extension and regional directors of state agricultural experiment stations in a state-by-state listing. Includes a name index.

ELECTRONIC SOURCES

849. Department of Agriculture. Cooperative State Research Service. **CRIS. (Current Research Information System)**. Database. Current projects, retrospective 3-4 years.
This research project directory describes government-sponsored research and projects related to agriculture, biology, forestry, and the life sciences. Also available on CD-ROM; as part of FEDRIP (entry 813); and on the USDA Extension Service gopher *URL http://www.sura.net/main/members/usda.shtml*.

850. Department of Agriculture. **USDA Economic and Statistics System**. *URL http://usda.mannlib.cornell.edu.usda.html*; or *URL telnet://usda.mannlib.cornell.edu* and type usda as ID.
Presents statistics on agricultural topics and data sets on food-related topics.

851. Food and Drug Administration. **FDA Bulletin Board System. (FDA BBS)**. Internet *URL http://www.fda.gov/bbs/bbs.html* or *URL telnet://fdabbs.fda.gov*, login as guest.
Contains information for health professionals about medicine and drugs, food labeling, regulations, and safety. Includes the index to *FDA Consumer* and the full text of selected articles, answers to frequently asked questions, and FDA regulatory summaries, a calendar of meetings, news releases, and enforcement reports.

852. National Agricultural Library. **ALF (Agricultural Library Forum)**. Electronic Bulletin Board. E-mail *alf@nalusda.gov*. Internet *URL telnet://fedworld.gov* or *URL http://www.fedworld.gov*.
Gives news about NAL products and services, policies, programs, workshops, job vacancies, and general reference materials. Information and a free user's guide are available from the National Agricultural Library, Reference and User Services Branch, Room 111, NAL Bldg., 10301 Baltimore Blvd., Beltsville, MD 20705-2351. The Department of Agriculture's Computerized Information Delivery Service (CIDS) electronic bulletin board is available commercially.

FOOD AND NUTRITION

853. Department of Agriculture. **Composition of Foods**. GPO, 1978- . Loose-leaf. (Agriculture Handbook 8). A 1.76:8-nos.

    8-1 Dairy and Egg Products

    8-2 Spices and Herbs

    8-3 Baby Foods

    8-4 Fats and Oils

    8-5 Poultry Products

    8-6 Soups, Sauces, and Gravies

    8-7 Sausages and Luncheon Meats

    8-8 Breakfast Cereals

    8-9 Fruits and Fruit Juices

    8-10 Pork Products

    8-11 Vegetables and Vegetable Products

    8-12 Nut and Seed Products

    8-13 Beef Products

    8-14 Beverages

    8-15 Finfish and Shellfish Products

    8-16 Legumes and Legume Products

    8-17 Lamb, Veal, and Game Products

    8-18 Baked Products

    8-19 Snacks and Sweets

    8-20 Cereal Grains and Pasta

    8-21 Fast Foods

    Supplements: 1989, 1990, 1991

These handbooks, consisting of the primary USDA nutrient tables, are revisions of the 1963 *Agriculture Handbook* no. 8, *Composition of Foods . . . Raw, Processed, Prepared.* Each handbook contains a table of nutrient data for raw, processed, and prepared food groups. Food values are given for energy, proximate composition, minerals, vitamins, fatty acids, cholesterol, phytosterols, and amino acids. Supplements update and expand nutrient data (A 1.76:8/yr./supp). A related title is *Calories and Weight: The USDA Pocket Guide* (A 1.75:364:yr.), which lists calories for servings of types of foods.

854. Department of Agriculture. Economic Research Service. **Food Consumption, Prices, and Expenditures**. GPO, 19??- . Annual. LC 87-655580. HD1751.A5 subser. 338.1/0973 s. OCLC 11607596. A 1.34/4: .

Historical data on U.S. food, income, and population, presented in tables and graphs, include the portion of the food dollar spent eating out, consumption by food group and specific foods, and food prices and expenditures for families and individuals.

855. Department of Agriculture. Nutrition Education Division. **Nutrient Content of the U.S. Food Supply, 1909-1988** prepared by Nancy R. Raper, C. Zizza, and J. Rourke. DA, 1992. 105p. LC 93-111333. TX1.U5 no.50. 640s. OCLC 27021892. A 1.87:50.

Also known as Home Economics Research Report #50, this provides historical data on the daily nutritional value in U.S. diets and comparable data from the Food and Agriculture Organization of the United Nations. Data are given for food energy, proteins, carbohydrates, fats, fatty acids, cholesterol, vitamins and minerals, along with major food groups and amount of food available for consumption.

856. National Agricultural Library. **Food and Nutrition Information Center**. 10301 Baltimore Blvd., Room 304, Beltsville, MD 20705-2351; E-mail *fnic@nalusda. gov*; (301) 504-5719. Internet *URL gopher://gopher.nalusda.gov* and select *NAL Information Centers/Food and Nutrition Information Center.*

The FNIC maintains a multimedia library and provides reference, referral, and database searching related to food service management, food labeling, foodborne illness, food technology, nutrition, and nutrition education.

857. National Agricultural Library. Food and Nutrition Information Center. **Selected Electronic Sources of Food and Nutrition Information** by Rebecca Thompson. NAL, 1994. Free (include title and a self-addressed gummed label): Public Services Division, Room 111, Beltsville, MD 20705. 70p. OCLC 31395329. A 17.2:F 73/7.

Economic data, recipes, research, press releases, regulations, food composition, and other sources of food and nutrition information available through databases, electronic bulletin boards, and the Internet are described, with access paths and costs noted. Listings include government, educational, and private entities.

FOREIGN AGRICULTURE

858. Department of Agriculture. Economic Research Service. Agriculture and Trade Analysis Division. **World Agricultural Trends and Indicators**. DA, 1988- . Biennial. LC 91-659194. HD1751.A5 subser. 338.1/0973s. OCLC 23664966. A 1.34:no.

Data on amount, value, trade, and indexes of country agricultural production and commodities since 1970 include labor force, population density, GNP, GDP, energy use, food consumption, land use, farming methods, and production.

859. Department of Agriculture. Economic Research Service. Commodity and Trade Analysis Branch. **Foreign Agricultural Trade of the United States**. GPO, 1962- . Bimonthly. LC 79-643738. HD9001.F654. 382/.41/0973. OCLC 4175706. A 93.17/7: .

FATUS provides data by commodity and country for the past two months for exports, imports, prices, and exchange rates. A supplement is issued semiannually (A 93.17/7-2:).

860. Department of Agriculture. Foreign Agricultural Service. **Dictionary of International Agricultural Trade** by Lawrence D. Fuell, David C. Miller, and Merritt Chesley. DA, 1988. Free: Room 5920-S, Information Division, Washington, DC 20250-1000. 96p. LC 88-602448. HD9000.5.F83 1988. 382/.41/0321. OCLC 18314177. A 1.76:411/988.

Terms related to commodities, policy, export, finance, documentation, transportation, storage, and agricultural programs are defined, with brief descriptions of agricultural commodities, U.S. commodity marketing years, units of measure, and conversion factors.

861. Department of Agriculture. Foreign Agricultural Service. **Foreign Agriculture**. FAS, 1989- . Annual. LC sn91-16163. OCLC 21423613. A 67.1/2: .

This fact book of country agricultural profiles focuses on production, marketing, policies, population, economy, and trade. Data since the 1970s are provided on population, GNP, diet and expenditures, harvest times, production regions, and agricultural products. Includes a glossary, a world agriculture atlas, maps, and graphics.

862. National Agricultural Library. **World List of Serials in Agricultural Biotechnology** by Robert D. Warmbrodt and Diana Airozo. NAL, 1993. Free: Biotechnology Information Center, 10301 Baltimore Blvd., 4th Floor, Beltsville, MD 20705-2351. 471p. LC 93-246290. Z5071.A1W37 1993. OCLC 28940084. A 1.60/3:116.
This subset of *World List of Agricultural Serials*, a commercially issued data file, is an interdisciplinary list of journals with non-English names, first year of publication, frequency, NAL call number, source of indexing, and variant titles. It includes indexes to place of publication, corporate name, and subject.

FORESTRY

863. Forest Service. **Atlas of United States Trees**. 6v. GPO, 1971-1981. LC 79-653298. S21.A46. 630/.8. OCLC 241660. A 1.38:nos. vary.

    Vol. 1. **Conifers and Important Hardwoods** by E. L. Little, Jr. 1971.

    Vol. 2. **Alaska Trees and Common Shrubs** by L. A. Viereck and E. L. Little, Jr. 1975.

    Vol. 3. **Minor Western Hardwoods** by E. L. Little, Jr. 1976.

    Vol. 4. **Minor Eastern Hardwoods** by E. L. Little, Jr. 1977.

    Vol. 5. **Florida** by E. L. Little, Jr. 1978.

    Vol. 6. **Supplement** by E. L. Little, Jr. 1981.

Large maps (and minimal text) illustrate the natural distribution or range of native tree species of the continental United States. Volume 1 includes an introduction to the series.

864. Forest Service. **Checklist of United States Trees (Native and Naturalized)** by Elbert L. Little, Jr. GPO, 1979. 375p. LC 78-600079. S21.A37 no.541. 630 s. OCLC 6553978. A 1.76:541.
This official standard for tree names in the Forest Service is a compilation of the accepted scientific names and synonyms, approved common names and other names in use, and the geographic ranges of native and naturalized forest trees in the continental United States. It is not illustrated.

865. Forest Service. **Diseases of Pacific Coast Conifers**. GPO, 1993. rev. June 1993. 199p. OCLC 28997156. A 1.76:521/REV.
This revision of Agriculture Handbook 521 is a manual for diagnosis of diseases attacking conifers along the Pacific coast and the western United States. It describes diagnosis; nomenclature; new diseases; abiotic, needle, and root diseases; rusts; mistletoes; rots; and cankers, diebacks, and galls. It includes color photographs, a glossary, and indexes to causal agents and host plants, with scientific equivalents. Omitted are diseases of seedlings and nursery-grown conifers.

866. Forest Service. **Eastern Forest Insects** by Whiteford L. Baker. GPO, 1972. 642p. LC 76-607316. S21.A46 no.1175. 630/.8. OCLC 702340. A 1.38:1175.
This is an identification manual for insects and related organisms found in North American forests and woodlands east of the 100th meridian and north of Mexico. Photos accompany descriptions of the insects, their damage, and remedies. Includes a diagnostic host index. Supersedes *Insect Enemies of the Eastern Forests*.

867. Forest Service. Pacific Northwest Region. **Growing Healthy Seedlings: Identification and Management of Pests in Northwest Forest Nurseries** edited by Philip B. Hamm, Sally J. Campbell, and Everett M. Hansen. FS, 1990. 110p. OCLC 22700332. A 13.2:Se 3/10.

This manual for growing Northwest bareroot conifers describes pests and pesticides, with color photographs and a glossary.

868. Forest Service. **Pesticide Background Statements**. 4v. FS, 1984-1989. LC 84-603501. S21.A37 no.-. 630s. OCLC 11408184. A 1.76: .

 Vol. 1. **Herbicides**. A 1.76:633.

 Vol. 2. **Fungicides and Fumigants**. A 1.76:661.

 Vol. 3. **Nursery Pesticides**. A 1.76:670.

 Vol. 4. **Insecticides**. A 1.76:685.

These are comprehensive reviews of the use, chemistry, toxicology, testing procedures, environmental fate, and hazards of pesticides. Volumes include a glossary, conversion factors, diet allowances, and references.

869. Forest Service. **The Principal Laws Relating to Forest Service Activities**. GPO, 1993. 1198p. LC 93-246865. KF5631.A3 1993. 346.7304/6784. OCLC 29215010. A 1.76:453/993.

The text of laws is arranged chronologically, with a title/popular name listing. Public Law number and *U.S. Code/Statutes at Large* citations and enactment date are noted.

870. Forest Service. **Western Forest Insects** by R. L. Furniss and V. M. Carolin. GPO, 1980. Microfiche. 654p. OCLC 9086879. A 1.38:1339/2.

This is an identification manual for insects and related organisms found in North American forests and woodlands west of the 100th meridian and north of Mexico. Photos accompany descriptions of the insects, their damage, and courses of action. Includes a diagnostic host index. Supersedes *Insect Enemies of Western Forests* (1938).

HISTORY OF AGRICULTURE

871. Department of Agriculture. Economic Research Service. **Chronological Landmarks in American Agriculture**. DA, 1990. rev. version, Nov. 1990. 106p. OCLC 23007352. A 1.75:425/990.

This chronological list of milestones in U.S. agricultural history includes inventions, laws, land policy changes, noteworthy people, institutional development, and new crops and livestock. Event notations give date, description, and references.

HORTICULTURE

872. Bureau of the Census. **Census of Horticultural Specialties (1988)**. GPO, 1991. 180p. LC 89-600343. HD1769.C46 1991. 338.1/0973/021. OCLC 20694530. C 3.31/12: 987/v.4.

Part of the Census of Agriculture, the Census of Horticultural Specialties provides national and state financial and establishment data for plant growers, with data on types of plants produced, containers, greenhouses, production expenses, sales, and number sold. Also available on diskette. A user guide is *Agriculture Specialty Publications and 1987 Public Use Files on CD-ROM: Technical Documentation.*

873. Congress. Joint Committee on the Library. **History of the United States Botanic Garden, 1816-1991** by Karen D. Solit. GPO, 1993. 112p. LC 94-149733. QK73.U62U557 1993. 580/.74/4753. OCLC 28830555. Y 4.L 61/2:B 65.

Provides the history of the botanic garden from its use in the Columbian Institute for the Promotion of the Arts and Sciences (1816-37), to the Wilkes Expedition (1838-49), new facilities (1850-1930), and today's garden (1931-91). Includes a bibliography.

874. National Park Service. **The White House Grounds and Gardens, 1988-1992**. NPS, 1993. 51p. OCLC 27780010. I 29.2:W 58/3/992.
Text and drawings detail the White House grounds during the Bush administration. This title supplements previous volumes covering the years 1984-88, 1980-84, and 1976-80.

INFORMATION CENTERS

875. National Agricultural Library. **Rural Information Center**. 10301 Baltimore Blvd., Room 304, Beltsville, MD 20705-2351; E-mail *ric@nalusda.gov*; (800) 633-7701; (301) 504-5372; Internet *URL gopher://gopher.nalusda.gov:70/1/ infocntr/ric_richs*.
The RIC provides information, referral, consulting, and database searching related to rural revitalization, including research, publications, and programs. It is also a good source of information on marketing and management, economic development, use of resources, employment alternatives, health, services, communities, families, and policy. The RIC issues the *Rural Information Center Publication Series* and operates a bulletin board. *A Rural Studies Bibliography* (A 1.60/3:112 and microfiche: A 1.60/3:127) and *Directory of Rural Studies Scholars and Educators* (A 17.2:D 62/2/994) are both free from RIC.

876. National Agricultural Library. **Water Quality Information Center**. 10301 Baltimore Blvd., Beltsville, MD 20705-2351; (301) 504-6077; E-mail *wqic@nalusda. gov*; Internet *URL gopher://gopher.nalusda.gov/* and select *NAL Information Centers/Water Quality Information Center* or *URL http://www.inform.umd.edu:8080/ EdRes/Topic/AgrEnv/Water*.
Offers reference, referral, and database searching related to water quality and agriculture research, education, and public policy. The Center also manages the Water Information Network (WIN), a computer conference on the NAL's electronic bulletin board, ALF (entry 852).

STANDARDS

877. Food Safety and Inspection Service. **List of Proprietary Substances and Non-food Compounds Authorized for Use Under USDA Inspection and Grading Programs**. GPO, 1982- . Annual. LC 84-645474. S21.A46 subser. 630 s. OCLC 8725108. A 110.15: .
Part 1 lists commercial substances used in preparing meat, poultry, and rabbit; part 2 lists nonfood agents used in federally inspected processing plants. Authorized proprietary substances and nonfood compounds are listed alphabetically by trade name under the marketing firm. A supplement is sometimes issued (A 110.15:yr.-no).

878. Food Safety and Inspection Service. Standards and Labeling Division. **Standards and Labeling Policy Book**. GPO, 19??- . Quinquennial. LC sn94-27928. OCLC 26624913. A 110.18: .
The "Policy Book" is a dictionary of foods and terminology related to food processing and distribution, with labeling requirements noted. It supplements *Meat and Poultry Inspection Regulations* (A 110.6/2:) and *Meat and Poultry Inspection Manual* (A 110. 8/2:).

STATISTICS

879. Agricultural Statistics Board. **Agricultural Statistics Board Catalog**. National Agricultural Statistics Service, 198?- . Annual. LC sn89-13301. OCLC 16892061. A 92.35/2: .

This list of commodities-estimates release dates covers reports on field crops, fruits and vegetables, livestock, poultry, dairy, prices, and expenditures. Includes an index.

880. Bureau of the Census. **Agricultural Atlas of the United States**. GPO, 1990. 199p. LC 89-600341. HD1769.C46 1990. 338.1/0973/021. OCLC 20694523. C 3.31/12: 987/v.2/pt.1.

Part of the Census of Agriculture, these thematic maps show U.S., state, and county data on farms and their sizes, types, and tenure; land use; irrigation; fertilizer and chemical use; value of sales; crops; livestock and poultry inventories and sales; production expenses; and machinery and equipment inventories. Replaces the Graphic Summary released for earlier censuses.

881. Bureau of the Census. **Census of Agriculture**. GPO, 1840- . Quinquennial. C 3.31/4: .

Also available on CD-ROM C 3.277:Ag 8/987/CD/v./rev.

The agriculture census provides a periodic statistical picture of the nation's farming, ranching, and related activities. Taken every five years, this census provides data on agricultural production, resources, and inventories for the nation, states, regions, and counties (including the only set of uniform county-level agricultural data). Data are released in printed reports, and on microfiche and computer tapes. Also available in *1992 Economic Census* on CD-ROM (entry 218). *Guide to the 1987 Census of Agriculture and Related Statistics* is a user guide and overview.

882. Bureau of the Census. Data User Services Division. **Agriculture Specialty Publications and 1987 Public Use Files [computer file]: 1988 A.E.L.O. Survey, 1988 F&R Irrigation Survey, 1988 Horticultural Census, Farms by ZIP Code (87 Census), Government Payments (87 Census), Public Use Files (State & U.S.)**. BC, 1993. CD-ROM. OCLC 29380989. C 3.277:AG 8/2/987/CD/993.

Also available on computer tape C 3.277:Ag 8/2/987/ .

Includes Agricultural Economics and Land Ownership Survey (1988), Farm and Ranch Irrigation Survey (1988), Government Payments and Market Value of Agricultural Products Sold, Census of Horticultural Specialties (1988), Public Use Files, and ZIP Code Tabulations of Selected Items from the 1987 Census of Agriculture. A user manual, *Agriculture Specialty Publications and 1987 Public Use Files on CD-ROM: Technical Documentation* (C 3.277:Ag 8/2/987/DOC), provides background on the survey, data collection, and statistics.

883. Department of Agriculture. **Agricultural Statistics**. GPO, 1936- . Annual. LC sn87-42980. HD1751.A43. 338.10973. OCLC 1773189. A 1.47: .

Presents comprehensive current and historical data since 1976 on agricultural production, supplies, population, consumption, facilities, costs, and returns. Statistics represent actual counts, survey estimates, and quinquennial censuses of agriculture.

884. Department of Agriculture. Economic Research Service. **Major Statistical Series of the U.S. Department of Agriculture**. 12v. DA, 1978-1990. 2d revision. LC 88-600806. S21.A37 no.671. 630s. OCLC 16903241. A 1.76:671/vol.

Vol. 1. **Agricultural Prices, Expenditures, Farm Employment, and Wages.**

Vol. 2. **Agricultural Production and Efficiency.**

Vol. 3. **Farm Income.**

Vol. 4. **Agricultural Marketing Costs and Charges.**

Vol. 5. **Consumption and Utilization of Agricultural Products.**

Vol. 6. **Land Values and Land Use.**

Vol. 7. **Crop and Livestock Estimates.**

Vol. 8. **Farmer Cooperatives.**

Vol. 9. **Market News.**

Vol. 10. **International Agricultural Statistics.**

Vol. 11. **The Balance Sheet.**

Vol. 12. **Costs of Production.**

1991. **Supplement.**

The 12 volumes in Agriculture Handbook No. 671 provide background and data underlying USDA statistical data series, with information about ongoing, new, and ceased series. A supplement was issued in 1991.

885. Department of Agriculture. Economic Research Service. **U.S.-State Agricultural Data** by Letricia M. Womack. GPO, 1993. Microfiche. 103p. OCLC 29923664. A 1.34:865.

Contains data for the 50 states and the nation related to population, land use, production, farms, and government payments.

886. Department of Agriculture. **Fact Book of Agriculture.** GPO, 1990- . Annual. LC sn91-23397. OCLC 23748075. A 1.38/2: .

This summary of trends in food, farms, rural development, the environment, research and education, and global agriculture is largely narrative, with some tables of data and a glossary.

887. Department of Agriculture. Foreign Agricultural Service. **Desk Reference Guide to U.S. Agricultural Trade.** DA, 19??- . Free: Room 5920-S, Information Division, Washington, DC 20250-1000. Irregular. LC sn93-27381. OCLC 27423648. A 1.76:683/ .

This comprehensive overview of agricultural imports and exports reveals trends since the 1950s, with forecasts for the upcoming year. Statistical tables show exports, imports, foreign trade, and trade balance.

888. Department of Agriculture. **Products and Services from ERS-NASS.** DA, 1995- . Free: ERS-NASS, 341 Victory Ave., Herndon, VA 22070. A 93.39: .

Also available through E-mail. Send E-mail to *almanac@esusda.gov* with the command *send ers-reports catalog.*

This new product listing for the USDA's economics agencies includes annotations, publication date, and price. Included are Economic Research Service situation, research, and outlook reports and periodicals; National Agricultural Statistics Service reports; and World Agricultural Outlook Board forecasts. USDA Economic Research Service situation and outlook reports and research are also available through the Internet on *ers-reports*: Send E-mail to *almanac@esusda.gov* with the command *subscribe ers-reports.*

WILDLIFE MANAGEMENT

889. Army. Corps of Engineers. North Pacific Division. **Fisheries Handbook of Engineering Requirements & Biological Criteria** by Milo C. Bell. ACE, 1986. rev. ed. 290p. OCLC 13311581. D 103.6/5:F 53/3.
This manual of fish culture covers the scientific management of fish, such as swimming speeds, spawning, toxicants, diseases, artificial guidance, and fishway structures. Chapters include references, charts, and tables.

890. Fish and Wildlife Service. **Federal Aid Handbook.** FWS, 1993. 168p. OCLC 28441429. I 49.6/2:F 52/7.
This guide to participation in Federal Aid in Wildlife Restoration, Federal Aid in Sport Fish Restoration, Coastal Wetlands Conservation, Endangered Species, and Anadromous Fish Conservation grant programs is a compilation of laws and regulations, with a glossary and references.

891. Fish and Wildlife Service. **Fisheries Review.** GPO, 1986- . Quarterly. LC 86-644719. SH1.S82. 639/.2. OCLC 13529972. I 49.40/2: .
This unannotated current awareness listing of publications on sport, fishery research, and management includes author, geographic, subject, and taxonomic indexes. Formerly *Sport Fishery Abstracts.*

892. Fish and Wildlife Service. Fisheries Statistics Division. **Fisheries of the United States.** GPO, 1959- . Annual. LC 73-640272. SH11.A349. 338.3/72/7092073. OCLC 1873631. C 55.309/2-2: .
   Supplemental. Annual. C 55.309/2-2: .
This statistical compendium on commercial and recreational fisheries, records numbers of fish caught in the U.S. Exclusive Economic Zones and international waters. It emphasizes the last decade, although some data go back to 1909. It covers world fish landings and U.S. fish trade, prices, consumption, production, and employment. Includes lists of publications and services, a glossary, and a statistical subject index. Also available on the *National Trade Data Bank* (entry 170) and the *National Economic, Social & Environmental Data Bank* (entry 172).

893. Fish and Wildlife Service. National Fisheries Center-Leetown. **Fish Culture: An Annotated Bibliography of Publications of the National Fisheries Center, Leetown, 1972-1980** by Joyce A. Mann et al. FWS, 1982. 124p. LC 82-603781. Z5970.F57 1982. 016.6393. OCLC 9128676. I 49.18:F 52.
This annotated bibliography includes an author index. It updates *Bibliography of Research Publications of the U.S. Bureau of Sport Fisheries, 1928-1972* (I 49.66:120).

894. Fish and Wildlife Service. Office of Administration-Fisheries. **Federal and State Listing of Fishery Offices.** FWS, 1992- . Annual. LC 93-648176. SH203.F43. OCLC 25780030. I 49.2:F 53/26/yr.
This directory of Washington and regional offices and federal fishery facilities includes names, addresses, and telephone and fax numbers. Also includes lists of fishery offices and personnel, and maps showing fishery offices and research offices.

895. Fish and Wildlife Service. Publications Unit. **Publications List.** FWS, 1993- . Biennial. LC sn95-27040. OCLC 32406651. I 49.18:P 96/ .
This unannotated list of general and technical publications, FWS leaflets, research, technical reports, bulletins, and free publications provides title, report number, author, and date.

896. Fish and Wildlife Service. **U.S. Fish and Wildlife Service Washington Office Directory.** FWS, 1992. 30p. OCLC 25584649. I 49.104:W 27/991-2.
Provides telephone numbers for Washington and regional FWS offices, along with fax numbers and information on booking conference rooms and locating shuttle buses for the Washington offices. Includes organizational, functional, and employee listings.

897. Fish and Wildlife Service. **Wildlife Abstracts: A Bibliography and Index of the Abstracts and Citations in Wildlife Review.** GPO, 1951- . Quinquennial. LC sn86-44025. SK351.U52. 016.33372. OCLC 1561529. I 49.17/2: .
These are five-year cumulations of citations since 1935 that originally appeared in *Wildlife Review*. Includes author, geographic, subject, and species indexes.

898. Fish and Wildlife Service. **Wildlife Review.** GPO, 1935- . Bimonthly. LC 53-17432. SK351.W58. 016.799. OCLC 1769882. I 49.17: .
This unannotated current awareness listing of world wildlife and natural resource literature covers journals, books, and symposia. Includes author, geographic, subject, and species indexes.

899. Forest Service. Wildlife and Fisheries. **The Fishery Resources of the National Forests: Extent, Uses and Economic Benefits, 1988** by Lisa Tripp and David B. Rockland. FS, 1990. 177p. LC 90-601941. SH221.T75 1990. 333.95/611/0973021. OCLC 23146939. A 13.2:F 53/7.
Tables of data for regions and the nation show types and extent of waters, use of fisheries in these waters, and species found in waters in national forests.

YEARBOOK

900. Department of Agriculture. **Yearbook of Agriculture.** GPO, 1894-1993. Annual. LC 86-659521. S21.A35. 630/.5. OCLC 7094188. A 1.10: .
Begun in 1894, each yearbook covered a single topic from 1936 to 1993, when it ceased publication. Cumulative indexes were published covering the years 1894-1915.

   1936-37. **Better Plants and Animals.**

   1938. **Soil and Men.**

   1939. **Food and Life.**

   1940. **Farmers in a Changing World.**

   1941. **Climate and Man.**

   1942. **Keeping Livestock Healthy.**

   1943-47. **Science in Farming.**

   1948. **Grass.**

   1949. **Trees.**

   1950-51. **Crops in Peace and War.**

   1952. **Insects.**

   1953. **Plant Diseases.**

   1954. **Marketing.**

   1955. **Water.**

   1956. **Animal Diseases.**

   1957. **Soil.**

   1958. **Land.**

1959. **Food.**

1960. **Power to Produce.**

1961. **Seeds.**

1962. **After a Hundred Years.**

1963. **A Place to Live.**

1964. **Farmer's World.**

1965. **Consumers All.**

1966. **Protecting Our Food.**

1967. **Outdoors USA.**

1968. **Science for Better Living.**

1969. **Food for Us All.**

1970. **Contours of Change.**

1971. **A Good Life for More People.**

1972. **Landscape for Living.**

1973. **Handbook for the Home.**

1974. **Shopper's Guide.**

1975. **That We May Eat.**

1976. **The Face of Rural America.**

1977. **Gardening for Food and Fun.**

1978. **Living on a Few Acres.**

1979. **What's to Eat?**

1980. **Cutting Energy Costs.**

1981. **Will There Be Enough Food?**

1982. **Food—From Farm to Table.**

1983. **Using Our Natural Resources.**

1984. **Animal Health.**

1985. **U.S. Agriculture in a Global Economy.**

1986. **Research for Tomorrow.**

1987. **Our American Land.**

1988. **Marketing U.S. Agriculture.**

1989. **Farm Management.**

1990. **Americans in Agriculture: Portraits of Diversity.**

1991. **Agriculture and the Environment.**

1992. **New Crops, New Uses, New Markets.**

1993. **Nutrition, Eating for Good Health.**

Astronomy

GENERAL WORKS

901. National Aeronautics and Space Administration. Public Affairs Division. **Photography Index**. NASA, 198?- . Irregular. LC 89-659094. TL521.3.P47. 629.4/0222. OCLC 16896858. NAS 1.43/4: .

This is an index to public domain black-and-white and color photographs available from NASA. Photos depict spacecraft, the moon and planets, astronauts, astronomy, aviation, and general interest topics.

902. Naval Observatory. Nautical Almanac Office. **Astronomical Phenomena for the Year. . . .** GPO, 1951- . Annual. LC 51-60475. QB9.U55. 525/.5. OCLC 2956636. D 213.8/3: .

Contains data on seasons, the moon, eclipses, occultations, planets, the sun, stars, comets, chronological cycles and eras, holidays, Gregorian calendar and Julian day numbers, and time.

COMETS

903. National Aeronautics and Space Administration. **The Comet Halley Archive Summary Volume** edited by Zdenek Sekanina. NASA, 1991. 332p. LC 93-102232. QB723.H2C6 1991. 523.6/42. OCLC 25472554. NAS 1.2:H 15.

Includes discussion of comets Halley and Giacobini-Zinner, the International Halley Watch, and the 1986 comet appearance and subsequent observations, along with a user manual for the Archive. Observations in the Archive database are arranged in nine disciplines: Astrometry, infrared studies, large-scale phenomena, meteor studies, near-nucleus studies, photometry and polarimetry, radio studies, spectroscopy and spectrophotometry, and amateur observations. The CD-ROM version will be titled the Halley Archive.

THE MOON

904. National Aeronautics and Space Administration. Scientific and Technical Information Division. **Where No Man Has Gone Before: A History of Apollo Lunar Exploration Missions** by William David Compton. NASA, 1989. 415p. LC 88-600242. TL789.8.U6A528 1989. 919.9/104. OCLC 18223277. NAS 1.21:4214.

This history of Project *Apollo* describes political and technological issues, people, major events, later missions, and results. Appendixes include references, technical and personnel data, a chronology, and a bibliographic essay on source materials. Indexed.

905. National Aeronautics and Space Administration. Scientific and Technical Information Office. **Apollo Over the Moon: A View from Orbit** edited by Harold Masursky, G.W. Colton, and Farouk El-Baz. GPO, 1978. 255p. LC 77-25922. QB595.A66. 559.9/1/0222. OCLC 3516272. NAS 1.21:362.

Contains black-and-white photographs of the lunar surface taken during the Apollo missions. Includes a glossary and bibliography.

NAVIGATION

906. Air Force ROTC. Curriculum Division. **Aerospace Science: The Science of Flight** by John G. Hamilton, Eric H. Petersen, and Kathleen W. Roush. 1v. Air Force Junior ROTC, 1990. LC 91-59990. OCLC 22768189. D 301.26/6:Ae 8/3/990.

This Air Force ROTC textbook offers an introduction to aeronautics, navigation, effects of flight on humans, the atmosphere, and weather. Includes an index and science activities.

907. Defense Mapping Agency. Hydrographic/Topographic Center. **American Practical Navigator: An Epitome of Navigation** originally by Nathaniel Bowditch. For Sale by Authorized Sales Agents of the Defense Mapping Agency, Office of Distribution Services, 1984- . OCLC 11892216. D 5.317:9/5/v.1,2.

Volume 1 covers fundamentals, practice and safety, piloting and dead reckoning, celestial navigation, oceanography, weather, and electronics. Volume 2 gives tables, formulas, and data, with instructions for dead reckoning, piloting, and celestial navigation. Often referred to as "Bowditch" because its original author was Nathaniel Bowditch (1802).

908. Naval Observatory. Nautical Almanac Office. **The Air Almanac.** GPO, 1953- . Annual. LC 52-61239. TL587.A36. 528/.05. OCLC 2257061. D 213.7: .

This is a handbook of astronomical data for air navigation, containing data on stars, planets, the moon, and the sky. It is published jointly with the Royal Greenwich Observatory, Great Britain, and replaces *The American Air Almanac. The Floppy Almanac* (computer file) reproduces data in the Air, Astronomical, and Nautical almanacs.

909. Naval Observatory. Nautical Almanac Office. **The Astronomical Almanac for the Year [ ].** GPO, 1981- . Annual. LC 80-647548. QB8.U6A77. 528. OCLC 6721508. D 213.8: .

Provides precise ephemerides of the sun, moon, planets, and satellites; eclipse data; and data for other astronomical phenomena, with brief explanations. Jointly published with the Royal Greenwich Observatory, Great Britain, it replaces *Astronomical Ephemeris for the Year [ ]* and *American Ephemeris and Nautical Almanac*. A companion source, the annual *Almanac for Computers*, provides mathematical series for positions of the sun, moon, planets, and stars for small computers. *The Floppy Almanac* (computer file) reproduces data in the Air, Astronomical, and Nautical almanacs.

910. Naval Observatory. Nautical Almanac Office. **The Nautical Almanac for the Year [ ].** GPO, 1960- . Annual. LC sc79-2685. 528. OCLC 1286390. D 213.11: .
This handbook of astronomical data for marine navigation contains "daily pages" of data for calculating the Local Hour Angle, with times for sunrise, sunset, moonrise, moonset, and twilight. It also contains calendarial and planning data and auxiliary tables, altitude corrections, and sight reduction procedures and tables. It is jointly produced by the Royal Greenwich Observatory and the U.S. Naval Observatory. Continues *American Nautical Almanac. The Floppy Almanac* (computer file) reproduces data in the Air, Astronomical, and Nautical almanacs.

PLANETS

911. National Aeronautics and Space Administration. **A Bibliography of Planetary Geology and Geophysics Principal Investigators and Their Associates, 1990-1991.** 1v. NASA, 1991. OCLC 26648658. NAS 1.26:4299.
Citations to recent publications supported by NASA are arranged by subject category and indexed by author. This is a companion to *Reports of the Planetary Geology and Geophysics Program, 1990*, a compilation of research report abstracts.

912. National Aeronautics and Space Administration. **Atlas of Mercury: Prepared for the Office of Space Sciences, National Aeronautics and Space Administration** authors and editors, Merton E. Davies et al. GPO, 1978. 128p. LC 78-603501. G1000.5.M4A8 1978. 912/.99/21. OCLC 5172128. NAS 1.21:423.
These photographs of Mercury were taken during the *Mariner 10* mission to Venus and Mercury.

913. National Aeronautics and Space Administration. Scientific and Technical Office. **Mission to Earth: Landsat Views the World** by Nicholas M. Short et al. GPO, 1976. 459p. LC 76-608116. QB637.M57. 910/.02/0222. OCLC 2190153. NAS 1.21:360.
Landsat color images show natural and cultural features, with captions describing well-known geographic points of interest, urban and cultural features, farm and industrial activities, vegetation, and geology. Forty percent of the photos are of the United States. A related title is *Planet Earth Through the Eyes of Landsat 4* (NAS 1.20:NF-138).

914. National Aeronautics and Space Administration. Scientific and Technical Information Branch. **On Mars: Exploration of the Red Planet, 1958-1978** by Edward Clinton Ezell and Linda Neuman Ezell. GPO, 1984. 535p. LC 82-22302. TL789.8.U6V524 1984. 629.43/543. OCLC 8975839. NAS 1.21:4212.
This is a history of the *Viking I* Mars landing and exploration, with photographs and tables of data.

915. National Aeronautics and Space Administration. Scientific and Technical Information Branch. **The Geology of the Terrestrial Planets** by Michael H. Carr et al. GPO, 1984. 317p. LC 83-16348. QB601.G47 1984. 559.9. OCLC 10277189. NAS 1.21:469.
This manual describes and compares the geology of the Moon, Mars, Mercury, Venus, and Earth, including maps and photographs.

916.   National Aeronautics and Space Administration. **The Magellan Venus Explorer's Guide** edited by Carolynn Young. NASA, 1990. 197p. LC 90-601993. TL799.V45M34 1990. 523.4/2. OCLC 22983382. NAS 1.12/7:90-24.

This guide to the 1990 *Magellan* mission to Venus features discussion of the planet's geology, the spacecraft, and the mission. Includes a glossary.

917.   National Aeronautics and Space Administration. Viking Lander Imaging Team. **The Martian Landscape**. GPO, 1978. 160p. LC 78-606041. QB641.V54 1978 Spec Format. 559.9/23/028. OCLC 3868087. NAS 1.21:425.

Presents photographs taken of Mars during the *Viking* landings, with an anecdotal account of the *Viking* program.

Biological Sciences

AQUACULTURE

918.   National Agricultural Library. **Aquaculture Information Center**. 10301 Baltimore Blvd., Room 304, Beltsville, MD 20705-2351; E-mail: *aic@nalusda.gov*; (301) 504-5558; Internet *URL gopher://gopher.nalusda.gov/NAL Information Centers/Aquaculture Information Center.*
AIC provides information, referral, and database searching related to plant and animal cultures in fresh, salt, or brackish water. Emphases include marketing, diseases, nutrition, and legislation.

919.   National Agricultural Library. Aquaculture Information Center. **Resource Guide to Aquaculture Information**. NAL, 1994. Free (include a self-addressed label): National Agricultural Library, Aquaculture Information Center, 10301 Baltimore Blvd., Beltsville, MD 20705-2351. 155p. OCLC 31090048. A 17.22:AQ 3/2.
This directory lists addresses, telephone numbers, and E-mail addresses for libraries, publications, online resources, associations, extension service contacts, state aquaculture coordinators, regional aquaculture centers, federal agencies, and equipment sources.

BIOTECHNOLOGY

920.   National Agricultural Library. **Biotechnology Information Center**. 10301 Baltimore Blvd., 4th Floor, Beltsville, MD 20705-2351; E-mail: *biotech@nalusda.gov*; (301) 504-5947; fax (301) 504-7098; Internet *URL http://www.inform.umd.edu:8080/EdRes/Topic/AgrEnv/Biotech*; or *URL gopher://gopher.nalusda.gov/NAL Information Centers/Biotechnology Information Center.*
Provides information, publications, and referral related to topics such as genetic engineering, monoclonal antibodies, immobilized enzymes, bioremediation, bioethics, and food processing and biomass applications.

BOTANY

921.   Agricultural Research Service. **A Checklist of Names for 3,000 Vascular Plants of Economic Importance** by Edward E. Terrell et al. GPO, 1986. rev. ed. LC 87-603106. S21.A37 no.505 1986. 630. OCLC 14697974. A 1.76:505/986.
Scientific names of vascular plants used anywhere in the world for food, spices, medicine, drugs, forage, or fiber (along with some noxious weeds, ornamentals, and lumber) are

listed, along with their common names and synonyms. A common-name to scientific-name list is included, with taxonomic and nomenclatural comments for some names.

922. Army. Corps of Engineers. Seattle District. **Wetland Plants of the Pacific Northwest** by Fred Weinmann et al. ACE, 1992. 85p. LC 93-122838. QK144.W48 1992. 582/.0526325/09795. OCLC 30158247. D 103.2:W 53/2.
This plant and habitat guide describes and illustrates 59 species of wetland plants occurring in eelgrass beds, marshes, wet meadows, and swamps. Although most representative of the state of Washington, it is applicable to Oregon, northern California, and other areas of the country as well. It includes a glossary, bibliography, and index.

923. Department of Agriculture. **Plant Genome Data and Information Center**. National Agricultural Library, 4th Floor, 10301 Baltimore Blvd., Beltsville, MD 20705-2351; E-mail: *pgenome@nalusda.gov* (301) 504-6613; Internet *URL gopher://gopher.nalusda.gov/NAL Information Centers/Plant Genome Data and Information Center.*
The Center maintains the Plant Genome Database (PGD) containing references, researcher information, data, genetic maps, and loci for key crops including maize, soybean, wheat, barley, oats, rice, and tomato, along with data on "Arabidopsis," an organism that has been used as a model for plant genetic research. PGD is available on CD-ROM and on the Internet *URL ftp://probe.nalusda.gov* or *URL gopher://probe.nalusda.gov/* or *URL http://probe.nalusda.gov:8300/plant/index.html.*

ZOOLOGY

924. Department of the Interior. National Wetlands Research Center. **National Atlas of Coastal Waterbird Colonies in the Contiguous United States, 1976-82** by Jeffrey A. Spendelow and Stephen R. Patton. DI, 1988. 326p. LC 88-600015. QL682.S64 1988. 598.29/24/0973. OCLC 17508845. I 49.89/2:88(5).
Surveys conducted between 1976 and 1982 are summarized, describing species, population, colony size, and breeding distribution.

925. Forest Service. **Forest and Rangeland Birds of the United States: Natural History and Habitat Use** by Richard M. DeGraaf et al. GPO, 1991. 625p. OCLC 23884254. A 1.76:688.
Descriptions are arranged by family and include color portraits; information on range, status, habitat, nest, and food; and bibliographic references. A section on bird/cover matrices describes bird uses of U.S. forest types, grasslands, and deserts. Includes an index to birds and families.

926. National Biological Service. Information Transfer Center. **Waterfowl Management Handbook [computer file]**. GPO, 1995. CD-ROM. OCLC 32623035. I 49.108:W 29/CD.
Short chapters written by subject experts are aimed at wildlife refuge managers and focus on the ecology and management of migratory birds.

927. Navy Department. Bureau of Medicine and Surgery. **Poisonous Snakes of the World: A Manual for Use by the U.S. Amphibious Forces**. GPO, 1990. rev. 212p. OCLC 30492271. D 206.6/3 Sn 1.
This illustrated guide to poisonous snakes on each continent includes information on avoiding snakebites, recognizing snake venom poisoning, and treating snakebites. Related titles are *Poisonous Snakes of Europe* (D 5.202:Sn 1) and *Snakes, Poisonous and Nonpoisonous Species* (D 103.49/3:Sn 1).

928. Smithsonian Institution. **An Annotated Catalog of the Halictid Bees of the Western Hemisphere (Hymenoptera, Halictidae)** by Jesus S. Moure and Paul D. Hurd, Jr. SI, 1987. 405p. LC 87-4929. QL568.H3M68 1987. 595.79/9. OCLC 15487847. SI 1.2:H 13.

The systematics, biology, and morphology of halictid bees in the family HALICTIDAE are described.

929. Smithsonian Institution. **Catalog of the Rutidermatidae (Crustacea: Ostracoda)** by Anne C. Cohen and Louis S. Kornicker. SI, 1987. 11p. LC 86-600283. QL1.S54 no.449. 591s. OCLC 14167072. SI 1.27:449.

References to the family prior to 1986 include information on distribution, habitat, material, life history, and ontogeny.

Earth Sciences

GENERAL WORKS

930. Army Cold Regions Research and Engineering Laboratory. **CRREL Technical Publications, 1950-75**. GPO, 1993. 273p. LC 93-118665. Z6005.P7U18 1992. 016.91/002. OCLC 28113219. D 103.39:C 67/950-975.
This annotated bibliography of reports of work sponsored by the Cold Regions Research and Engineering Laboratory includes author and subject indexes. Supplements were issued for the years 1976-90 and 1990-92: *CRREL Technical Publications: Supplement, [date]* (D 103.39:C 67/date).

931. Geological Survey. **Minerals, Lands, and Geology for the Common Defence [sic] and General Welfare: A History of Public Lands, Federal Science and Mapping Policy, and Development of Mineral Resources in the United States** by Mary C. Rabbitt. 3v. GPO, 1979-86. LC 79-601846. QE76.R3. 353.008/55. OCLC 5403354. I 19.2:M 66/9/vol.
This is a history of the U.S. Geological Survey and its place in U.S. history, geology, and allied sciences. Volume 1 describes the Survey's establishment, with black-and-white photographs and an extensive bibliography. Volume 2 covers the first 25 years of the Survey, 1879 to 1904; the evolution of public lands; and federal science, mapping policies, and mineral resources. Volume 3, covering the years 1904-39, looks at the conservation movement under Theodore Roosevelt through the start of World War II. Includes name and subject indexes. A fourth volume is planned.

CLIMATOLOGY

General Works

932. National Climatic Data Center. **Products & Services**. NCDC, 1990- . Free: Federal Building, Asheville, NC 28801-2696; or E-mail: *orders@ncdc.noaa.gov.* Irregular. OCLC 31062533. [SuDocs number not available].
This is a catalog of NCDC online systems, CD-ROMs, databases, and publications.

933. National Oceanic and Atmospheric Administration. National Environmental Satellite, Data, and Information Service. **National Climatic Data Center**. Federal Building, Asheville, NC 28801-2696; Satellite Data Services Division, Princeton Executive Center, Room 100, Washington, DC 20233; Internet *URL http://www. ncdc.noaa.gov/.*

Originally the National Weather Records Center, the NCDC has been the official depository of U.S. weather records since 1950. The NCDC records current and historical world climate data, maintaining a weather database, disseminating publications, and providing information. OASIS, offering online access to selected NCDC data and metadata files, is available through the Internet *URL http://hurricane.ncdc.noaa.gov/codiac/oasis-www.html.*

934. National Oceanic and Atmospheric Administration. National Environmental Satellite, Data, and Information Service. **Selective Guide to Climatic Data Sources** by Warren L. Hatch. 1v. NOAA, 1988. rev. ed. LC 89-601732. Z6685.U64 no.4.11 1988. 551.5 s. OCLC 21165979. C 55.219:4.11/988.

This annotated list of weather data identifies data sets filed in the National Climatic Data Center (NCDC), statistical and special studies, manuscripts and autographic records, microforms, historical publications, periodic publications, subscriptions, and indexes in which categories of data (temperature, precipitation, wind, humidity, etc.) are depicted.

935. National Weather Service. **National Weather Service Offices and Stations**. NWS, 1971- . Irregular. LC sn91-23805. OCLC 9901597. C 55.102:Of 2/yr.

First- and second-order offices and stations operated under the auspices of the NWS are arranged by state, with type and location, and the nature of observation programs.

936. National Weather Service. **Selected Worldwide Marine Weather Broadcasts**. GPO, 1982- . Annual. LC 84-644830. QC994.U63. 551.6/5162. OCLC 8880316. C 55.119: .

SWMWB provides information and schedules for worldwide English-language marine weather broadcasts (foreign-language broadcasts when English is unavailable), and includes station name, call sign, broadcast times, radio frequencies, class of emission, power, content, and language. Part 1 is arranged by regions and countries. Part 2 is a reprint of the latest *Worldwide Marine Radiofacsimile Broadcast Schedules*. It is updated by the weekly *Notice to Mariners* (D 5.315:) and the quarterly *Mariners Weather Log* (C 55.299/2:). This title continues *Worldwide Marine Weather Broadcasts*.

Atlases

937. National Climatic Data Center. **Climatic Atlas of the Outer Continental Shelf Waters and Coastal Regions of Alaska** by William A. Brower, Jr. et al. 3v. GPO, 1988. LC 89-675183. G1532.C6C8B7 1988. 551.69798/0223. OCLC 20994227. C 55.281:A 1 1 s/988/v.1-3.

Maps, graphs, and tables present a detailed weather profile of Alaskan marine and coastal regions, 1872-1974. Statistics are provided on wind, visibility, weather, sea level pressure, air and sea surface temperature, clouds, waves, storm surges, tides, sea ice, cyclone tracks, surface currents, bathymetry, detailed weather, and aviation weather. Consists of three volumes: I. *Gulf of Alaska*, II. *Bering Sea*, and III. *Chukchi and Beaufort Seas*.

938. National Climatic Data Center. **Climatic Atlas of the United States**. NCDC, 1983. 80p. LC 77-372701/MAP. OCLC 11837546. C 55.22:C 61.

This reprint of the 1968 edition depicts monthly and annual distribution and variation of the U.S. weather during the years 1931-60. It includes climate maps, graphs, and tabulations depicting distribution and variation of temperature, precipitation, wind, barometric pressure, humidity, dew point temperature, sunshine, sky cover, heating degree days, solar radiation, and evaporation. A 1993 reprint of the 1983 edition was issued by the National Climatic Data Center (nondepository).

Statistics

939. National Climatic Data Center. **Climatological Data**. NCDC, 19??- . Monthly. Microfiche. QC983.A5. C 55.214/no.: .

Published monthly for each state, the Pacific islands, Puerto Rico, and the Virgin Islands, CD reports daily temperature and precipitation records, monthly averages and totals, and extremes. Some weather stations report daily snowfall and depth, evaporation, soil temperature, and heating and cooling degree days. The July issue recaps monthly heating degree days and snow data for the past season. Annual state summaries record monthly and average temperatures and extremes, precipitation totals, freezes, soil temperatures, evaporation, and cooling degree days.

940. National Climatic Data Center. **Comparative Climatic Data for the United States Through. . . .** NCDC, 1978- . Annual. LC 79-644434. QC983.C65. 551.6973/02/12. OCLC 5629209. C 55.202:C 61/2/yr.

CCD tables of monthly and annual climate averages, totals, and extreme weather for about 300 major cities allow comparisons of temperature, rain, snow, wind, cloudiness, humidity, and sunshine.

941. National Climatic Data Center. **Local Climatological Data**. NCDC, 1983- . Monthly. C 55.286/6-no.

Monthly issues of LCD provide data from National Weather Service stations: Temperatures, dew point temperatures, heating and cooling degree days, weather, precipitation, snowfall, pressure, wind, sunshine, and sky cover. The annual issue summarizes the year's data, provides a climatological narrative, a "Normals, Means, and Extremes" table, and tables listing monthly, yearly, and seasonal statistics for the last 30 years.

942. National Climatic Data Center. **Monthly Climatic Data for the World**. NCDC, 1948- . Monthly. LC 79-643843. QC982.U442. 551.6/02/12. OCLC 4512269. C 55.211: .

Compiled from data gathered at weather stations around the world, MCDW provides tables showing pressure, temperature, vapor pressure, precipitation, sunshine, and upper air data for countries and selected cities. Also available on the *National Economic, Social & Environmental Data Bank* (entry 172).

943. National Climatic Data Center. **World Weather Records**. GPO, 1930- . Decennial. LC sn87-43443. QC982.W6. OCLC 3408684. C 55.281:W 89/yr.

These volumes form a complete listing of weather records since earliest recorded times. Tables represent 10-year periods since 1920 and before, with monthly averages of station pressure, sea level pressure, temperature, and precipitation for weather stations worldwide. A related title, *Climates of the World* is a short brochure summarizing temperature and precipitation averages, with maps and brief narrative descriptions of each continent's climate.

944. Weather Bureau. **Storm Data**. GPO, 1959- . Monthly. LC 78-646611. QC943.5.U6S82. 551.5/5/0973. OCLC 2468803. C 55.212: .

This state-by-state chronological list and description of the month's storms and unusual weather includes data on storm paths, deaths, injuries, and property damage. An "Outstanding Storms of the Month" section includes photographs, storm tracks, and maps. The

December issue gives annual summaries of tornadoes, lightning, and North Atlantic tropical cyclones.

GEOLOGY

945. Geological Survey. **Annotated Bibliography of Studies on the Geology, Geochemistry, Mineral Resources, and Geophysical Character of the Early Mesozoic Basins of the Eastern United States, 1880-1984** by Jacob Margolis, G. R. Robinson, Jr., and C. M. Schafer. GPO, 1986. 492p. LC 86-600147. QE75.B9 no.1688. 557.3s. OCLC 13642393. I 19.3:1688.
Citations related to land and water Mesozoic geology of Massachusetts, Connecticut, New Jersey, Pennsylvania, Virginia, Maryland, and the Carolinas are listed by author. Includes location, subject, and map indexes.

946. Geological Survey. **Bibliography of North American Geology.** GPO, 1906/07-1970. Annual. LC gs09-427. QE75.B9. 016.557. OCLC 2177447. I 19.3:nos. vary.
Citations to publications on the geology of North America, Greenland, the West Indies, Guam, Hawaii, and Panama include journal articles, books, professional papers, and *Dissertation Abstracts* titles. Includes subject and geographic indexes. In 1971, it was incorporated into the *Bibliography and Index of Geology*, published by the American Geological Institute. Cumulative editions: *Geologic Literature on North America, 1785-1918* (I 19.3:746,747), *Bibliography of North American Geology, 1919-1928* (I 19.3:823), *Bibliography of North American Geology, 1929-1939* (I 19.3:937), *Bibliography of North American Geology, 1940-1949* (I 19.3:1049), *Bibliography of North American Geology, 1950-1959* (I 19.3:1195).

947. Geological Survey. **Catalogue and Index of Contributions to North American Geology, 1732-1891** by Nelson Horatio Darton. GPO, 1896. 1045p. LC gs05-696. QE75.B9 no. 127. OCLC 1927564. [no SuDocs number].
This is a chronological listing of geologic literature published in North America, plus literature about North America (except Greenland and Central America). Some entries are annotated; some include references to reviews in journals.

948. Geological Survey. **GEOINDEX [computer file].** Online Computer Library Center, Inc. (OCLC), 19??- . Quarterly. CD-ROM.
This is a bibliographic database for geologic maps of the U.S. and its territories.

949. Geological Survey. **New Publications of the U.S. Geological Survey.** GS, 1984- . Monthly. LC 85-3385. OCLC 10827199. I 19.14/4: .
This is a bibliography of recent USGS special interest and outside publications, books, maps, and CD-ROMs, with general and author indexes and availability information. Monthly issues are cumulated annually in *Publications of the U.S. Geological Survey* (I 19.14/1:879-961, I 19.14:962-70, and I 19.14:971-81, with annual issues since 1982).

950. Geological Survey. **Stratigraphic Nomenclature Databases for the United States, Its Possessions and Territories [computer file].** GS, 1994. Release 2. CD-ROM. OCLC 30663342. I 19.121:6/994.
Also known as DDS-0006, this is a computerized lexicon of U.S. geologic and stratigraphic units that can be sorted by name, stratigraphic rank, age, province or region, state, author, or keywords. It includes the Geologic Names Unit Lexicon (GNULEX) and Geologic Names of the United States (GEONAMES). GNULEX is a computerized lexicon of U.S. historical geology and paleoecology. GEONAMES lists geological names, with pertinent

data such as location, geologic age, USGS usage, lithology, geologic province, thickness, lexicon reference, and unique identifier.

951. Smithsonian Institution. **A Brief History of Geomagnetism and a Catalog of the Collections of the National Museum of American History** by Robert P. Multhauf and Gregory Good. SI, 1987. 87p. LC 86-600156. QC816.M85 1987. 538/.7/09. OCLC 13665623. SI 1.28:48.

A brief history of terrestrial magnetism precedes an illustrated catalog of geomagnetic instruments held in the Museum of American History.

INFORMATION CENTER

952. National Oceanic and Atmospheric Administration. **National Geophysical Data Center**. NOAA, Code E/GC4, Dept. ORD, 325 Broadway, Boulder, CO 80303-3328; E-mail: *info@mail.ngdc.noaa.gov*; Internet *URL http://ftp.ngdc.noaa.gov/*; *URL http://gopher.ngdc.noaa.gov/*; *URL http://www.ngdc.noaa.gov/*.

The NGDC gathers data related to solid earth geophysics, marine geology and geophysics, solar-terrestrial physics, and paleoclimatology. The Center maintains digital and analog databases and distributes data on CD-ROM, magnetic tapes, and floppy diskettes, and in publications, maps, slides, and educational tools. Many data sets are available on the Internet. Materials and services are summarized in *Data, Products, and Services* (C 55.202:G 29/5).

MINERALOGY

953. Bureau of Mines. **Bureau of Mines Publications and Articles ... (With Subject and Author Index)**. GPO, 1993- . Biennial. LC sn94-28425. OCLC 30987665. I 28.5: .

Annual and five-year cumulations provide citations and abstracts for series, open file reports, outside and sales publications, patents, and reprints. There is a time lag before publication. Updated by the monthly *New Publications* of the Bureau of Mines (entry 958).

954. Bureau of Mines. **Directory of Mineral-Related Organizations**. BM, 19??- . OCLC 29510397. I 28.151: .

This list of public and private organizations offering mineral-related data, technical guidance, and advice is arranged by state.

955. Bureau of Mines. **Mineral Commodity Summaries**. BM, 1978- . Annual. LC 78-640742. HD9506.U6U48b. 338.2/0973. OCLC 3673088. I 28.148: .

This annual report provides market profiles from the Bureau of Mines and the USGS for nonfuel mineral commodity and commodity groups. Included are data on production, employment, earnings, expenditures, production, capacity use, tariffs, world reserves, and industry developments. Complementary sources are the monthly and quarterly *Mineral Industry Surveys: Monthly Mineral Surveys* (I 28.no:) and the annual *Mineral Industry Surveys: Annual Advance Summaries and Annual Reviews by Commodity* (I 28.no:).

956. Bureau of Mines. **Mineral Facts and Problems**. GPO, 1956- . Quinquennial. LC sn92-34158. OCLC 1779113. I 28.3/2:nos. vary.

This standard reference on key metals and minerals includes data on U.S. and world industry patterns, technology, reserves, supply and demand, consumption, economic factors, environmental considerations, and future uses. Since 1980 it has covered nonfuel minerals only, with the Department of Energy reporting fuel data. Chapters are issued separately as preprints and reprints. Updates during the five year cycle appear as MCP, *Mineral Commodity Profiles* (I 28.37/3:).

957.	Bureau of Mines. **Minerals Yearbook**. GPO, 1933- . Annual. LC 33-26551. TN23.U612. 338.2/0973. OCLC 1847412. I 28.37: .
Presents summaries of economic and technological developments in mineral industries in three separate volumes: Volume 1, Metals and Minerals, provides data arranged by metallic and industrial commodity for production and trade consumption, plus discussion of survey methods, a summary of nonfuel minerals, and trends in mining and quarrying. Volume 2, Area Reports: Domestic, reviews the minerals industry of each of the 50 states, Puerto Rico, the Northern Marianas, Island Possessions, and Trust Territory; describes survey methods for data collection; and presents a statistical summary of domestic nonfuel minerals. Volume 3, Area Reports: International, provides mineral data, trends, location maps, and industry structure tables for foreign countries, presented as five area reports and one world overview: Mineral Industries of Africa, Mineral Industries of Asia and the Pacific, Mineral Industries of Latin America and Canada, Mineral Industries of Europe and Central Eurasia, Mineral Industries of the Middle East, and Mineral Industries in the World Economy. Coverage for the series began in 1932. A related title is *Minerals in [year]* (I 28.156/3:), with profiles of key minerals.

958.	Bureau of Mines. **New Publications**. BM, 1910- . Monthly. LC sc77-188. OCLC 1348790. I 28.5/2: .
This is an annotated bibliography of publications, open file reports, and journal articles by Bureau authors, with availability notes.

959.	Bureau of Mines. **Statistical Compendium [computer file]**. GPO, 1994. CD-ROM. OCLC 31155866. I 28.37/6:970-90.
Contains longitudinal mining and minerals data that were previously published in *Minerals Yearbook*.

960.	Bureau of the Census. **Census of Mineral Industries**. GPO, 1840- . Quinquennial. C 3.216/: .
Data on the number of establishments, employment, payroll, hours worked, materials costs, value added, capital expenditures, products shipped, and materials consumed are collected every five years. An introduction is available in *Guide to the 1987 Economic Censuses and Related Statistics* (entry 219).

OCEANOGRAPHY

961.	National Oceanic and Atmospheric Administration. **National Oceanographic Data Center**. User Services Branch, NOAA/NESDIS E/OC21, 1825 Connecticut Ave., N.W., Washington, DC 20235; (202) 606-4549; E-mail: *services@nodc.noaa.gov*; Internet *URL http://gopher.nodc.noaa.gov/* or *URL http://www.nodc.noaa.gov/*.
The NODC is a repository and dissemination facility for global physical, chemical, and biological ocean data collected by federal, state, foreign, and local governments, universities, and industry. Data can be purchased on magnetic media, on CD-ROM, or transferred over computer networks through File Transfer Protocol (FTP). The Center also manages the NOAA Library and Information Network, with sites throughout the U.S. offering collections of books, journals, CD-ROMs, videos, and audiotapes.

962.	National Oceanic and Atmospheric Administration. Office of Undersea Research. **NOAA Diving Manual: Diving for Science and Technology**. 1v. GPO, 1991. LC 93-101737. VM981.U6228 1991. 627/.72. OCLC 25692377. C 55.8:D 64/991.

This is a manual of instructions, recommendations and guidance on a broad range of underwater living conditions and dive situations. Emphasis is on diving techniques and technology at depths of less than 250 feet. Includes photographs, illustrations, and a glossary.

963. National Oceanic and Atmospheric Administration. **The Directory of U.S. Marine CD-ROMs.** NOAA, 1991. Free: NOAA Central Library, 6009 Executive Blvd., Rockville, MD 20852. 48p. OCLC 23248521. C 55.48:M 33.

Describes CD-ROMs containing government marine and oceanic data and provides availability information.

PALEONTOLOGY

964. Geological Survey. **Index of Generic Names of Fossil Plants, 1820-1965** by Henry N. Andrews. GPO, 1970. 354p. LC 76-604645. QE75.B9 no.1300. 016.561. OCLC 109398. I 19.3:1300.

965. **Index of Generic Names of Fossil Plants, 1966-73** by Anna M. Blazer. GPO, 1975. 54p. LC 74-14995. QE75.B9 no.1396. 557.3/08s. OCLC 1008243. I 19.3:1396.

966. **Index of Generic Names of Fossil Plants, 1974-1978: Based on the Compendium Index of Paleobotany of the U.S. Geological Survey** by Arthur D. Watt. GPO, 1981. 63p. LC 80-606811. QE75.B9 no.1517. 557.3s. OCLC 7178058. I 19.3:1517.

The index lists generic names of fossil plants, exclusive of the diatoms, published from 1820 through 1978. It is based on the USGS Compendium Index of Paleobotany and its accompanying bibliography. Lengthy bibliographies give full citations for references listed in the index.

SEISMOLOGY

967. Environmental Data and Information Service. **Earthquake History of the United States** edited by Jerry L. Coffman, Carl A. von Hake, and Carl W. Stover. GPO, 1982. rev. ed. (through 1970), repr. 1982 with supplement (1971-80). 270p. OCLC 8968342. C 55.228:41-1/3.

This nontechnical chronology of major U.S. earthquakes through 1980 briefly describes major, intermediate, and minor earthquakes of intensity V or higher, and includes a section on Puerto Rico. Also contains bibliographies, photographs, and tables.

968. Geological Survey. **Earthquakes & Volcanoes.** GPO, 1986- . Bimonthly. LC 87-658056. QE531.N32a. 551.2/2/05. OCLC 15041297. I 19.65: .

Articles and tables provide current information on earthquakes, seismology, volcanoes, and landslides, with tables of earthquake activity by state, eyewitness accounts, and newspaper clippings. Each issue includes totals of U.S. earthquake activity and lists of locations, magnitudes, and fatalities for earthquakes during the previous two months.

969. Geological Survey. **United States Earthquakes.** GPO, 1928- . Annual. LC 75-640209. QE535.2.U6U55. 551.2/2/0973. OCLC 1798128. I 19.65/2:yr.

Contains detailed technical reports of all earthquakes registered in the United States and its territories during the year. Includes a list of all cities reporting earthquakes, samples of seismograph and tilt-graph readings and photographs, and detailed damage descriptions.

970. Geological Survey Photographic Library. **Photographs from the U.S. Geological Survey Photographic Library [computer file]: Earthquakes, Volcanoes, Geologic Hazards, and Other Phenomena** by Joseph K. McGregor and Carl Abston. GS, 1992. CD-ROM. OCLC 27122738. I 19.121:8.

Color and black-and-white images from the USGS Photographic Library collection include photos of earthquakes and volcanoes.

971. National Earthquake Information Center. **Guide to Products and Services.** NEIC, 19??- . Annual. LC sn94-27620. OCLC 29766973. I 19.15/3:P 94/ .

Products and services of the NEIC, the key source of current earthquake data, include CD-ROMs, software, maps and posters, database services, and publications.

972. National Geophysical Data Center. **Catalog of Significant Earthquakes, 2150 B.C.-1991 A.D., Including Quantitative Casualties and Damage** by Paula K. Dunbar, Patricia A. Lockridge, and Lowell S. Whiteside. NGDC, 1992. 320p. OCLC 26846102. C 55.220/5:49.

Data tables show date and time, epicenter, depth, magnitude, intensity, deaths, damage, tsunami, and location of historical earthquakes worldwide that were 7.5 or greater magnitude and X or greater intensity, and resulted in moderate damage and more than nine deaths. Earthquakes are listed chronologically and geographically. Also available as the Significant Earthquake Data Base.

973. National Geophysical Data Center. **United States Tsunamis: (Including United States Possessions): 1690-1988** by James F. Lander and Patricia A. Lockridge. NGDC, 1989. 265p. LC 89-602734. GC 220.3.L36 1989. 551.47/024. OCLC 20337032. C 55.202:T 78.

Tables of data and descriptions of tsunamis in Hawaii, Alaska, the coastal U.S., American Samoa, Puerto Rico, and the Virgin Islands are augmented by a general overview of tsunami characteristics and warning systems. Includes a place name index.

974. National Oceanic and Atmospheric Administration. World Data Center A for Solid Earth Geophysics. **Directory of World Seismograph Stations.** 2v. WDC, 1980, 1986. LC 80-603927. QE500.W67a. 551. OCLC 7738760. C 55.220/5:25.

Vol. 1. **The Americas** by Barbara B. Poppe.

Vol. 2. **East Asia—China, Japan, Korea, and Mongolia** compiled by S. Miyamura.

Volume 1 is a directory of stations in the United States, Canada, and Bermuda. Volume 2 covers China, Japan, Korea, and Mongolia. Additional volumes are planned.

Energy

Energy Information Administration:
*URL http://*www.eia.doe.gov/; or
URL http://gopher.eia.doe.gov/; or
URL http://ftp.eia.doe.gov/.

GENERAL WORKS

975. Energy Information Administration. **Historical Monthly Energy Review**. EIA, 1988- . LC 95-648072. HD9502.A1H57. 333.79/0973/021. OCLC 31161444. E 3.2:H 62/2.

This companion to *Monthly Energy Review* (entry 977) is a comprehensive summary of energy statistics for the U.S. and selected foreign countries. Statistics for coal, electricity, natural gas, nuclear power, and petroleum depict trends in production, use, import and export, stock, and prices, with additional detail for petroleum data. Data are presented for home, commercial, industrial, transportation, and electric utility use. Also available on diskettes as HMERDB, the *Historical Monthly Energy Review Database* (E 3.2:H 62/2/floppy) and through the *Federal Bulletin Board* (entry 35).

976. Energy Information Administration. **International Energy Annual**. GPO, 19??- . Annual. LC 82-641118. TJ163.13.I573. 333.79/11/0212. OCLC 7138645. E 3.11/20: .

Data can be downloaded through the Internet *URL http://www.eia.doe.gov/.*

Data on primary energy production, consumption, trade, stocks, and reserves in foreign countries, dependencies, and areas of special sovereignty are provided. The report covers petroleum, natural gas, coal, hydroelectric power, nuclear electric power, and electricity. Also available electronically through the *National Trade Data Bank* (entry 170).

977. Energy Information Administration. **Monthly Energy Review**. GPO, 1974- . Monthly. LC 75-640927. HD9564.M66. 333.7. OCLC 1798576. E 3.9: .

Also available on diskette: E 3.9/2: .

MER provides the most recent comprehensive monthly summary of U.S. energy statistics, with current and historical (about 20 years back) data for key U.S. energy series: Production, consumption, stocks, imports and exports, and prices. Also includes some international data for crude oil, petroleum, and electricity produced from nuclear power.

The EIA's electronic bulletin board, EPUB (entry 994), includes all tables from *Monthly Energy Review*. Also available through the *Federal Bulletin Board* (entry 35) and the *Economic Bulletin Board* (entry 169). The Monthly Energy Review Data Base is available from NTIS and GPO on diskette (E 3.9/2:).

978. Energy Information Administration. National Energy Information Center. **Energy Facts**. GPO, 1984-1992. Annual. LC 86-648047. HD9502.U5E524. 333.79/0973/021. OCLC 12144131. E 3.49: .

This was a quick reference compendium of domestic and international energy data on trends, petroleum, natural gas, coal, electricity, nuclear power, and renewable energy. Historical and current data were provided, along with a glossary.

979. Energy Information Administration. Office of Energy Markets and End Use. **Annual Energy Review**. GPO, 1982-. Annual. LC 83-645824. TJ163.25.U6U532a. 333.79/0973. OCLC 9563095. E 3.1/2: .

Also available from NTIS and GPO on diskette.

Presents historical data (since about 1949) for U.S. energy consumption and imports and exports. Also contains data on key energy commodities and fuel price, inventory, and reserve data. Key international data for major energy sources and activities are included. Continues volume 2 of the EIA *Annual Report to Congress*. Selected data and text are also available through the *National Economic, Social & Environmental Data Bank* (entry 172).

980. Energy Information Administration. Office of Energy Markets and End Use. **Short-Term Energy Outlook. Quarterly Projections**. GPO, 1982- . Quarterly. LC 84-641696. TJ163.25.U6S45. 333.79/0973. OCLC 10488812. E 3.31: .

Short-Term Energy Outlook. Annual Supplement. E 3.31: .

STEO forecasts energy supply, demand, stocks, and prices, and makes projections for petroleum, crude oil, gasoline, fuel oil, natural gas, coal, and electricity. The *Annual Supplement* discusses previous forecast errors. Also available through EPUB (entry 994) and the *Economic Bulletin Board* (entry 169).

981. Energy Information Administration. Office of Integrated Analysis and Forecasting. **Annual Energy Outlook**. GPO, 1982- . Annual. LC 83-645822. TJ163.25.U6A55. 333.79/0973. OCLC 9587622. E 3.1/4: .

Also available on diskettes (E 3.1/5:) and on the Internet *URL http://www.eia. doe.gov/*.

AEO presents projections of the U.S. domestic energy market, with projected supply, demand, and prices for electricity and major fuels. A supplement is sometimes issued (E 3.1/4:). Also available through EPUB (entry 994). The annual *Assumptions for the Annual Energy Outlook* (E 3.1/4-3:) discusses methodologies. AEO continues the EIA *Annual Report to Congress, Volume 3: Energy Projections*. International projections are given in the companion source, *International Energy Outlook* (E 3.11/20:) and its companion diskettes *World Energy Projection System (WEPS)* (E 3.11/20-3:).

BIBLIOGRAPHIES

982. Energy Information Administration. **EIA Directory of Electronic Products**. EIA, 19??- . Free: National Energy Information Center, EI-231, Energy Information Administration, Forrestal Bldg., Room 1F-048, Washington, DC 20585. Quarterly. LC 94-648417. TJ163.17.E35. 025.06/33379. OCLC 30771606. E 3.27/7: .

Descriptions of data files, computer models, CD-ROMs and online files include an abstract, technical contact person name, character set, media, ordering information, and documentation.

983. Energy Information Administration. **EIA Publications Directory**. EIA, 1978- . Free: National Energy Information Center, EI-231, Energy Information Administration, Forrestal Bldg., Room 1F-048, Washington, DC 20585, or request by E-mail: *infoctr@eia.doe.gov*. Annual. LC 80-641854. Z5853.P83U53a. 016.33379. OCLC 4943360. E 3.27: .

This is a bibliography with abstracts, availability, and report numbers noted. Indexed by subject, title, and report number. Also available through EPUB (entry 994). Updated by the bimonthly *EIA New Releases* (E 3.27/4:), also free from NEIC. Supplements *EIA Publications Directory, 1977-1989* [DOE/EIA-0149(77-89)].

COAL

984. Energy Information Administration. Office of Coal, Nuclear, Electric, and Alternate Fuels. **Coal Data, A Reference**. GPO, 1978- . Irregular. LC sn92-23008. OCLC 8995369. E 3.11/7-7: .

A compendium of current and some historical data on coal reserves, production and mining, supply and disposition, consumption, exports, and prices, with coal classifications.

985. Energy Information Administration. Office of Coal, Nuclear, Electric, and Alternate Fuels. **Quarterly Coal Report**. GPO, 1982- . Quarterly. LC sc83-1108. 338. OCLC 8911051. E 3.11/9: .

Also known as QSCR, this provides current and historical data (since 1982) on U.S. coal and coke production, distribution, exports, imports, receipts, prices, consumption, and stocks. A glossary is included. Also available through EPUB (entry 994).

986. Energy Information Administration. Office of Coal, Nuclear, Electric, and Alternate Fuels. **Weekly Coal Production**. GPO, 19??- . Weekly. LC sc84-8. OCLC 8517081. E 3.11/4: .

WCPR provides data on U.S. production of bituminous, lignite, and anthracite coals for the preceding two weeks, a corresponding week from the previous year, and for the previous 52 weeks and the preceding year, with percentage changes. Data are also provided on U.S. and state production, the number of railroad cars loaded, coal and coke exports and imports, state coal profiles, and coal use at the electric utilities. Also available through EPUB (entry 994).

DIRECTORIES

987. Department of Energy. **U.S. Department of Energy National Telephone Directory**. DE, 1994- . LC sn94-20641. OCLC 29700196. E 1.12/3: .

Lists DOE Washington and field personnel, with address and telephone number. Also includes a directory of other government agencies.

988. Energy Information Administration. **Energy Information Directory**. EIA, 1981- . Free: National Energy Information Center, EI-231, Energy Information Administration, Forrestal Bldg., Washington, DC 20585. Annual. LC 81-643400. HD9502.U5E526. 025.4/933379/0973. OCLC 6437469. E 3.33: .

Provides sources of energy information in DOE headquarters, field offices, project offices, labs, and power marketing administrations; other federal executive departments; energy congressional committees; independent federal agencies; state energy offices, governors' offices, and public service commissions; and trade associations. Also available through EPUB (entry 994) and the *National Economic, Social & Environmental Data Bank* (entry 172).

ELECTRIC

989. Energy Information Administration. Electric Power Division. **Electric Power Annual**. GPO, 1982- . Annual. LC 83-641417. HD9685.U4E39. 333.79/32/0973. OCLC 9121513. E 3.11/17-10: .

Presents national, regional, and state electric utility data on generation, consumption, finances, stocks, sales, revenue, gaseous emissions, environmental equipment, and electric power transactions.

990. Energy Information Administration. Office of Coal, Nuclear, Electric, and Alternate Fuels. **Electric Power Monthly**. GPO, 1980- . Monthly. LC 82-641981. TK23.E52. 363.6/2. OCLC 7056394. E 3.11/17-8: .

Also known as EPMS, this provides summaries of electric utility statistics for the nation, census divisions, and states for net generation, consumption, stocks, quantity and quality, cost, sales, and average retail prices of electricity. Some plant level and North American Electric Reliability Council region level data are also given. Also available through EPUB (entry 994).

INDEXES AND ABSTRACTS

991. Department of Energy. **Energy Science and Technology**. Database. 1974- .

This online equivalent of *Energy Research Abstracts* (entry 992) is a database of report literature on solar and geothermal energy, fuels, nuclear and fusion energy, electric power engineering, and many other subjects. Materials abstracted and indexed include technical reports, patent applications, theses, conference papers and proceedings, audiovisuals, electronic media, and engineering drawings. Available on magnetic tape from NTIS and from commercial vendors; also accessible via the Department of Energy's online system, DOE/RECON. Formerly Energy Data Base (EDB).

992. Department of Energy. Technical Information Center. **Energy Research Abstracts**. GPO, 1977- . Semimonthly. LC 78-642308. Z5853.P83U544b. 621. OCLC 3568399. E 1.17: .

ERA provides abstracts of energy-related reports from the DOE, other government agencies, and U.S. and foreign private sources. Since 1991, ERA has been limited to literature in report form, including technical reports, patent applications, theses, conference papers and proceedings, audiovisuals, electronic media, and engineering drawings. ERA's online equivalent is the DOE Energy Science and Technology Database (entry 991).

INFORMATION CENTER

993. Energy Information Administration. **National Energy Information Center**. Energy Information Administration, Forrestal Bldg., EI-231, Room 1F-048, Washington, DC 20585. E-mail: *infoctr@eia.doe.gov*.

The Center responds to requests for energy statistics, provides referral, and maintains a public reading room.

MACHINE-READABLE DATA

994. National Energy Information Center. **EPUB; Electronic Publishing System. (Electronic Bulletin Board).** Current month only. Accessed by dialing (202) 586-2557 or through FedWorld *URL http://www.fedworld.gov/govtbbs.htm.*
EPUB provides news releases and timely statistics from EIA publications, including all tables from the *Monthly Energy Review* (entry 977). Other EIA files of disaggregated data on which aggregate tables appearing in EIA publications are based are available through the *Federal Bulletin Board* (entry 35). *EPUB User's Guide* (E 3.8:El 2) is available online or free from the National Energy Information Center, Forrestal Bldg., EI-231, Room 1F-048, Washington, DC 20585; E-mail: *infoctr@eia.doe.gov.*

NATURAL GAS

994a. Energy Information Administration. Office of Oil and Gas. **Natural Gas Annual.** GPO, 1980- . Annual. LC 83-641511. HD9581.U49N37. 338.2/7285/0973. OCLC 8702847. E 3.11/2-2: .

Also available on diskettes.

A compendium of data on the supply and disposition of natural gas from production to use, including supplemental supplies. Tables show recent statistics for each Census division and the 50 states, with annual historical data for the nation. Includes a glossary.

995. Energy Information Administration. Office of Oil and Gas. **Natural Gas Monthly.** GPO, 1982- . Monthly. LC 84-650685. TN880.A1N314. 338.2/7285/0973021. OCLC 9314116. E 3.11: .
Presents monthly and annual data on state and national gas supply, disposition, production, prices, storage, imports and exports, interstate pipelines, and consumption. Includes a discussion of data sources and a glossary, plus feature articles.

PETROLEUM

996. Energy Information Administration. Office of Energy Markets and End Use. **International Petroleum Statistics Report.** GPO, 1989- . Monthly. LC 89-656177. HD9560.1.I566. 338.2/728/021. OCLC 19688109. E 3.11/5-6: .
Provides historical and current data on international oil production, exports, imports, consumption, and stocks.

997. Energy Information Administration. Office of Oil and Gas. **Petroleum Marketing Annual.** GPO, 19??- . Annual. LC 87-654128. HD9561.P424. 338.4/36655/0973021. OCLC 15233107. E 3.13/4-2: .
Data on crude oils and refined petroleum products include costs, sales, and prices.

998. Energy Information Administration. Office of Oil and Gas. **Petroleum Marketing Monthly.** GPO, 1983- . Monthly. LC sc83-9424. 338. OCLC 9583990. E 3.13/4: .
Data for states and for U.S. Petroleum Administration for Defense Districts indicate sales and prices for petroleum products by seller and type of sale.

999. Energy Information Administration. Office of Oil and Gas. **Petroleum Supply Annual.** GPO, 1981- . Annual. LC 83-645629. HD9561.P428. 338.4/76655/0973. OCLC 8771430. E 3.11/5-5: .
Final statistics on supply and disposition of crude oil and petroleum products in the U.S. replace data previously published in *Petroleum Supply Monthly* (entry 1000).

1000. Energy Information Administration. Office of Oil and Gas. **Petroleum Supply Monthly**. GPO, 1982- . Monthly. LC 82-647181. HD9561.P43. 338.2/7282/0973. OCLC 8517121. E 3.11/5: .

Data and articles about supply and disposition of crude oil and petroleum products in the U.S. include current and historical data describing monthly production, imports and exports, inter-Petroleum Administration for Defense District movements, and inventories.

1001. Energy Information Administration. **Weekly Petroleum Status Report**. GPO, 1981- . Weekly. LC sn87-43154. 338. OCLC 9978225. E 3.32: .

WPSR provides data on U.S. petroleum supply for the week and month, with some historical data. It describes the U.S. petroleum balance sheet, refinery activity, stocks, imports, products, and prices. Includes a glossary and list of data sources. Also available through EPUB (entry 994).

THESAURUS

1002. Department of Energy. Office of Scientific and Technical Information. **International Energy: Subject Thesaurus**. NTIS, 1990- . LC 91-641241. Z695.1. P68E54. 025.4/933379. OCLC 23185742. E 1.2:T 34/2/ .

Contains descriptors for international energy research, development, and technology; nuclear energy; energy resources; conservation; safety; environmental impact; and regulation. Formerly *Energy Information Database: Subject Thesaurus*.

Engineering

AERONAUTICAL AND SPACE ENGINEERING

General Works

1003. National Aeronautics and Space Administration. **NASA Thesaurus**. NTIS, 19??- .
Triennial. LC sn88-6124. 025. OCLC 13801500. NAS 1.21: .
This is a controlled vocabulary of descriptors assigned to documents in the NASA
scientific and technical information database. Volume 1, Hierarchical Listing, contains
descriptors and cross-references; Volume 2, Access Vocabulary, refers from other terms to
descriptors in Volume 1; and Volume 3, Definitions, defines descriptors. Updated semiannually by the *NASA Thesaurus Supplement* (NAS 1.21:7064-suppl-3).

1004. National Aeronautics and Space Administration. Scientific and Technical Information Division. **NASA Thesaurus Aeronautics Vocabulary**. NTIS (N91-
16847/6/HDM), 1991. 215p. OCLC 23840935. NAS 1.15:104230.
Descriptors for aeronautical documents in the NASA scientific and technical information
database are listed in this subset of the 1988 *NASA Thesaurus* and its supplements. It
also covers terminology for fluid dynamics, propulsion engineering, test facilities, and
instrumentation.

Indexes and Abstracts

1005. National Aeronautics and Space Administration. Scientific and Technical Information Program. **Aeronautical Engineering**. NTIS, 1970- . Monthly. LC 71-
613342. Z5063.A2A28. 016.62913. OCLC 1664053. NAS 1.21:7037(nos.).

> Beginning with January 1996, only available on the Internet *URL http://www.
> sti.nasa.gov/.*

Contains selected, annotated citations to classified reports and journal articles related to
aircraft engineering, design, and operation, along with aerodynamic and aeronautical
research. Titles were added to the NASA scientific and technical information system and
announced in *Scientific and Technical Aerospace Reports* (entry 1006) and *International
Aerospace Abstracts*.

1006. National Aeronautics and Space Administration. Scientific and Technical Information Program. **Scientific and Technical Aerospace Reports**. GPO, 1963-1995. Semimonthly. LC 64-39060. TL500.S35. 629.1./05. OCLC 1645472. NAS 1.9/4: .

> Beginning with January 1996, only available on the Internet *URL http://www. sti.nasa.gov/.*

STAR covers all aspects of aeronautics and space research, plus aerospace aspects of earth resources, energy development, conservation, oceanography, environmental protection, and urban transportation. It indexes and abstracts unclassified technical reports of NASA and its contractors and grantees, federal agencies, universities, private firms, and U.S. and foreign institutions; translations in report form; NASA-owned patents and patent applications; and dissertations. An annual cumulated index is published separately (NAS 1.9/5:). Indexing is based on the *NASA Thesaurus* (entry 1003).

Space Exploration

1007. House. Committee on Science and Technology. **Investigation of the Challenger Accident: Report of the Committee on Science and Technology, House of Representatives, Ninety-Ninth Congress, Second Session**. (H.Rpt.v 99-1016). GPO, 1986. 442p. LC 86-603145. KF32.S39 1986. 363.1/24. OCLC 14767125. (Serial Set 13713). Y 1.1/8:99-1016.

The report on the investigation of the January 28, 1986 space shuttle *Challenger* accident is based on oversight hearings.

1008. House. Committee on Science, Space, and Technology. **Astronauts and Cosmonauts Biographical and Statistical Data: Report** prepared by the Congressional Research Service, Library of Congress. GPO, 1994. 605p. LC 94-189480. TL789.85.A1A87 1993. 629.45/0092/273. OCLC 30304037. Y 4.SCI 2:103/I.

Presents biographies and statistics about living and dead astronauts, cosmonauts, and foreign personnel and trainees. Includes an index and black-and-white photographs.

1009. House. Committee on Science, Space, and Technology. **Space Activities of the United States, Soviet Union, and Other Launching Countries-Organizations, 1957-1993: Report** by Marcia S. Smith. GPO, 1994. 170p. LC 94-190840. TL788.5.S583 1994. 629.4/0973. OCLC 30652634. Y 4.SCI 2:103-K.

Provides a chronicle of U.S. and Soviet human flight, applications flights, space science, military activities, and the space program. Includes projections and a comprehensive list of launches and flights. Space activities of other nations and organizations are also discussed.

1010. National Aeronautics and Space Administration. **Aeronautics and Space Report of the President . . . Activities**. GPO, 19??- . Annual. LC 81-642321. TL789.8.U5U57a. 629.4/0973. OCLC 5924866. (Also in the Serial Set). NAS 1.52: .

Summarizes federal activities in space and provides information on expenditures and launch vehicles. Includes chronologies and policy documents.

1011. National Aeronautics and Space Administration. **Astronautics and Aeronautics**. GPO, 1963-1985. Annual. OCLC 3490304. NAS 1.21: .

This chronology summarizes events in aeronautics, aviation, and space, citing sources of further information. It includes tables of "Satellites, Space Probes, and Manned Space Flights," lists of major NASA launches and NASA History Series titles, and an index.

1012. Presidential Commission on the Space Shuttle Challenger Accident. **Report to the President**. 5v. PCSSCA, 1986. LC 86-602211. TL867.U55 1986. 363.1/24. OCLC 13742794. Pr 40.8:Sp 1/R 29.
The report of the Presidential Commission investigation of the January 28, 1986 space shuttle *Challenger* accident describes the background and causes of the accident. Volumes 2 and 3 are appendixes; volumes 4 and 5 provide hearings transcripts.

1013. Senate. Committee on Commerce, Science, and Transportation. **Soviet Space Programs: 1981-87**. (S.Prt. [100]-107, 101-32). 2v. GPO, 1988, 1989. LC 89-603494. TL789.8.S65S6852 1988. 354.470087/78. OCLC 18130405.
   Pt.1. **Soviet Space Programs: 1981-87, Piloted Space Activities, Launch Vehicles, Launch Sites, and Tracking Support**. Y 4.C 73/7:S.prt.101-107/pt.1.
      This report focuses on manned space activities, including a historical summary, details on *Salyut 7* and the Russian Space Station, MIR, and discussion of space medicine and biology, facilities, and support services. Future activities are projected. Also included are descriptions of surface vessel support ships and their missions.
   Pt.2. **Soviet Space Programs: 1981-87, Space Science, Space Applications, Military Space Programs, Administration, Resource Burden, and Master Log of Spaceflights**. Y 4.C 73/7:S.prt. 101-32/pt.2.
      This report covers automated space programs and administration of the program, with a historical overview (1957-83) and a discussion of military space activities.

1014. Entry not used.

1015. Senate. Committee on Commerce, Science, and Transportation. **Space Law and Related Documents: International Space Law Documents, U.S. Space Law Documents**. GPO, 1990. 605p. LC 90-601621. JX5810.S6786 1990. 341.4/7/026. OCLC 22146333. Y 4.C 73/7:S.prt. 101-98.
Part 1 contains texts of U.S. and international law and policy materials governing space exploration and use, including U.S.-Soviet bilateral agreements; U.N. treaties, resolutions, and agreements; multilateral agreements; and international communications satellite agreements. Part 2 contains texts of U.S. space law and policy documents.

1016. Smithsonian Institution. National Air and Space Museum. **Rockets, Missiles, and Spacecraft of the National Air and Space Museum, Smithsonian Institution** complied by Gregory P. Kennedy. SI, 1983. rev. ed. 165p. LC 83-600049. TL 506.U6W376 1983. 629.47/0973074/0153. OCLC 9394138. SI 9.2:R 59.
This catalog of descriptions and photographs of the definitive U.S. Space Program collection includes artifacts originating between 1844 and 1983. It also lists all manned spacecraft and their locations.

CIVIL ENGINEERING

1017. Army. Corps of Engineers. **Officer and Warrant Officer Directory**. GPO, 1982- . Irregular. LC 82-643045. UG23.U46b. 358/.2/02573. OCLC 8401553. D 103.71: .
Lists names of general, engineer, and warrant officers, and U.S. Military Academy engineer faculty members, along with a numerical listing by grade/sequence number. Tables provide name, unit, station, active duty grade code, permanent grade, component,

date of rank, basic pay entry date, specialty, birth date, engineer registration, and state of registration.

1018. Army. Corps of Engineers. **The History of the U.S. Army Corps of Engineers.** ACE, 1993. 3d ed. LC 92-38521. UG23.H68 1993. 358/.22/0973. OCLC 26853336. [SuDocs number not available].

Military and civil activities of the Corps since the Revolutionary War are reviewed, including wartime operations; flood control; involvement with lighthouses, the Panama Canal, and the Manhattan Project; and military construction. Biographical sketches of the chief engineers since 1775 are included. Related titles are *A Century on the Mississippi: A History of the Memphis District, U.S. Army Corps of Engineers, 1876-1981* (D 103.2:M 69/10) and *The Southwestern Division: 50 Years of Service* (D 103.2:So 8/2).

1019. Coast Guard. **Bridges Over the Navigable Waters of the United States.** 4v. CG, 1984. OCLC 24031261. TD 5.2:B 76/[region]/984.

       Great Lakes. 1991. TD 5.2:B 76/great lakes/991.

This directory of bridges notes ownership, clearance height, and use. Volumes cover the following regions: Atlantic Coast, Great Lakes, Gulf Coast and Mississippi River System, and Pacific Coast.

1020. Federal Highway Administration. **Standard Specifications for Construction of Roads and Bridges on Federal Highway Projects.** GPO, 1992. 701p. OCLC 27313755. TD 2.8:C 76/2/992.

This is a construction handbook for Federal Highway Administration FP-92 standards, including general requirements, earthwork, embankments, aggregate courses, surface treatments, bridge construction, incidental construction, and materials. Includes an index.

1021. Forest Service. Engineering Staff. **Timber Bridges: Design, Construction, Inspection, and Maintenance** by Michael A. Ritter. 1v. FS, 1990. OCLC 22146724. A 13.84/2:7700-8.

A manual for designing, building, inspecting, and maintaining timber bridges. Includes a glossary.

1022. Occupational Safety and Health Administration. **Construction Industry Digest.** GPO, 1991- . Irregular. LC sn94-28132. OCLC 30481841. L 35.6/4:C 76/ .

This is a compilation of frequently overlooked safety and health standards, including those for hazardous situations.

NUCLEAR ENGINEERING

1023. Nuclear Regulatory Commission. Division of Freedom of Information and Publications Services. **Nuclear Regulatory Commission Issuances.** GPO, 1975- . Monthly. HD9698.U5A332. LC sf88-36009. 343.73/0925. OCLC 2274907. Y 3.N 88:11-2/ .

Contains the text of opinions, decisions, denials, memoranda, and orders of the NRC, the Atomic Safety and Licensing Boards, and the Administrative Law Judges, and Directors. Issues are cited in this format: 35 NRC 236 (1992), which represents volume 35 (1992) of *Nuclear Regulatory Commission Issuances*, page 236. Cumulated semiannually (Y 3.N 88:11/).

1024. Nuclear Regulatory Commission. Division of Freedom of Information and Publications Services. **Indexes to Nuclear Regulatory Commission Issuances.** Y 3.N 88:11-2/yr-yr/cum.ind.no.
Indexes and digests of issuances from the NRC, the Atomic Safety and Licensing Boards, the Administrative Law Judges, and Directors refer to the full text through issuance and docket numbers. Included are case name, legal citation, subject, and facility indexes.

1025. Nuclear Regulatory Commission. Division of Freedom of Information and Publications Services. **Title List of Documents Made Publicly Available.** GPO, 1979- . Monthly. LC 90-656630. Z5162.R42T57. 016.62148/35/0973. OCLC 5182879. Y 3.N 88:21-2/ .
Also known as NUREG-0540, this lists NRC publications and materials received by the NRC related to nuclear power plants, radioactive material, and regulatory records. It includes NRC-docketed regulatory records related to civilian power plants and uses of radioactive materials, and nondocketed NRC material related to its regulatory role. Includes author, corporate, and report number indexes. A related title is *Local Public Document Room Directory* (Y 3.N 88:31:0088/REV.3) for commercial power plants.

1026. Nuclear Regulatory Commission. **Licensed Operating Reactors, Status Summary Report.** GPO, 198?- . Annual. LC 81-643876. TK1343.U56b. 621.31/25/0973. OCLC 7465682. Y 3.N 88:15/ .
Operating data for commercial American nuclear power plants relate to licensed thermal power, maximum dependable capacity, power level restrictions, hours reactor was critical, reserve shutdown hours, energy generated, shutdowns scheduled during the next six months, and average daily power level. Each entry includes a utility contact and telephone number. Features a glossary.

1027. Nuclear Regulatory Commission. **NRC Telephone Directory.** GPO, 198?- . Irregular. LC sn90-20295. 353. OCLC 22271388. Y 3.N 88:14/ .
The directory lists personnel on the Commission, committees and boards, staff offices, program offices, and regions. Includes organizational abbreviations. A related source is *Directory of Contacts for Technical Issues* (Y 3.N 88:52/C 76).

1028. Nuclear Regulatory Commission. Regulatory Publications Branch. **Regulatory and Technical Reports.** GPO, 198?- . Quarterly. LC sn91-23472. OCLC 24252005. Y 3.N 88:21-3/ .
This abstract journal cites and summarizes regulatory and technical reports from the NRC and its contractors (cited NUREG-xxxx). Indexes provide access by secondary report number, author, subject, organization, contract sponsor/contractor, international organization, and licensed facility.

PUBLIC SAFETY ENGINEERING

1029. National Geophysical Data Center. **The Natural Hazards Data Resources Directory: A Resource for the Disaster and Hazard Management Community of Practitioners and Research Scholars** compiled and edited by Leaura M. Hennig. NGDC, 1990. 247p. LC 90-60033. Z6004.N3H46 1990. 363.3/4. OCLC 21502240. C 55.219/2:23.
This is a directory of federal, state, and international organizations active in geological and meteorological hazards studies, management, and mitigation. It includes organizations active in emergency preparedness and disaster relief.

Motor Vehicle Safety

1030. National Highway Traffic Safety Administration. **Safety Related Recall Campaigns for Motor Vehicles and Motor Vehicle Equipment, Including Tires.** GPO, 1979- . Quarterly. LC sn89-23263. OCLC 7498758. TD 8.9/2: .

Recalls of foreign and domestic vehicles and of domestic equipment and tires are listed by company, with make, model, year, number recalled, system, vehicle description, description and consequence of defect, notification date, and corrective action.

Natural Disasters

1031. Federal Emergency Management Agency. **FEMA Publications Catalog.** FEMA, 1985- . LC sn90-20431. OCLC 22600005. FEM 1.24:P 96/ .

Lists publications and training materials, including civil preparedness guides, technical reports, handbooks, research summaries, instructor guides, student manuals, kits, and posters, along with availability information. Includes a title index.

Environmental Sciences

GENERAL WORKS

1032. Bureau of Land Management. **Public Land Statistics**. GPO, 1962- . Annual. LC
79-647223. HD183.B87a. 333.1/0973. OCLC 1197130. I 53.1/2:yr.
Data from Bureau of Land Management administration of public lands in the U.S. and its
territories covers land disposition and use; management of wild horses and burros, habitat,
range, and forests; conservation and development; outdoor recreation; wilderness resources; energy and minerals resources; and classifications and investigations, protection,
surveys, and government administration and finance. Information about administration of
the BLM includes public land surveys, fire protection, unauthorized use, and finance.
Includes an index and a glossary.

1033. Bureau of Reclamation. **Environmental Glossary** by Wayne O. Deason et al. BR,
1986. rev. and enl. 79p. OCLC 15174209. I 27.2:En 8/2/986.
Environmental terms used in algology, archaeology, bacteriology, chemistry, dendrology,
fish and wildlife biology, geology, hydrology, and physiology are briefly defined. Featured
are tables of unit prefixes and conversions.

1034. Bureau of Reclamation. **Publications for Sale**. BR, 19??- . Annual. LC 75-
644787. Z5853.H9P82. 016.627/0973. OCLC 2242068. I 27.10/2: .
This selected list of sale publications from the Bureau of Reclamation includes title, price,
and publication date for each item.

1035. Center for Environmental Research Information. **Geographic Index of Environmental Articles**. CERI, 1990- . Annual. LC 94-649659. Z5861.G46. 016.3637.
OCLC 26220203. EP 1.23/6:600/ .
Citations to journal articles and proceedings related to environmental issues and research
are arranged by geographic locations and by source documents.

1036. Environmental Protection Agency. Office of Toxic Substances. **Toxic Release
Inventory**. EPA, 1987- . Annual. Microfiche. OCLC 21401259. EP 5.22: .
Also available from GPO on CD-ROM EP 5.22:T 65/ .
TRI includes information about toxic chemicals released into the environment. It can
be purchased from GPO or NTIS, accessed through commercial vendors, or searched
on MEDLINE as TOXNET. Also available on the *Federal Bulletin Board* (entry 35)
and the *National Economic, Social & Environmental Data Bank* (entry 172). The *Toxic
Release Inventory Fiche Search Guide* (EP 5.22:ind./990) is a guide to searching the TRI
microfiche.

1037. Executive Office of the President. Council on Environmental Quality. **Environmental Trends**. GPO, 1989. 152p. LC 91-600503. TD171.E575 1989. 363.7/00973. OCLC 21111260. PrEx 14.2:T 72.

This colorful, visual summary of U.S. environmental trends depicts data and projections with maps, tables, charts, and narrative. Subjects include minerals, energy, water, climate, air quality, land resources, wetlands, wildlife, parks, transportation, and environmental hazards.

1038. National Oceanographic Data Center. **Ecosystems of the Florida Keys: A Bibliography** compiled, edited, and indexed by Linda Pikula and Stanley Elswick. NODC, 1992. 189p. LC 92-247703. Z5322.E2P55 1992. 574.5/09759/41. OCLC 25910801. C 55.229:F 66.

This annotated bibliography includes books, articles, and reports. Indexed by author, subject, and geographic region.

AIR POLLUTION

1039. Environmental Protection Agency. **Building Air Quality: A Guide for Building Owners and Facility Managers**. GPO, 1991. 229p. OCLC 24674320. EP 4.8:Ai 7/7.

This is a manual for developing a building profile to prevent air quality problems, create a quality plan, identify problems and solutions, and determine when outside technical advice is needed. Includes a glossary and an index.

1040. Environmental Protection Agency. Office of Air and Radiation. **Directory of State Indoor Air Contacts**. EPA, 1991. 149p. LC 92-178325. TD883.2.D57 1991. 363.73/92. OCLC 23964774. EP 1.102:St 2/2.

Experts on indoor air problems are listed by state and type of problem. State agencies are also listed.

1041. Environmental Protection Agency. Office of Air Quality Planning and Standards. **National Air Pollutant Emission Estimates**. GPO, 19??- . Annual. LC sn93-28131. OCLC 26442751. EP 4.24: .

This summary is retrospective to 1940, giving trends and estimates for particulates, sulfur oxides, nitrogen oxides, reactive volatile organic compounds, carbon monoxide, and lead. Sources of each pollutant are noted.

1042. Environmental Protection Agency. Office of Air Quality Planning and Standards. **National Air Pollutant Emission Trends, 1900-1994**. 1v. EPA, 1995. OCLC 33396085. [SuDocs number not yet available].

Pollution from transportation, combustion of stationary fuel, industry, solid waste disposal, and fires is summarized by source, state, and region for particulates, sulfur oxides, nitrogen oxides, volatile organic compounds, carbon monoxide, and lead. Information is presented in charts and tables.

1043. Environmental Protection Agency. Office of Air Quality Planning and Standards. **National Air Quality and Emissions Trends Report**. GPO, 1981- . Annual. LC 85-643610. TD883.2.N27. 363.7/3922/0973. OCLC 12568641. EP 4.22/2: .

Summarizes particulates, sulfur dioxide, nitrogen dioxide, carbon monoxide, ozone, and lead in the air for the nation, Metropolitan Statistical Areas (MSAs), and foreign countries, with trends dating back a decade. Presents information in maps, charts, and tables.

1044. Environmental Protection Agency. Office of Air Quality Planning and Standards. **National Air Toxics Information Clearinghouse: Bibliography of Selected Reports and Federal Register Notices Related to Air Toxics: Index, 1990: Final Report** prepared by Carol A. Owen, Linda Y. Cooper, and Carolyn E. Norris. EPA, 1990. 482p. OCLC 23742385. EP 4.25:AI 7/IND.
This is a cumulative index to reports and *Federal Register* notices published since 1974.

CONSERVATION

1045. Federal Interagency Committee for Wetland Delineation. **Federal Manual for Identifying and Delineating Jurisdictional Wetlands: An Interagency Cooperative Publication.** 1v. GPO, 1989. OCLC 19985573. I 49.6/2:W 53/2.
Gives technical criteria, field indicators, and methods for identifying jurisdictional wetlands and delineating their upper boundaries.

1046. Fish and Wildlife Service. **Endangered and Threatened Species of the Southeastern U.S.** 1v. FWS, 1991. OCLC 26040784. I 49.2:R 24/7.
This guide, better known as The Red Book, lists national, regional (Carolinas, Georgia, Florida, Alabama, Tennessee, Kentucky, Mississippi, Arkansas, Louisiana, Puerto Rico, and the Virgin Islands), and individual endangered and threatened plants, mammals, invertebrates, reptiles, fish, and mussels. Descriptive entries include *Federal Register* citation; status; family; description; biological, reproductive, and developmental information; habitat; management and protection; bibliographic references; and contact persons. Includes the text of the Endangered Species Act.

1047. Fish and Wildlife Service. **Endangered and Threatened Species Recovery Program: Report to Congress.** GPO, 1990- . Biennial. LC 92-657338. QH76.E54. 333.95. OCLC 24617666. I 49.77/3: .
Contains progress reports on the status of endangered and threatened plants and animals (land and freshwater species) managed by the FWS. Features length of time listed, priority, recovery plan status, and state native species lists. Includes a species common name index.

1048. Fish and Wildlife Service. **Field Guide to Nontidal Wetland Identification** by Ralph W. Tiner, Jr. FWS, 1988. 283p. LC 88-623549. QH87.3.T56 1988. OCLC 18694842. I 49.6/2:W 53.
This guide for nonspecialists describes wetlands, soils, and hydrology, along with 200 wetland plants common to Maryland and other Northeastern states.

1049. Fish and Wildlife Service. **Handbook of Toxicity of Pesticides to Wildlife** by Rick H. Hudson, Richard K. Tucker, and M. A. Haegele. GPO, 1984. 2d ed. 90p. LC 84-600011. S914.A3 no.153. 333.95/4/0973. OCLC 10458120. I 49.66:153.
Information is provided on toxicity estimates, use, lethal doses, and signs of intoxication for individual chemicals or formulations. Includes a species index.

1050. Fish and Wildlife Service. Publications Unit. **Publications List.** FWS, 1993. 40p. OCLC 28595914. I 49.18:P 96.
This unannotated bibliography of technical series publications includes biological reports, resource publications, research reports, leaflets, bulletins, posters, brochures, and the "biologue" series of single-page life histories of species. No index.

1051. National Park Service. Rivers, Trails and Conservation Program. **River Conservation Directory.** GPO, 1990- . Biennial. LC 91-641858. QH76.R58. 333.91/6216/02573. OCLC 22055709. I 29.126:R 52/ .

Lists public and nonprofit agencies concerned with river conservation, with address, telephone number, contact person, and a brief description. Includes an agency index.

EPA PUBLICATIONS

1052. Environmental Protection Agency. **Access EPA**. GPO, 1991- . Annual. LC 92-657336. Z675.E75U55a. 027.6/9. OCLC 24771439. EP 1.8/13:Ac 2/ .
This guide to EPA and other environmental resources includes library and information sources, clearinghouses and hot lines, environmental databases, dockets, records management programs, EPA scientific models, and state environmental libraries. Includes indexes to subjects, acronyms, agency names, titles, and acts.

1053. Environmental Protection Agency. Architectural Management and Planning Branch. **EPADOC [computer file]**. GPO, 1992- . Irregular. CD-ROM. LC 95-641394. TD171u. OCLC 29838837. EP 1.104/2: .
This compendium of general interest EPA documents includes the EPA Processing Division's Operations Policies Manual, information about EPA software and hardware contracts, E-mail guides, and records management policies.

1054. Environmental Protection Agency. Library Systems Branch. **EPA Publications Bibliography; Quarterly Abstract Bulletin**. NTIS, 1977- . Quarterly. LC 79-644595. Z5863.P7U58a. 016.3637. OCLC 3806538. EP 1.21/7: .
Bibliographic citations and abstracts are provided for EPA technical reports and journal articles added to the NTIS collection. Indexes by title, keyword, corporate and personal author, contract number, sponsoring EPA office, and accession/report number are cumulated in the fourth quarterly issue. Cumulations (titled *EPA Publications Bibliography, [date]*) are available for the years 1984-90, 1977-83, and 1970-76 (EP 1.21/7-2:).

1055. Environmental Protection Agency. Office of Administration and Resources Management. **EPA National Publications Catalog**. GPO, 1994- . LC 94-648702. Z5863.P7U58c. 016.3637/00973. OCLC 31507666. EP 1.21:P 96/5/ .
This bibliography of EPA publications, journals, and electronic information products provides EPA number, source, and ordering number. Includes agency, title, EPA number, and subject indexes. Publications are listed by agency, title, EPA number, and subject.

1056. Environmental Protection Agency. Office of Administration and Resources Management. **Headquarters Telephone Directory**. GPO, 1984- . Semiannual. LC sn89-10528. OCLC 10425891. EP 1.12: .
EPA telephone numbers are arranged in organizational, alphabetical, headquarters subject, regional, hot line, and agency directories, along with organizational and regional contact people and E-mail addresses. Also included are organization charts, abbreviations, descriptions, and selected government acronyms.

WASTE DISPOSAL

1057. Department of Defense. **Hazardous Material Control & Management [computer file]: HMC&M; Hazardous Material Information System: HMIS**. Defense General Supply Center, 1991- . Quarterly. CD-ROM. LC 93-648935. T55.3.H3 u. OCLC 25494925. D 212.16: .
Data from the Material Safety Data Sheet (MSDS) Database are augmented by transportation information, hazard warning label information, and disposal criteria used by the DoD and civilian federal agencies.

1058. Environmental Protection Agency. Office of Emergency and Remedial Response. **Catalog of Superfund Program Information Products**. EPA, 199?- . OCLC 31726134. EP 1.21:SU 7/ .
This is an annotated list of EPA publications, diskettes, microfiche, CD-ROMs, and magnetic tape related to cleanup of abandoned and uncontrolled hazardous waste sites. Includes a subject index.

1059. Environmental Protection Agency. **RCRA Information Center (RIC)**. Office of Solid Waste, 401 M. St., S.W. (Mail Code 5305), Washington, DC 20460; (800) 424-9346, in Washington, DC area (703) 412-9810.
Information to the public about recycling, treatment, and disposal of hazardous and nonhazardous solid waste is provided by RIC using documents also designed for writing regulations under the Resource Conservation and Recovery Act and EPA publication.

1060. Environmental Protection Agency. Solid Waste and Emergency Response. **Catalogue of Hazardous and Solid Waste Publications**. EPA, 19??- . Free: Office of Solid Waste, RCRA Information Center, 401 M. St., S.W. (Mail Code 5305), Washington, DC 20460.
    Annual. LC 93-660720. Z5853.S22U4285a. 363.72/87/005. OCLC 27245460. EP 1.2:H 33/30/.
This annotated bibliography of documents issued by the EPA's Office of Solid Waste includes title, subject, and report number indexes.

WATER

1061. Bureau of Reclamation. **Ground Water Manual: A Guide for the Investigation, Development, and Management of Ground-Water Resources**. GPO, 1985. rev. reprint. 480p. LC 85-602665. TD403.G7155 1985. 628.1/14. OCLC 12951671. I 27.19/2:G 91/985.
This handbook for groundwater investigations, management, and development covers occurrence and flow, well-aquifer relationships, data collection, investigations and tests, estimating aquifer yield, wells, dewatering systems, and pumps.

1062. Bureau of Reclamation. **Summary Statistics. Water, Land, and Related Data**. BR, 1988- . Annual. LC sn91-23349. OCLC 23993486. I 27.1/4: .
This is the Bureau of Reclamation's annual report on crops, water deliveries, recreation, and land use. Includes current and historical data (some dating back to 1906), plus narrative analyses of irrigation, municipal and industrial water, power, recreation, and flood control in western states and Hawaii.

1063. Environmental Protection Agency. Office of Water. **National Water Quality Inventory: Report to Congress**. EPA, 1974- . Biennial. LC 74-603176. TD223.U52d. 363.6/1. OCLC 2469418. EP 2.17/2: .
This summary of pollution in rivers, streams, lakes, reservoirs, ponds, Great Lakes and ocean shorelines, estuaries, wetlands, and groundwater is based on state reports required by the Clean Water Act of 1972. State water quality, pollution causes and control, and progress toward goals are summarized.

1064. Geological Survey. **Annual State Water-Data Reports [computer file]: A Digital Representation of the Hydrologic Records of the United States For. . . .** Books and Open-File Reports Section, 1990- . Annual. CD-ROM. LC 94-645243. GB 701. OCLC 25500414. I 19.76: .

Hydrologic records of the United States include data for states and territories from the open-file report series. SWDRS are searchable by state, gaging station or location, well location, latitude, or type of information desired. This is the CD-ROM version of the annual *Water Resources Data for [state]* (I 19.53/2:).

1065. Geological Survey. **National Water Summary**. GPO, 1983- . Biennial. LC 85-644161. GB701.N36. 553.7/0973. OCLC 12379142. I 19.13/3: .
Provides data on river and stream pollutants, their sources, and environmental factors for states, along with data on pollution levels of dissolved oxygen and solids, bacteria, nitrate, phosphorus, sediment, and other components. Includes national and state maps, discussion of water quality trends, and a chronology of floods, droughts, water use, and supply.

1066. Geological Survey. **Water Resources Abstracts**. 1985- . Database.
This bibliographic database cites worldwide water-resource journal articles, monographs, reports, patents, conference proceedings, and court cases related to water conservation, control, use, and management. It is searchable through commercial vendors, on CD-ROM, and on magnetic tape. Corresponds to *Selected Water Resources Abstracts* (I 1.94/2:), which ceased in 1991.

1067. National Archives and Records Service. **United States Hydrographic Office Manuscript Charts in the National Archives, 1838-1908** compiled by William J. Heynen. NARS, 1978. 250p. LC 78-606193. CD3034.H9U54 1978. 016.353008/775. OCLC 3728733. GS 4.7:43.
The Navy's Hydrographic Office, established in 1830, is one of three federal agencies engaged in hydrographic surveying and charting. This list describes manuscript hydrographic and oceanographic survey charts and cartographic records in Record Group 37, the pre-1908 Hydrographic Office holdings of the National Archives. Arranged geographically, entries give the date of the original survey or chart compilation or receipt. Includes indexes to subjects, people, places, and ships. Other textual and cartographic records in Record Group 37 are described briefly in "Inventory of the Records of the Hydrographic Office" (1971).

1068. National Ocean Service. **Great Lakes Water Levels**. NOS, 1970- . Quinquennial. LC 85-641035. GB1627.G8G753. 551.48/2/0977. OCLC 7394511. C 55.420/2: .
Sixty-six water level gauge records are given in meters, with monthly and annual averages, and the highest and lowest monthly levels.

Medical Sciences

GENERAL MEDICINE

1069. Health Care Financing Administration. **HCFA's Laws—Titles XI, XVII, XIX; Regulations—Titles 42, 45; Manuals [computer file]**. GPO, 199?- . Monthly. CD-ROM. LC sn93-28660. OCLC 28897520. HE 22.8/22: .
This CD-ROM includes the text of updates from HCFA program manuals and memoranda, with laws, regulations, and reproductions of Medicare and Medicaid forms.

1070. Public Health Service. Office of Disease Prevention and Health Promotion. **National Health Information Center**. Box 1133, Washington, DC 20013-1133; (800) 336-4797, (301) 565-4167.
The NHIC refers health professionals and consumers to health organizations specializing in diseases, statistics, educational materials, programming, nutrition, exercise, and other health topics. The NHIC referral database is also accessible through DIRLINE (entry 1096). NHIC publications include the free "ODPHP Publications List" and the Healthfinders series.

AIDS

1071. Centers for Disease Control. **National AIDS Clearinghouse**. Box 6003, Rockville, MD 20849-6003; (800) 458-5231; Internet *URL http://cdcnac.aspensys.com:86/.*
The CDC National AIDS Clearinghouse is a source of information on educational materials, funding, and organizations providing AIDS services. Reference specialists (including those fluent in French or Spanish) answer questions, make referrals, and help identify publications. CDC NAC Online, a computerized information network link to the clearinghouse and to health professionals, includes *AIDS Daily Summary* and AIDS-related *Morbidity and Mortality Weekly Report* articles. To register, contact CDC NAC. *CDC National AIDS Clearinghouse HIV/AIDS Materials* is a free list of publications, posters, information services, videotapes, displays, and kits from the clearinghouse.

1072. National Library of Medicine. **AIDSLINE**. 1980- . Database.
Citations to worldwide scientific articles, books, conference abstracts, government reports, theses, and audiovisuals are gleaned from MEDLINE (entry 1102), HEALTH (entry

1134), CANCERLIT (entry 1100s), CATLINE (entry 1078), and AVLINE (entry 1074). Entries usually note author, title, journal citation, ISSN, language, and abstract. AIDSLINE is searchable through MEDLARS (entry 1100), numerous commercial vendors, and available on CD-ROM. Related NLM databases are AIDSTRIALS, with information on clinical drug and vaccine trials, and AIDSDRUGS, with information about agents being tested in clinical drug and vaccine trials. All three of NLM's AIDS-related databases may be searched without incurring online charges.

1073. National Library of Medicine. Reference Section. **AIDS Bibliography**. GPO, 1988- . Quarterly. LC sn88-40093. OCLC 18035434. HE 20.3615/3: .

> Available through Internet *URL http://gopher.nlm.nih.gov:70/11/bibs/aids* or *URL gopher://gopher.nlm.nih.gov:70/11/bibs/aids.*

This is a list of all preclinical, epidemiologic, diagnostic, and prevention AIDS-related citations from AIDSLINE (entry 1072) added to these NLM databases: MEDLINE, HEALTH, CANCERLIT, CATLINE, and AVLINE (entries 1100, 1100s, 1100s, 1078, and 1074). The bibliography is divided into subject (MeSH) and author sections, similar to *Index Medicus* (entry 1121). The June and December issues include a listing of new serials about AIDS. A related pamphlet, *Guide to NIH HIV/AIDS Information Services: With Selected Public Health Service Activities* (HE 20.3008:Aq 5) is free from Office of Public Information, National Library of Medicine, 8600 Rockville Pike, Bethesda, MD 20894. The paper edition was discontinued after vol.8, no.12; this publication is now available only via the Internet.

Audiovisual Materials

1074. National Library of Medicine. **AVLINE**. 1975- . Database.

> Available on MEDLARS, Grateful Med, and through NLM Locator (the NLM's public access catalog) accessible through the Internet *URL telnet://locator. nlm.nih.gov* and login as *locator*.

This is the NLM bibliographic database of biomedical audiovisuals and computer software cataloged since 1975. Entries usually include author's name and affiliation, title, imprint, language, price, availability, abstract, review data, series, and notes.

1075. National Library of Medicine. **National Library of Medicine Audiovisuals Catalog**. GPO, 1977-1993. Quarterly. LC 79-640065. R835.U49b. 016.61. OCLC 4108612. HE 20.3609/4: .

This bibliography of audiovisuals cataloged by the NLM was drawn from AVLINE and ceased after the 1993 cumulation. Most entries include abstracts, source notes, MeSH headings, NLM call number, audience level, and citations to reviews. The annual cumulation was issued as the fourth quarterly issue. Data are now available through AVLINE (entry 1074). Audiovisuals cataloged before 1975 are listed in *NLM Current Catalog*; those between 1975 and 1976 in *The National Library of Medicine AVLINE Catalog* (HE 20.3602:Au2/975-76); and those for 1977 in *NLM Current Catalog* and cumulated in the 1977 *NLM Audiovisuals Catalog*.

Bibliographies

1076. Center for Devices and Radiological Health. Publications Support Branch. **Center for Devices and Radiological Health Publications Index**. CDRH, 1988- . Biennial. LC 89-646107. Z6671.7.U47a. 616.07/57/0289. OCLC 19170149. HE 20.4609/2: .

CDRH Publications Index lists journal articles, abstracts, and technical reports related to medical devices and radiology, issued since 1978 by the CDRH. Includes keyword, author, and ICC Accession Number indexes.

1077.   Health Care Financing Administration. Office of Research and Demonstrations. **Publications Catalog**. HCFA, 1992. 43p. OCLC 29760191. HE 22.22:C 28.
This annotated bibliography of publications available from GPO, NTIS, or free from the HCFA also lists by author and title the cumulative contents of issues of *Health Care Financing Review* (entry 1103) during the years 1979-92.

1078.   National Library of Medicine. **CATLINE**. 1965- . Database. Searchable on MEDLINE, Grateful Med, and through the Internet *URL telnet://locator.nlm. nih.gov* and login as *locator*.
Citations to books and serials cataloged by the NLM include author and affiliation, title, imprint, language, price, abstract, reviews, source, series, and notes.

1079.   National Library of Medicine. **Current Bibliographies in Medicine**. GPO, 1988- . Irregular. LC 88-644761. Z6660.U66b. 610. OCLC 17913615. HE 20.3615/2: .
    Also available on the Internet *URL gopher://gopher.nlm.nih.gov: 70/11/bibs/cbm*.
These current awareness bibliographies on biomedical topics (excluding AIDS, covered in *AIDS Bibliography* [entry 1073]) continue the defunct Literature Search Series and Specialized Bibliography Series. About 15 popular bibliographies are released in the CBM series annually and announced in NLM *News, Index Medicus*, and *Abridged Index Medicus* (entries 1116, 1121, and 1118).

1080.   National Library of Medicine. **National Library of Medicine Current Catalog**. GPO, 1988-1993. Quarterly, with annual cumulation. LC sn91-23346. 610. OCLC 23985263. HE 20.3609/2: (quarterly); HE 20.3609/3: (annual cumulation).
This bibliography of publications cataloged by the National Library of Medicine ceased after the 1993 cumulation. It superseded *National Library of Medicine Catalog*. NLM cataloging is currently available in CATLINE (entry 1078) and AVLINE (entry 1074).

1081.   Public Health Service. Agency for Health Care Policy and Research. **AHCPR Publications Catalog**. PHS, 19??- . Free: AHCPR Publications Clearinghouse, Box 8547, Silver Spring, MD 20907. LC 95-641022. OCLC 33322524. [SuDocs number not available].
This annotated bibliography of AHCPR publications, programs, research reports, funding opportunities, and health care technology assessments includes author and title indexes.

Medical History

1082.   Army. Center of Military History. **The Army Medical Department, 1775-1818** by Mary C. Gillett. GPO, 1990. 299p. LC 80-12502. UH223.G54. 353.3/45/0973. OCLC 21056280. D 114.19:M 46/775-818/990.
    Army Medical Department, 1818-1865. D 114.19:M 46/818-865.
    Army Medical Department, 1865-1917. D 114.19:M 46/865-917.
This projected four-volume series will provide a history of the Army Medical Department from 1775 to 1941. Each volume includes an index.

1083. National Library of Medicine. **A Catalogue of Sixteenth Century Printed Books in the National Library of Medicine** compiled by Richard J. Durling. GPO, 1967. 698p. LC 67-62303. Z6659.U59. 016.610/9/031. OCLC 160443. FS 2.209:Si 9.

Citations include physical descriptions (such as defects) and bibliographic history (including information about authors and editors). Name and geographic indexes of printers and publishers and a short title catalog are also provided. Continues *A Catalogue of Incunabula and Manuscripts in the Army Medical Library* (1950). A supplement was published in 1971: Peter Krivatsy, *A Catalogue of Incunabula and 16th Century Printed Books in the National Library of Medicine*.

1084. National Library of Medicine. **A Catalogue of Seventeenth Century Printed Books in the National Library of Medicine** compiled by Peter Krivatsy. NLM, 1989. 1315p. LC 89-602290. Z6659.N38 1989. 016.61/09/032. OCLC 21871061. HE 20.3614:Se 8.

The fifth in a series of book catalogs of pre-19th-century works in the NLM collection is culled from CATLINE and cites books, dissertations, broadsides, pamphlets, and serials printed between 1601 and 1700. Others in the series are *A Catalogue of Incunabula and Manuscripts in the Army Medical Library* (1950), *A Catalogue of Sixteenth Century Printed Books in the National Library of Medicine* (entry 1083), *A Catalogue of Incunabula and 16th Century Printed Books in the National Library of Medicine* (entry 1083[n]), and *A Short Title Catalogue of Eighteenth Century Printed Books in the National Library of Medicine* (entry 1085).

1085. National Library of Medicine. **A Short Title Catalogue of Eighteenth Century Printed Books in the National Library of Medicine** compiled by John B. Blake. GPO, 1979. 501p. LC 79-602137. Z6659.U6 1979. 016.61. OCLC 5650414. HE 20.3614:C 28.

This is a list of holdings in the NLM history of medicine collection printed between 1701 and 1800. About one-third were never recorded in either the *Index-Catalogue of the Library of the Surgeon General's Office* or the *National Union Catalog, Pre-1956 Imprints* (entry 109).

1086. National Library of Medicine. **Bibliography of the History of Medicine**. GPO, 1965- . Annual with quinquennial cumulations. LC 66-62950. Z6660.B582. 016.61/09. OCLC 1532763. HE 20.3615: .

This selective bibliography of recent medical history literature includes journal articles, books and book chapters, plus analytics for symposia, congresses, and other composite publications. There are no limitations on time period or place. Entries list author and affiliation, journal citation, abstract, and language. It is cumulated every five years. Citations also appear in HISTLINE (entry 1100s), NLM's database for the history of medicine.

1087. National Library of Medicine. **Online Images from the History of Medicine**. Database. Internet *URL http://www.nlm.nih.gov/hmd.dir/oli.dir/index.html.*

IHM contains medical caricatures, photographs, prints, ephemera, portraits, and illustrations since the Renaissance. It also contains 20th-century images, primarily before World War II.

Biotechnology

1088. **Biotechnology Information Center**. National Agricultural Library, Beltsville, MD 20705-2351; E-mail: *biotech@nalusda.gov.*

The Center provides information and publications related to biotechnology, including genetic engineering, monoclonal antibodies, food processing, and biomass applications.

1089. National Institutes of Health. **Biosafety in Microbiological and Biomedical Laboratories** edited by Jonathan Y. Richmond and Robert W. McKinney. GPO, 1993. 3d ed. 177p. LC 94-161991. QR64.7.B56 1993. 614.4/5. OCLC 28529255. HE 20.7002:B 52/993.
This guide to containment of infectious agents in microbiology laboratories describes practices, facilities, and safety equipment for four biosafety levels. Includes a discussion of risk assessment, summaries of six types of infectious agents, and an index.

1090. National Library of Medicine. National Center for Biotechnology Information. **Entrez Document Retrieval System [computer file]**. GPO, 1994-1996. Bimonthly. CD-ROM. LC 94-646734. QP625.N89. 016. OCLC 31189688. HE 20.3624: .
Available on the Internet *URL http://www.ncbi.nlm.nih.gov/*.
This is a molecular biology database of DNA and protein sequence data, along with associated MEDLINE entries for papers containing molecular sequence data, nucleotide sequences from GenBank, protein sequences from Protein Identification Resource, and data from the Merck Gene Index. It includes a Sequence disk (molecular sequence and bibliographic citations in the sequence databases) and a References disk (MEDLINE citations).

1091. National Library of Medicine. National Center for Biotechnology Information. **GenBank**. Internet *URL http://www.ncbi.nlm.nih.gov/*.
Also available on CD-ROM in flat file format (data only, without retrieval software). Bimonthly. GPO, 1993- .
GenBank is the genetic sequence database aimed at collecting all DNA sequences from around the world. Formerly NCBI-GenBank.

Directories

1092. Department of Health and Human Services. **Telephone Directory**. GPO, 1980- . Annual. LC sn85-14237. OCLC 6550017. HE 1.28: .
The directory lists personnel, DHHS units, and regional offices.

1093. National Center for Education in Maternal and Child Health. **Comprehensive Clinical Genetic Services Centers: A National Directory**. GPO, 1985- . Irregular. LC 87-658577. RB155.C59. 362.1/892. OCLC 13749785. HE 20.9112/3: .
Centers providing diagnosis, medical management, counseling, and follow-up care are listed by state and city.

1094. National Institutes of Health. **Health Hotlines: Toll-Free Numbers from the National Library of Medicine's DIRLINE Database**. NIH, 1992. Free: National Library of Medicine, 8600 Rockville Pike, Bethesda, MD 20894. 64p. OCLC 27152534. HE 20.3602:H 34/6/992.
This list of toll-free numbers for organizations dealing with AIDS, cancer and other diseases, maternal and child health, aging, poison control, substance abuse, disabilities, and mental health is culled from DIRLINE (entry 1096). It includes federal, state, and local government agencies, information centers, professional societies, support groups, and voluntary organizations.

1095. National Institutes of Health. **Telephone and Service Directory**. GPO, 19??- . Irregular. LC sn86-20216. OCLC 7809968. HE 20.3037: .

The directory lists the telephone numbers, unit, building, and room for personnel. Includes a directory of NIH units and abbreviations code.

1096. National Library of Medicine. **DIRLINE**. Database. Quarterly. Searchable through MEDLINE, Grateful Med, and through the Internet *URL telnet://locator.nlm. nih.gov* and login as *locator*.
This is an online directory of health and biomedical organizations, government agencies, information centers, professional societies, voluntary organizations, support groups, academic institutions, and research facilities. Entries note address, telephone number, holdings, publications, services, and criteria for use.

1097. Office of Disease Prevention and Health Promotion. National Health Information Center. **Health Information Resources in the Federal Government**. ODPHP, 1987- . Irregular. LC sn91-23495. OCLC 24007325. HE 20.37: .
This directory of government resources providing health information describes services, databases, and publications. It is produced from the more comprehensive MEDLARS database, DIRLINE (entry 1096). It includes indexes by keyword, subject, organization, and Healthy People 2000 Priorities.

Machine-Readable Data

1098. Health Care Financing Administration. Bureau of Data Management and Strategy. **Public Use Files Catalog As of January 1, 1994: Medicare/Medicaid Data Files**. HCFA, 1994. Free: 1-A-9 Oak Meadows Bldg., 6325 Security Blvd., Baltimore, MD 21207. 35p. OCLC 30082245. [SuDocs number not available].
Descriptions of data files cover price, media, and time covered. Order forms are included.

1099. National Center for Health Statistics. **Catalog of Electronic Data Products from the National Center for Health Statistics**. NCHS, 19??- . Free: Data Dissemination Branch, Division of Data Services, 6525 Belcrest Rd., Hyattsville, MD 20782. LC 93-656154. RA407.3.N28c. 362.1/0973/021. OCLC 27347162. HE 20.6209/4-6: .
Also available on CD-ROM.
Descriptions of NCHS public use data files on tape, CD-ROM, and diskette include vital statistics; household interview and health examination surveys; surveys of hospitals, nursing homes, physicians, and other health care providers; and other health-related data. They include content, source of data, technical characteristics, documentation, and ordering information. Updated by the free *Electronic Data Products Update* (HE 20.6202:El 2/2/).

1100. National Library of Medicine. **MEDLARS**. Database.
MEDLARS is a family of NLM databases searchable through NLM Online Centers, through commercial vendors, and on CD-ROM from commercial vendors. MEDLARS includes the following databases:

> AIDSLINE - (entry 1072)
>
> AVLINE - (entry 1074)
>
> BIOETHICSLINE - literature on euthanasia, human experimentation, abortion, and other bioethical topics
>
> BIOTECHSEEK - biotechnology citations from journals not covered by MEDLINE
>
> CANCERLIT - worldwide cancer literature

CATLINE - (entry 1078)

CHEMLINE - online chemical dictionary (entry 808)

DBIR - *Directory of Biotechnology Information Resources*

DIRLINE - (entry 1096)

HEALTH - worldwide literature on health care delivery (companion print source: *Hospital Literature Index*)

HISTLINE - literature on the history of medicine (companion print source: *Bibliography of the History of Medicine*)

HSDB - (Hazardous Substances Data Bank) data on hazardous chemicals, toxins, environmental safety, chemical emergency response

HSTAR - citations to health services research

MEDLINE - journal articles (entry 1102)

POPLINE - citations to worldwide literature related to population, family planning, fertility, contraception, maternal and child health, AIDS, demography, censuses, and vital statistics

RTECS (Registry of Toxic Effects of Chemical Substances) - toxic chemicals

SERLINE - serials cataloged by NLM (microfiche counterpart: *Health Sciences Serials* (entry 1115n)

TOXLINE - worldwide literature on toxicology

TRI (Toxic Release Inventory) - toxic chemicals released into the environment (entry 1036)

1101.	National Library of Medicine. MEDLARS Management Section. **Online Services Reference Manual**. 1v. NLM, 1988. OCLC 18254456. HE 20.3608:On 1/988.
This NLM database search manual is a guide to commands, search techniques, and accessing databases.

1102.	National Library of Medicine. **MEDLINE**. Database. 1966- .
MEDLINE contains citations (and many abstracts) to world biomedical journal literature (including *International Nursing Index* and *Index to Dental Literature)* and chapters and articles from selected monographs from the years 1976-81. MEDLINE is searchable through numerous commercial vendors and available on CD-ROM.

Medical Research

1103.	Health Care Financing Administration. **Health Care Financing Review**. GPO, 1979- . Quarterly. LC 79-644454. RA410.53.H415. 338.4/33621/0973. OCLC 5527522. HE 22.18: .
Each issue of HCFA Review focuses on an aspect of Medicare, Medicaid, or the health care system, presenting information and analyses on health care financing and delivery. Includes information formerly in *Medicare and Medicaid Data Book*, which ceased in 1991.

1104.	Health Care Financing Administration. Office of Research and Demonstrations. **Status Report**. GPO, 1983- . Annual. LC 84-641426. RA410.53.S73. 338.4/33621/ 0973. OCLC 10452482. HE 22.16/2: .
Summaries of intramural and extramural research projects related to Medicare and Medicaid provide researcher's name and address, federal project officer, description, and status. Newly awarded funding and results from research and demonstration projects are often reported in *Health Care Financing Review* (entry 1103).

1105.   National Agricultural Library. **Animal Welfare Information Center**. 10301 Baltimore Blvd., Room 205, Beltsville, MD 20705-2351; (301) 504-6212; E-mail:
awic@nalusda.gov; Internet *URL gopher://gopher.nalusda.gov/NAL Information
Centers/Animal Welfare Information Center.*
AWIC provides information, referral, and literature searches related to humane handling
of warm-blooded animals for research, testing, exhibition, and education. AWIC maintains
a file of electronic documents on the Internet and issues a free quarterly publications list,
Animal Welfare Information Center Newsletter (A 17.27/2:). *Animal Welfare Information
Center Scope Notes* (A 17.27:6) is an indexing guide to animals and animal-related
subjects. *Animal Welfare Bibliographies*, published as part of the *Quick Bibliographies*
(entry 839) and *Special Reference Briefs* (entry 840) series, list materials in the AGRI-
COLA database.

1106.   **National Institutes of Health**. Internet *URL gopher://gopher.nih.gov:70/77/gopherlib/
indices/localmenu/index?aids bibliograph.*
Contains information about NIH health and clinical issues, grants and research projects,
publications, the CancerNet database, conferences, calendars, and press releases.

1107.   National Institutes of Health. Animal Research Advisory Committee. **Using Ani-
mals in Intramural Research: Guidelines for Investigators and Guidelines for
Animal Users**. 1v. NIH, 1994. OCLC 31313603. HE 20.3008:AN 5/3/1994.
This guide to ethical, humane care of research animals discusses scientific and ethical
issues, laws and regulations, alternatives to animal use, and the Animal Welfare Act.
Includes a bibliography.

1108.   National Institutes of Health. Committee on Care and Use of Laboratory Animals.
Guide for the Care and Use of Laboratory Animals. NIH, 1985. 83p. LC
86-658043. SF406.G8. 636.08/85/05. OCLC 4923005. HE 20.3008:An 5/985.
This reference manual for animal care discusses housing, sanitation, husbandry, and
veterinary care. Includes appendixes of laws and a bibliography.

1109.   National Institutes of Health. Division of Research Grants. **Biomedical Index to
PHS-Supported Research**. GPO, 1988- . Annual. LC 90-648299. RA440.6.U47.
610/.72073. OCLC 21141009. HE 20.3013/2: .
BI is a list of biomedical extramural and intramural research supported by the Public Health
Service; the Alcohol, Drug Abuse, and Mental Health Administration; and the Food and
Drug Administration. Volume 1 is a subject listing based on the *CRISP Thesaurus*; volume
2 lists projects by project number and investigator. Entries include activity code, funding
organization, duration, initial review group, principal investigator, and institutional affiliation. Formerly *Research Awards Index.*

1110.   National Institutes of Health. **NIH Almanac**. NIH, 1978- . Annual. LC 85-640026.
RA11.D293. 353.0077/05. OCLC 4158997. HE 20.3016:yr.
This compendium of facts about the nation's primary biomedical research agency includes
information about the NIH's research institutes and divisions, the National Library of
Medicine, the Clinical Center, the National Center of Nursing Research, the National
Center for Research Resources, and the John E. Fogarty International Center for Advanced
Study in the Health Sciences. It also includes data on NIH history, staff, property and
facilities, field units, lectures, and Nobel laureates. Related publications are *NIH Databook*
(HE 20.3041:), a statistical compendium on NIH programs and national health activities;
NIH Guide for Grants and Contracts (HE 20.3008/2:), describing new programs and grant
opportunities; and *NIH Publications List* (HE 20.3009:), a list of printed publications
available from NIH units (many of which are free).

1111.   National Institutes of Health. Office of Extramural Research. **NIH/ADAMHA Extra-mural Programs**. NIH, 1992- . LC sn93-38164. OCLC 27056227. HE 20.3053/2: .
This is a directory of the National Institutes of Health and the Alcohol, Drug Abuse, and Mental Health Administration units that award grants, cooperative agreements, and contracts. Entries describe research focus, contacts, and procedures.

1112.   National Institutes of Health. Research Documentation Section. **Biomedical Research Information [computer file]**. GPO, 1992- . Quarterly. CD-ROM. LC sn94-27648. OCLC 29838785. HE 20.3013/2-4: .
Also known as CRISP on CD-ROM, this is a research-in-progress database of projects funded by the National Institutes of Health and the Substance Abuse and Mental Health Services Administration. Entries include project number and name, performing organization, principal investigator, and a project description. Also available through FEDRIP (entry 813).

1113.   National Institutes of Health. **The Medical Staff Fellowship Program at the National Institutes of Health: Catalog**. Medical Staff Fellowship Program, 1982- . Annual. LC sn83-11998. OCLC 8948406. HE 20.3015: .
Provides descriptions and application instructions for research and training opportunities open to physicians and dentists. Continues *Associate Training Programs in the Medical and Biological Sciences*.

1114.   Public Health Service. **CRISP Thesaurus**. PHS, 1986- . Annual. LC 94-642940. Z695.1.M48U47a. 025.3/361. OCLC 19675857. HE 20.3023: .
This controlled vocabulary of indexing terms used with CRISP, the Public Health Service's research project data file, covers many diversified areas of medicine, dentistry, mental health, and allied public health. Formerly *Medical and Health Related Sciences Thesaurus*.

Periodicals and Serials

1115.   National Library of Medicine. **Health Sciences Serials**. GPO, 1979- . Quarterly. Microfiche. LC sn79-4274. 610. OCLC 4094060. HE 20.3614/3: .
Derived from SERLINE, this is a catalog of the NLM's holdings of serials and numbered congresses, along with some titles not in the NLM collection. It is available in microfiche only, with each issue superseding the previous one. Entries describe current holdings and provide bibliographic information, including NLM call number and control number, ISSN, CODEN, and index and abstract coverage. SERLINE, its companion online serials database, is searchable free through MEDLINE, Grateful Med, and the Internet *URL telnet://locator.nlm.nih.gov* and login as *locator*.

1116.   National Library of Medicine. **News**. NLM, 1956- . Free: 8600 Rockville Pike, Bethesda, MD 20894. Bimonthly. LC sn79-8324. OCLC 3439741. HE 20.3619: .
A newsletter announcing new health sciences developments and publications.

Indexes and Abstracts

1117.   National Aeronautics and Space Administration. Office of Management, Scientific and Technical Information Division. **Aerospace Medicine and Biology**. NTIS, 1964- . Monthly, with annual cumulative index. LC 65-62677. Z6664.3.A36. OCLC 1832161. NAS 1.21:7011/ .

Beginning with September 1995, only available through the Internet *URL http://www.sti.nasa.gov/*.

Also known as *NASA AP-7011*, this is an annotated index to unclassified reports and journal articles announced in the NASA STI Database. Emphasis is on the biological, physiological, psychological, and environmental effects of flight in Earth's atmosphere or in space. Citations include *Scientific and Technical Aerospace Reports* (STAR) (entry 1006) and *International Aerospace Abstracts* accession numbers. There are subject, author, corporate, foreign technology, contract, report number, and accession number indexes.

1118.   National Library of Medicine. **Abridged Index Medicus**. GPO, 1970- . Monthly. LC sc78-2350. 016. OCLC 1752727. HE 20.3612/2: .
Aimed at physicians and small hospital and clinical libraries, AIM covers 119 English-language biomedical journals. An annual cumulation was sold separately: *Cumulated Abridged Index Medicus* (HE 20.3612/2-2:), abbreviated CAIM; it was discontinued with volume 25—the information is now available on MEDLINE (entry 1102). AIM uses *Medical Subject Headings* (MeSH) (entry 1150).

1119.   National Library of Medicine. **Centenary of Index Medicus, 1879-1979** edited by John B. Blake. GPO, 1980. 115p. LC 80-603763. Z6659.5.C45. 610/.5. OCLC 7814727. HE 20.3602:C 33/879-979.
This history of *Index Medicus* (entry 1121) is a collection of scholarly papers written by librarians, historians, and physicians about bibliography, librarianship, and publishing.

1120.   National Library of Medicine. **Cumulated Index Medicus**. GPO, 1960- . Annual. LC 62-4404. Z6660.I422. 016.61. OCLC 1565584. HE 20.3612/3: .
CIM is an annual compilation of citations from the previous year's *Index Medicus* (entry 1121), arranged by author and subject. The cumulation also includes *Medical Subject Headings* (entry 1150), *List of Journals Indexed* (entry 1122), and *Bibliography of Medical Reviews*. Annual cumulations were published by the American Medical Association from 1960 to 1964. Since 1965 they have been published by GPO as separate subscriptions.

1121.   National Library of Medicine. **Index Medicus**. GPO, 1960- . Monthly. LC 61-60337. Z6660.I42. 016.61. OCLC 1752728. HE 20.3612: .
This bibliography of biomedical journal literature worldwide includes subject and author indexes (including names of biographees). Both *Index Medicus* and *Cumulated Index Medicus* contain "Bibliography of Medical Reviews" sections, listing reviews of current thinking on biomedical topics, including scholarly, classical, or exhaustive reviews; tutorial, didactic, or subject reviews; multicase or epidemiologic reviews; consensus conferences; reviews of cases; and state-of-the-art reviews. Companion resources are MEDLARS and MEDLINE; *Medical Subject Headings* (also in part 2 of each January *Index Medicus* issue); and *List of Journals Indexed in Index Medicus* (included in the January *Index Medicus*, with subsequent monthly issues listing only those added or discontinued).

1122.   National Library of Medicine. **List of Journals Indexed in Index Medicus**. GPO, 1960- . Annual. LC 73-642296. Z6660.U66a. 016.61. OCLC 2760305. HE 20.3612/4: .
Journals are listed by title, abbreviated title, subject field, and country of publication. LJI entries include NLM call number and title control number, ISSN, and MeSH headings. Also included is a list of newly indexed journals, titles no longer indexed, and title changes during the past year (all updated in the monthly *NLM Technical Bulletin*). A list of indexed journals is also included in the July *Index Medicus*. LJI is produced from SERLINE, NLM's online serials database.

1123. National Library of Medicine. **List of Serials Indexed for Online Users**. NTIS, 1983- . Annual. LC 84-649762. Z6660.L66. 016.61/05. OCLC 9199853. HE 20.3618/2: .

This is a bibliography of serials cited in these MEDLARS subfiles: BIOTECHSEEK, MEDLINE, HEALTH, and POPLINE. Citations include journal title abbreviation, place of publication, NLM call number, date and volume of first issue (and last, when appropriate), ISSN, journal title code, indexing, and NLM title control number. Produced from SERLINE.

1124. President's Council on Physical Fitness and Sports. **Physical Fitness/Sports Medicine: A Publication of the President's Council on Physical Fitness and Sports**. GPO, 1978-1994. Quarterly. LC 84-644930. Z6664.6.P48. 016.617/1027. OCLC 3622655. HE 20.111: .

Provides citations to journal articles and selected conferences, retrieved from the MEDLARS database and related to exercise physiology, sports injuries, physical conditioning, and medical aspects of exercise. Non-English periodicals with English abstracts are included. Entries are arranged by MeSH headings, with an author index and a list of serials indexed. The Spring 1994 issue was the last.

Statistics

1125. Center for Environmental Health and Injury Control. Biometrics Branch. **Injury Mortality Atlas of the United States, 1979-1987**. CEHIC, 1991. 141p. LC 93-676578/MAP. G1201.E24I6 1991. 363.1/02/0973022. OCLC 27817091. HE 20.7502:In 5/979-87.

Thematic maps show the prevalence of deaths from firearms, homicide, suicide, motor vehicles, falls, burns and fires, drowning, and poisoning. Data are shown for the nation, counties and states, and by sex, age, year of death, and race. Includes maps showing the geographic distribution of homicides for Black males and mortal falls for people over 53.

1126. Congress. Office of Technology Assessment. **International Health Statistics: What the Numbers Mean for the United States**. OTA, 1993. 163p. LC 93-247959. RA407.I59 1993. 614.4/2. OCLC 29443436. Y 3.T 22/2:2 H 34/7.

Data for the years 1979-90 and projections to 2025 cover sociodemographics, infant mortality, mortality and morbidity, and health-affecting behaviors for the U.S. and 12 Organization for Economic Cooperation and Development (OECD) ountries.

1127. Federation of American Societies for Experimental Biology. Life Sciences Research Office. **Nutrition Monitoring in the United States: An Update Report on Nutrition Monitoring**. GPO, 1989. 158p. LC 89-14529. TX360.U6N86 1989. 363.8/2/0973021. OCLC 20357841. HE 20.6202:N 95/989.

This report, with recommendations, summarizes American eating habits and the relationship between nutrition and health. Includes a description of the National Nutrition Monitoring System (NNMS), along with data on food and alcohol consumption, nutritional and dietary factors related to heart disease, and iron intake and deficiency. Results are summarized in *Nutrition Monitoring in the United States: Chartbook I: Selected Findings from the National Nutrition Monitoring and Related Research Program* (HE 20.6202:N 95/14). *Nutrition Monitoring in the United States: The Directory of Federal Nutrition Monitoring Activities* (HE 20.6228:N 95) describes NNMS activities and summarizes involvement of federal agencies in nutrition monitoring.

1128. Health Care Financing Administration. Bureau of Data Management and Strategy. **Data Compendium**. HCFA, 19??- . Annual. LC 93-642689. HD7102.U4D26. 338.4/33621/097305. OCLC 28642535. HE 22.2:D 26/yr.

Tables, graphs, and charts summarize current, historic, and projected data on Medicare enrollment and Medicaid recipients, expenditures, and use. Provides information on budget, costs, income, financing, and providers. General national health-related data are also included.

1129. Health Resources and Services Administration. Division of Disadvantaged Assistance. **Health of the Disadvantaged Chartbook**. GPO, 1986- . Irregular. LC sn91-23303. OCLC 23284041. HE 20.9302:D 63/2/ .

Charts, tables, and narrative describe trends in demographics, health, use of services, expenditures, and enrollment in health training programs for racial and ethnic minorities and low-income populations. Some data go back to the 1960s.

1130. House. Committee on Ways and Means. **Health Care Resource Book**. GPO, 1993. 123p. LC 93-232908. RA407.3.H42 1993. 362.1/0973. OCLC 28135397. Y 4.W 36:WMCP 103-4.

This chartbook of the nation's health care system includes graphs depicting federal, state, and personal health spending; sources, coverage, and costs of health insurance; and access to health care.

1131. National Center for Health Statistics. **Advance Data from Vital and Health Statistics of the Centers for Disease Control and Prevention/National Center for Health Statistics**. NCHS, 1976- . LC 79-643688. RA407.3.U57c. 362.1/6/0973. OCLC 2778178. HE 20.6209/3:nos.

These summary reports provide the first release of selected NCHS data. Many *Advance Data* reports are followed by detailed publications in the *Vital and Health Statistics* series (entry 1138), including Series 16, *Compilations of Advance Data from Vital and Health Statistics*.

1132. National Center for Health Statistics. **Catalog of Publications of the National Center for Health Statistics**. NCHS, 1980- . Free: Scientific and Technical Information Branch, Data Services, 6525 Belcrest Rd., Room 1064, Hyattsville, MD 20782; (301) 436-8500. Annual. LC 81-643666. Z7553.M43N35a. 016.3621/0973/021. OCLC 7062972. HE 20.6216/4: .

This is an annotated bibliography of NCHS reports (including *Advance Data from Vital and Health Statistics* and the *Vital and Health Statistics* series), a list of staff publications, and an index to selected health topics covered in NCHS reports (continuing *Current Listing and Topical Index to the Vital and Health Statistics Series* [HE 20.6209/2:]). Catalogs have been published for the years 1962-79 (*Catalog of Publications of the National Center for Health Statistics, 1962-1979*), 1980-89, and 1990-92.

1133. National Center for Health Statistics. **Detailed Diagnoses and Procedures, National Hospital Discharge Survey**. GPO, 1987- . Annual. LC 92-650236. RA407.3.A349 subser. 362.1/0973/021. OCLC 21869494. HE 20.6209/9: .

Diagnoses or procedures, organized by *The International Classification of Diseases, 9th Revision, Clinical Modification* (entry 1166), show age, sex, and region.

1134. National Center for Health Statistics. **Health, United States**. GPO, 1975- . Annual. LC 76-641496. RA407.3.U57a. 362.1/0973. OCLC 3151554. HE 20.6223: .

Also available on the *National Economic, Social & Environmental Data Bank* (entry 172).

This annual report to the President and Congress is a statistical handbook of longitudinal health care trends and comparisons. It has two parts: (1) a chartbook on minority health and (2) charts depicting health status and determinants, use, health care resources, and expenditures. It includes a table index, a description of data sources, and a glossary. Every third year since 1989 this source is titled *Health, United States . . . and Prevention Profile. Health, United States (Highlights)* (HE 20.6223:). *Health, United States 1993, Statistical Tables on Lotus Spreadsheets* (HE 20.7042/4:993) is available on floppy diskette.

1135.   National Center for Health Statistics. **Monthly Vital Statistics Report: Provisional Statistics from the National Center for Health Statistics.** NCHS, 1952- . Monthly. LC 66-51898. HA203.A43. 312/.0973. OCLC 1685363. HE 20.6217: .
Contains monthly and cumulative provisional data on births, marriages, divorces, deaths and infant deaths for states and the nation. Includes brief analyses. Shows death rates (estimated from a sample of death certificates) by cause, age, color, and sex.

1136.   National Center for Health Statistics. **National Health Interview Survey: [Report] [computer file].** GPO, 1987- . Annual. CD-ROM. LC 94-641427. RA407.3. 614. OCLC 23062568. HE 20.6209/4-3:10/no.⁻
Data from Series 10 of the *Vital and Health Statistics* series (entry 1138) include NHIS core files on AIDS knowledge and attitudes, child health, illness, injuries, pregnancy and smoking, and use of health services.

1137.   National Center for Health Statistics. **National Hospital Discharge Survey [computer file]: [report].** GPO, 1990- . Annual. CD-ROM. LC 94-641426. RA407.3u. 362. OCLC 29266566. HE 20.6209/7-2:13/ .
This CD-ROM, part of Series 13 of *Vital and Health Statistics* (entry 1138), provides hospital use data based on a sample of discharged-patient records from nonfederal short-stay hospitals. Newborn and non-newborn data show discharges, days of care, average stay, and diagnostic and therapeutic procedures, all cross-tabulated by age, sex, and race; region; and payment source. A print summary is also issued (HE 20.6209/7:).

1138.   National Center for Health Statistics. **Vital and Health Statistics.** HE 20.6209: .
This series describes background information and research findings from NCHS programs. Includes more than 500 individual publications grouped into the subseries described below. Updated by *Advance Data from Vital and Health Statistics* (entry 1131).

> Series 1. Programs and Collection Procedures.
> NCHS data collection programs.
>
> Series 2. Data Evaluation and Methods Research.
> Studies of new statistical methods.
>
> Series 3. Analytical and Epidemiological Studies.
> Analyses based on vital and health statistics.
>
> Series 4. Documents and Committee Reports.
> Final reports of committees concerned with statistics and documents.
>
> Series 5. International Vital and Health Statistics Reports.
> U.S. health compared with other nations, and international data.
>
> Series 6. Cognition and Survey Measurement.
> Reports from the National Laboratory for Collaborative Research in Cognition and Survey Measurement.
>
> Series 10. Data from the National Health Interview Survey.
> Statistics on illness, injuries, disability, use of health services. (Also available on CD-ROM.)

Series 11. Data from the National Health Examination Survey, the National Health and Nutrition Examination Surveys, and the Hispanic Health and Nutrition Examination Survey.
Data from examination, testing, and measurement of individuals.

Series 13. Data from the National Health Care Survey.
Health care resources data (incorporates the former series 12 and 14). Also available on CD-ROM.

Series 15. Data from Special Surveys.
Surveys not part of the continuing data systems of NCHS.

Series 16. Compilations of Advance Data from Vital and Health Statistics.
Early data releases on specific topics from NCHS health and demographic surveys, each with a distinct title. Some releases are followed by detailed reports in series 10 through 13.

Series 20. Data on Mortality.
Mortality data omitted from other reports, with analyses by cause of death, demographics, geography, and trends.

Series 21. Data on Natality, Marriage, and Divorce.
Statistics omitted from other reports, with analyses by health and demographic variables, geography, and trends.

Series 23. Data from the National Survey of Family Growth.
Factors affecting birth rates, adoption, family planning and fertility medical care, and maternal and infant health.

Series 24. Compilations of Data on Natality, Mortality, Marriage, Divorce and Induced Terminations of Pregnancy.
Highlights and summaries based on final data from supplements to the *Monthly Vital Statistics Report* (entry 1135), later expanded in *Vital Statistics of the United States* (entry 1138).

1139. National Institutes of Health. National Heart, Lung, and Blood Institute. **A Mortality Study of 1.3 Million Persons by Demographic, Social, and Economic Factors: 1979-1985 Follow-Up: U.S. National Longitudinal Mortality Study** by Eugene Rogot et al. NIH, 1992. 481p. LC 93-104366. HB1335.M684 1992. 304.6/4/0973. OCLC 28345322. HE 20.3202:M 84/2/979-85.
This second follow-up to the National Longitudinal Mortality Study (HE 20.3202:M 84/2) gives demographic data for leading causes of death: Disease, septicemia, cancer, cardiovascular and cerebrovascular disease, respiratory disease, pneumonia and influenza, chronic obstructive pulmonary disease, liver disease and cirrhosis, nephritis and nephrosis, accidents, suicide, and murder. Data are given for census division, city or noncity residence, birthplace (U.S. or foreign), Hispanic origin, education, income, household size, marital status, employment, state, and large metropolitan statistical areas (MSAs), and cross-tabulated by cause of death, sex, age, and race.

Substance Abuse

1140. Bureau of Justice Statistics. **State Drug Resources . . . National Directory**. Drugs & Crime Data Center & Clearinghouse, 1990- . Biennial. LC 92-660680. HV5825.S66. 362.29/18/02573. OCLC 22250455. J 29.2:D 84/2/ .
This directory of state agencies addressing drug abuse provides addresses and telephone numbers, with appendixes listing federally sponsored drug control offices, national clearinghouses and associations, national drug abuse or criminal justice resources, and state drug control or statistical agencies.

1141.   Department of Health and Human Services. Office for Substance Abuse Prevention. **National Clearinghouse for Alcohol and Drug Information**. Box 2345, Rockville, MD 20852; (301) 468-2600, (800) 729-6686.
The NCADI provides information and referral, maintains a library and research database, and distributes publications (many of which are free) related to alcohol and drug problems. It can also refer individuals to their state center in the Regional Alcohol and Drug Awareness Resource (RADAR) Network. The *NCADI Publications Catalog* is free (entry 1144). The Alcohol and Alcohol Problems Science Database is available from commercial vendors.

1142.   Department of Transportation. Office of the Secretary. **Drug Testing Procedures Handbook**. 1v. GPO, 1990. OCLC 24269074. TD 1.8:D 84.
Provides guidelines for workplace drug testing, with procedures for urine collection and interpretation of test results.

1143.   House. Committee on Government Operations. **Drug Abuse and Its Control: Glossary of Selected Terms: A Report**. GPO, 1990. 87p. LC 92-246846. HV5825.D767 1990. OCLC 23116247. Y 4.G 74/7:D 84/26.
Presents terms related to narcotics and other dangerous drugs, including slang, colloquialisms, and acronyms.

1144.   National Clearinghouse for Alcohol and Drug Information. **NCADI Publications Catalog**. NCADI, 1988- . Free: Box 2345, Rockville, MD 20852. Semiannual. LC sn91-23036. OCLC 22455195. HE 20.8012/2: .
This is an annotated list of NCADI print and audiovisuals about alcohol and other drugs.

1145.   National Institute on Drug Abuse. **Drug Abuse and Drug Abuse Research**. GPO, 1984- . Triennial. LC 85-645373. HV5825.D764. 362.2/93/0973. OCLC 11824701. HE 20.8220/2: .
This report summarizes for Congress the extent of drug abuse in the U.S., its health implications, and advances in treatment and prevention. It is largely narrative, with some tables and bibliographies.

1146.   National Institute on Drug Abuse. **National Directory of Drug Abuse and Alcoholism Treatment and Prevention Programs**. GPO, 1982- . Annual. LC 93-649082. HV5825.N323. 362.29/18/02573. OCLC 10720918. HE 20.8320: .
Federal, state, local, and private treatment and prevention facilities, services, state authorities, state prevention contacts, and activities in the U.S., Guam, Puerto Rico, and the Virgin Islands are listed. Entries include address, telephone number, services, capacity and use, client characteristics, funding, and staffing.

1147.   National Institute on Drug Abuse. **National Household Survey on Drug Abuse. Main Findings**. NIDA, 19??- . Irregular. LC 92-645988. HV5825.N343. 362.29/12/0973021. OCLC 24486289. HE 20.402:D 84/ .
Data portray the use of marijuana, cocaine, inhalants, hallucinogens, heroin, alcohol, tobacco, and the nonmedical use of psychotherapeutic drugs by Americans age 12 and older, and by the population of the Washington, D.C., Metropolitan Statistical Area (MSA). Companion volumes are *National Household Survey on Drug Abuse: Population Estimates 1990* (HE 20.8202:H 81/2/990) and *National Household Survey on Drug Abuse: Highlights 1990* (HE 20.8202:H 81/3/990).

1148. Public Health Service. Office on Smoking and Health. **Bibliography on Smoking and Health**. GPO, 1963- . Annual. LC sn86-16558. Z6673.U515. 016.6138/5. OCLC 2884349. HE 20.7610/2: .

These annotated lists of international articles, technical reports, subject bibliographies, books, book reviews, and annual reports related to smoking and tobacco use serve as a companion to the Smoking and Health Database, available from commercial vendors.

1149. Public Health Service. Office on Smoking and Health. **Directory, On-Going Research in Smoking and Health**. GPO, 1980- . Biennial. Microfiche. LC 83-644832. RA1242.T6D57. 615.9/52374. OCLC 7362454. HE 20.25: .

Project descriptions for current research worldwide related to smoking, tobacco, and tobacco use are arranged by country. Includes a summary of research trends, and indexes to principal investigators, organizations, sponsors, and subjects.

Thesauri

1150. National Library of Medicine. **Medical Subject Headings (MeSH)**. GPO, 1960- . Annual. LC 60-62415. Z695.1.M48U5. 025.3/361. OCLC 2482950. HE 20.3612/3-8: .

The "black MeSH" is the subject authority list of descriptors used in *Index Medicus* and MEDLARS. *MeSH* is divided into two sections: (1) Alphabetic List and (2) Tree Structures. The January *Cumulated Index Medicus* also includes *MeSH*.

1151. National Library of Medicine. Medical Subject Headings Section. **Medical Subject Headings: Annotated Alphabetic List**. NTIS, 19??-. Annual. LC 80-644513. Z695.1.M48U52c. 025.4/961. OCLC 6392946. HE 20.3612/3-4: .

Annotated MeSH ("green MeSH") is an expanded version of *MeSH* aimed at indexers, catalogers, and MEDLINE searchers, and providing a synthesis of indexing scope and policy. It contains information omitted from the *MeSH* aimed at *Index Medicus* users, adding subject headings, cross-references, geographic headings, non-MeSH terms, check tags, tree numbers, and notes for indexers, catalogers, and online searchers. An annotated version of *MeSH* is also available online through MEDLINE. Annotated MeSH is supplemented by *Medical Subject Headings. Tree Structures*; *Permuted Medical Subject Headings*; and *Medical Subject Headings, Supplementary Chemical Records* (entries 1153, 1155, and 1152).

1152. National Library of Medicine. Medical Subject Headings Section. **Medical Subject Headings: Supplementary Chemical Records**. NTIS, 1983- . Annual. LC sn84-10085. 025. OCLC 9379687. HE 20.3612/3-7: .

Chemical subject headings in this compilation are more detailed than those in *MeSH*, with records of chemicals mentioned in journals indexed in MEDLINE since 1970. The list omits chemical descriptors from the D category of *MeSH*.

1153. National Library of Medicine. Medical Subject Headings Section. **Medical Subject Headings: Tree Structures**. NTIS, 1972- . Annual. LC 77-646753. Z695.1.M48U52b. 025.3/361. OCLC 1778210. HE 20.3612/3-5: .

Subject headings (including geographic and minor descriptors) are arranged hierarchically, showing relationships between broader and narrower terms, with annotations preceding each subcategory in the hierarchy. The Tree Annotations introduce each tree and are meant to supplement the Annotated MeSH. *Tree Structures* also appears as the second section of the January *Index Medicus*. *Tree Structures* supplements *Medical Subject Headings: Annotated Alphabetic List* and *Permuted Medical Subject Headings* (entries 1151 and 1155). This title absorbed *Medical Subject Headings. Tree Annotations* in 1990 and is supplemented by *Medical Subject Headings. Tree Annotations, 1977-1984*.

1154. National Library of Medicine. **National Library of Medicine Classification: A Scheme for the Shelf Arrangement of Library Materials in the Field of Medicine and Its Related Sciences.** GPO, 1994. 5th ed. 507p. OCLC 31378402. HE 20.3602:C 56/994.

This classification scheme for medicine and allied sciences contains the schedules and index to the classification. The schedules (QS-QZ and W) have been permanently removed from the Library of Congress classification.

1155. National Library of Medicine. **Permuted Medical Subject Headings.** NTIS, 1977- . Annual. LC 80-645349. Z695.1.M48U52d. 025.4/961. OCLC 3467406. HE 20.3612/3-3: .

The *Permuted MeSH* is a computer-generated list of MeSH terms in context. Listings include citation type, check tag, and geographic descriptors from the Annotated Alphabetic MeSH. The *Permuted MeSH* supplements *Medical Subject Headings: Tree Structures* and *Medical Subject Headings: Annotated Alphabetic List* (entries 1153 and 1151).

DENTISTRY

1156. National Center for Health Statistics. **Use of Dental Services and Dental Health, United States, 1986** by Susan S. Jack and Barbara Bloom. NCHS, 1988. 84p. LC 88-19553. RA407.3.A346 no.165. 362.1/0973/021. OCLC 18134850. HE 20.6209:10/165.

Based on data collected in the 1966 National Health Interview Survey, this report estimates dental visits, dental insurance coverage, fluoride and sealant use, and dentition status.

1157. National Institute of Dental Research. Epidemiology and Oral Disease Prevention Program. **Oral Health of United States Adults: The National Survey of Oral Health in U.S. Employed Adults and Seniors, 1985-1986: National Findings.** National Institutes of Health, 1987. 168p. LC 87-602350. RK52.2.O7 1987. 614.5/996/0973021. OCLC 16793503. HE 20.3402:Or 1/2.

Presents dental health data for people aged 18-64 and 65 and older by sociodemographic and demographic characteristics. Data for working people are also frequently shown by race. Statistics depict number of teeth; decayed and filled teeth and root surfaces; type of calculus; and gum pocket depth, attachment loss, bleeding, detachment, and receding gums. Data for regions of the United States are given in *Oral Health of United States Adults: Regional Findings* (HE 20.3402:Or 1/3).

1158. National Institutes of Health. **National Institute of Dental Research.** 9000 Rockville Pike, Bethesda, MD 20892.

The Institute oversees clinical and laboratory research on tooth decay and oral-facial disorders. Its annual indexes (HE 20.3401/2:) summarize research projects.

DISEASES AND DISABILITIES

General Works

1159. Americans with Disabilities Act. Technical Assistance Manuals.

Equal Employment Opportunity Commission. **A Technical Assistance Manual on the Employment Provisions (Title I) of the Americans with Disabilities Act.** 1v. GPO, 1992. OCLC 25213327. Y 3.Eq 2:8 T 22.

Department of Justice. Civil Rights Division. Public Access Section. **The Americans with Disabilities Act: Title II Technical Assistance Manual: Covering State and Local Government Programs and Services**. 1v. GPO, 1993. LC 94-149456. KF480.A32A2 1993. 346.7301/3. OCLC 29342500. J 1.8/2:AM 3/TITLE 2/993.

Department of Justice. Civil Rights Division. Public Access Section. **The Americans with Disabilities Act: Title III Technical Assistance Manual: Covering Public Accommodations and Commercial Facilities**. 1v. GPO, 1993. LC 94-149458. KF480.Z9A465 1993. OCLC 29394551. J 1.8/2:AM 3/TITLE 3/993.

Title I of the ADA provides guidance on legal requirements and EEOC compliance for employers with more than 15 employees. Title II, applicable to state and local governments, and Title III, pertaining to public and commercial facilities, cover eligibility, policies, practices, procedures, program accessibility, auxiliary aids and communication, and construction and remodeling. The subscriptions provide a basic manual and updates.

1160. Architectural and Transportation Barriers Compliance Board. **Americans with Disabilities Act: Accessibility Guidelines for Buildings and Facilities, Transportation Facilities, Transportation Vehicles**. 1v. GPO, 1994. OCLC 31441654. Y 3.B 27:8 AM 3/2/994.

Checklists for ADA compliance are useful in surveying barriers to access in buildings, parking lots, entrances, bathrooms, and stairs. Includes instructions, diagrams, and lists of ADA requirements.

1161. Department of Education. **National Rehabilitation Information Center**. 8455 Colesville Rd., Suite 935, Silver Spring, MD 20910-3319; (800) 346-2742.

The NARIC is an information and referral source for materials related to rehabilitating people with sensory, physical, mental, or psychiatric disabilities. Publications include *NARIC Quarterly* (ED 1.79/2:) and *NARIC Disability Research Resources* (ED 1.79:).

1162. Department of Education. Office of Special Education and Rehabilitative Services. **Clearinghouse on Disability Information**. Room 3132, Switzer Bldg., Washington, DC 20202-2524; (202) 205-8241.

The clearinghouse is an informational, referral, and educational resource for people with disabilities.

1163. Department of Education. Office of Special Education and Rehabilitative Services. **Compendium of Products by NIDRR Grantees & Contractors**. DE, 1993- . Annual. LC 95-640916. 362. OCLC 31744730. ED 1.2:C 73/7/ .

This is a bibliography of manuals, brochures, posters, videos, audiocassettes, computer programs, training materials, and reports produced with NIDRR funding.

1164. Department of Education. Office of Special Education Programs. **National Information Center for Children and Youth with Disabilities**. Box 1492, Washington, DC 20013-1492; (800) 695-0285; (202) 884-8200; E-mail: *nichcy@aed.org*.

The NICHCY, operated for the Department of Education by the Academy for Educational Development, is a national clearinghouse of free information on disabilities from childhood through age 22. The center offers information and referral, database searches, free publications (request GR8, "Publications List"), and assistance to parents and professional groups.

1165. Equal Employment Opportunity Commission. **Americans with Disabilities Act Handbook.** 1v. GPO, 1992. 344.730159. OCLC 25588747. Y 3.Eq 2:8 Am 3.

> Also available on the *Federal Bulletin Board*, in braille, large print, audiotape, and CD-ROM.

This basic source on the ADA covers Titles I, II, and III of the law. It features detailed background information, rulemaking history and analysis of revisions, "plain English" summaries of the regulations, definitions, and answers to commonly asked questions. It includes *Americans with Disabilities Act: Accessibility Guidelines for Buildings and Facilities* (entry 1160) in the appendixes.

1166. Health Care Financing Administration. **The International Classification of Diseases, 9th Revision, Clinical Modification: ICD-9-CM.** 3v. GPO, 1989. 3d ed. LC 89-601758. RB115.I49 1989. 616/.0012. OCLC 21445032. HE 22.2:In 8/2/989/v.1-3.

> Vol. 1. **Diseases Tabular List.**

> Vol. 2. **Diseases Alphabetic Index.**

> Vol. 3. **Procedures—Tabular List and Alphabetic Index.**

> Also available from GPO on CD-ROM HE 22.41/2:992.

Based on the World Health Organization's *International Classification of Diseases*, *ICD-9-CM* is used to classify mortality and morbidity statistics and to index hospital records. Volume 1 is a numerical list of three-digit class numbers for diseases, factors affecting health, injury, poisoning, and contact with health services. Volume 2 refers from diseases to class numbers, with a table of drugs and medicines, and an index to causes of injury. Volume 3 is a numerical tabular list and index to diagnostic, nonsurgical, and surgical procedures.

1167. House. Select Committee on Children, Youth, and Families. **Respite Care: A Listing of Resources: A Report of the Select Committee on Children, Youth, and Families, One Hundred First Congress, Second Session.** (H.Rpt.101-1001). GPO, 1990. 189p. OCLC 23101451. (Serial Set 14028). Y 1.1/8:101-1001.

This state-by-state directory describes respite care services for families with disabled children.

1168. National Center for Chronic Disease Prevention and Health Promotion. **CDP File [computer file].** GPO, 1991- . Semiannual. CD-ROM. LC 94-660798. RA644.6. 613. OCLC 25355073. HE 20.7616: .

This index to published and unpublished health promotion information in articles, books, curricula, AV materials, and programs comprises databases focusing on health promotion and education, AIDS, school health education, cancer, contacts for chronic disease prevention, and state programs and contacts. It includes the Health Promotion and Education Database (HPED), the Comprehensive School Health Database (CSHD), the Cancer Prevention and Control Database (CPCD), the Prenatal Smoking Cessation Database, the Chronic Disease Prevention Directory (CDPD), and the Epilepsy Education and Prevention Activities Database. All are also part of the Combined Health Information Database (CHID), available through a commercial database vendor.

1169. National Institute on Disability and Rehabilitation Research. **Digest of Data on Persons with Disabilities** prepared by Robert C. Ficke. NIDRR, 1992. Free: NARIC, 8455 Colesville Rd., Suite 935, Silver Spring, MD 20910-3319. 179p. LC 92-235298. HV1553.F53 1992. 362.4/0973/021. OCLC 26145987. ED 1.2:D 26/3/992.

Tables and charts of aggregate data give an overview of the size and characteristics of the disabled population: Prevalence and characteristics, work disability, and disability in long-term care facilities. The report also discusses definition and measurement of disability, and federal benefit programs. It includes the text of the Americans with Disabilities Act. Related titles are *Chartbook on Disability in the United States* (ED 1.2:D 63/8), which uses graphics, tables, and text to show statistics on the disabled population and notes data sources, and *Chartbook on Work Disability in the United States* (ED 1.2:D 63/8/991), which depicts labor force participation.

1170. National Institute on Disability and Rehabilitation Research. **Directory of National Information Sources on Disabilities.** NIDRR, 1991- . LC sn93-38096. OCLC 24821313. ED 1.30/2:D 63.
This nationwide directory of organizations providing disability-related information, referral, and direct services notes address, telephone number, type of client and disability, and information services, including databases. The index allows searching by function, location, type of facility, activities, and disability.

1171. National Institute on Disability and Rehabilitation Research. **Program Directory.** National Rehabilitation Information Center, 19??- . Annual. LC 90-655182. HV1553.N42a. 362/.0425. OCLC 22731022. ED 1.215: .
Funded projects are described, noting name, address, and telephone number of principal investigator; project number; dates; funding; objectives; activities; and publications.

1172. Public Health Service. Agency for Health Care Policy and Research. **Clinical Practice Guideline Series.** HE 20.6520: .
Concise guides for practitioners and patients describe treatment for specific conditions, with references, algorithms, flowcharts, and figures.

Alzheimer's Disease

1173. National Institute on Aging. **Alzheimer's Disease Education and Referral Center.** Box 8250, Silver Spring, MD 20907-8250; (800) 438-4380.
The ADEAR disseminates information about Alzheimer's disease and related disorders, diagnosis, treatment, and research, along with audiovisuals, training materials, and free packaged searches from the Combined Health Information Database (CHID), publications, and information updates. The Center's database is available through CHID, available through a commercial database vendor.

Arthritis

1174. National Institutes of Health. National Institute of Arthritis and Musculoskeletal and Skin Diseases. **National Arthritis and Musculoskeletal and Skin Diseases Information Clearinghouse.** Box AMS, 9000 Rockville Pike, Bethesda, MD 20892; (301) 495-4484.
The NAMSIC is an informational, referral, and educational resource about rheumatic and musculoskeletal diseases, sports medicine, and skin diseases. The Clearinghouse maintains a subfile on the Combined Health Information Database (CHID), available through a commercial database vendor, and distributes publications (many of which are free).

Blood Diseases

1175. Centers for Disease Control. **Atlas of Blood Cells in Health and Disease** by Marguerite Candler Ballard. CDC, 1987. 159p. LC 86-72102. RB145.B26 1987. 616.1/5/00222. OCLC 17637198. HE 20.7002:B 62/2.
This pictorial microscopic guide shows characteristic morphological features of healthy and diseased blood and bone marrow cells, including nonmalignant disease, anemia, agranulocytosis, lupus, anomalies, leukemia, metastatic tumor cells, metabolic storage disease, and microorganisms.

Cancer

1176. National Cancer Institute. Office of Cancer Communications. **Publications List for Health Professionals.** NCI, 19??- . Quarterly. LC sn84-45771. OCLC 11476188. HE 20.3183/2: .
This is a short, annotated list of free NCI professional pamphlets.

1177. National Cancer Institute. Office of Cancer Communications. **Publications List for the Public and Patients.** NCI, 19??- . Free: Office of Cancer Communications, Bldg. 31, Room 10A 24, Bethesda, MD 20892. Irregular. LC sn88-40530. OCLC 18362562. HE 20.3183: .
This is an annotated list of free NCI pamphlets, including some in Spanish.

1178. National Cancer Institute. **Survey of Compounds Which Have Been Tested for Carcinogenic Activity.** GPO, 1941- . Biennial. LC sn87-42356. OCLC 3228744. HE 20.3187: .
Published carcinogenesis data for tested organic, inorganic, and unclassified compounds are cited. Citations include the test subject, site, survival data, and duration of the experiment. Includes author, chemical name, CAS registry number, site, species, and tumor site indexes. Cumulative indexes for the 16 volumes through the 1989-90 edition have been issued (HE 20.3187:[years]/ind).

1179. National Institutes of Health. **Atlas of U.S. Cancer Mortality Among Nonwhites: 1950-1980** by Linda Williams Pickle et al. NIH, 1990. 186p. OCLC 28344534. HE 20.3152:M 84/3.
Death rates are shown for state economic areas for men and women and for racial groups.

1180. National Institutes of Health. **Atlas of U.S. Cancer Mortality Among Whites: 1950-1980** by Linda Williams Pickle et al. GPO, 1987. 184p. LC 87-601908/MAP. RC276.A89 1987. 614.5/999. OCLC 16158056. HE 20.3152:M 84/2/950-80.
Death rates for three decades are shown for state economic areas for white men and women.

Deafness

1181. National Institutes of Health. **National Institute on Deafness and Other Communication Disorders.** 1 Communication Ave., Bethesda, MD 20892-3456; (800) 241-1044.
The NIDCD is a source of information on normal and disordered communication, including hearing, balance, smell, taste, voice, speech, and language. Its bibliographic and educational database is available through the Combined Health Information Database (CHID), available through a commercial database vendor.

Diabetes

1182. National Institutes of Health. National Institute of Diabetes and Digestive Kidney Diseases. **National Diabetes Information Clearinghouse**. Box NDIC, 9000 Rockville Pike, Bethesda, MD 20892-3560; (301) 654-3327.

The NDIC is an informational, referral, and educational resource for patients and health professionals. The clearinghouse distributes publications (many of which are free); a free publications list, "Professional and Patient Education Publications"; and a free newsletter, *Diabetes Dateline* (HE 20.3310/3:).

Hepatitis B

1183. National Institute of Diabetes and Digestive and Kidney Diseases. **Hepatitis B Prevention: A Resource Guide, 1990**. NIDDKD, 1990. 245p. OCLC 23839804. HE 20.3308:H 41.

This is a directory of national, state, and local prevention programs. It features a bibliography of books, brochures, pamphlets, and AV and other materials about the hepatitis B virus. Includes an index.

Intestinal Diseases

1184. National Institutes of Health. National Institute of Diabetes and Digestive Kidney Diseases. **National Digestive Diseases Information Clearinghouse**. 2 Information Way, Bethesda, MD 20892-3570; (301) 654-3810.

The NDDIC is an informational, referral, and educational resource for patients and health professionals. The Clearinghouse maintains the Digestive Diseases subfile of the Combined Health Information Database (CHID), available through a commercial database vendor, and distributes publications (many of which are free) and a free publications list, "Professional and Patient Education Publications."

Mental Retardation

1185. President's Committee on Mental Retardation. **International Directory of Mental Retardation Resources** edited by Rosemary F. Dybwad. GPO, 1989. 3d ed. 317p. LC 89-603211. HV3004.D97 1989. 362.3/8/025. OCLC 22115410. HE 23.102:R 31/3.

Country listings describe government agencies, voluntary organizations, research organizations, research, publications, and program areas. Also listed are activities of international organizations and "Tips for Travellers."

Venereal Disease

1186. Centers for Disease Control. **Survey of Research on Sexually Transmitted Diseases**. Division of Sexually Transmitted Diseases, 1981- . LC 88-657510. Z6664.V45U52. 616. OCLC 9863947. HE 20.7312:Se 9.

Includes abstracts of journal articles related to sexually transmitted diseases. Formerly *Sexually Transmitted Diseases: Abstracts and Bibliography*.

PHARMACOLOGY

1187. Food and Drug Administration. Center for Food Safety and Applied Nutrition. Industry Programs Branch. **Cosmetic Handbook**. FDA, 1989. 96p. LC 89-602918. OCLC 20568570. HE 20.4508:C 82.
Presents excerpts of key FDA regulations and policies for cosmetics production, labeling, and self-inspection.

1188. National Institute of Mental Health. **Psychopharmacology Bulletin**. GPO, 1966- . Quarterly. LC sn81-1211. OCLC 1643323. HE 20.8109: .
Describes recent and ongoing research results worldwide. The first two issues of the year focus on the annual New Clinical Drug Evaluation Unit meeting; the third issue provides summaries of papers presented at the annual American College of Neuropsychopharmacology meeting; the fourth issue focuses on proceedings of NIMH workshops, reviews, and special issues on selected themes.

PSYCHIATRY
AND MENTAL HEALTH

1189. National Institute of Mental Health. **Mental Health and Rural America, 1980-1993: An Overview and Annotated Bibliography** by Morton O. Wagenfeld et al. NIMH, 1994. 116p. OCLC 31477916. [SuDocs number not available].
Provides an overview of the field, along with an annotated bibliography.

1190. National Institute of Mental Health. **Mental Health Directory**. GPO, 1964- . Irregular. LC 85-645729. RA790.A1U52. 362.2/025/73. OCLC 2264049. HE 20.8123: .
This directory of government, public, and private mental health organizations gives addresses and telephone numbers for organizations in each state and city. Includes a list of state mental health agencies.

1191. National Institute of Mental Health. **Mental Health, United States**. GPO, 1983- . Biennial. LC 88-640621. RA790.6.M463. 362.2/0973. OCLC 10720813. HE 20.8137: .
This snapshot of the nation's mental health service system includes data on availability, volume, staffing, expenditures, clients, specialty mental health services in each state, revenues and expenditures, and staff availability.

1192. National Institute of Mental Health. **Publications from the National Institute of Mental Health**. NIMH, 19??- . Free: Information Resources and Inquiries Branch, 5600 Fishers Lane, Room 7C-02, Rockville, MD 20857; fax (301) 443-5158. LC sn95-27373. OCLC 31991159. HE 20.8113/6: .
This is a short, annotated list of free and for-sale pamphlets, books, and journals.

1193. National Institute of Mental Health. **Schizophrenia Bulletin**. GPO, 1969- . Quarterly. LC sf79-10393. RC514.S336. OCLC 1345919. HE 20.8115: .
Information and abstracts of recent multidisciplinary literature on schizophrenia are presented from articles, descriptions of treatments, news items, and an annual listing of grants awarded by NIMH. A related title is *Special Report: Schizophrenia*, with reviews of ongoing research and developments (nondepository).

PUBLIC HEALTH

1194. Centers for Disease Control. **Health Information for International Travel**. GPO, 1974- . Annual. LC 77-649068. RA783.5.C45a. 614.4/2/02491. OCLC 2905736. HE 20.7315: .

This handbook for international travelers lists vaccination requirements and advises travelers on health protection. It is updated by the biweekly "Blue Sheet," *Summary of Health Information for International Travel* (HE 20.7315/2:), which lists countries with outbreaks of cholera, plague, smallpox, or yellow fever.

1195. Centers for Disease Control. **Morbidity and Mortality Weekly Report: MMWR**. GPO, 1976- . Weekly. LC 83-644022. RA407.3.A37. 614.4/273. OCLC 3454113. HE 20.7009: .

> Also available on the Internet *URL gopher://gopher.niaid.nih.gov*; select *AIDS Related Information/Morbidity and Mortality Weekly Report.*

MMWR provides data and analysis of death and disease in the U.S., with articles on timely public health issues and statistics for the nation, states, regions, and major cities. The National AIDS Clearinghouse (entry 1071) distributes reprints of AIDS-related *Morbidity and Mortality Weekly Report* articles.

1196. Food and Drug Administration. **Foodborne Illness Education Information Center**. Food and Nutrition Information Center, Room 304, National Agricultural Library, 10301 Baltimore Blvd., Beltsville, MD 20705-2351; (301) 504-5719; E-mail: *croberts@nalusda.gov*; Internet *URL gopher://gopher.nalusda.gov:70/11/ infocntr/fnic/foodborne.*

Part of the NAL's Food and Nutrition Information Center, the *Foodborne Illness Education Information Center* maintains a database of consumer and food worker education materials. It can also be accessed through ALF (entry 852).

TOXICOLOGY

1197. National Institute for Occupational Safety and Health. **Registry of Toxic Effects of Chemical Substances**. GPO, 1975-1993. Quarterly. Microfiche. LC 93-640597. 615. OCLC 4508155. HE 20.7112/3: .

> Available on CD-ROM from NTIS, on MEDLARS, and from commercial vendors.

RTECS contains data on toxicity and biological effects of toxic chemicals on people and animals, including substance prime name, update, Chemical Abstracts Service name and registry number, molecular weight, molecular formula, synonyms, toxicity data, cited reference, aquatic toxicity rating, reviews, standards and regulations, criteria documents, and status. *Registry of Toxic Effects of Chemical Substances (RTECS): Comprehensive Guide to the RTECS* (HE 20.7108:T 65) is a guide to the data and their format. *Registry of Toxic Effects of Chemical Substances, RTECS* (HE 20.7112:) is a slide and tape introduction to using RTECS.

1198. National Library of Medicine. **TOXNET**. (TOXicology Data NETwork). Internet: individuals with MEDLARS accounts may telnet to *medlars.nlm.nih.gov*; or *gopher.nlm.nih.gov*; or ftp to *public.nlm.nih.gov*; or *URL http://www-toxnet.nlm. nih.gov/*; or *URL http://tarnas.nlm.nih.gov/.*

This system of toxicological data banks includes the Hazardous Substances Data Bank, Toxic Release Inventory (entry 1036), and *Registry of Toxic Effects of Chemical Substances* (entry 1197).

VETERINARY MEDICINE

1199. Department of Agriculture. Animal and Plant Health Inspection Service. **Animal Disease Thesaurus**. DA, 1984. 223p. OCLC 17975851. A 101.2:D 63/3/984. Terminology for animal and other diseases is indexed and coded and presented in alphabetical and hierarchical arrangement.

 Transportation

GENERAL WORKS

1200. Bureau of the Census. **Census of Transportation**. GPO, 1995- . Quinquennial.
   C 3.233/3: ; C 3.233/5: .
The Census of Transportation includes establishment data for transportation industries and products, and the Truck Inventory and Use Survey (TIUS), which records data on the physical and operational characteristics of the nation's private and commercial trucks since 1992 (C 3.233/5:TC92-T-nos). These data are also available in *1992 Economic Censuses on CD-ROM* (entry 218). *Guide to the 1987 Census of Agriculture and Related Statistics* is a user guide and overview. *Transportation Statistics* (Factfinder for the Nation no.13; C 3.252:13/2/yr) is available free from the Census Bureau.

1201. Bureau of Transportation Statistics. **Transportation Statistics Annual Report**.
   GPO, 1977- . Annual. LC 78-643715. HE203.T76a. 380.5/0973. OCLC 3967204.
   TD 10.9: .
Data for aviation, highways, water, rail, and pipelines summarizes financial, inventory, and performance during the past year.

1202. Federal Transit Administration. **Accessibility Handbook for Transit Facilities**.
   NTIS (PB93-112498/HDM), 1992. 242p. OCLC 26785508. TD 1.8:T 61/2.
Presents information for designers and planners for constructing or renovating transit facilities in compliance with the Americans with Disabilities Act. Includes discussion of siting, entrances, interior, and boarding areas. Contains an index and a glossary.

1203. Federal Transit Administration. **Characteristics of Urban Transportation Systems**.
   tems. FTA, 1993. 7th rev. ed. 143p. OCLC 27838115. TD 7.2:C 37/992.
Data on speed, capacity, capital and operating costs, labor, energy use, pollution, and accidents are summarized for rail; bus; car, truck, and highway; high-occupancy vehicle lanes; and automated guideway transit.

1204. Transportation Research Board. Transportation Research Information Service.
   TRIS. Database. 1968- .
Contains citations, with abstracts, to current research and international literature about transportation, including air, highway, rail, maritime, and mass transit. Available from commercial vendors.

AVIATION

1205. Customs Service. **U.S. Customs Guide for Private Flyers (General Aviation Pilots)**. GPO, 19??- . Irregular. LC sn87-30203. OCLC 6430006. T 17.23: .
Provides customs requirements for private flights to and from foreign countries. Includes a list of airports with Customs Service and their location, hours, FAA flight plan notification procedure, Customs Service phone number, and policies.

1206. Defense Mapping Agency. **Defense Mapping Agency Public Sale Aeronautical Charts and Publications**. National Oceanic and Atmospheric Administration, 1994- . Free: NOAA Distribution Branch, N/CG33, National Ocean Service, Riverdale, MD 20737-1199. LC sn94-27874. OCLC 31304891. C 55.418/3: .
Defense Mapping Agency aeronautical charts and Flight Information Publications (FLIPs) are distributed by the National Ocean Service. This booklet describes and illustrates public sale DMA aeronautical charts (showing areas primarily outside the U.S.) and FLIPs, and provides ordering information. The booklet contains brief chart descriptions, including currency, size, scale, style, layout, and uses, with references to related publications, a directory of chart sales agents, and ordering information. Chart currency can be verified in the quarterly NOAA/NOS "Dates of Latest Edition (Aeronautical)," free from NOAA Distribution Branch, N/CG33, National Ocean Service, Riverdale, MD 20737-1199.

1207. Department of Transportation. Transportation Systems Center. **U.S. International Air Travel Statistics**. DOT, 1979- . Annual. LC 94-643022. HE9787.5.U5U17. 387.7/0973/021. OCLC 8274678. TD 1.40/3: .
Travel on commercial airlines between the U.S. and foreign countries is summarized for citizens, aliens, flag carriers, selected ports, and foreign country. Five-year trends are given.

1208. Federal Aviation Administration. **A Guide to Aviation Education Resources**. FAA, 1993. Free: National Coalition for Aviation Education, Box 28068, Washington, DC 20038. 31p. OCLC 29462958. TD 4.8:ED 8/3.
This pamphlet describes titles available from member organizations in the National Coalition for Aviation Education.

1209. Federal Aviation Administration. **Aeronautical Information Manual: Official Guide to Basic Flight Information and ATC Procedures**. GPO, 1995- . OCLC 33167438. TD 4.12/3: .
Revised every 112 days, this is a manual of flight information and ATC procedures. It includes medical and health facts, flight safety information, a glossary of Air Traffic Control terms, and information on safety, accident, and hazard reporting. The information parallels that in the internationally distributed *U.S. Aeronautical Information Publication*, or AIP (TD 4.308/2:).

1210. Federal Aviation Administration. Air Traffic Rules and Procedures Service. Air Traffic Publications Branch. **International Flight Information Manual**. GPO, 19??- . Annual. LC sf85-9750. WMLC L 83/922 u. OCLC 5192872. TD 4.309:vol.
This preflight and planning guide for U.S. nonscheduled operators and business and private aviators notes foreign entry requirements and provides an airport directory, with regulations and restrictions. Updated by the biweekly *International Notices to Airmen* (TD 4.11:).

1211. Federal Aviation Administration. **FAA Aviation Forecasts**. FAA, 1989- . Annual. LC 81-641480. HE9803.A1O36a. 387.7/4/0973. OCLC 4341789. TD 4.57/2: .
This guide to projected domestic activity at metropolitan hub area airports for 10-year periods, with historical data since 1960, shows economic and demographic characteristics of passengers and operational data. Includes maps, charts, and tables.

1212. Federal Aviation Administration. **FAA Organizational Directory**. GPO, 1992- . Annual. LC 93-648678. HE9803.A1F43f. 353.008/77/025. OCLC 27450289. TD 4.52: .
Provides names, addresses, and telephone numbers for FAA officials in branches, regions, centers, and at Washington headquarters. A related title is *The FAA International Answer Book: Answers to Commonly Asked Questions About FAA Regulations and Procedures* (TD 4.2:In 8/4/992).

1213. Federal Aviation Administration. **FAA Statistical Handbook of Aviation**. GPO, 1959- . Annual. LC 73-609572. TL521.A41612. 387.7/0973. OCLC 2707503. TD 4.20: .
Data on FAA-regulated aviation include the National Airspace System Operations, airports, aviation activity, carriers, personnel, accidents, and aircraft production and trade. Includes maps of FAA regions and air traffic hubs, acronyms, and a glossary.

1214. Federal Aviation Administration. **Guide to Federal Aviation Administration Publications**. FAA, 1977- . Free: Public Inquiry Center, APA-230, Office of Public Affairs, Federal Aviation Administration, Washington, DC 20591; (800) FAA-SURE. Annual. LC sn89-23258. OCLC 5202771. TD 4.17/6: .
This annotated list includes regulatory and technical documents, test books and test standards, educational materials, and specifications, along with other FAA information sources. Related titles are *Advisory Circular Checklist (And Status of Other FAA Publications for Sale by the U.S. Government Printing Office (GPO)* (TD 4.8/5:), *FAA Forms Catalog* (TD 4.8/2:), and *Index of Aviation Technical Standard Orders* (TD 4.8/5:).

1215. Federal Aviation Administration. Office of Management Systems. **Census of U.S. Civil Aircraft**. GPO, 1964- . Annual. LC 76-641161. HE9803.A1A27. 387. 7/33/40973. OCLC 1136794. TD 4.18: .
The annual FAA count of all registered U.S. civil aircraft by manufacturer (for each of the 50 states) includes the type and number of engines and aircraft size. The number of U.S. registered aircraft kept in foreign countries is also given.

1216. Library of Congress. Science and Technology Division. **Wilbur & Orville Wright; A Bibliography Commemorating the Hundredth Anniversary of the Birth of Wilbur Wright, April 16, 1867** compiled by Arthur G. Renstrom. LC, 1968. Free: Science and Technology Division, Washington, DC 20540-5446. 187p. LC 68-60013. Z8986.33.R4. 016.629133/34/0922. OCLC 452451. LC 33.2:W 93.
This bibliography is an expansion of *Papers of the Wright Brothers* (McGraw-Hill, 1953), with annotated entries arranged chronologically under subject headings. Indexed by name and institution.

1217. Library of Congress. Science and Technology Division. **Wilbur & Orville Wright; A Chronology Commemorating the Hundredth Anniversary of the Birth of Orville Wright, August 19, 1871** by Arthur G. Renstrom. LC, 1975. Free: Science and Technology Division, Washington, DC 20540-5446. 234p. LC 74-11244. TL540.W7R46. 629.13/0092/2. OCLC 948116. LC 33.2:W 93/2.

This chronology and flight log traces the Wright brothers' activities from 1867, including events following their deaths, through 1971. Includes a name and geographic index.

1218. Library of Congress. **Wilbur & Orville Wright, Pictorial Materials: A Documentary Guide** by Arthur G. Renstrom. LC, 1982. Free: Science and Technology Division, Washington, DC 20540-5446. 200p. LC 82-600194. TL540.W525R46 1982. 016.62913/0092/2. OCLC 8495548. LC 1.6/4:W 93.

This is a guide to photographic research using Library of Congress aeronautical holdings and NASA's Wright brothers photographic collection. Includes an index of people, institutions, and places, and an appendix listing microfiche, audiotapes, slides, recordings, and films.

1219. National Oceanic and Atmospheric Administration. National Ocean Service. **Aeronautical Charts and Related Products**. NOAA, 19??- . Free: Distribution Branch, N/CG33, National Ocean Service, Riverdale, MD 20737-1199. Irregular. LC sn94-27619. OCLC 29559360. C 55.418/2: .

Contains descriptions and ordering information for U.S. civil aeronautical charts and flight information publications, plus information on obtaining foreign charts.

1220. National Oceanic and Atmospheric Administration. National Ocean Service. **Airport/Facility Directory**. NOAA, 19??- . Every 8 weeks. C 55.416/2: .

 East Central U.S. C 55.416/2:EC/ .

 North Central U.S. C 55.416/2:NC/ .

 Northeast U.S. C 55.416/2:NE/ .

 Northwest U.S. C 55.416/2:NW/ .

 South Central U.S. C 55.416/2:SC/ .

 Southeast U.S. C 55.416/2:SE/ .

 Southwest U.S. C 55.416/2:SW/ .

Seven regions of the U.S., Puerto Rico, and the Virgin Islands are described in the seven volumes of this pilot's manual. Volumes include data about airports, seaplane bases, heliports, NAVAIDs (navigational aids), communications, special notices, and operational procedures.

HIGHWAYS

1221. Federal Highway Administration. Federal Works Agency. **Highway Statistics. Summary to ... [year]**. GPO, 1945- . Decennial. LC sn90-20070. OCLC 3803026. TD 2.23/2: .

Historical data summarize key series, featuring earlier data than those of the annual volumes (entry 1223).

1222. Federal Highway Administration. **Highway Safety Performance [year] Fatal and Injury Accident Rates on Public Roads in the United States**. FHA, 1982- . Annual. LC 84-645525. HE5614.2.U563a. 363.1/252/0973021. OCLC 10686769. TD 2.30/13: .

The number and rate of highway accidents, deaths, and injuries are given by state and highway/road type for the nation, with a summary for Puerto Rico. Other data include highway and vehicle miles, average daily travel, accident and casualty rates for urban/rural locations and highway type, and miles traveled and accidents/casualties per capita/driver/vehicle.

1223.   Federal Highway Administration. **Highway Statistics**. GPO, 1945- . Annual. LC 74-648854. HE355.A3A25. 388.1/0973. OCLC 1796740. TD 2.23: .

>   Also available on the *National Economic, Social & Environmental Data Bank* (entry 172).

This is a compilation of statistics on motor fuel, vehicles, driver licensing, highway user taxes, state highway finance, mileage, and federal aid. Related titles are *Our Nation's Highways: Selected Facts and Figures* (TD 2.2:H 53/29/992) and *Selected Highway Statistics and Charts* (TD 2.23:yr/charts).

1224.   House. Committee on Public Works and Transportation. **The Status of the Nation's Highways, Bridges, and Transit: Conditions and Performance: Report of the Secretary of Transportation to the United States Congress, Pursuant to Section 307(h) of Title 23, United States Code, and Section 308(e) of Title 49, United States Code**. GPO, 1993- . Biennial. LC 94-643053. OCLC 28102828. Y 4.P 96/11: .

This series of biennial reports to Congress provides a snapshot of characteristics, finance, and trends.

1225.   National Highway Traffic Safety Administration. **Fatal Accident Reporting System [year]**. GPO, 1979- . Annual. LC 82-643414. HE5614.2.U58b. 312/.279/0973. OCLC 7211598. TD 8.27: .

Data on deaths, circumstances, and people/vehicles involved in fatal motor vehicle accidents for the nation and Puerto Rico with trends back to 1966 are compiled from the NHTSA's computerized Fatal Accident Reporting System (FARS). Data are cross-tabulated by time of day, month, and day of week; class of highway, speed limit, traffic flow, number of lanes, weather and light, type of junction and traffic control, city, urban/rural location; vehicle type, vehicle involved, maneuver/collision type, point of impact, rollover or fire, medical response time; and victim demographics, injury, ejection, restraint use, helmet use, driving record, and alcohol level.

MERCHANT VESSELS AND PORTS

1226.   Army. Corps of Engineers. Water Resources Support Center. **Port Series**. GPO, 1979- . Irregular. LC 86-730992. HE554. D 103.8: .

Information about U.S. coastal, inland, and Great Lakes ports includes a description of conditions, location, tidal range, anchorages, bridges, weather, port and harbor facilities, oil handling and bunkering, coal and dry bulk handling, grain elevators, warehouses, open storage, hoisting equipment, repair and drydocking, and rail lines. Maps, charts, and aerial and ground photographs are included.

1227.   Coast Guard. **Merchant Vessels of the United States**. GPO, 1925- . Annual. LC sn90-20391. OCLC 4057799. TD 5.12/2: .

This is a listing of American merchant and recreational vessels documented by law in the Marine Safety Information System Database, noting official number, tonnage, dimensions, prop and hull type, when and where built, type of service, trade licenses, owner, and home port. Includes an index of managing owners. This publication was discontinued from 1982 to 1989 because of the transition to a new computer system. It continues *Annual List of Merchant Vessels of the United States . . . and List of Vessels Belonging to the U.S. Government with Distinguishing Signals* and offers coverage back to 1924.

1228. Department of the Interior. Office of the Secretary. **The Secretary of the Interior's Standards for Historic Vessel Preservation Projects: With Guidelines for Applying the Standards.** DI, 1990. 101p. OCLC 22141983. I 29.9/2:St 2.
Standards for registering historic nautical vessels include guidelines for acquisition, protection, documentation, stabilization, preservation, rehabilitation, restoration, and interpretation.

1229. Department of Transportation. Maritime Administration. **Marad Publications.** DT, 1978- . Annual. LC sn87-18226. OCLC 4537917. TD 11.9/2: .
This unannotated bibliography of publications related to the U.S. merchant marine includes addresses and phone numbers of Department of Transportation regional offices.

1230. Department of Transportation. Maritime Administration. **Merchant Fleets of the World.** DOT, 1955- . Annual. LC 59-61277. HE735.U5. OCLC 2223151. TD 11.14: .
Ship data include area profiles detailing fleet composition, number of ships, and tonnage; new ship construction; the top 15 maritime nations ranked by tonnage, with new ships, losses, and ship type; and the number of freighters, bulk carriers, and tankers in the privately owned U.S. merchant fleet.

1231. Naval Oceanography Command. **National Oceanographic Fleet Operating Schedules for [year].** . . . Naval Oceanographic Office, 1983- . Annual. LC 84-645010. GC57.N27. 551.46/0072. OCLC 10862262. D 203.33: .
Provides operating schedules for academic, government, and commercial vessels that are specifically configured, deep-ocean-capable, oceanographic, or hydrographic. Included with the ship schedules is information on ship characteristics, engineering and deck equipment, and a contact person. Replaces *Oceanographic Ship Operating Schedules.*

1232. Navy Hydrographic Office. **World Port Index.** GPO, 1953. Biennial. LC 58-60168. HE552.W67. 387.1/5/05. OCLC 6928389. D 5.317:150/.
This guide to location, characteristics, facilities, and services of selected ports, shipping facilities, and oil terminals around the world consists largely of tables, with some charts. The chart and Sailing Direction are given for each place listed.

NAVIGATION

1233. Coast Guard. **Light List.** 7v. GPO, 19??- . Annual. LC sn82-3992. OCLC 2923471. TD 5.9: .

> Vol. 1. **Atlantic Coast, St. Croix River, Maine to Toms River, New Jersey.**
> Vol. 2. **Atlantic Coast, Toms River, New Jersey to Little River, South Carolina.**
> Vol. 3. **Atlantic and Gulf Coasts from Little River, South Carolina to Econfina River, Florida.**
> Vol. 4. **Gulf of Mexico, Econfina River, Florida to the Rio Grande, Texas.**
> Vol. 5. **Mississippi River System.**
> Vol. 6. **Pacific Coast and Pacific Islands.**
> Vol. 7. **Great Lakes, United States and Canada.**

These are listings of lights, fog signals, buoys, daybeacons, radio-beacons, and U.S. racon and loran stations on the U.S. Pacific coast and Pacific islands, as well as those maintained by British Columbia between the U.S. coast and Alaska. They are not intended to substitute for navigational charts and coast pilots. Updated by *Notice to Mariners* and *Local Notice to Mariners*.

1234.   Coast Guard. **Loran-C User Handbook**. GPO, 1992. 232p. OCLC 28552437. TD 5.8:L 88/992.
Known as the "Green Book," the Loran-C radio-navigation system handbook describes installation and use of technological advances and guidance, including position determination and accuracy, marine navigation tips, sources of interference, and Loran-C charts. Includes updated data sheets and coverage diagrams.

1235.   Coast Guard. **Navigation Rules, International-Inland**. GPO, 1992. 212p. LC 93-196504. KF2566.A2 1992. 343.7309/64/02632. OCLC 27819636. TD 5.6:In 8/992.
This official Coast Guard manual presents the International Regulations for Prevention of Collision at Sea (known as 72 COLREGS) and the Inland Navigational Rules side by side for comparison. Included are the amendments and revisions to the rules, illustrations, and COLREGS Demarcation Lines.

1236.   Defense Mapping Agency. **Defense Mapping Agency Nautical Charts and Publications Public Sale**. National Oceanic and Atmospheric Administration, 1994- . Free: NOAA Distribution Branch, N/CG33, National Ocean Service, Riverdale, MD 20737-1199. C 55.440: .

> Region 1. United States and Canada. C 55.440:1/
>
> Region 2. Central and South America, and Antarctica. C 55.440:2/
>
> Region 3. Western Europe, Iceland, Greenland, and the Arctic. C 55.440:3/
>
> Region 4. Scandinavia, Baltic, and the former Soviet Union. C 55.440:4/
>
> Region 5. Western Africa and the Mediterranean. C 55.440:5/
>
> Region 6. Indian Ocean. C 55.440:6/
>
> Region 7. Australia, Indonesia, and New Zealand. C 55.440:7/
>
> Region 8. Oceania. C 55.440:8/
>
> Region 9. East Asia. C 55.440:9/

Each of these nine catalogs covers a different region of the world. The catalogs contain product and ordering information, chart lists for regions, illustrations of chart locations, and a list of sales agents. A free, quarterly *Dates of Latest Editions: Defense Mapping Agency Public Sale Nautical Charts and Publications* (DMA Nautical DOLE), available from the NOAA/NOS, is a list of chart numbers with edition number and date.

1237.   National Ocean Survey. **United States Coast Pilot**. 9v. GPO, 19??- . Annual. C 55.422: .

> Vol. 1. **Atlantic Coast. Eastport to Cape Cod**.
>
> Vol. 2. **Atlantic Coast. Cape Cod to Sandy Hook**.
>
> Vol. 3. **Atlantic Coast. Sandy Hook to Cape Henry**.
>
> Vol. 4. **Atlantic Coast. Cape Henry to Key West**.
>
> Vol. 5. **Atlantic Coast. Gulf of Mexico, Puerto Rico, and Virgin Islands**.
>
> Vol. 6. **Great Lakes, Lakes Ontario, Erie, Huron, Michigan, and Superior and St. Lawrence River**.
>
> Vol. 7. **Pacific Coast. California, Oregon, Washington, and Hawaii**.
>
> Vol. 8. **Pacific Coast. Alaska, Dixon Entrance to Cape Spencer**.
>
> Vol. 9. **Pacific and Arctic Coasts. Alaska, Cape Spencer to Beaufort Sea**.

Information in this series on U.S. coastal and intracoastal waters and the Great Lakes supplements nautical charts. Subjects covered include local navigation regulations, weather, shoreline features, tides, and navigational hazards. Each of the volumes is available on magnetic tape.

1238.   National Oceanic and Atmospheric Administration. National Ocean Service. **Guide to NOAA Nautical Products and Services.** NOAA, 19??- . Free: National Ocean Service, Riverdale, MD 20737-1199. OCLC 19746678. C 55.418:6/ .
Describes publications, charts, maps, and other NOAA products.

1239.   National Oceanic and Atmospheric Administration. National Ocean Service. **Nautical Chart Symbols, Abbreviations, and Terms: Chart No. 1, United States of America.** NOAA, 1990. 9th ed. 99p. LC 90-600586. OCLC 21742583. C 55.402: Sy 6.
Contains symbols, abbreviations, and terms on National Ocean Service, Defense Mapping Agency, Hydrographic/Topographic Center, and International Hydrographic Organization charts, along with those on foreign charts reproduced by the DMA Hydrographic/ Topographic Center.

RAILROADS

1240.   Interstate Commerce Commission. **Transport Statistics in the United States. Part 1: Railroads. Part 2: Motor Carriers.** GPO, 1980- . Annual. LC sn87-42339 and LC sn87-42336. OCLC 6881764 and OCLC 8731125. IC 1.25: .
This is a compendium of detailed statistics on traffic, operations, equipment, finances, and employment for carriers subject to the Interstate Commerce Act. Part 1 covers railroads; part 2 covers motor carriers. Supersedes *Statistics of Railways in the United States* (1887-1953).

TIDES

1241.   National Ocean Service. **Tidal Current Tables. Atlantic Coast of North America.** NOS, 1958- . Annual. LC 78-615555. VK781.C87. 623.89/49/091634. OCLC 2458466. C 55.425: .
Accompanying the rise and fall of tides is a periodic horizontal water flow known as the tidal current. The annual tidal current tables give daily predictions of times of slack water, rotary tidal currents, and times and speeds of flood and ebb currents for reference stations along the U.S. Atlantic coast. It is expected that NOAA's National Ocean Service will distribute a CD-ROM with tidal current and tide tables for the U.S. for 1996.

1242.   National Ocean Service. **Tidal Current Tables. Pacific Coast of North America and Asia.** NOS, 1958- . Annual. LC 77-616576. VK747.A16. 623.89/49/09164. OCLC 2458480. C 55.425/2: .
Daily predictions of times of slack water, rotary tidal currents, and times and speeds of flood and ebb currents are given for reference stations along the coasts of Alaska, Washington, Japan, China, the Philippines, British Columbia, and the Aleutian Islands. Correction factors for calculating other currents and at other locations are given. Includes an index by station name and a glossary. It is expected that NOAA's National Ocean Service will distribute a CD-ROM with tidal current and tide tables for the U.S. for 1996.

1243. National Ocean Service. **Tide Tables, High and Low Water Predictions.** 4v. National Oceanic and Atmospheric Administration, 1958- . Annual. C 55.421/ .

> **Alaskan Supplement.** C 55.421/ : .
>
> **Central and Western Pacific Ocean and Indian Ocean.** C 55.421/4: .
>
> **East Coast of North and South America, Including Greenland.** C 55.421/2: .
>
> **Europe and West Coast of Africa, Including the Mediterranean Sea.** C 55.421/3: .
>
> **West Coast of North and South America, Including the Hawaiian Islands.** C 55.421: .

Tables show predicted times and heights of high and low tides at reference stations for every day of the year, with correction factors for calculating at other locations and for calculating the tide height at any time of day. Includes an index by station name and a glossary. It is expected that NOAA's National Ocean Service will distribute a CD-ROM with tidal current and tide tables for the U.S. for 1996.

PART FOUR

Humanities

Architecture

HISTORIC PRESERVATION

1244. Library of Congress. Prints and Photographs Division. **America Preserved: A Checklist of Historic Buildings, Structures, and Sites**. Cataloging Distribution Service, 1995. 60th Anniversary ed. 1152p. LC 94-19453. E159.A37 1995. 973. OCLC 30623682. LC 1.2:H 62/7.
This state/territory and county checklist features buildings, structures, and sites recorded by the Historic American Buildings Survey (HABS) and Historic American Engineering Record (HAER) of engineering and industrial sites. Included are architectural drawings, photographs, and written documentation in the HABS and HAER collections in the Library of Congress and National Park Service. The volume notes LC shelflist numbers and includes ordering instructions, essays, drawings, black-and-white photographs, and a city index to counties. A related title is *Historic American Engineering Record Catalog* (I 29.84/2:C 28/976), which lists documentation available in the HAER collection in the Library of Congress. Supersedes *Historic American: Buildings, Structures, and Sites* (1983).

1245. National Park Service. Cultural Landscape Program. **Cultural Landscape Bibliography: An Annotated Bibliography on Resources in the National Park System** by Katherine Ahern. NPS, 1992. 150p. LC 93-198610. Z1251.A2A34 1992. 016.973. OCLC 27521881. I 29.82:C 89.
This annotated bibliography describes research reports written between 1940 and 1991 about historic sites and historic ethnographic, designed, and vernacular landscapes.

1246. National Park Service. Cultural Resources. **Catalog of Historic Preservation Publications**. NPS, 1990- . Biennial. LC sn93-27515. OCLC 27750383. I 29.82:P 96/2/ .
This is an annotated bibliography of preservation-related books, slide-tapes, and databases published since 1989. Titles relate to preservation and architectural assistance, park historic architecture, interagency resources, history, the Historic American Buildings Survey/Historic American Engineering Record, curatorial services, and anthropology. Addresses of NPS regional offices are included. Supersedes the NPS *Publication Catalog*.

1247. National Park Service. Cultural Resources Programs. **Federal Historic Preservation Laws** compiled by Sara K. Blumenthal. NPS, 1989, 1990. 61p. LC 89-603533. KF4310.A3 1989. 344.73/094. OCLC 20801409. I 29.2:P 92/8.
The text of laws governing National Historic Preservation Programs, National Historic Landmarks, the Federal Archeology Program, Federal Preservation Tax Incentives, and

other major federal historic preservation laws is provided. An appendix of regulations governing National Historic Preservation Programs cites title and part of the *Code of Federal Regulations.*

1248. National Park Service. Historic American Buildings Survey/Historic American Engineering Board. **Historic American Buildings Survey/Historic American Engineering Record: An Annotated Bibliography** compiled by James C. Massey, Nancy B. Schwartz, and Shirley Maxwell. NPS, 1992. 170p. LC 92-37310. Z5944.U5M39 1992. 016.36369/0973. OCLC 26801613. I 29.74:B 47.

This is a list of Historic American Buildings Survey (HABS) and Historic American Engineering Record (HAER) publications recording historic structures between the years 1933 and 1991. Not included are National Park Service publications using HABS/HAER records. The bibliography includes a section on lists and finding aids and an index to authors, cooperating organizations, and publishers.

1249. National Park Service. History Division. **Catalog of National Historic Landmarks.** NPS, 19??- . Irregular. LC 89-641105. E159.C33. 917.3/025. OCLC 17966977. I 29.120: .

This directory of landmarks is arranged by state. Included in each listing are address, city and county, historic dates, date of designation as a National Historic Landmark, architect, and a description.

1250. National Park Service. Interagency Resources Division. **Guidelines for Completing National Register of Historic Places Forms. Part A, How to Complete the National Register Registration Form.** 1v. GPO, 1991. OCLC 25384243. I 29.76/3:16 A.

Instructions for completing NPS 10-900 forms documenting historic properties for eligibility determination or nomination to the National Register of Historic Places include how to document classification, function, description, and significance. Includes a bibliography and glossary. Related titles are *Guidelines for Completing National Register of Historic Places Forms. Part B. How to Complete the National Register Multiple Property Documentation Form* (I 29.76/3:16), *The Secretary of the Interior's Standards for Rehabilitation and Illustrated Guidelines for Rehabilitating Historic Buildings* (I 29.9/2:R 26/992), and *Guidelines for Evaluating and Documenting Historic Aids to Navigation* (I 29.76/3:34).

1251. National Park Service. **Metals in America's Historic Buildings: Uses and Preservation Treatments.** NPS, 1992. 2d ed. 167p. LC 92-34883. NA3940.M47 1992. 721/.0447. OCLC 26722649. I 29.2:M 56/2/992.

This guide to use, identification, and replacement of architectural metals includes surveys of frequently used types in buildings, sculpture, foundations, and "street furniture." Also contains background information on deterioration and preservation. Includes a bibliography.

1252. National Park Service. Preservation Assistance Division. **Preserving and Revitalizing Older Communities: Sources of Federal Assistance** by Lesley Slavitt; edited by Susan Escherich. GPO, 1993. 146p. LC 94-143459. E159.S63 1993. OCLC 29569420. I 29.2:P 92/12.

This directory of federal programs for revitalizing declining historic neighborhoods includes program objectives and results, types of assistance, eligibility criteria, financial information, and contacts. Includes a glossary and an index to eligibility, assistance type, and subject.

1253. National Park Service. Preservation Assistance Division/Catalog of Landscape Records in the United States, US ICOMOS Historic Landscapes Committee. **Historic Landscape Directory: A Source Book of Agencies, Organizations, and Institutions Providing Information on Historic Landscape Preservation** edited by Lauren G. Meier; compiled by Sarah S. Boasberg et al. NPS, 1991. 96p. LC 92-201615. E159.H7135 1991. OCLC 25321011. I 29.126:H 62.

This is a directory of national, state, and local agencies (both public and private) active in historic landscape preservation. It also lists academic programs with curricula in landscape architecture or historic preservation, archival and library collections, and organizations and publications related to historic plant materials. Includes an index. A related title is *Guidelines for Evaluating and Documenting Rural Historic Landscapes* (I 29.76/3:30).

THE CAPITAL

1254. Architect of the Capitol. **Art in the United States Capitol.** (H.Doc.94-660). GPO, 1978. 455p. OCLC 4231757. (Serial Set 13150). X 94-2:H.doc.660.

Portraits, paintings, busts, statues, reliefs, frescoes, exterior sculpture, and murals in the U.S. Capitol are reviewed, using color photographs and descriptions.

1255. Commission of Fine Arts. **Massachusetts Avenue Architecture.** 2v. GPO, 1973, 1975. LC 73-603051. NA735.W3U5 1973. 975.3. OCLC 1093287. FA 1.2:M 38/v.1,2.

This is a detailed survey of beaux-arts buildings on Massachusetts Avenue in northwest Washington, D.C. Includes illustrations, technical descriptions, permits, deeds, biographies of occupants, and physical and social histories.

1256. Commission of Fine Arts. **Sixteenth Street Architecture** by Sue A. Kohler and Jeffrey R. Carson. 2v. GPO, 1978, 1988. LC 79-603275. NA735.W3K644. 975.3. OCLC 5847373. FA 1.2:Si 9/v.1-2.

This guide to beaux-arts structures in Washington, D.C., includes historical and current photos and floor plans. Volume 1 describes residences in the 16th Street area of northwest Washington, D.C., many of which had nationally prominent architects or owners. Volume 2 contains descriptions of churches, hotels, houses, and other buildings.

1257. Library of Congress. **The White House: Resources for Research at the Library of Congress.** GPO, 1992. 150p. LC 92-12623. Z1270.W3G85 1992. 016.9753. OCLC 25675495. LC 1.2:H 81.

This is an annotated bibliography of books, magazine articles, manuscripts, prints, and photographs in the Library of Congress related to the history of the White House since its construction in 1792. It includes descriptions of related materials in LC's Prints and Photographs and Manuscript Divisions. Updates *The White House: A Bibliographical List.*

1258. National Park Service. Preservation Assistance Division. **The Interior Building: Its Architecture and Its Art** by David W. Look and Carole L. Perrault. NPS, 1986. 201p. LC 86-21710. NA4227.W2L6 1986. 725/.12/09753. OCLC 14166186. I 29.104:In 8/corr.

Presents descriptions, with photographs, of the exterior, entrances, grand stairs, corridors, offices, murals, sculpture, floor plans, and architectural highlights of the Department of the Interior building constructed during the period 1935-36. Includes a bibliography.

1259. National Park Service. Preservation Assistance Division. **White House Stone Carving: Builders and Restorers** by Lee H. Nelson. GPO, 1992. 32p. LC 92-21388. NK8700.5.U62W26 1992. 725/.17/09753. OCLC 26632170. I 29.2:W 58/5.

This is an introduction to the building and recent restoration of the White House, "the finest eighteenth century stone house in the United States."

1260. Office of the Chief of Engineers. Historical Division. **"To the Immortal Name and Memory of George Washington": The United States Army Corps of Engineers and the Construction of the Washington Monument** by Louis Torres. GPO, 1985. 145p. LC 85-601652. F203.4.W3T67 1985. 975.3. OCLC 12085597. D 103.43:870-1-21.

This history of the planning and construction of the Washington Monument covers through the 1940s, with photographs, a bibliography, and an index.

1261. Senate. **The Dome of the United States Capitol: An Architectural History** (S.Doc.102-7) by William C. Allen. GPO, 1992. 84p. OCLC 27022759. (Serial Set number not yet available). Y 1.1/3:102-7.

This illustrated history of the building of the initial and the current U.S. Capitol domes includes construction details and biographical sketches of architects and engineers, along with an index.

1262. Smithsonian Institution. **Washington Deco: Art Deco Design in the Nation's Capital** by Hans Wirz and Richard Striner. SI, 1984. 128p. LC 84-600183. NA735.W3W57 1984. 720/.9753. OCLC 10912880. SI 1.2:D 35.

Photographs and descriptions of art deco buildings and homes in Washington, D.C., Maryland, and Virginia built between 1925 and 1945 are presented, along with text describing the art deco era. Includes a list of buildings, with address, use, architect/ developer, building permit number, and year constructed. Indexed.

1263. White House Historical Association. **The White House: An Historic Guide**. WHHA, 1994. 18th ed. 159p. LC 94-60794. OCLC 32502454. Y 3.H 62/4:8 W 58.

Using color photographs, this official guide describes history, rooms and historical furnishings of the White House. Includes an index.

Fine Arts

1264. Library of Congress. **Exhibit Catalogs of the German-Speaking Countries of Europe, 1958-1988: A Selective Bibliography** by Margrit B. Krewson. LC, 1990. Free: Office Systems Services, Printing and Processing Section, Washington, DC 20540-5446. 329p. LC 89-600103. Z2000.K72 1990. 016.94/0097/531. OCLC 20015810. LC 1.12/2:G 31/5.

Citations describe the Library of Congress's collection of auction and exhibit catalogs published in Austria, Germany, and Switzerland during the last 30 years. Exhibits include those on art as well as intellectual, social, and technical history. Includes an index.

1265. Library of Congress. **Library of Congress Prints and Photographs: An Illustrated Guide.** LC, 1995. 80p. LC 94-17438. NE53.W3L49 1995. 760/.074/753. OCLC 30544001. LC 1.6/4:P 93.

This introduction to LC's pictorial collections describes holdings that include watercolor views, portraits, architectural drawings, posters, news photographs, and printed ephemera.

1266. Library of Congress. Prints and Photographs Division. **Farm Security Administration, Historical Section: A Guide to Textual Records in the Library of Congress** prepared by Annette Melville. LC, 1985. 48p. LC 85-600147. TR820.5.M44 1985. 779/.997391. OCLC 12342689. LC 25.8/2:F 22.

This is a finding aid to written records of the FSA photographic unit, including microfilmed office files, scrapbooks, captions, and photographic prints, negatives, and transparencies.

1267. Library of Congress. Prints and Photographs Division. **Graphic Sampler** compiled by Renata V. Shaw. LC, 1979. Free to U.S. Libraries and Institutions: Office Systems Services, Printing and Processing Section, Washington, DC 20540-5446. 367p. LC 79-12124. NE400.G7. 760/.074/0153. OCLC 4857518. LC 25.2:G 76.

This selection of images from the Prints and Photographs Division was determined by rediscovery of a group of drawings or prints, or by the newness or interest of recent acquisitions. It includes pictures created between the 15th century and 1800; prints and drawings from the 19th century; and prints, drawings, and paintings from 1900 to the 1960s.

1268. Library of Congress. Prints and Photographs Division. **The Polish Poster: From Young Poland Through the Second World War: Holdings in the Prints and Photographs Division, Library of Congress** by Elena Millie and Zbigniew Kantorosinski. LC, 1993. Free: European Division, Washington, DC 20540-5530. 104p. LC 94-123647. NC1807.P6L5 1993. 741.6/74/09438074753. OCLC 30509142. LC 25.2:P 75.

This checklist of LC's Prints and Photographs Division collection lists Polish posters by artist and title, with a description of the image, medium, publisher, date, size, signature, and bibliographic sources in which the poster is illustrated or cited. It includes biographical notes on artists, primarily from previously untranslated Polish sources, a historical perspective, and a bibliography.

1269. Library of Congress. **Visual Arts in Poland: An Annotated Bibliography of Selected Holdings in the Library of Congress** compiled by Janina W. Hoskins. GPO, 1993. 219p. LC 92-27991. Z5961.P57L5 1993. 016.7/09438. OCLC 26308852. LC 1.2:P 75/7.

This is an annotated checklist of books, periodicals, and articles about art and cultural life in Poland, published since the 19th century and particularly since World War II. Titles are primarily in Polish, but some also appear in English, French, German, and Italian. Includes a name index.

1270. Smithsonian Institution. **Finders' Guide to Decorative Arts in the Smithsonian Institution** by Christine Minter-Dowd. SI, 1984. 213p. LC 82-600320. NK460.W3S67 1984. 745/.074/0153. OCLC 8930463. SI 1.20:D 35.

This directory describes collections of decorative arts and of archaeological, ethnological, and technological artifacts found in the Smithsonian's museums and offices. Excluded are painting, printmaking, drawing, photography, and sculpture. The guide describes the Smithsonian unit's collection objectives and strengths, purpose, scope, count, lending policy, and finding aids. It also cites publications describing or illustrating the collection. Includes an index of names, places, titles of works, artistic materials, object types, and subjects.

1271. Smithsonian Institution. **Guide to Photographic Collections at the Smithsonian Institution** by Diane Vogt O'Connor. 3v. SI, 1989-1992. LC 89-600116. Q11.S79 1989. 026/.779/074753. OCLC 19741738. SI 3.10:P 56.

This selected guide to the Smithsonian Institution's vast holdings of still photographs includes photonegatives, photoprints, phototransparencies, and direct positive processes. Entries include collections, dates of photos, origins, subjects, arrangement, captions, finding aids, and restrictions. Indexed by creator, form and process, and subject. Five volumes are planned: vol. 1 *National Museum of American History*; vol. 2 *National Museum of Natural History, National Zoological Park, Smithsonian Astrophysical Observatory, Smithsonian Tropical Research Institute*; vol. 3 *Cooper-Hewitt Museum, Freer Gallery of Art, National Museum of American Art, National Portrait Gallery, Arthur M. Sackler Gallery, Office of Horticulture*. No information available on volumes 4 and 5.

Literature

GENERAL WORKS

1272. Library of Congress. Center for the Book. **The History of Books: A Guide to Selected Resources in the Library of Congress** by Alice D. Schreyer. GPO, 1987. 221p. LC 86-10493. Z1002.S35 1987. 027.573. OCLC 13581359. LC 1.6/4:H 62.
This is a guide to scholarly collections relating to the history of books and printed materials held in units of the Library of Congress.

1273. Library of Congress. Latin American, Portuguese, and Spanish Division. **The Archive of Hispanic Literature on Tape; A Descriptive Guide** compiled by Francisco Aguilera and edited by Georgette Magassy Dorn. LC, 1974. Free: Hispanic Division, Washington, DC 20540-5446. 516p. LC 73-19812. Z1609.L7U54 1974. 016.86/008. OCLC 749835. LC 24.2:H 62/2.
The archive consists of recordings, dating back to 1943, of writers from Latin America and the Iberian peninsula reading their own prose and poetry. Selections from novels, poetry, essays, and commentaries are read in Spanish, Portuguese, French, Catalan, and the Indian languages of Zapotec, Nahuatl, and Quechua. Entries provide a biographical author sketch, a discussion of the author's work, a listing of archive holdings, and a bibliography.

1274. Library of Congress. Rare Book and Special Collections Division. **Library of Congress Rare Books and Special Collections: An Illustrated Guide**. LC, 1992. Free: Washington, DC 20540. 64p. LC 92-32163. Z881.U5 1992. 026.09/09753. OCLC 26502042. LC 23.8:B 64.
This is a guide to books, broadsides, pamphlets, theater playbills, title pages, prints, posters, photos, medieval and Renaissance manuscripts, incunabula, and separate collections in LC's Rare Book and Special Collections Division. The collection encompasses American history and literature, Europe, the book arts, and the illustrated book.

1275. Library of Congress. Rare Book and Special Collections Division. **Vision of a Collector: The Lessing J. Rosenwald Collection in the Library of Congress**. LC, 1991. Publishing Office, Box J, Washington, DC 20540-8620. 427p. LC 91-32821. Z997.R817V57 1991. 026/.0007475. OCLC 24380200. LC 23.2:V 82.
Accumulated from LC's foremost donor of rare books, the Rosenwald Collection in LC's Rare Book and Special Collections Division consists of Western European and American

illustrated books, with a special emphasis on 15th-century titles, 16th-century imprints from the Low Countries, 18th-century French books, books by William Blake, and 20th-century livres d'artiste. The guide is in the form of essays and is indexed by name.

BIBLIOGRAPHIES

1276. Library of Congress. **Contemporary Authors of the German-Speaking Countries of Europe: A Selective Bibliography** by Margrit B. Krewson. LC, 1988. Free to U.S. Libraries and Institutions: Office Systems Services, Printing and Processing Section, Washington, DC 20540-5446. 306p. LC 88-600010. Z2233.K79 1988. 016.83/08/00914. OCLC 17439792. LC 1.12/2:G 31/4.

This is an unannotated bibliography of LC holdings for prominent writers from Austria, Germany, and Switzerland. The works cited include reference materials and works by and about the authors, including belles lettres, music, radio plays, social criticism, travelogues, and some children's literature.

1277. Library of Congress. European Division. **Czech and Slovak Literature in English: A Bibliography** by George J. Kovtun. LC, 1988. Free to U.S. Libraries and Institutions: Office Systems Services, Printing and Processing Section, Washington, DC 20540-5446. 2d ed. 152p. LC 87-17004. Z2138.L5K68 1988. 016.8918/6. OCLC 16717322. LC 1.12/2:C 99.

This bibliography of translations published as monographs between the years 1832 and 1982 includes prose, poetry, criticism, literary history, journalism, and folklore. Children's literature is excluded. Includes an index of authors, translators, and editors.

Individual Authors

Cervantes

1278. Library of Congress. Hispanic Division. **Works by Miguel de Cervantes Saavedra in the Library of Congress** compiled by Reynaldo Aguirre. GPO, 1994. 107p. LC 92-34038. Z8158.L52 1994. 016.863/3. OCLC 26673936. LC 24.7/2:C 33.

This is an updated, comprehensive bibliography of multilingual collected and selected works, anthologies, abridged and juvenile editions, individual works, and translations held in the Library of Congress. Includes a name index of editors, compilers, commentators, translators, and illustrators.

Mark Twain

1279. Library of Congress. Children's Book Section. **Samuel Langhorne Clemens: A Centennial for Tom Sawyer; An Annotated, Selected Bibliography** compiled by Virginia Haviland and Margaret N. Coughlan. LC, 1977. Free: Office Systems Services, Printing and Processing Section, Washington, DC 20540-5446. 86p. LC 76-608129. Z8176.H38. 016.818/4/09. OCLC 2284644. LC 1.12/2:C 59.

This annotated list of materials includes first editions, foreign-language editions, bio-critical works, and bibliographies related to Mark Twain and his novels, travel books, essays, and short stories.

CHILDREN'S LITERATURE

1280. Library of Congress. Children's Literature Center. **Books for Children**. GPO, 1985- . Annual. LC 85-643487. Z1037.C542. 011/.62. OCLC 11884747. LC 2.11: .

No. 1. 1985. Photoduplication Service, Washington, DC 20540-5230.

No. 2. 1986. Free: Children's Literature Center, Washington, DC 20540.

No. 3. 1987. Photoduplication Service, Washington, DC 20540-5230.

No. 4. 1988. Free: Children's Literature Center, Washington, DC 20540.

No. 5. 1989. Photoduplication Service, Washington, DC 20540-5230.

No. 6. 1990. Free: Office Systems Services, Printing and Processing Section, Washington, DC 20540-5446.

No. 7. 1991. GPO.

No. 8. 1992. GPO.

These short, annotated pamphlets list new, recommended children's picture books, fiction, folklore, poetry, biography, history, and nonfiction. Entries are organized by reader's age, and include publisher, price, LC card number, and ISBN. *The Best of Children's Books, 1964-1978* is a compilation (LC 1.12/2:C 43/5/964-78).

1281. Library of Congress. Children's Literature Center. **Children & Poetry: A Selective, Annotated Bibliography** compiled by Virginia Haviland and William Jay Smith. LC, 1979. Free: Children's Literature Center, Washington, DC 20540. 2d ed. rev. 84p. LC 78-57071. Z1037.H36 1979. 010. OCLC 3915400. LC 1.12/2:P 75/979.

This is a selective annotated bibliography of rhymes and more serious poetry, old and new, in English and translated from other languages.

POETRY

1282. Library of Congress. Poetry Office. **Literary Recordings: A Checklist of the Archive of Recorded Poetry and Literature in the Library of Congress** compiled by Jennifer Whittington. LC, 1981. Free to U.S. Libraries and Institutions: Office Systems Services, Printing and Processing Section, Washington, DC 20540-5446. rev. and enl. ed. 299p. LC 79-607981. PS306.5.Z9U53 1981. 016.811/5. OCLC 5727688. LC 4.2:L 71/2.

This inventory of Library of Congress recordings of renowned poets reading their own work at lectures, poetry readings, and plays is current to May 1975. Poem titles and first lines of untitled poems are listed, along with the poet's name and place and date of the reading. Includes an index of poets who have recorded for the Archive. Copies of many of the recordings may be purchased for noncommercial educational and cultural use.

Music

GENERAL WORKS

1283. Library of Congress. Cataloging Distribution Service. **The Music Catalog**. LC, 1990- . Quarterly. Microfiche. LC sn91-1915. ML136.U5N9. 016. OCLC 23209415. [SuDocs number not available].

1981-1990 Cumulated Indexes and Register.

This is a microfiche list of scores, sound recordings, and books and serials about music cataloged since 1981 by the Library of Congress. It is issued in two parts: (1) the Register and (2) an Index to numbers, names, titles, subjects, and series. It continues *Music, Books on Music, and Sound Recordings*, and updates *Library of Congress Catalog: Music and Phonorecords* (LC 30.8/6:), published during the years 1953-72.

1284. Library of Congress. Music Division. **Library of Congress Music, Theater, Dance: An Illustrated Guide**. GPO, 1993. 80p. LC 93-27720. ML136.U5M8 1993. 791/.09753. OCLC 28377121. LC 1.6/4:M 97/2.

This guide to LC holdings emphasizes music—including manuscripts, instruments, and photographs—with descriptions of materials in theater and dance.

1285. Library of Congress. Music Division. **The Music Manuscripts, First Editions, and Correspondence of Franz Liszt (1811-1886) in the Collections of the Music Division, Library of Congress** compiled by Elizabeth H. Auman and Raymond A. White, with the assistance of Gail L. Freunsch and Robert J. Palian. LC, 1991. Free: Music Division, Washington, DC 20540. 126p. LC 86-20875. ML134.L7L5 1991. 016.78/092/4. OCLC 14966737. LC 12.2:L 69.

Part 1, a bibliography of LC holdings related to composer Franz Liszt, includes music manuscripts written in his own hand and printed editions with his holography annotations. Part 2 is a list of the Music Division's first-edition Liszt music, and part 3 is an inventory of autographed Liszt letters in the Division. Indexed by music title and composer.

1286. Library of Congress. Music Division. **The Sousa Band, A Discography** compiled by James R. Smart. LC, 1970. Free: Music Division, Washington, DC 20540. 123p. LC 70-604228. ML156.4.B3S6. 789.9/136/50671. OCLC 93178. LC 12.2:So 8.

This is a recording history of the Sousa Band, along with U.S. Marine Corps band recordings made during Sousa's three years of leadership (1890-92) and two Philadelphia Rapid Transit Company band recordings performed under Sousa's direction. Foreign releases of Sousa band records are omitted. Both cylinder and disk recordings are documented, arranged by title under record manufacturer (there is no title index). An appendix contains a chronological list of Victor recording sessions, indexed by soloist, composer, and conductor.

1287. Library of Congress. **Musical Instruments in the Dayton C. Miller Flute Collection at the Library of Congress: A Catalog** compiled by Michael Seyfrit. 1v. LC, 1982. Free to U.S. Libraries and Institutions: Office Systems Services, Printing and Processing Section, Washington, DC 20540-5446. LC 81-14274. ML462.W33L545 1982. 788/.5/0740153. OCLC 7774191. LC 12.2:F 67/3/v.1.

Describes flutes and other woodwind instruments in the Miller Collection. Entries include accession number, location, system, lowest pitch, maker, place, date, key(s), sections, measurements, case, and plate number. Includes many photographs, and indexes to instrument makers, cities, symbols, and sources.

1288. Library of Congress. **Yiddish American Popular Songs, 1895 to 1950: A Catalog Based on the Lawrence Marwick Roster of Copyright Entries** by Irene Heskes. GPO, 1992. 527p. LC 92-6519. ML128.J4H49 1992. 016.78242164/089/924073. OCLC 25372754. LC 1.12/2:Y 5/2.

Titles from the Hebrew Publishing Company inventory of American Yiddish sheet music are presented chronologically. Entries list copyright, composers, lyricists, arrangers, theaters, imprint, and notes. The catalog includes illustrations, a bibliography, a publishers list, and indexes to composers, arrangers, lyricists, and song titles.

BRAILLE

1289. Library of Congress. National Library Service for the Blind and Physically Handicapped. **Dictionary of Braille Music Signs** by Bettye Krolick. LC, 1979. National Library Service for the Blind and Physically Handicapped, Washington, DC 20542-5304. 199p. LC 78-21301. MT38.K76. 781/.24. OCLC 4494734. LC 19.2:B 73/10.

Braille music signs used since 1888 are defined, with explanations of formats used by publishers over time. Musical terms are not defined. Available in both print and braille.

1290. Library of Congress. National Library Service for the Blind and Physically Handicapped. **Music and Musicians**. Free: National Library Service for the Blind and Physically Handicapped, Washington, DC 20542-5304.

> **Braille Scores Catalog. Choral.** 1979. 110p. Available in braille and large print editions. LC sn82-21350. 784. OCLC 5725221. LC 19.2:M 97/8/ .
>
> **Braille Scores Catalog. Instrumental.** 1980. 92p. Available in braille and large print editions. LC 77-649584. ML136.U52B7. 016.7808. OCLC 7372621. LC 19.2:M 97/11/ .
>
> **Braille Scores Catalog. Organ.** 1978. 62p. Available in braille and large print editions. LC 79-642728. ML136.U52M86. 016.7868. OCLC 4823026. LC 19.2:M 97/4/ .
>
> **Braille Scores Catalog. Piano.** 1979. 209p. Available in braille and large print editions. LC sn82-20323. 784. OCLC 5419103. LC 19.2:M 97/7/ .
>
> **Braille Scores Catalog. Vocal. Parts I-II, Classical and Popular Music.** 2v. 1983. Available in braille and large print editions. LC 90-649430. 780. OCLC 9737313. LC 19.2:M 97/13/ .

Part II, Popular, Supplement A. 1992. 44p. Available in braille and large print editions.

Instructional Cassette Recordings Catalog. 1991. 104p. Available in 15/16 ips cassette and large print editions. LC 77-649579. ML156.2.N39. 016.7899/12. OCLC 4445748. LC 19.11:M 97/ .

Instructional Disc Recordings Catalog. 1987. 42p. Available in large print and 8 rpm phonodisc editions. LC 80-647735. ML156.2.U6. 016.7899/12/07. OCLC 6606404. LC 19.11/3-2: .

Large-Print Scores and Books Catalog. 1991. 81p. Available in large print edition only. LC 79-640268. ML136.U52M9. 016.7808. OCLC 4525695. LC 19.2:M 97/3/ .

These are lists of music materials available on loan to blind and physically disabled people.

Performing Arts

1291. Library of Congress. Copyright Office. **Catalog of Copyright Entries. Cumulative Series. Motion Pictures.** NTIS, 1951-1971. LC 53-60032. PN1998.U615. OCLC 2478026. LC 3.8:M 85/date.

> Cumulation for 1894-1912. 92p. NTIS (PB85-194751/HDM), 1953.
> Cumulation for 1912-1939. 1256p. NTIS (PB85-194777/HDM), 1951.
> Cumulation for 1940-1949. 599p. NTIS (PB85-194769/HDM), 1953.
> Cumulation for 1950-1959. 494p. NTIS (PB85-194785/HDM), 1960.
> Cumulation for 1960-1969. 744p. NTIS (PB85-194793/HDM), 1971.

This comprehensive catalog of motion pictures registered with the Copyright Office between 1894 and 1969 cites title, production company, physical description, author, copyright date, and registration number. Includes title and name indexes.

1292. Library of Congress. **Information Resources in the Arts: A Directory** compiled by Lloyd W. Shipley. LC, 1986. Free to U.S. Libraries and Institutions: Office Systems Services, Printing and Processing Section, Washington, DC 20540-5446. 161p. LC 85-600227. NX110.S48 1986. 700/.25/73. OCLC 12665030. LC 1.2:In 3.

This directory of performing arts organizations is drawn from the Library of Congress's National Referral Center database and includes federal, state, and local agencies; arts education programs; dance; theater; music; film; television, video, radio, broadcasting, and cable; and international arts organizations. Entries include address and telephone number, sponsor, scope, holdings, publications, and information services. Includes geographic, organization, and subject indexes.

1293. Library of Congress. Motion Picture, Broadcasting, and Recorded Sound Division. **Early Motion Pictures: The Paper Print Collection in the Library of Congress** by Kemp R. Niver. LC, 1985. Free: Office Systems Services, Printing and Processing Section, Washington, DC 20540-5446. 509p. LC 84-600185. Z5784.M9L5 1985. 016.79143/75. OCLC 10912882. LC 40.9:Ea 7.

This is a catalog of paper prints submitted to the Library of Congress before 1912, when films were unprotected by copyright. Paper prints are strips of photographic paper with reproductions of individual frames of film. Entries give title, producer, production credits, length and LC location number, identification information, and summary. Includes a credits index by actor, cameraman, director, scriptwriter, and author; and a subject and name index that includes company and personal names.

1294.   Library of Congress. Motion Picture, Broadcasting, and Recorded Sound Division. **The George Kleine Collection of Early Motion Pictures in the Library of Congress: A Catalog** prepared by Rita Horwitz and Harriet Harrison, with the assistance of Wendy White. LC, 1980. Free to U.S. Libraries and Institutions: Office Systems Services, Printing and Processing Section, Washington, DC 20540-5446. 270p. LC 79-607073. PN1998.A1U57 1980. 016.79143/7. OCLC 5098300. LC 40.2:K 67.

This catalog describes materials in the collection purchased in 1947 from the Kleine estate and incorporated into LC's National Film Collection. Included are films produced between 1898 and 1926 (later copies on 16-mm acetate film) by Thomas A. Edison, Gaumont and Pathe of France, Cines and Ambrosio of Italy, and others, as well as scripts, stills, pressbooks, posters, correspondence, and other materials.

1295.   Library of Congress. Motion Picture, Broadcasting, and Recorded Sound Division. **3 Decades of Television: A Catalog of Television Programs Acquired by the Library of Congress, 1949-1979** compiled by Sarah Rouse and Katharine Loughney. GPO, 1989. 688p. LC 86-20098. PN1992.9.L53 1989. 016.79145/75. OCLC 14242172. LC 40.2:T 23.

This annotated list of TV programs held in the Library of Congress is arranged alphabetically by title and is indexed by genre-subject. Program notes include copyright registrant, producer, dates televised and number of episodes, regular cast, and a description. Includes photographs, definitions, and a bibliography on the history of television.

1296.   Library of Congress. Motion Picture, Broadcasting, and Recorded Sound Division. **Wonderful Inventions: Motion Pictures, Broadcasting, and Recorded Sound at the Library of Congress** edited by Iris Newsom. GPO, 1985. 384p. and 2 sound discs analog, 33 1/3 rpm, mono.; 12 in. LC 83-600369. PN1994.W62 1985. 791.4. OCLC 10374960. LC 40.2:W 84.

Early works of film, radio, phonograph records, and television in LC's holdings are described in essays illustrated with photographs and musical examples. Includes an index.

1297.   Library of Congress. **Music for Silent Films, 1894-1929: A Guide** compiled by Gillian B. Anderson. GPO, 1988. 182p. LC 87-26248. ML128.M7A5 1988. 016.7828/5. OCLC 16755104. LC 1.6/4:M 97.

This is a guide to microfilmed silent film scores and cue sheets in the LC Music Division, the Museum of Modern Art, the Arthur Kleiner Collection, the George Eastman House, the New York Public Library Music Division, and the Federation Internationale des Archives du Film. Arranged alphabetically by film title, entries include literary source, adaptor, screenplay author, director, film company, distributor, composer/compiler, musical series title, instrumentation, copyright, notes, projection time and film footage, LC or MOMA call number, pagination and height, microfilm and item number, and music publisher, place, and date. Includes an index.

1298.   Library of Congress. **Radio Broadcasts in the Library of Congress, 1924-1941: A Catalog of Recordings** compiled by James R. Smart. LC, 1982. Free to U.S. Libraries and Institutions: Office Systems Services, Printing and Processing Section, Washington, DC 20540-5446. 149p. LC 81-607136. PN1991.9.L5 1982. 011/.38. OCLC 7976772. LC 40.2:R 11/924-41.

This chronological listing of live radio broadcasts includes a wide range of topics and performers, from President Roosevelt's "Fireside Chats" to Adolf Hitler; the announcement of the Hindenburg explosion to Mae West. Most of the recordings are rare or unique. Entries note broadcast date, program title, length, performers or newscaster, and station call letters.

1299. Library of Congress. **The Federal Theatre Project Collection: A Register of the Library of Congress Collection of U.S. Work Projects Administration Records on Deposit at George Mason University.** LC, 1987. 320p. LC 87-600067. PN2270.F43L52 1987. 016.792/0973. OCLC 15550972. LC 4.10:61.

This checklist of the FTP includes letters, memos, reports, forms, lists, scripts, costume and set designs, posters, manuals, publications, bulletins, charts, blueprints, research studies, addressograph plates, newspaper clippings, photographs, oral histories, playbills, and scrapbooks, in four major categories: Administrative, play service and research, library, and production records. Most span the years 1935-39. Entries note provenance, content, and series description.

1300. National Endowment for the Humanities. Humanities Projects in Media. **Media Log: A Guide to Film, Television, and Radio Programs Supported by the National Endowment for the Humanities, Division of Public Programs, Humanities Projects in Media.** NEH, 1993. Free: Media Log, Public Information Office, 1100 Pennsylvania Ave., N.W., Room 407, Washington, DC 20506. 162p. LC 93-198502. P96.D622U66 1993. 016.0701/8. OCLC 27869155. NF 3.8:M 46/2/992.

This annotated list of film, TV, and radio programs funded by the NEH for use in colleges and libraries describes dramas, documentaries, and children's programs, noting format, length, distributor, production credits, ancillary materials, and awards.

Philosophy and Religion

1301. Library of Congress. **Medieval and Renaissance Manuscript Books in the Library of Congress: A Descriptive Catalog** by Svato Schutzner. GPO, 1989. LC 85-600260. Z6621.U58M64 1989. 091/.09753. OCLC 12721992. LC 23.2:M 46/vol.

> Vol. 1. **Bibles, Liturgy, Books of Hours**. 1989. 421p.

Volume 1 of this projected three-volume set, *Bible, Liturgy, Books of Hours*, is a catalog of LC holdings, with indexes, notes, and illustrations.

1302. Library of Congress. **The Holy Koran in the Library of Congress: A Bibliography** compiled by Fawzi Mikhail Tadros. GPO, 1993. 449p. LC 93-26271. Z7835.M6T32 1993. 016.297/122. OCLC 28633621. LC 41.12:K 84.

This selected, illustrated bibliography describes manuscripts, facsimiles, and Arabic texts of the Koran; manuscript fragments; translations; commentaries; books; articles; microfilm; and sound recordings in LC's collections. Includes a name, title, subject, and series index.

Appendix:
Subject Bibliographies

(see entry 107)

These Subject Bibliographies identify publications, subscriptions, and electronic products for sale by the Superintendent of Documents, U.S. Government Printing Office (GPO). Numbers refer to the SB number that covers that subject.

Accident Prevention
    (see–Safety/229)
    (see also—Occupational Safety and
        Health/213)
Accidents
    (see–Safety/229)
    (see also—Occupational Safety and
        Health/213)
Accounting and Auditing/42
    (see also—General Accounting
        Office/250)
Adolescence
    (see–Childhood and Adolescence/35)
Aeronautics
    (see–Aerospace/222)
Aerospace/222
Africa/284
African Americans
    (see–Minorities/6)
Aging/39
Agriculture/162
    (see also—Census of Agriculture/277)
AIDS (Acquired Immune Deficiency
    Syndrome)/315
    (see also—Diseases/8)
Air Force Manuals/182
    (see also—Aviation/18)
Air Pollution/46
Aircraft
    (see–Aviation/18)
Airman's Information Manual
    (see–Aviation/18)

Airplanes
    (see–Aviation/18)
    (see also—Federal Aviation
        Regulations/12)
Airports
    (see–Aviation/18)
Airways
    (see–Aviation/18)
Alcohol, Tobacco and Firearms/246
    (see also—Substance Abuse/163)
American Revolution/144
Americas (The)/287
Animals, Domestic
    (see–Agriculture/162)
Animals, Wild
    (see–Wildlife Management/116)
    (see also—Birds/177)
Annual Reports/118
Anthropology
    (see–Social Sciences/205)
Aquatic Life/209
Archeology
    (see–Social Sciences/205)
Architecture
    (see–Buildings, Landmarks and
        Historic Sites/140)
    (see also—Census of Construc-
        tion/157)
    (see also—Home (The)/41)
Armed Forces/131
    (see also—Military History/98)

Armies
(see–Armed Forces/131)
(see also—Army Corps of
Engineers/261)
(see also—Military History/98)
Arms Control/127
Army Corps of Engineers/261
Art and Artists/107
(see also—Posters and Prints/57)
Artists
(see–Art and Artists/107)
Asia/288
(see also—China/299)
(see also—Middle East/286)
Asian Americans
(see–Minorities/6)
Associations
(see–Directories/114)
Astronomy
(see–Aerospace/222)
Astrophysics
(see–Aerospace/222)
Atlases
(see–Maps and Atlases/102)
Atomic Energy
(see–Nuclear Power/200)
Atomic Power
(see–Nuclear Power/200)
Audiovisual Materials
(see–Films and Audiovisual Informa-
tion/73)
Auditing
(see–Accounting and Auditing/42)
(see also—General Accounting
Office/250)
Automation/51
Automobiles
(see–Motor Vehicles/49)
Aviation/18
(see also—Air Force Manuals/182)
Awards
(see–Grants and Awards/258)

Background Notes/93
(see also—Foreign Country
Studies/166)
Banking
(see–Financial Institutions/128)
Banks
(see–Financial Institutions/128)
Birds/177

Blacks
(see–Minorities/6)
Boats
(see–Transportation/40)
(see also—Naval History/236)
Bonds
(see–Securities and Investments/295)
Budget of the United States Government
(see–Economic Policy/204)
Building Trades
(see–Construction Industry/216)
(see also—Census of Construc-
tion/157)
Buildings, Landmarks and Historic
Sites/140
Bureau of Land Management/256
Bureau of Reclamation/249
Business/4
(see also—Census of Business/152)
(see also—Federal Trade Commis-
sion/100)
(see also—Small Business/307)
Business Management
(see–Business/4)

Camping
(see–Recreation/17)
Canada
(see–Americas (The)/287)
Cancer/316
(see also—Diseases/8)
Cardiovascular System
(see–Diseases/8)
Career Education/110
(see also—Elementary and Secondary
Education/196)
(see also—Higher Education/217)
Caribbean
(see–Americas (The)/287)
CDROM
(see–Electronic Information
Products/314)
(see also—Automation/51)
Census of Agriculture/277
Census of Business/152
Census of Construction/157
Census of Governments/156
Census of Manufactures/146
Census of Mineral Industries/310
Census of Population and Housing/181
Census of Transportation/149

Diet
  (see–Nutrition/291)
Directories/114
Disability
  (see–Physically Challenged/37)
Disarmament
  (see–Arms Control/127)
Disaster Preparedness
  (see–Safety/229)
Discrimination
  (see–Civil Rights and Equal Opportu-
    nity/207)
  (see also—Labor Management Rela-
    tions/64)
  (see also—Minorities/6)
  (see also—Women/111)
Diseases/8
  (see also—Health Care/119)
Disks
  (see–Automation/51)
  (see–Electronic Information
    Products/314)
Domestic Animals
  (see–Agriculture/162)
Drinking
  (see–Substance Abuse/163)
Drugs and Drug Abuse
  (see–Substance Abuse/163)

Earth Sciences/160
Earthquake
  (see–Earth Sciences/160)
Economic Development/319
Economic Policy/204
Economy (The)/97
Education
  (see–Career Education/110)
  (see–Educational Statistics/83)
  (see–Elementary and Secondary
    Education/196)
  (see–Higher Education/217)
  (see also—School Facilities/223)
Educational Statistics/83
Elections
  (see–Voting and Elections/245)
Electricity and Electronics/53
  (see also—Utilities/298)
Electronic Information Products/314
Elementary and Secondary Educa-
  tion/196
Employment and Occupations/44

Energy/303
  (see also—Nuclear Power/200)
  (see also—Solar Energy/9)
Engineering/308
  (see also—Army Corps of Engi-
    neers/261)
  (see also—Census of Construc-
    tion/157)
Environmental Protection/88
Equal Opportunity
  (see–Civil Rights and Equal Opportu-
    nity/207)
Europe/289
  (see also—Russia/279)
Export/Import/317

Factories
  (see–Census of Manufactures/146)
Factory and Trade Waste
  (see–Waste Management/95)
Farms and Farming
  (see–Agriculture/162)
  (see also—Census of Agriculture/277)
Federal Aviation Regulations/12
Federal Communications Commis-
  sion/281
Federal Government/141
  (see also—Census of Govern-
    ments/156)
  (see also—Congress/201)
  (see also—Forms/90)
  (see also—Intergovernmental
    Relations/211)
Federal Trade Commission/100
Films and Audiovisual Information/73
Financial Aid to Students
  (see–Student Financial Aid/85)
Financial Institutions/128
Fire Prevention
  (see–Safety/229)
Firearms
  (see–Alcohol, Tobacco and
    Firearms/246)
Firefighting
  (see–Safety/229)
Fish and Marine Life
  (see–Aquatic Life/209)
Flowers
  (see–Home (The)/41)
Food
  (see–Nutrition/291)

Food Relief
 (see–Social Welfare/30)
Foreign Affairs of the United States/75
 (see also—Foreign Relations of the
   U.S./210)
Foreign Countries
 (see–Africa/284)
 (see–Americas (The)/287)
 (see–Asia/288)
 (see–China/299)
 (see–Europe/289)
 (see–Middle East/286)
 (see–Pacific Rim/318)
 (see–Russia/279)
Foreign Country Studies/166
 (see also—Background Notes/93)
Foreign Languages
 (see–Languages/82)
Foreign Relations of the United
   States/210
 (see also—Foreign Affairs of the
   U.S./75)
Foreign Trade and Tariff
 (see–International Trade/123)
Forest Fires
 (see–Safety/229)
 (see also—Trees, Forest Management
   and Products/86)
Forest Management
 (see–Trees, Forest Management and
   Products/86)
Forest Products
 (see–Trees, Forest Management and
   Products/86)
Former Soviet Union
 (see–Russia/279)
 (see also—Asia/288)
 (see also—Europe/289)
Forms/90
Fungicides
 (see–Pest and Weed Control/227)

Gardening
 (see–Home (The)/41)
General Accounting Office/250
 (see also—Accounting and Audit-
   ing/42)
General Services Administration/247
Geography
 (see–Foreign Country Studies/166)
 (see also—Earth Sciences/160)
 (see also—Africa/284)

 (see also—Americas (The)/287)
 (see also—Asia/288)
 (see also—China/299)
 (see also—Europe/289)
 (see also—Middle East/286)
 (see also—Pacific Rim/318)
 (see also—Russia/279)
Global Change/320
Government
 (see–Federal Government/141)
 (see also—Census of Govern-
   ments/156)
 (see also—Congress/201)
 (see also—Intergovernmental
   Relations/211)
Government Forms
 (see–Forms/90)
Government Printing Office/244
Government Procurement
 (see–Procurement/129)
Government Purchasing
 (see–Procurement/129)
Government Specifications and
   Standards
 (see–Specifications and
     Standards/231)
 (see also—National Institute
     of Standards and
     Technology/290)
Grants and Awards/258
 (see also—Student Financial Aid/85)
Graphic Arts/77
Guidance
 (see–Personnel Management/202)
Guns
 (see–Alcohol, Tobacco and
     Firearms/246)

Handicapped
 (see–Physically Challenged/37)
Health
 (see–Health Care/119)
 (see–Mental Health/167)
 (see–Occupational Safety and
     Health/213)
 (see–Vital and Health Statistics/121)
 (see also—Diseases/8)
Health Care/119
Health Statistics
 (see–Vital and Health Statistics/121)
Hearing
 (see–Health Care/119)

Hearing Disability
(see–Physically Challenged/37)
Herbicides
(see–Pest and Weed Control/227)
High School Debate Topic/43
High Schools
(see–Elementary and Secondary
Education/196)
(see also—School Facilities/223)
Higher Education/217
Highway Construction and Safety
(see–Road Construction and Safety/3)
Hispanics
(see–Minorities/6)
Historic Sites
(see–Buildings, Landmarks and
Historic Sites/140)
History
(see–American Revolution/144)
(see–Buildings, Landmarks and
Historic Sites/140)
(see–Civil War/192)
(see–Military History/98)
(see–National Park Service
Handbooks/16)
(see–Naval History/236)
Home (The)/41
Home Construction
(see–Home (The)/41)
(see also—Census of Construc-
tion/157)
(see also—Construction Industry/216)
Home Economics
(see–Home (The)/41)
(see also—Nutrition/291)
Home Maintenance
(see–Home (The)/41)
Housing
(see–Housing and Development/280)
(see also—Census of Population and
Housing/181)
(see also—Census Tracts and Blocks
(Maps)/312)
(see also—Census Tracts and Blocks
(Publications)/311)
Housing and Development/280
How to Sell to Government Agencies
(see–Procurement/129)

Immigration
(see–Citizenship/69)

(see also—Census of Population and
Housing/181)
Immunization
(see–Customs, Immunization and
Passports/27)
(see also—Health Care/119)
Indians of North America
(see–Minorities/6)
(see–Smithsonian Institution/252)
Industrial Relations
(see–Labor-Management
Relations/64)
Industrial Safety
(see–Safety/229)
(see–Occupational Safety and
Health/213)
Industry
(see–Census of Construction/157)
(see–Census of Manufactures/146)
(see–Census of Mineral Indus-
tries/310)
(see–Construction Industry/216)
Infant Care
(see–Childhood and Adolescence/35)
Insecticides
(see–Pest and Weed Control/227)
Insects
(see–Home (The)/41)
Insurance/294
Insurance, Social
(see–Social Security/165)
Intellectual Property
(see–Copyright/126)
(see–Patents and Trademarks/21)
Intergovernmental Relations/211
Internal Revenue Cumulative
Bulletins/66
International Economic Relations
(see–Foreign Affairs of the U.S./75)
(see also—Economy (The)/97)
(see also—International Trade/123)
International Obligations
(see–Foreign Relations of the
U.S./210)
International Trade/123
Internet
(see–Telecommunications/296)
Investments
(see–Security and Investments/295)

Judiciary
(see–Criminal Justice/36)

Pollution
 (see–Air Pollution/46)
 (see–Environmental Protection/88)
 (see–Waste Management/95)
 (see–Water Management/50)
Population
 (see–Census of Population and
  Housing/181)
 (see also—Census Tracts and Blocks
  (Maps)/312)
 (see also—Census Tracts and Blocks
  (Publications)/311)
Postal Service/169
Posters and Prints/57
 (see also—Art and Artists/107)
Poultry
 (see–Agriculture/162)
Power
 (see–Nuclear Power/200)
 (see–Utilities/298)
Preservation
 (see–Buildings, Landmarks and
  Historic Sites/140)
Presidents/106
Prices
 (see–Cost of Living/226)
Prints
 (see–Posters and Prints/57)
 (see also—Art and Artists/107)
Printing
 (see–Graphic Arts/77)
Prisons
 (see–Criminal Justice/36)
Procurement/129
Public Buildings
 (see–Buildings, Landmarks and
  Historic Sites/140)
Public Health
 (see–Health Care/119)
Public Utilities
 (see–Utilities/298)
Public Welfare
 (see–Social Welfare/30)

Radar
 (see–Electricity and Electronics/53)
Radiation/48
Radio
 (see–Telecommunications/296)
Radioactivity
 (see–Radiation/48)

Railroads
 (see–Transportation/40)
Recipes
 (see–Nutrition/291)
Reclamation
 (see–Bureau of Reclamation/249)
Recreation/17
Refuse Disposal
 (see–Waste Management/95)
Research
 (see–Scientific Research/243)
Retirement/285
Road Construction and Safety/3
Rockets
 (see–Aerospace/222)
Rodenticide
 (see–Pest and Weed Control/227)
Rural Conditions
 (see–Housing and Development/280)
 (see also—Agriculture/162)
Rural Electrification Administration
 (REA)/168
Russia/279
 (see also—Asia/288)
 (see also—Europe/289)

Safety/229
 (see also—Occupational Safety and
  Health/213)
Salvage
 (see–Waste Management/95)
Satellites
 (see–Aerospace/222)
 (see also—Space Exploration/297)
Savings and Loan Institutions
 (see–Financial Institutions/128)
School Facilities/223
Schools
 (see–Elementary and Secondary
  Education/196)
 (see–Higher Education/217)
 (see–School Facilities/223)
 (see also—Teaching/137)
Science
 (see–Earth Sciences/160)
 (see–Oceanography/32)
 (see–Scientific Research/243)
 (see–Social Sciences/205)
 (see also—Aerospace/222)
 (see also—Energy/303)
 (see also—Health Care/119)
 (see also—Nuclear Power/200)

Index

Numbers indicate entry numbers. Those entry numbers with an (n) indicate annotation entry. Those entry numbers with an (s) indicate subentries. Bold entries are general categories listed in the book with inclusive entry numbers.